SEXUAL DESIRE AND LOVE

ERIC FUCHS ———————

Sexual Desire and Love

Origins and History
of the Christian Ethic
of Sexuality and Marriage

Translated from the French by
MARSHA DAIGLE

James Clarke & Co / Cambridge
The Seabury Press / New York

1983

James Clarke & Co. Ltd.   The Seabury Press
7 All Saints' Passage   815 Second Avenue
Cambridge   CB2   3LS   New York, N.Y. 10017
U.K.   U.S.A.
Originally published as *Le Désir et La Tendresse* copyright © 1979 by
Edition Labor et Fides, 1, rue Beauregard CH-1204 Genève.

The poem on pp. 201–203 was translated by John Ratti.

Printed in the United States of America

Library of Congress Cataloging in Publication Data

Fuchs, Eric, 1932-
   Sexual desire and love.

   Translation of: Le désir et la tendresse.
   Bibliography: p. 269
   Includes indexes.
   1. Sex—Religious aspects—Christianity. 2. Marriage
—Religious aspects—Christianity. I. Title.
BT708.F813 1983   241'.66   82-19703
ISBN 0-8164-2467-5 (U.S.)
   0   227   67876   1   (U.K.)

Contents

Introduction

The following book results both from a protest and a conviction. First the protest: for a long time now we have tolerated with discomfort something called "Christian morality." As a believer first converted to the gospel through Saint Paul, and as a pastor, I have continued to ask myself—at first hesitantly, then more vigorously as my pastoral experience progressively convinced me of the merits of that protest (in view of the disasters engendered by this particular ethic)— how a teaching so foreign to the spirit of the New Testament could still be categorized as Christian. By what mysterious alchemy did the liberating gospel of the Christ who unconditionally accepted wounded humanity become transformed into moral requirements that were so guilt-forming? Through having to help men and women who had been hampered by so many inhibitions resulting from Christian education, I finally came to see that it was time to examine more closely what is referred to as the "taboos of Judaeo-Christian morality," and not to leave that investigation only to the adversaries of Christianity. After all, it really should be the Christians who denounce the errors of the Church.

This book, then, sprang from a simple recognition that the distance between primordial faith and its translation into an ethic was now too great. And also from a conviction based upon discovering that the uneasy silences of some were counterbalanced only by the all-directional apologetics of others. Apologetics per se is not the main point of interest and this project does not aim to justify the whole of Christianity; but embarrassed silence abandons Christians to an evergrowing chaos, even though the biblical tradition carries a wealth of meaning and of promise entirely capable of dealing with the questions of our time. My departure point is pastoral: I have not begun this study with the detached objectivity of a scholar but with the intensity of someone who needs answers. However, this protest is really also a polemic presentation of a theological conviction which this work does wish to justify: that scriptural tradition insofar as we accept the theological risk of interpreting it in a way that takes into account the research and findings of the social sciences, does have the liberating potential of reshaping the Christian ethic of sexuality.

"Liberating"—that's the modern cry. The a priori conclusion of all modern books on sexuality. As I have said, it is not my intention to write an apologetic for traditional Christian morality; but, on the other hand, this does not imply I am accepting every idea on the subject just as long as it is modern. Being fashionable, i.e. speaking about sexual liberation because everyone is talking about it, is not my aim. My motive is the theological conviction that the source of our understanding of morality is to be found neither in the sciences nor in the consciousness or "praxis" of modern man, but in the revelation of the meaning of human existence in the life of Jesus of Nazareth as it has been transmitted through scriptural tradition. This conviction is of course controversial since it challenges the predominant stance of sexology, the new ideology of "advanced, liberated" society; if Christian morality has often eclipsed the gospel, the stance of sexology under all its multiple forms eclipses man himself. It is neither feasible nor right to allow people to believe that the new morality, one without restrictions (so they say) is liberating. That is simply a lie; we only need to look around, but, better yet, let's look at the gospel. Let it be clear that the attempt at a reformulation of a Christian ethic is not mere complicity with the new morality of "sexual liberation."

My motivation is twofold: pastoral and theological. The first justifies the self-criticism which this book demonstrates with regard to various moral traditions of Christianity; the second motivation explains why, in a polemic aimed against fashionable ideology, I advocate a return to scriptural tradition as the very source for our our ethical understanding. In so doing, I am not acting as an historian or an archaeologist but as a theologian, professing with the whole church that the Word of God finds its privileged and normative place through the testimony of biblical tradition.

Is an ethic possible between these two extremes? Certainly, as long as no one expects a catalogue of formulas which dispenses with any risk of free, individual commitment. I intend this to be a book of ethics, but there will be no discussion of problems generally treated in the works of sexology or casuistry, nor advice on the correct or permissible methods of sexual intercourse. It is more urgent, it seems, to discuss the fundamental stakes involved in an ethic of sexuality and of marriage. What is seriously lacking today is not recipe books, but the conviction that cooking still has a real meaning and significance. . . .

My investigation is devoted to these fundamental issues and that is the only topic of this book. For between sexual desire and love there is a pathway of humanization, where genuine love, which is the awe-inspiring recognition of the otherness of a person, controls the sense of desire, and where desire, a life-force and gift of joy, can become the source of all possible tenderness. This humanizing pathway is the issue, the ground which I intend to cover.

*   *   *

I must also mention the limits to this project. During the course of this study, methodological choices have been made, the most significant of which are these:

—In Chapter I, on the human significances of sexuality, I have chosen two particular (and therefore limited) points of discussion in the dialogue with the social sciences: the question of social control of sexuality through symbolic rituals (the ethnological and sociological approach) and the question of the significance which language, both in culture and in the unconscious, gives to sexuality. This defines my area of interest and the limits of the dialogue with social science.

—Chapters II and III, devoted to the study of scriptural tradition, do not claim to resolve all of the exegetical questions raised by the texts. Since my interest is primarily ethical, I have taken account of the most recent works in the historical and critical domain but only to draw out of them the elements that are relevant to a normative morality—something that in general holds little interest for professional exegetes! But their focus and mine are not the same: I am going to the text with a particular intention, i.e., to make these texts meet the ethical questions of the modern reader head on. For even though the first consideration, of course, is understanding these biblical texts, we must not stop there; we must go further and make these texts deal critically with today's problems. This describes the emphasis as well as the limits of my discussion.

—Chapter IV (on history) is equally fragmentary. It is impossible to completely encompass the subject because of the sheer abundance of documents; for each period of church history a significant figure has been chosen as representing the ethical position of his time, with its question, its problems and its difficulties: Clement of Alexandria (end of the second and beginning of the third century); Gregory of Nyssa and Augustine (fourth century East and West), the same Augustine and Hugh of Saint

Victor (the Middle Ages); Luther and Calvin (sixteenth century). This particular pattern of selection is obviously arbitrary, since other figures could have been chosen, and since the history of moral practices does not necessarily correspond to the history of ideas on morality. It has been necessary, therefore, to make somewhat relative choices, for what I have sought to understand—even more than the actual Christian practices throughout history—is the reason why the Christian ethic evolved so far from its gospel sources. And on this point, the contribution of the theologians was decisive.

Finally, in the last chapter, I wanted above all to delineate the foundation upon which the credibility of a Christian ethic of sexuality and marriage is based. There again, I have refused to enter technical and quasi-casuistic debates. Once the major axes of the Christian ethic have been specified, the rest is a personal matter: by the grace of God, every man and woman is absolutely unique and the manner in which he or she will live out the demands and the awesome wonder of the love-encounter is also equally unique. Therefore, I refuse to discuss specific cases: they belong to inter-personal dialogue and not to the anonymity of a written text.

Having specified all these limits, without enumerating those that the reader will discover for himself, I hope that this attempt does not testify too unskillfully to my conviction that a renewed Christian ethic is a way out, if not the only way out, of the profound demoralization that characterizes the end of this century.

In ending this introduction, I would like to thank those who made this book possible. First of all, my friends from the Centre Protestant d'Études and elsewhere, who encouraged me in their reassurance that this was a necessary book and that it was of consequence to them. I would also like to thank those who gladly read my work and offered useful criticism both on form and content; in particular, the members of the thesis committee and the professors of the Theology Department in Geneva: Pierre Bonnard (of Lausanne); André Dumas (of Paris) who associated himself from the beginning with this research and encouraged me in it; François Bovon, Olivier Fatio and Gabriel Ph. Widmer. Thanks are due to my dear friends Béatrice Perregaux of the Humanities Department, Pierre Reymond, François Vouga and Marc Faessler, who all confirmed to me that authentic intellectual and theological work is a community work. Equal thanks are due to Mrs. Marguerite Ravex-Nicolas who ensured, with her usual competence, the typing of my manuscript.

I would also like to express my gratitude for financial aid to the Fonds national de la Recherche scientifique, who in the past granted me a scholarship for a year and a half; to the University of Geneva, which contributed to the publishing of this book by a subsidy; and to the Société auxiliare de la Faculté autonome de Théologie, whose generosity allowed this book to see the light of day in good financial condition.

Introduction

I

Human Significances
of Sexuality

So that my attempt at reformulating the terms of a
Christian ethic of sexuality and marriage has an opportunity to succeed,
it is necessary to recognize the context of this attempt. If, indeed, as a
theologian, I am compelled to confront a priori the Word of God as it
is attested to in scriptural tradition, it is certainly not irrelevant to know
the context in which this confrontation takes place, for theology is not
the rational structuring of eternal truths but the critical confrontation of
the teaching of the Church with its scriptural basis. But what kind of a
teaching would it be if it were inattentive to the cultural, social, and
contingent reality of the people to whom it is addressed?

If every ethic must clearly indicate by what authority it makes its
pronouncements (which is the topic of Chapters II and III), it must also
clearly recognize the context in which it speaks, if only to be honest about
its own basic assumptions! But also, more fundamentally, context is
important because an ethic is born out of the distance which a society
discovers (and which it quickly seeks to make up) between the factual
situation and the justifications given in defense of its values and moral
norms which it is defending. It is always current circumstances which
more or less forcibly call into question accepted moral values. The current state of affairs dictates the agenda of discussion! An ethic is thus
called for, at least at first, because of the context. Next, however, it is
necessary that the values now in question (insofar as they are not totally
disqualified) exert a critical influence on the newly arisen practices or
trends so that a new equilibrium between practices and standards can be
achieved, which affords a certain security to social groups as well as to
individuals.

7

In Christian ethics, the same process is true: the questions of modern man, or more precisely the questions that our secularized society presents to modern man, be he Christian or not, seriously challenge the manner in which the Church, or Churches, justify the standards they propose. Current circumstances, once again, call the Churches to account for their understanding of the teaching of the Bible. A new debate has opened, not only between Christianity and modern culture, but also within Christianity, on its own comprehension of the ethical consequences of the biblical message. It is thus evident that the manner in which contemporary society understands and speaks of sexuality determines a priori our ethical approach.

It would be foolish to neglect the contribution of social sciences which offer us a more developed understanding of human sexuality: here again the evolution of knowledge affects the ethics-formulator: he must determine if and how scientific contributions have modified the past justifications of values and standards and whether that modification is fundamental or superficial. To tackle an ethic of sexuality today while ignoring the input of psychology or ethnology, for example, would be to condemn the project to an impertinent and pretentious discussion. That would be to prejudge, to confuse (once more, O Galilee!) judgment with condemnation. But this does not mean that an ethic need only line up the "objective givens" of science and thereby organize human behavior. That would be the same misunderstanding in reverse. Confronted with the contributions of social sciences, the Christian theologian must critically analyze them, in the name of the Word which is his reference point. This critique must pay particular attention to the hidden assumptions of these sciences which so often lead them to enclose man and morality in a new system that becomes sacred but which lacks transcendence and liberty.

Thus, although we begin our investigation by listening attentively to the social sciences vis-à-vis sexuality, we approach them as valuable partners but also as adversaries to be criticised. For if the type of questioning which characterizes our age and our society has sprung from their sector, then they should not be the ones who are asked to justify the ethical standards which seem right to us; that will be left to the testimony of biblical tradition.

The following considerations involve two stages: first, an investigation of the symbolic control of sexuality as presented by sociologists and ethnologists to promote understanding of the importance of the instances of control which all human societies (our own included!) organize against sexuality; and next, a consideration of how man has attempted to give meaning (and by what language) to the force of desire which dwells in him, and the language he has used in this attempt.

1. The Symbolic Control of Sexuality

Sexuality is one of the fundamental ambiguities of human society, to the extent that it must be situated both with regard to nature (from which it comes and which it must use) and with regard to culture which defines its role . . . . Sexuality itself, then, can never become the ultimate source of uncleanness, under penalty of destroying the very culture which might claim to eradicate it as a foul thing. A system of prohibitions, on the other hand, demarcates the limits of sexual activity, its incompatability with some daily functions (work) or with some bodily functions (menstruation, etc.). Sexuality is the domain par excellence of rules, the primary domain where culture is unwittingly hinged to nature. Its ideology is evidence, to a greater or lesser extent, of an unsettled conscience, pulled this way and that by insurmountable contradictions. Sexuality is not classifiable, it is the one true mystery: it does not belong to the universe of uncleanness, for far from being repulsive, it is thrilling. It is, however, dangerous—an inexhaustible source of troubles, for the individual and for society. But it cannot be prohibited, because society would then extinguish itself. We are forced, then, to make it a carefully monitored and contingent activity: to forbid it at certain times, to warn against certain types of women, to decree it incompatible with hunting, war or the blacksmith shop, to isolate it, to circumscribe it in such a way as to avoid becoming overwhelmed by it.

Luc de Heusch (Preface to *De La souillure,* Paris, 1971)[1]

The following reflections aim at understanding the connection between the two affirmations presented by anthropological study vis-à-vis human sexuality, i.e. that sexuality is always and everywhere the object of rigorous social control / and that it nevertheless is also the locus from which a meaning or significance emerges which always in some way goes beyond the boundaries of social regulations which attempt to restrict it. That is what is meant by the *symbolic* value of sexuality and the *controls* that are placed upon it.

Although necessary for the survival of any social group, sexuality is at the same time feared because of the violent disorder that it can bring into society's working order. Thus, a right and good use of sexuality must be ascertained while the serious disorder that it can cause is simultaneously avoided. This is the reason for the many rituals that surround sexuality, the taboos and prohibitions—the first and most fundamental being against incest—which rigorously specify the social expression of sexuality. As opposed to animals, whose sexual activity is regulated by entirely instinctive seasonal cycles, man has no built-in regulation to channel his sexual instinct. Human sexuality is characterized by a continuous state of readiness and by the lack of connection between the sensation of pleasure and ultimate biological goal. "This excess of sexual urges, together with the absence of reactions that are conditioned by instinct, constitutes, from the biological point of view, an extreme danger for man."[2]

From the beginning, humanity has had to come to grips with the need to channel the sex drive, which is potentially deadly, towards life. This necessity, often costly to the individual, has nonetheless an important civilizing aspect: "The sublimation of instincts is an especially conspicuous feature of cultural development; it is what makes it possible for higher physical activity, scientific, artistic or ideological, to play such an important part in civilized life . . . civilization is built upon a renunciation of instinct."[3]

Freud is right: it is the renunciation of instinct which is at the origin of civilization. But on this point, Freud's subsequent explanation in *Civilization and Its Discontents* seems more like science fiction than science. If sexuality constitutes a possibly deadly menace, it is because it has the power of constantly awakening the mimetic rivalry within a social group and of re-initiating a cycle of violence. It is therefore necessary to prohibit the closest sexual object (for instance, the women in the group) and to remove the danger of mimetic contagion. Man thus renounces the immediate satisfaction of his sexual desires because he knows from experience that to do otherwise would create a violent conflict with the other members of the group, whose desires also seek immediate satisfaction. It is therefore necessary to have prohibitions against the sexual objects nearby and to put off satisfaction until later when other women, coming from outside the group, could, without risk, be paired off to each man.[4]

Thus, human sexuality is from the outset a social matter, as signified in its collective implications by behavioral standards that retain importance even if their content varies according to time and place. These standards all aim at keeping violence at a distance and at channeling instinctive drives towards social tasks as well as freeing the individual from the stress of having constantly to risk behavior that would expose him to violent conflict with others. Assured of a stable framework and of constant reference points, the individual can, within this clearly delineated space, freely organize behavior patterns that are directed to the accomplishment of cultural tasks. The rules which restrict simultaneously create a social space that is protected from aggressive instincts.

Paradoxically, it is when these standards are the most deeply interiorized and accepted that they appear "natural." And from this "naturalness" man shapes his own personal direction. There is no surer indication of the crisis of credibility of any particular moral standard than the challenge which questions its "natural" foundation.

It can be said, then, that the function of standards for sexual morality is to allow for the fulfillment of the biological goals of reproduction as well as for the instinctive needs for pleasure, and to structure this fulfillment into a socially coherent scheme, for example, work, or family, where the individual can be conscious both of his social function and his own personal creativity.[5] Every society aims at integrating sexuality, pleasure, love and the safety of the group.

This importance of the symbolic control of sexuality can readily be understood, in view of fear of the violence that sexuality potentially harbors.

Sexual desire can use excessive force to achieve its goals. Rape is a violent expression of sexual desire, the extreme point to which it can lead.[6] Always linked to eroticism (which from this point of view is only an attempt to transform the force of desire into an expression which can organize and therefore humanize the power of eros), violence indicates the deadly menace which inhabits a person: this drive, this desire can destroy his being, not only becuase it can override his control, but especially because it is a latent threat to relationships with all others; the fragile edifice of personal and social life is constantly threatened by it. Of course not all violence is sexual in origin, and sexual desire does not necessarily express itself in violence, but violence and passion are often interchangeable terms and man knows it: he knows that he must constantly sidestep this danger.[7]

The force of sexual desire, even when controlled, i.e. partly repressed in the subconscious, remains an ever-threatening reality. But that same powerful force bespeaks the fact that sexual desire, like life, is more complex, richer than any system that socializes it. It points to the deadly ruin which threatens the City of Man (thus the *Bacchae* of Euripides), but also points to the festive celebration which broadens man's horizon. That is why sexuality must be continually controlled and must have times and places (rituals and celebrations) provided for it, where its dangerous character is both invoked and exorcised. Celebration banters with and even mimes violence, consenting momentarily to it in order to better curb or subdue it. For social life is only possible where the sex drive is contained and diverted to other objectives, which is what work accomplishes: "Work demands the sort of conduct where effort is in a constant ratio with productive efficiency. It demands rational behavior where the wild impulses worked out on feast days and usually in games are frowned upon. If we were unable to repress these impulses we should not be able to work, but work introduces the very reason for repressing them. These impulses confer an immediate satisfaction on those who yield to them. Work, on the other hand, promises to those who overcome them a reward later on whose value cannot be disputed except from the point of view of the present moment. From the earliest times work has produced a relaxation of tension thanks to which men cease to respond to the immediate urge impelled by the violence of desire. No doubt it is arbitrary always to contrast the detachment fundamental to work with tumultuous urges whose necessity is not constant. Once begun, however, work does make it impossible to respond to these immediate solicitations which could make us indifferent to the promised desirable results. Most of the time work is the concern of people acting collectively and during the time reserved for work the collective has to oppose those contagious impulses to excess, to violence, that is. Hence the human collective, partly dedicated to work, is defined by taboos without which it would not have become the world of work that it essentially is."[8]

Thus sexuality is in several ways a threat to social order. It is irreducible in its essense to clear language; it belongs to the pre-technical existence of man; it is, in fact, anti-institutional. It contradicts the order among men that is organized through language—the rational order which allows for communication, communal projects, morality; it defies a clear-headed exercise of will power. Augustine even saw in it a proof of sin which had left its indelible stamp on man: "The undeniable truth is that a man by his very nature is ashamed of sexual lust. And he is rightly ashamed because there is here involved an inward rebellion which is a standing proof of the penalty which man is paying for his original rebellion against God. For lust is a usurper, defying the power of the will and playing the tyrant with man's sexual organs. It is here that man's punishment particularly and most properly appears, because these are the organs by which that nature is reproduced which was so changed for the worse by its first great sin."[9]

Sexuality is a way of being present to the world that differs from the way in which the man with technological intelligence is present. The latter distances the world through the mediation of the Tool. In a certain way, sexuality is the refusal to accept being distanced: "In sexual desire and pleasure a radically 'other' experience is revealed which is not to be numbered with the other modes of presence in the world. In it, the body discovers that it cannot allow itself to be imprisoned by the daily routine of tasks or work for which it is only used as an instrument by the man who chooses these projects. He discovers his body and its independent existence precisely for this type of presence, freed from having to do or to work! Simply to be and to be present, ready for adventure or encounter. . . . This experience can only occur when someone is temporarily freed of responsibilities and the care of transforming the world. It is play, or poetry."[10] The fulfillment promised by sexual desire enters into conflict with the long-term fulfillment promised by the technical or work adventure. It is not sheer chance that modern society, committed like none before it to technical adventure, engages in so much nostalgic fantasy about the joys and promises of eroticism, but, more often than not, only on the level of voyeurism.

This is the reason that the appropriate time for sexuality cannot be accommodated with social time, which is the time necessary to every institution, every project, beginning with the institution of marriage. The whole problem of marriage is encapsulated in this challenge of institutionalizing what by definition refuses institutionalization.

Enigma and threat, sexual desire should nevertheless be submitted to some kind of order. We must pause here for a moment to consider the relationship between sexuality and language. Man must "voice" his sexuality to socialize it. Without language, sexuality would remain in the domain of impulse only, the domain of the undifferentiated, and the very meaning of the sexualization of man and woman would be lost. But language is also a choice which brings only one element of understanding to the level of consciousness. Everyone has the occasion of experiencing this ambiguity. The boy and the girl become truly such only when social language delineates precisely the role each must play. To be a man means to belong to a certain community whose rituals, symbols and expression define and recall social functions; to be a woman, the same is true, but with this difference, that in our society the rituals and symbols of the feminine community are subtly devalued, which tends to discredit the female with reference to the male. Social language categorizes roles, offers a meaning to them and guarantees a kind of order by ritualizing certain dangers inherent in the sexual act. This determining (even repressive) aspect of language exerts a very real and heavy pressure on all of us. What we call "common sense" is often only the expression of language-determinism that has become unconscious. There is a trap, therefore, set by words that must be guarded against.[11]

This ambivalence of the social function of language, i.e. stating a plausible meaning of masculinity and femininity and thereby excluding other possible meanings, is indeed particularly apparent when it exerts itself in the definition of roles of men and women.[12] The work of ethnologists—for instance, the often conclusive research of Margaret Mead—has long demonstrated the variability of this definition from one culture to another. Sociology has demonstrated the extent of this same variability even within a particular society where it functions according to social groupings based on class, religion or levels of education.[13]

The separation of roles is first of all social, i.e. linked to the demands of work. It's a question of knowing, among the multiplicity of possibilities, "who does what." This appears to be the decisive criteria, especially for the definition of the sexual roles of a couple. It does seem right to affirm that the need to define the forms of collective production takes priority over that of clarifying the standards of the sexual activity of men and women.

How do these very general observations apply to our *contemporary society*? The old standards, especially religious ones, have become more and more secularized; in any case they no longer constitute the needful reference point for western society. Are we to say, as certain heroes of sexual liberation ingenuously do, that we have entered an era where sexuality shall escape the former need of social regulation and now will be left purely to the individual choice?

In our secularized society, the task of regulating sexuality has been transferred to "scientific" authority. Sexuality has become an object for scientific study. The positive side of this fact is known; it would be repetitious to explain how much our consciousness has changed and been broadened with regard to sexual issues through the contribution of the social sciences. But there is a more subtle consequence which must be noted: at the social level there is a massive demand that this research proffer moral standards that are "objective" and (therefore!) indisputable. In reality, popularized sexology[14] acts as the new master of morality, wherein, I believe, we can see the two fundamental values of what I would call the objectifying of sex and the activism of pleasure. The new sexual normality requires dealing with sex as an object of study, i.e. as an object of discussion. We must speak about sex, but as an object whose presence is everywhere pursued by the multiplicity of discourses concerning all the possible methods of expressing it. There is something like hostility in the attempt to leave nothing in the dark: the mystery, the enigma (and to call it such is considered hypocrisy) must be grabbed by the throat and strangled in an attempt to do away with the disquieting anguish which, in spite of everything, is still attached to sex. The more said, the more that needs to be said in order to finally wipe out the remaining element which always ultimately escapes being objectified. One can't help but think that this constant emphasis on sex, at least in language, really hides an anguished search for a new morality which is capable of regulating sexuality, of giving it meaning in a secularized society in which relationship to the world is defined by technology. But at the same time, this objectification through language can only in the last analysis be an illusion, a dream, a subtle way of avoiding the face to face encounter with the real. The "all is permitted" theory of popularized sexology (since we can also say all!) comes up against a reality now more difficult to face, since no law allows the structuring of sexuality into a scheme that can socialize it.

The new sexual morality is marked by the requirement of having to discuss all aspects of sex; it is also characterized by the duty to succeed. This activism of pleasure to which contemporary man must yield requires steep sacrifice. He must take courses—for this area is too tricky for improvisation!—, read books, listen to the advice of specialists,[15] ask himself constantly if his partner has finally reached orgasm, wherein one finds one's ultimate raison d'être and freedom. According to the canons of the new sexuality, sexual success is of major value. Whoever is incapable, or barely capable, is abnormal in the primary sense of the word: he doesn't correspond to the norm. From this comes a new distress that seems to characterize perfectly well today's man, as is apparent from letters to specialized journals and from the questions most frequently directed to psychological consultants: the anguish of not "knowing how" to make love according to the new norms of required performance.

What does this new normality mean? Its prophets, i.e. Wilhelm Reich or David Cooper, speak of the revolutionary, liberating value of the successful sexual act. There would be, then, behind this search for sexual success, a profound protest against the alienation that man is subjected to in liberal, capitalistic society. Orgasm is a political act. For society is sexually sick, as Reich says;[16] the patriarchal society in the West is completely repressive: it imposes an absolute suppression of sexuality or prohibits the complete discharge of hormonal energy. To heal sexuality would be to liberate forces capable of promoting a true "affirmation of life ... in its subjective form of the affirmation of sexual pleasure and in its objective social form of a planned work democracy."[17] It is thus no longer the Revolution that brings happiness, but happiness, considered as successful orgasm, which will lead us to the Revolution.

Still more subtly, David Cooper demonstrates that orgasm is a political act because it allows for a purifying experience of death, a radical negation which gives rise to a new consciousness, liberated from alienating feelings caused by property.[18] This quasi-Buddhist perspective of the annihilation of the self in a sexual nirvana also becomes an almost anarchist vision: sexuality will be liberated only when it ceases expressing a patriarchal or bourgeois feeling towards property.

Thus, to seek after sexual success is to be a missionary in the new society. A whole morality is, of course, implicitly expressed here, which places a duty on each man to work for the success of the whole society by liberating himself from all that could deflect his quest for "orgasmic ecstasy." But this morality is based upon a powerful deification of sex: sex, (once it is "natural," as Reich says) is alone capable of giving man meaning and happiness. Sex here plays the role of God, who is adored and who, it is hoped, will graciously care for the needs of its servants.[19] We are probably witnessing a return here to pantheistic religion which seeks, through sexuality, to integrate the individual into the world, into the Whole, and by means of the repudiation of any and all "otherness," avoids the difficulty of the confrontation between society and pleasure.[20] One can't help but see here a desperate (and regressive) attempt to pitch a tent in imaginary places where repression and institutions no longer reign.[21]

However, we must consider underneath its theoretical justifications and commercial exploitation whether this new demand is expressing something important—perhaps a protest against the inability of our societies to fulfill the basic needs of the individual. In a world where all relationships tend to be mediated by means of a cumbersome and complex technical and political structure, eroticism is perhaps one of the last possibilities of expressing and experiencing the fundamental vulnerability in existence and a profound nostalgia for a sensual relation to the world and to "nature."[22]

The problem for our culture is that this protest, whose social importance was attested to by the events of May 1968, is itself a victim of what it implicitly denounces. It seeks to safeguard individual liberty in a super-organized world; and to accomplish that, it tends to encourage behavior that is abnormal, irregular and eccentric. Sexuality seems to have become the domain of non-conformists, the place for social decontrol. But modern society, like previous societies, cannot actually consent to this non-conformity. It is now constrained to use this non-conformity itself as the best means of a social integration: it becomes the current equivalent to the celebrations of former times, which guarded against violence by partially consenting to it.

We can readily see this in the use that is made of psychological language. Because of its technicality, the individual is given the illusion that his individuality and uniqueness is taken seriously. In fact, that language represents a social norm which must be conformed to for happiness. The paradox is that an individual achieves happiness by being like everyone else, i.e. convinced that he has succeeded in transgressing taboos and prohibitions! Psychology thus continues to present itself as the means by which transgressions become possible, while all along, everyone ascribes to this same method. In other words, the more that sexuality is made a private affair, the more room there is for stricter social control. Likewise, when the utopia of unrestricted desire presents itself as the counter-model of capitalistic society, standing against marriage as a symbol of the defense of private property, it ends up unwittingly reproducing one of the most predominant models of the neo-liberal society. Let me elaborate that statement:[23] the ideology of bourgeois marriage expressed the needs of a society that was based on the values of real estate, and the requirement of fidelity was motivated by the comparable economic necessity not to sell off the land. Challenging this concept of bourgeois ideology could signify that liberal capitalism no longer needs this ideology of property in order to function. Isn't the utopia of sexual desire—freedom to go wherever and do whatever it pleases really the ideology of a society where capital is also free to go and be wherever it pleases? A certain kind of contemporary discussion on fidelity, which is interpreted as faithfulness to self, to one's own duty, to one's own expansion, to one's pleasure—doesn't that correspond to an economic discussion about investment which should show some profit or else be pulled out? To be faithful means to invest desire wherever it can get the expected returns. The partner becomes the locus of investment—a locus which is more or less desirable and thus more or less compatible with any given scheme. This whole approach to sexuality and sexual desire reproduces, while desiring to fight against, a model of liberal capitalism founded on the free circulation of money (i.e. desire) and free trade. Here again, the social norm is subtly functioning, just when people think they are ridding themselves of any norms. Even the freedom of movement given to desire, which is sometimes asserted as the essence of liberation in the face of an oppressive bourgeois society, is quite suited to capitalistic liberalism, for it assures a better adaptation of individuals to the system, an integration into the models of social order.

But just like any system of exchange, sexuality will also have its own third-world, its forgotten ones, its under-developed—under-developed not through lack of desire, but through lack of means of becoming desired. Therefore, some compensation must be offered to all these, lest the new social norms and requirements arouse a yet stronger violence, on the part of those who revolt. And this is the basis of transforming sexuality into an object, a saleable item. This is the diversionary function of the erotic pictures which are abundant throughout the world: they function exactly as religion according to Marx, as the opium of the people. Precisely the measure in which social normality (beauty, masculinity, etc.) becomes sexual exploitation, it becomes tolerable only in the guise of a dream, an illusion. To protest against daily misery only reinforces the misery, reinforces in the last analysis the "pedantic hatred of reality" (to use Laplantine's expression) which characterizes our society.

In our society, we find both sides of the coin, control as well as protest, which characterize the social symbolism of sexuality. Despite appearances, it seems that the control, at the expense of the protest, has a tendency to be stronger than ever. This has occurred because the protest is still seeking an embodiment, a language which allows it to call itself a legitimate celebration, part of the collective symbolism which grounds man in a scheme, which is at the same time an underlying meaning and a critique of our society.

To examine this point further we must step back and try to shed more light on the relationship between sexuality and speech.

2. Sexuality and Speech

> You arrived the afternoon split the earth
> And the earth and men changed direction
> . . . . .
> You arrived I was very sad I said yes
> Starting with you I said yes to the world
>
> Pierre Eluard ("Dominique aujourd'hui présente,"
>   trans. by Marilyn Kallet)

Language, as we have seen, both represses and expresses sexual desire. The sociological analysis is convincing. There is no humanization of sexuality without language, be it symbolic, juridical, ritual, moral, etc. It is always a matter of integrating sexuality, so mysterious and threatening in its essence, into a possible framework of meaning, thereby orienting and controlling it.

But it is not sufficient to simply state the phenomenon and take note of the plurality of possible meanings given to sexuality by men. The ethical issue, always related to the issue of meaning, calls for an examination of the validity of those meanings. Which one is the best, the most authentic, the most valid, the most correct, the most moral? Whatever form the question takes, it is an imperative question. Even if we were to find ourselves hesitating in regard to the proper analysis, it is imperative that we answer the question, although it be a provisional answer. But before concluding, along with so many of our contemporaries, that the meaning is whatever we choose it to be and that there are no prior absolutes in this area, let us consider some other kinds of analyses besides the sociological ones.

a) The "Truths" of Physiology

We could be tempted to demand an answer from biology and physiology. What could be more "natural" after all, than to begin with the basic fact of the difference between the sexes: isn't that fact full of meaning prior to all elaboration? Sexuality is indeed structured by social language, but doesn't it also, and even first, structure that language? To be a man or a woman is to be man or woman in a certain way which is shaped by culture. But it is also to be present to the world in a certain way which, this time, is shaped by the physiological constraints which accompany the particular sex of a person. Is it possible to distinguish between what comes from culture and what belongs to the "natural"? All that we can be sure of is that there is a mutual interaction between the two. For physiological reasons, men and women do not live out their sexuality in the same way. The sexual desire of man expresses itself in temporary urges and impulses which are brief and intense. Masculine sexuality often displays this characteristic through aggression, a certain violence in obtaining immediate satisfaction, with no concern for consequences. It is oriented towards the point of fulfillment. "It (the desire) is action turned towards the other, a giving which is fulfilled at the moment it is given."[1] Feminine sexuality, on the other hand, is linked to the regular ovulation cycle with its discomfort and troublesomeness, independent of human choice. Because of this, even as a young girl, a woman begins to experience her sexuality as a burdensome constraint. Moreover, feminine sexuality is obviously tied to maternity, i.e. to something that links the present sexual act to a possible future pregnancy and a child to be brought into the world. Even if contraceptives have freed women from the fear of unwanted pregnancy, women, much more than men, are conditioned even by the structure of their bodies to link sexuality with duration, sexuality with project.[2]

Here is a report of the experience a woman has of her body:

"First, there are the cycles which punctuate my life according to a curving rhythm with alternating highs and lows: the times when I rule my body and the times when I bow to its rule, the moments when I approach life as a conqueror and the moments when my vulnerability rises to the surface. With regularity and obstinance, these cycles call me back to a fixed order and prevent me from imagining myself other than I am.

Pregnancy taught me what it means to wait, a waiting that is full of promise, full of concern too, the time (long and full) necessary for new life to issue forth.[3]

Birth was the moment of my life when I intensely experienced a rupture, the violent separation necessary for the appearance of another being. At the moment when the close tie which united us to each other was dramatically exposed, at that very moment the proof of that life's unique otherness also was revealed. Hardly come out of me, he was other than I; flesh of my flesh, yet never my double. It was at this moment that I understood the tremendous value of a life: that a child is unique, infinitely precious, and nothing could ever require that he be sacrificed.

Finally, nursing showed me the price paid so that a life could continue. A price of self-sacrifice, from the depths of one's being, a price that allows no cheating.

My female body recalls me continually to the confines it imposes on me; it teaches me, once a new life appears, about the value of time—of long duration—and the high price I must personally pay; it also reveals to me in an incontrovertible fashion the otherness of every human being, even if he be conceived within me. This instruction by my body, if I am willing, opens me to certain dimensions of life that I would not have so cleary perceived without it. It also disciplines me, if I am faithful to it, to certain choices which are not automatic today: respect for rhythms and the long time inherent to the development of every person, a welcoming of the other and of what in him cannot be reduced to me, a recognition of what it will eventually cost me."[4]

These remarks, however, should not be over-valued, for if "the morphological differentiation imposes rhythms (and) . . . assigns tasks in the function of reproduction, it is only in the world of culture where these differences are invested with value, that they function as destiny, i.e. as boundaries to human possibility."[5]

Thus, even if there is "testimony from a woman" on sexuality which reveals the uniqueness of a person and reveals a consciousness of her body vastly different from that of man, that testimony is an inseparable mixture of cultural conditioning and a physically-rooted experience.[6] Even if it be true that we are far from having understood and explored all the richness of the physical existence of both man and woman, that knowledge belongs to an order other than physiological; for once the body has been acknowledged (which is obviously important!), the problem is understanding how to live in that body, i.e. what meaning we are to assign to it. We must stop believing that there exists somewhere behind the language of culture a fundamental language, which is clear and incontestable. The meaning of the body is not "naturally" hidden in physiology; it arises from elsewhere.

It seems that a consensus would largely be admitted on this point today; here are two testimonies chosen from different ends of the spectrum in the scientific field. First a biologist:

"As a biologist, I take issue against two unwarranted concepts:

—the concept of a "punitive" and alienating biology which irremediably consigns woman to a kind of fatalism because of her anatomophysiology, when, on the contrary, it would be proper to redefine the biological data, not in order to confine woman within the limitations dictated by the data, but in order to "correct" them, to revise them so that these limitations no longer represent a social *handicap*;

—the concept which likens sexual behavior in general to mating behavior and reproductive behavior. If the mating behavior and reproductive behavior, which sometimes (but these days not always) flows from the mating behavior, are at least in large part determined by anatomophysiological givens of men and women, the same is not true for sexual behavior in the larger sense (erotic and generally relational function) nor for *social* behavior a fortiori. The roles of men and women and their social status . . . no longer have much to do with biology. It is important to "chaperon" biology in this respect. Two biological differences are incontestable . . . muscular strength (woman's is 570/1000 that of man's) and aggressiveness (linked in part to male hormones); these are able, *at the beginning,* to explain the attributing of certain social functions to the men, and especially the establishment of their domination. However, these two factors aside, nothing biological could justify in the past, and even less *in our time,* the perennialization of this state of affairs. . . . *Biology introduces no value judgment about the differences between the sexes that would allow for any inequalities to be made."*[7]

And here's the opinion of a psychoanalyst:

"*. . . for us, 'anatomy is not destiny.' But this does not mean that anatomy counts for nothing.* Anatomy causes the castration complex to take the form of penis envy in the girl which explains the prevalence in her of what would be called the *privative* aspect of all imaginary identification, whereas the boy imagines himself 'coupled' with the *object*—which is as Lacan explains, an 'affliction.'

"For even if it is true that the ego of the girl builds itself along the same principle of *Lust,* as that of the boy, and that therefore there is nothing astonishing in the fact that she undergoes the same fear of castration, it is nonetheless true that her tranquility on this matter is much greater."[8]

b) The Developments in Culture

We could turn now to cultural history and see if men have progressively unlocked the secret of the engima of the Sphinx.

As I have said, it does seem that the first attempt to give meaning to sexuality consisted in relating it to the forces of the sacred: ". . . the first properly human meaning given to sexuality appeared in phallic cults where it was associated with the cosmic forces that lead the frenzied dance of the life-and-death cycles. Sexuality drew its meaning from that cosmic dimension by which man participated in a vital energy that transcended his expending himself in the dissemination of life and returning to the indefinite cycles of nature by death."[9] Linked to the rhythms of nature as primitive man percieved them (i.e. life and death, and life once again rising out of death), sexuality is interpreted here as a divine force, and therefore sacred (that is to say, both good and evil).[10] Through this divine force, man becomes associated, in the orgiastic festivity which symbolizes and ritualizes it, with the resuscitated and resuscitating power of nature: but this association is also the occasion of perceiving the link between sexuality and violence, i.e., between sexuality and the disorder that threatens the Laws of the City. To make sexuality sacred bespeaks its terrifying aspect associating man with a force which dominates him and which he can control only at the cost of constant deception; celebration is a sign of that, as it lifts prohibitions but within a framework that has lines carefully pre-drawn.

Sexuality is sacred because it risks precipitating the return of non-differentiation at any moment, a resurgence of evil forces which submerge the fragile city of man. Itself a conquest over nature, the city cannot but fear whatever profoundly reminds it of the violence from which it has come. But sexuality is also sacred because it is a means of organizing the world, of distinguishing between man and woman, the child and the adult, favorable and unfavorable times (for example, the woman's regulating cycles, and her menstrual period). It risks casting men headlong into nondifferentiation, but it can also organize the city, structure exchanges with other groups, and qualify social and economic roles. . . .

If making sex sacred means integrating it into a social scheme while acknowledging its threat, it also, in the same breath, means placing it on the side of anonymous cosmic forces which come upon man at will. Man can, of course, play tricks with these forces, try to appease them, but they remain a sign of his radical dependence. But, in order for man to affirm his uniqueness, he must deny whatever so obviously enslaves him to instinctive forces. Isn't the fact of sexuality which man shares with animals, a sign of the non-human that man seeks to disengage himself from? It is at this point that man defines himself as a spirit, or reason, and thus dissociates himself from the world and gives himself to a transcendent and abstract God. Man takes his destiny in hand, refusing to allow himself to be imposed upon by his instinctive urges.

The spiritualization of man, the rejection of the animal side of sexuality, the finite and moral nature, causes sexuality to lose its divine character and also allows for the transition from ritual to ethic. It is at this moment that reflection on standards appears, in Greece through the playwrights and the philosophers as well as in Israel through the prophets and lawmakers. Without a doubt, this interpretation has stamped all of western civilization. This will be seen more fully in Chapter IV. It must be acknowledged that this de-sacredizing of sexuality, replaced by reason in Greece, and by faith in the Word of God in Israel, was crucial in the evolution of man's consciousness of himself. This break, this putting aside of sex, was probably needed so that the human person could emerge. But, separated from the development of a person, sex, now stripped of its sacred prestige, risks being reduced to a genital function with no symbolic meaning.

We know the results: the most serious has, without doubt, been that for a long time sexuality and love have been dissociated, since love was conceived of as only a communion of souls with the divine and in the divine, i.e. on the other side of death. A dream of eternal love which nourishes itself more from itself than from the beloved-other, and which in the last analysis is nothing but a love of self-eternally-dreamt, far removed from the contingencies that sexuality incessantly, and rightly so, recalls in us.

Considering sexuality as a negative factor necessarily gave rise to contrary interpretations: suppose this negativity was itself the possibility for man's affirmation of freedom with regard to God? The transgression of moral and social law through sexuality, then, becomes the very sign of strength for the libertine.

In the libertine interpretation—the other basic current that runs through our culture—sexuality is certainly recognized and exalted, but as the potential for increasing the power of an individual in continual triumph over the other: this explains why the game of seduction must relentlessly be played. What is Don Juan, or Valmont in *Liasons dangereuses,* searching for? "After all, the growth of a passion has infinite charm, and the true pleasure of life is in its variety. How deliciously sweet to lay siege to a young heart; to watch one's progress day by day; to overcome by means of vows, tears and groans, the delicate modesty of a soul which sighs in surrender; to break down little by little the weakening resistance, the maidenly scruples that her honor dictates, and bring her at last where we would have her to be. But once we have our desire, there is no more to wish for. The best is behind. And we rest on our laurels until a new object appears to reawaken our desire, and lure us on with the charms of a new conquest."[11] Don Juan must continually prove his strength, and that is why, as Molière understood so well, the libertine must also affirm in a hundred ways that he is above communal laws, including the most sacred one of Christianity which places the weak, the poor, under God's protection (Act III, ii). At his worst, Don Juan, like Sade, defies God by using sex as a weapon to prove the inanity of moral law and the impunity of rebellion. As an anarchist, even to the point of sapping the ideology of his own class, Don Juan is a black hero, a sadist who uses sexuality as the most efficient method given to the strong man to enable him to dominate the weak, to crush them and reduce them to begging. And this is done to affirm, in the presence of the conquered, the omnipotence of the liberated man, of superman. He announces a world in which by conquering bodies man thinks himself rid of the mystery which inhabits flesh. A bizarre reversal. Don Juan, the free man, cannot even admit his own vulnerability and thus remains engulfed in a sphere of resentment. Believing himself freed of the restrictions of laws, he can only affirm this freedom by prohibiting the existence of others, because the other, by the very fact that he is, reminds the libertine of the fundamental law which he is afraid of confronting. To reduce the other to a body to be conquered and possessed and consequently cast aside is to deny that the other is word, an irreducible otherness, and that the other always somehow eludes the childish claims of the omnipotence of the libertine. The libertine's triumph is in each instance a bitter failure. If Don Juan is a tragic person it's because he is deceived from the beginning about what he is doing: he blindly thinks he is fighting for freedom and does not realize that his freedom lies with those he is overpowering, in their irreducible aspect which ever eludes him.

The interest around the Don Juan myth is in the admission of this failure; in the myth, our western civilization expressed very clearly, although indirectly, its tremendous desire for power and yet its conviction that this desire leads to death. . . .

The libertine, the shadowy double of Tristan, links, like Tristan, sexuality to death, which alone can ultimately fulfill the promises of desire. However, neither Don Juan nor Tristan are the major characters in the drama of western morality. They represent instead the antitype of the less prestigious character who has sought throughout the ages to reconcile his need for order with his need for love. What dominates in the West is really an interpretation of sexuality which links its meaning, if not all the practice of it besides, to the formation of the stable couple—in other words, a conjugal couple. Sexuality is given meaning within the framework, of a stable and faithful couple.[12] We might summarize this interpretation by saying that sexuality will be called human when it will allow or express a successful love relationship. The obviously ambiguous word "successful" should be elaborated: a love relationship is successful when it is free, mature, creative and integrated. Free, because there cannot be authentic sexual encounter without freedom of the partners; rape, which has ever been the vehicle of phantasm, has never been recognized by humanity as a model of successful encounter! Mature, because in this perspective, a sexual relationship requires the partners to be as free as possible from their childish dependencies; physical and psychical maturity do not necessarily equal each other! Creative, because it seeks to create a new reality which is other than and more than the sum of the two individual parts: a child is the ultimate sign of the new reality carved out by the partners together, but not the only sign: a whole network of connections is woven between the two partners and also because of them, and this constitutes a new social, cultural and affective reality. Finally, integrated, because we cannot separate sexuality from the rest of existence; it is called upon to signify and to allow a more total relationship, inclusive of the whole activity of the two people and not just of their sexual desire.

Such is the essence of the dominant ethical stance of western civilization today. It is diffuse in personal and social applications where it functions as the norm by whose authority many, and probably the majority of people, judge the success of their lives. But this stance itself is being shaken. On one hand, as we have pointed out, it is being challenged by the new standard which makes success in sex (in the quasi-technical meaning) a more decisive criteria than that of love. The subtle objectifying of sexuality tends to shatter the ideal of a system in which it is fundamentally linked with love.

But it is mostly the facts that challenge this interpretation: placing too much value on the couple per se, at a time when a great number of traditional social restraints are losing their effectiveness, does burden the partners with a very heavy responsibility.[13] If the couple is to be both a social counter-model (where, for example, equality between man and woman can be lived out in a way that is not acknowledged elsewhere in society), as well as a place for refuge sheltered from the reach of society where man and woman can come to full development, then such a scheme establishes terribly rigorous objectives. And difficult to attain: the growing number of divorces and the growing phenomenon of "trial marriages" is proof of that. That scheme, however, does indicate the power of the utopian concept of a long-lasting and loving couple, especially since the facts unfortunately do not match up with it. It must be that somehow this utopia sins in its idealism, that in one way or another it misunderstands the reality of sex.[14]

We could say that about all the interpretations described so far (which have been a sample and not an exhaustive list!) in this brief journey through history and civilization. Each of these interpretations illuminates certain aspects of the problem, but in the end they fail to resolve the tension that arises from trying to integrate sexuality into a system that would humanize it; the obstacles which sexual, and also social, reality present to such a system quickly and cruelly emphasize the limitations of any clear word and thus of any ethic of sexuality.

The connection between sexuality and verbal expression is more profound and more crucial than has been stated up to this point. Here, at this juncture, the contribution of analytical anthropology is needed.

c) The Law of Language and the Humanization of Sexuality

We have seen that without language there is no human sexuality. But the contribution of the quasi-evidence of physiology and of the other stances elaborated by culture have not yet made clear the connection between sexuality and language which strives to give it meaning. For up until now we have treated sexuality as an object—"here-it-is"—which language is supposed to explain; but psychoanalysis tells us that in reality sexuality becomes human only because it runs up against the inflexible law of language which precedes and structures it. Let us rapidly describe this head-on encounter in order to grasp the ethical stakes that are involved.

The most decisive experience, which in the end conditions all the subsequent expressions that man can give to his sexual existence, occurs when the child passes from the first stage (non-distinguishing), in which he knows himself necessarily organic, to that of being a subject. Now this experience is radically linked to language. It is really the spoken word of the other which gives the child his identity by *naming* him. This is what Jacques Lacan brought to light while studying what he calls the "mirror stage."[15] In order for a child to abandon the imaginary identification of the "I" with his body, or with separate parts of the body of the other, he must be able to see *himself.* That is impossible, contends Lacan, unless the *voice* of the other *names* him something, i.e. addresses him as a being other than his body, as a symbolic unity which his name represents. This is literally nothing except the expression of desire by the other that the child live, as other-reality, as otherness. In the mirror the child sees not the visual image, but the name he hears. When the child sees what he hears, he becomes a subject, i.e. that invisible reality which cannot be named. Through his name, the subject is set apart: "This setting apart releases him from an obsession with himself as object and leads the subject to the refusal of being a thing so that now he only sees it or has it (body)."[16] He is no longer the thing he sees (or imagines), he is someone who links his real body to his imaginary one (that of the desire of the other).

It is precisely here that we encounter the law, a reality that is attested to in the word of the other which sets apart the subject.[17]

The law then is linked to the structure of language. In effect, it is through the mode of language that this setting apart of the subject occurs, his disentanglement from identification with things. Language is both an instrument of communication and a means of bringing one into contact with the real. By its very meaning, language permits the linking of individuals (or objects) through the perspective of distance. As a pre-established system in which the child finds himself, but in which he must and should participate in order to communicate with others, language compels a renunciation of the satisfaction of immediate pleasure: "The child does not agree to the symbolization of his urges until the direct appeasement of the body by the body. . . . is no longer possible. At this point he can invent a long detour which goes through vocal, mimetic, and gestural expression."[18] An individual does not accept the order brought through language except by renouncing the satisfaction of the body by the body. He does not become a subject except by yielding to the symbolic order of communication—distanced by a renunciation on the imaginary level of a participation which fuses him with the other.

Thus it is through a renunciation of the security of non-distinction that the child gains access to the possibility of a communication between his "I" and another. And this is the equivalent for him of also admitting his own limitation: I am not the whole, I am only this "I" which lives through the desire of others and their recognition. For what language says between the lines, "inter-dict," is the fundamental law which the father symbolizes, the prohibition against incest, which simultaneously bars access to the mother and creates a necessary space for life, a shelter from the sexual aggression of those near at hand.

The function of the name of father is the prohibiting of immediate fulfillment. The father must oppose the child's identification of himself with what he believes to be his mother's desire with regard to him. He achieves this by separating the mother from the child. This is done in the name of the "law" which is no longer represented in our societies by an initiation rite, but expressed through reciprocal desire which bond the father and mother together. (Heaven help him if their desires are pathogenic!) The law is anterior even to the conception of the child: "The Oedipal context is characterized by the setting into motion of a law prior to the conception of the child, to the extent that the law of language governs the parental covenant. . . . It is on the level of unconscious desire, which links the child to the body of the mother (his wife), that the word which is 'spoken-between' in the alliance (i.e. his child) emerges— it is on this level that the prohibition against incest takes form."[19]

What is prohibited is the identification of the child with his fantasy. He must run up against this established boundary which is the desire of the parents and their unity in encounter. "The law . . . prohibits the subject from confusing himself with the multiplicity of functions and impulses that take place within him. At the same time, the Other becomes the bearer of Law—the Other who is and who becomes the reference point."[20]

We can try, with P. David, to somewhat clarify what is meant by *the law*. The prohibition against incest expresses itself in regulations concerning consanguinity and marital union. This covenant, a contractual union with mutual commitment, and consanguinity, the bond of rights that exist between a mother and a father and their offspring (signified through the bestowal of the family name) are the historical conditions wherein the symbolic encounter is expressed. This is what makes the marital union and family ties possible. "It is an act of recognition and mutal esteem which entails the respecting of certain regulations"[21] It thus implies the recognition of the otherness of others according to certain rules, some of which belong to the conscious realm of customs and habits, and some of which belong to the unconscious realm, which psychoanalysis has shown can lead to serious consequences if ignored.

In other words, it is the word of union and mutual recognition which the parents have addressed to each other which becomes important. In this respect, the family name is much more than the insertion of an individual into a group; it is proof of the implicit or explicit pact between the progenitors themselves and between the progenitors and their offspring. Psychoanalysis, along with other sciences, testifies what it costs the child if this pact is scorned.

Thus the law expresses itself in the recognition of sexual difference as otherness and in the acknowledgement of the pact which unites and links the parents together and also prohibits the child at the same time with regard to sex with his mother.

To summarize what this brief selection from psychoanalysis has helped us to understand; it is the law of language which gives human meaning to sexuality, that is, which establishes it as a locus of experiencing otherness and of experiencing one's own limits, and as a potential locus for union (covenant) with another. These two points are fundamental, in my opinion: they indicate the crux of a meaning—the same meaning that an ethic must elaborate with a view towards formulating a norm.

Sexuality, then, is the locus of experiencing otherness, because the law prohibits the identification of a subject with his urges or with his fantasy and separates him from himself to turn his gaze outward to the Other, the father who carries the law, and with him, the Other, world, things, reality. The law establishes a limit, a check whereby the subject is halted. But the law also grounds the human subject in the twofold reality (which he is forced to accept) of precedence and limitation. Man is not his own origin, nor his own foundation, rather he is the consequence of the words of a union (covenant) pronounced before he came to be; and he is not the whole, but simply some "one" in a given place and time, sexed in a certain way, forever separated from his mother who is not himself. Precedence and limitation are the conditions of the expression of desire. Because I can be spoken, I can speak. The order of language constitutes me. Man exists only to consent to the word which precedes him.

The recognition of this foundational limit is also the potential pathway to communication with others, and even to the exchange of a spoken covenant (union) between specific and unique men and women. Thus we recognize that we are not our own beginning nor our own foundation and that we live only to speak (and not to keep for ourselves) the word of love which precedes us.

Sexuality, then, cannot be, without perversion, the locus of abolishing limitation or difference. The gnostic dream of a return to the Undifferentiated Whole is really a denial of the law of language, and thus a rejection of that which by its imposition of limitation is the very condition for the possibility of a communication. Likewise sexuality cannot become human except through the acceptance of the irreducibility of the other who becomes united to me to the same extent that he is not myself and never will be, a refusal of narcissism through consenting to one's limitation and through rejecting the violence which would attempt to reduce otherness: these are the conclusions, negatively expressed, of this brief analysis.

3. Conclusion

At the beginning of this first part, I said we were trying to understand the actual context in which we are situated. Now we can concentrate on this point.

The context of all moral reflection is that of a vivid consciousness that sexuality is never without a social language that controls and organizes it, corrects it, and assigns meaning to it. Even when we try to throw off the restraints imposed by social standards, as is the case in our western society, we see that it is done less to abolish standards than to propose more acceptable ones. It remains to be seen for whom these new standards are more acceptable: is it for the real needs of modern man, or for the advantage of ruling power (today more economic and technocratic than political)?

As we approach the biblical texts and those of Christian tradition, we should keep in mind this close link between morality and social needs. We can no longer accept just any moral position, even one full of biblical references, as the real thing; in any case, moral standards are at the service of the social group (and the important thing to know is to what extent!) in defense against the centrifugal forces that threaten it; the truth of moral position is then, to some extent, only limited and contingent.

But, and this was especially apparent as we analyzed the new values of contemporary sexual morality, the discourse on morality cannot be reduced to this unique social function because it also expresses a rebellion against the reduction of man to merely useful social functions; it bespeaks the possible meaning of sexuality which always in a certain way goes beyond how society lives it out or accepts it. Thus the modern stance of "sexual freedom" certainly does carry an aspect of social control: it corresponds only too well to the needs of our technical and objectifying society, but it also bespeaks the nostalgia and even the hope of a relationship between people that is not purely functional, of a larger space given to desire and its inventions, a need for freedom in the acknowledged vulnerability of bodies. . . .

We must try to take this protest into account when we approach the ethical domain directly. Apart from that, we cannot say that our contemporary society is more capable than its predecessors of giving a meaning to sexuality which simultaneously ensures both social life and individual life. The brief excursion into the history of culture pointed out that all the interpretations offered up until now demonstrate by their very diversity that so far no objective truth has been established. At the very most, and certainly this counts for something, analytic anthropology presented two themes, i.e. otherness and union, which perhaps have an important ethical significance but only if we can say what direction they are moving in, that is, what kind of otherness and what kind of union is really at issue. By determining that, we can measure just how conclusive, or limited, the contribution of the humanities is vis-à-vis morality. Conclusive, because they define the conditions for the anthropological possibility of an ethical reflection; limited because they cannot (and do not wish to) comment on the validity of the meaning which man ascribes to it. We partly know what cannot be said about sexuality without risking a flight from reality, but we do not yet know by what authority to speak about a human significance of sexuality.

The meanings which man has given sexuality are multiple and I have referred to some of them already. Certain ones really seem aberrant (but perhaps we are out of touch with the social context from which they emerged: we will have to bear this in mind as we deal with the complex history of Christian sexual morality); other interpretations appear to be the immediate and direct expression of the needs of the social group that proposes them; others seem to aspire to a tension between the necessities of reality and the transcendence of liberty. I say "seem" and "appear" because we do not have the necessary criteria to pronounce a value judgment. By what authority can we say that this or that way of dealing with sexuality is valid or invalid? But if we want to propose an ethical system we have to ask the question about validity while remaining aware of the weight of social imperatives concerning the manner in which we ask the question.

The Christian formulator of ethics cannot escape; he also must in turn tell by what authority he proposes the particular perspective which seems better to him than others. That is the topic of the next two chapters of this book.

II

Man and Woman in the Image of God: Scriptural Theology of Sexuality

Social sciences demonstrate that sexuality is always socialized, i.e. rigorously controlled. Nevertheless sexuality always, in a certain way, eludes social control to become the place of the discovery and sudden revealing of a person, a possible escape from social restraint, and indeed a challenge to it. The human significance of sexuality is to be found in the difficult and precarious inter-relation between the social language which imposes standards, and thereby creates a meaning, and the individualized spoken word which discovers a place for its affirmation of freedom in the context of a sexual relationship. The ethical issue is found in this tenuous relation between the needs of society, the conditions necessary to its very existence, and the hope that animates some people in the task of liberation. It remains for us, of course, to define the validity of social standards and the system that contests them. In the preceding chapter, we saw that the question could not be entirely settled by scientific analyses; these help define the problem but do not offer judgments on the validity of the solutions which men have suggested. If we now wish to address the question, we cannot merely describe the facts, but must make value judgments and consequently also discuss their rationale.

By what authority do I, as a Christian theologian, enter the debate on the value of certain moral standards concerning sexual matters? On the grounds of my conviction that the Word of God,[1] as expressed with all the ambiguity of human language, nevertheless reveals the ultimate

33

issues of human existence, and puts them in a perspective which reveals their theological meaning. With regard to this conviction, let me simply say for now that I will try to demonstrate its relevance during the biblical exegesis I will be undertaking. It is for the reader to determine at the end of this study whether or not the demonstration has convinced him. One note must be added: to approach biblical tradition in order to find ultimate enlightenment on the fundamental stakes of existence does not mean abandoning all spirit of criticism in the face of biblical language— on the contrary! What I am really interested in is to see how, within the ambiguity of this truly human language, i.e. language in context, men have tried to understand and speak forth the Word which by faith we believe comes from God, i.e. from this Other who presents Himself as the Alpha and the Omega of the truth of existence. In order to discover this Word, we must first acknowledge the complexity of the human events wherein this Word is always "made flesh," and try to perceive how the texts themselves express that which is contained in them and comes through them.

My study presupposes, then, a critical exegesis of the texts, which is required by scientific honesty and which is itself supported by the conviction that the biblical texts can become the source of the revelation of a Word having both a significant value and a liberating power—which thereby attests to its unique authority. This is the reason I am investigating biblical tradition. My investigation will be done in two stages. First of all I will look at the traditions which approach sexuality with regard to its dangerous aspect and which place restrictive controls upon it. These ancient traditions, transmitted especially by the priestly milieu under the form of statutes, represent an initial ethical development on sexuality. This became the reference point, even if and when later opposed, by which the more theologically developed traditions, which we will look at next, were defined. If the former place the emphasis on the threat of sexuality, the latter insist on the sudden coming forth of the word which sexuality allows between a man and a woman. In distinguishing these two stages, I am not thereby introducing a hierarchy, but merely wish to highlight how, in biblical tradition itself, the social aspect of the order of differentiation is closely linked to the order of otherness which is more strictly theological.

1. The Order of Differentiation: Sexuality Between Life and Death

In biblical tradition as elsewhere, sexuality is the locus of an ambiguous, and therefore dangerous, experience. This ambiguity is highlighted, in the oldest traditions, by a whole series of prohibitions whose function is to protect society as a whole from certain dangers to which sexuality exposes men, and to propose positive significations allowing sexuality to be integrated into a constructive scheme.

The "priestly" tradition[1] has preserved, particularly in the book of Leviticus, countless notations of these prohibitions. What do they mean? In chapters 11–16 of Leviticus, there is a whole series of instructions on the clean and the unclean; a strange succession of prohibitions and permissions unfolds with no apparent logic: sometimes they concern animals (Chapter 11), sometimes the woman who has just given birth (12), or the leper (13–14), or sexuality (15) and the purification rite for the Day of Atonement (16). What is the link in all these instances of uncleanness? I think I can risk presenting the following hypothesis: those things and those people are declared unclean who do not, in one way or another, correspond to the integration of the order of things willed by God.

For instance, the animals:[2] we notice first of all that the animals declared clean are those which are necessary to the life of man, in the context of being an Israelite, who is shepherd and not a hunter, sedentary and not a nomad. The animals blessed by God, the clean, are those with whom man has formed a covenant of familiarity, of service; for the Israelite this means ruminants with cloven hooves.[3] By extension, animals without these characteristics are reputed to be unclean. The distinction between clean and unclean serves to organize the world into an order by which man can dwell in his own space: this becomes even more apparent when examining the system of classification for the other animals.

Animals are classified into three categories (following the order of Creation, cf. Genesis 1:20, 25, 28) according to their natural habitat: there are beasts of the earth (Lev. 11:2–8) which, as we have discussed, are classified as clean and unclean; then there are aquatic creatures (Lev. 11:9–12); and finally winged creatures (Lev. 11:13–23). The latter two categories also contain clean and unclean animals: the clean are those that are specifically adapted to their habitat, at least from the vantage point of an empirical observer. Thus aquatic creatures that are clean have fins and scales (Lev. 11:9) because they are adapted to the requirements of water life; the same is true for the clean birds: they have feathers and wings and fly. By contrast, animals who are not adapted to their habitat are unclean, i.e. the water animals who lack fins and scales, and the animals with wings that do not fly (Lev. 11:20), as well as the animals that dwell on land but do not walk (Lev. 11:42), etc. In brief, all the animals who do not conform to the characteristics of world order, such as the Israelite conceives them, are unclean, i.e. they carry a peril for those who touch them. What peril? The danger of disorder, the sudden appearance of primeval chaos which is always a potential (cf. Gen 1:2) and which can engulf the world and men. Every animal that bears the mark of disorder, in being an ill-defined or hybrid creature, must scrupulously be avoided. And even more so when it is dead (Lev. 11:24, 28, 32–38), for then it is doubly dangerous: as an abnormal animal and as a corpse—which again is a hybrid state, i.e. it has the appearance of life but already is something else, a decomposing body, a body on its way to becoming a non-body.

The rest of Leviticus seems to confirm this hypothesis. The woman who has just given birth (Lev. 12) is unclean because she was for a moment—at the time of giving birth—a hybrid being, in some way double: she is herself as well as the other which has come out of her. For an instant she represented a threat of disorder, like a dangerous space that has opened up in the order of things: one cannot become two without causing, at the moment when it occurs, the appearance of disorder! Likewise the leper (Lev. 13–14), who was a well-known and fearful danger to ancient societies, is a spectacular example of a physical monstrosity who, like a deadly disorder, risks infecting the other members of the community. Leprosy is contagious, and therefore similar to the disorder which "de-structures" the group and abandons it to the death of its internal hostilities.

Sexuality is also categorized along these lines. The text (Lev. 15) describes the many instances of "sexual uncleanness" which is to say the times when sexuality does not function according to the norms of the accepted order. When a man experiences "discharge from his body," i.e., venereal disease (Lev. 15:1–15) or loss of semen (Lev. 15:16–17), the disorder arises from the fact that man's sperm should not be discharged elsewhere but into the woman (and this is the same reason that onanism [Gen 38:9ff.] is condemned). What comes out of the man or what escapes from him is dangerous because it symbolizes the lack of enclosure around man and around the openings which are in him.[4] Something escapes out of man (sperm) or out of woman (flow of blood, etc. cf. Lev. 15:19–27) which represents a loss of wholeness; for what flows out of man is himself but also other than himself, something which blurs the clear-cut boundary lines of a body. And this is valid since the sperm and the blood have to do with life itself (cf. Lev. 17 on specific prohibitions concerning blood, the seat of life); any outflow from man or woman blurs the most essential boundary line (like the corpse who is the best example of the unclean), the line which separates life from death.

Another very interesting "uncleanness" in view of this discussion: "If a man lies with a woman and has an emission of semen, both of them shall bathe themselves in water, and be unclean until evening." (Lev. 15:18). The act of intercourse also causes some kind of risk to occur, since it causes uncleanness. Why? In my opinion, because the sexual act is the instance where man and woman abolish the line that separates and differentiates them, and where they risk, for a moment, forming a hybrid being, a kind of undifferentiated androgen. Here again, the threat lies in the disappearance of set limits. Under these circumstances, then, men and women should never forget, even if it seems to be abolished by the sexual act, the "ordering" role appointed to sexual difference, respect for which guarantees world order.

This idea reappears in Chapter 18 of Leviticus which presents a long list of prohibitions concerning sexuality: incest (Lev. 18:7–18), sexual relations with a woman during her cycles (18:19), adultery (18:20), child-sacrifice (21), homosexuality (22), sodomy (23). All these practices defile the land. All these instances issue from the same far-reaching logic: whatever sows confusion, in this case whatever abolishes sexual difference, is forbidden because it carries a latent deadly threat.[5] Thus homosexuality is an "abomination," as are sodomy and child-sacrifice, and of course incest, which abolishes the line between the interior and the exterior of the clan. In all these cases, the law of God has been violated, the law which Leviticus summarizes this way: "I am the Lord thy God; consecrate yourselves therefore and be holy, for I am holy." (Lev. 11:44; 19:2). This signifies that one must respect the order of things fixed by God, the order which is so lyrically celebrated by the priestly tradition in the great hymn of the creation of the world (Gen. 1:1–2:4). Thus we read in Lev. 19:19 (Deut. 22:9–11): "You shall keep my statutes. You shall not let your cattle breed with a different kind; you shall not sow your field with two kinds of seed; nor shall there come upon you a garment of cloth made of two kinds of stuff." Holiness, in this context, becomes the rejection of hybrids.[6]

There is, then, an order which God has established to which sexuality must be referred, but which is elsewhere expressed by sexuality in its own way. A quick look at the other texts of the priestly tradition reveals the essential elements of this.

a) God's order is victorious against the threatening forces of chaos (Gen. 1:2). God structures the world by successively separating diverse elements (Gen. 1:4,6) which are established in their respective places, and thus differentiated: primeval chaos with its reign of non-differentiation is succeeded by God's created world which is marked by differentiation. Thus, diverse living species are created "after their kind" (Gen. 1:11, 12, 21, 24, 25). And finally man, in the image of God, is created male and female, with a sign of differentiation stamped into his very flesh (Gen. 1:27; cf. Gen. 5:2). Sexuality is not an unfortunate accident, but rather the high point of God's creative act: man is not only created other than the world and other than the animals, he is created in God's image—in a structural relationship to someone other than himself, experiencing even in his flesh the order of differentiation which he crowns and dominates (Gen. 1:28).

We can see the importance of this order of differentiation in the very sign of the covenant which God entered into with Abraham, the father of the chosen people, namely circumcision. It is in fact by the sign of circumcision that the elective covenant of God is marked from generation to generation (cf. Gen. 17:10–14). Precisely what is the meaning of this ritual? An interesting interpretation of the Jewish tradition sees it as an act which brings about manhood, and as a sharper differentiation between the sexes: . . . [it is] a misinterpretation to liken circumcision to castration even if—or especially since—circumcision, because of certain western cultural influences, could more or less totally lose its true significance and be contaminated by the castration complex. In its original meaning, it was an *unveiling*—(the Zohar, using the example of a nut and its shell, states that everything has a covering but is also a covering itself). . . . It's a matter, then, of coming into manhood. The foreskin, moreover, on account of certain embryological hypotheses and because of its form as a "sheath". . . constitutes a female symbol. Circumcision then is the emergence of virility away from animality and is at the same time a more clear-cut differentiation with reference to femininity."[7]

Thus, at the moment when God seals the covenant with Abraham, He does so while emphasizing the importance of sexual differentiation, in instituting this very difference as a sign itself of His covenant. Because man has entered into a covenant relationship with God, he can truly consent to the differentiation: a difference vis-à-vis God that sexual differentiation symbolizes. Man can recognize in that which constitutes a limitation for him—his sexual character fully acknowledged—the very condition for a love relationship which recognizes the other as a partner in a covenant. The union of man and woman can thus be in the image of the one between God and man, not a relationship of non-differentiation and confusion, but the relationship of partners who are different and separate.

As a key to the whole order of differentiation which structures the world, sexuality should be lived out by the man and the woman as the very meaning of all differentiation, that is, recognized as a call to a relationship that is organizational and creative, like a call to arms against the constant threat of disorder and chaos, whose most insidious form is the confusion of the sexes.

b) Based on this, the blessing of God upon sexual life takes on a whole significance. In the recitation of creation already quoted (Gen. 1:27ff.), the blessing of God—"Be fruitful and multiply, and fill the earth and subdue it"—is in fact the consequence of the creation of man in God's image as "male and female." We must avoid making procreation the primary rationale or the only rationale for sexuality, for the text clearly shows that it is not central. On one hand, the same blessing is pronounced upon the animals (Gen. 1:22) so it therefore is not the specific characteristic of man's relationship to the woman; on the other hand, it is sexuality as representing differentiation, and not as representing fruitfulness, that is pronounced in the text (Gen. 1:27) as the sign of being in the image of God. This specific point is important in understanding the theological meaning of the link the Bible makes between sexuality and procreation: only the blessing of God can make procreation a creative act, a participation in the very creation of God. The human couple is not truly fruitful, in the biblical sense, unless they consent to live out the differentiation as the possible locus of the revelation of and the acceptance of the other (God, partner, child). Procreation itself is thus not the meaning of sexuality, but rather the promise attached to it if it does not lose sight of the image of God which it manifests.

In reading the Old Testament, one can sense a certain tension about this last point. The priestly tradition has a tendency to highlight the positive aspect of procreation as the means of securing the permanence of a people "from generation to generation."[8] The blessing of God is irreversible and therefore assures a continuity of history; thus, man and woman need only enter into that blessing in order to be assured of descendants. However, the yahwist and elohist traditions[9] are much more conscious of procreation as a miraculous gift of love from God: "natural" procreation alone does not suffice to ensure the continuity of the promise. It is not Ishmael, the natural offspring of Abraham, who receives the promise, but Isaac, the child of promise, the child of a quasi-miracle (cf. Gen. 17:15–21; 18:10–14). What these traditions seek to demonstrate is that procreation receives its true meaning only when it is situated within the plan of God. To give birth to children is first of all to agree to this: the life which is transmitted does not really belong to the transmitter but is entrusted to him as a promise and as a gift. What is primary is its aspect as gift—gift of God and by extension gift of man to the woman and of woman to the man,[10] of which the child becomes the living sign. Thus, man and woman experience the creative reality of love which is the foundation for and precedes the procreative aspect of sexuality. The yahwist and elohist traditions emphasize that procreation is a blessing from God insofar as it expresses the continuity of the promise of God to man and woman which enables them to receive and accept one another in love (which is related so well in the accounts of Isaac's love for Rebecca and of Jacob's for Rachel, Gen. 24 and 29).

Whatever nuances there may be, it is clear that the scriptural tradition as a whole links sexuality to the blessing of God on life. Sexuality is a creative force: God does not take back His promise, and men and women have always experienced this fact. But it is creative in the truest sense only when it accepts being preceded on one hand and pre-ordained on the other hand. Preceded, that is, by the creative Word of God: man is not his own beginning, and his sexuality must not be the opportunity of asserting his lust or his dream of omnipotence; but, on the contrary, it is the occasion of consenting to his finiteness and his incompleteness, in which he can rejoice and in which he can perceive the traces of the love that precedes him and is his very foundation. Preceded and pre-ordained. Pre-ordained in this great battle that the Bible wages continually against idolatry. Since God is the creator of the whole world and not of a world or a part of the world, and since He is Other, and different, sexuality must signify our humanity, and not our participation in the supernatural forces that inhabit the world. The difference attested to by sexuality also attests to our humanity: we are not God. Better yet, the difference is given as the potential for a relationship of persons who can never become the other, as God is to us! Potential for a relationship where the other can be accepted, recognized, loved. Every effort to minimize the difference always ends in death, which is why it is an "abomination"; it is idolatrous because it manifests a fascination with self, a closing in on oneself, a deadly refusal of the other. Because human sexuality can function as an acknowledgment of difference but can just as easily function as an exaltation of the idolatrous pride of man, it thus always hovers between life and death.

2. In the Beginning, Otherness. . .

An ambiguous social fact—that's the picture of sexuality in the texts we have seen. But more than that! Even if it can be the means through which the deadly peril of disorder can enter the community (cf. the prohibitions on sexual uncleanness in Leviticus), sexuality can also be, as we have seen, the locus of experiencing something of the order of the world as structured by God according to the separation of kinds and species and a clear affirmation of that differentiation. Moreover, man and woman, through sexuality, participate in the creative blessing of God on life; they themselves experience the creative force of relationship.

It is this latter insight which other texts of the biblical tradition pursue in depth, in linking theological reflection to anthropological study in a more definite fashion. How is sexuality related to the fact that man is a creature of God? How exactly can the relationship of a man with a woman manifest something of a relationship with God? These are the questions addressed to the texts that I come to now. I will begin with the teaching of Jesus who takes up and comments on the previous biblical tradition, in particular that of Genesis. This background to the evangelical tradition, especially the extraordinary passage which the yahwist tradition devotes to sexuality in Genesis 2 and 3, deserves some serious study. Finally, I will examine how sexuality, subsequent to the evangelical tradition, was lived out in a hellenistic Christian community, i.e. Corinth, and how that influence developed the Apostle Paul's reflections on the body.

a) "What God Has Joined Together": The Teaching of Jesus

Jesus expressed Himself very little on sexuality: His teachings in this area are certainly much less plentiful than those on money, power, violence or hyprocrisy. The only warning *against* sexuality is actually a warning against lust, which certainly can be expressed in sexuality, but covers a much broader range than that, as is shown by the context of the words of Jesus.[1] In itself, sexuality is not a problem for evangelical tradition; as a human given, it is caught up in all the ambiguities of man himself. If man is brought to his true humanity through the call of the Gospel, his sexuality then will also find its genuine relational dimension.[2]

But this does not mean that sexuality becomes a secondary issue in evangelical tradition. On the contrary. This becomes evident in the most important New Testamant text on sexuality, Matt. 19:4–6 (also Mark

10:6–9)[3]: "Have you not read that he who made them from the beginning made them male and female and said, 'For this reason a man shall leave his father and mother and be joined to his wife, and the two shall become one'? So they are no longer two but one. What therefore God has joined together, let no man put asunder."

This text, posited as directly from Jesus Himself, is evidently a major endorsement; it defines what could be called the evangelical and Christian tradition on sexuality. With regard to divorce, or rather the repudiation of the woman by the husband, the question of do's and don'ts in that area is presented to Jesus. He answers indirectly by returning to the very foundation of human life, i.e. the creative will of God as it is described in Genesis (1:27 and 2:24). "In the beginning" symbolically signifies the primary will of God. Jesus opposes the primary and foundational will of God to the Mosaic Law professed by the Pharisees. Faced with those who want to translate that which is contingent and historic—v. 8: "your hardness of heart" or the evil which constrains a legislator to intervene—into terms of destiny ("divine law"), Jesus recalls that the norm for all practices is found in the original will of God.

Jesus chooses, therefore, that which in biblical tradition seems to define the primary will of God—His intention, that which is "in the beginning"—in the name of which He judges the validity of the interpretations made by the people of Israel in the course of their history about this original intention. The functioning of the Law of Moses is thus judged by this key to interpretation. In so doing, Jesus confers primary authority on these texts at the beginning of Genesis. Christian tradition will never cease referring to them.

Jesus cites two different fragments: first of all, He hearkens back to Genesis 1:27, i.e. the culminating point of the first account of creation;[4] next, He quotes the conclusion of the second creation account, Genesis 2:24[5] to which He adds a brief parenthetical commentary. His choice is, to a certain extent, itself an interpretation. It is essential to notice which points Jesus insists on and which He leaves aside when He returns to the original text of Genesis.

What Jesus proves first is that sexual differentiation—"male and female he made them" (Matt. 19:4/Gen. 1:27)—is willed by God Himself as the fundamental anthropological structure. Sexuality is then neither an evil nor a misfortune; it is, rather, a gift from the Creator. This point is crucial with regard to all religious attempts (Christian included!) to disqualify sexuality. Scriptural tradition attests the fundamental goodness of sexuality. In a certain way, Jesus reinforces this affirmation by not quoting the following verse (Gen. 1:28) where sexuality is immediately interpreted as the potential to procreate, to fill the earth and subdue it. That point is not brought out by the text in the evangelical tradition. The quotation from Genesis immediately takes on a specific emphasis: sexual differentiation has something to do with God's very intention to make man in His image (Gen. 1:26). The experience of otherness which is made possible through sexual differentiation refers to and finds its meaning in the experience of the otherness of God.[6] But let's not go too fast. One conclusion is established from here on: in contrast to all dualistic and gnostic pessimism which assigns sexuality to the side of evil, misfortune or sin, evangelical tradition—supported by the authority of Christ—affirms that sexuality, a "good creation" by God, is part of man that, from the beginning, is willed by the Creator.

A second point can be emphasized. Sexuality is given to man as a means of his humanization. It was Georges Crespy who brought attention to the fact[7] that in the Gospel text (Matt. 19:4–5; Mark 10:6–7), the regrouping of the two quotes from Genesis (1:27 and 2:24) signifies this movement towards humanization by a transition from the sexual qualifier "male/female," the starting point, to the anthropological qualification "man/woman," a new reality that is infinitely more complex. There is, then, an indication in the text itself of a movement from nature to culture; sexuality is not human until it also signifies this transition, i.e. the recognition of the other (man or woman) in the impulse of sexual desire. That is what is indicated in the end of the verse from Gen. 2:24 "and the two become one flesh." The goal of sexuality is in this unity, which the sexual act at one and the same time allows for and expresses. This is a confirmation that sexuality concerns first of all the realm of relationship and is not primarily biological. Man and woman become one not primarily to procreate children but to encounter one another in the unique manner where, through sexuality, something of the ultimate mystery of human life, as God calls it to be, is revealed. It is therefore not scriptural to affirm, as nonetheless the tradition of western Catholic morality has, that procreation is the only ultimate goal of sexuality. Jesus in speaking of sexuality says not one word about its procreative function. This indicates that there is a depth to the meaning of sexuality which is far from being exhausted by its ultimate biological goal. That meaning concerns encounter, as indicated in the text by the expression "one flesh." The text not only notes the strength of the force of desire, i.e. stronger than the family ties of man to his parents, but also shows the promise that is linked to sexuality. Jesus recalls this text at the moment that He is being questioned about divorce, that is to say about the failure of relationship. Sexual desire can and should lead right up to this encounter which by the union of bodies symbolizes and allows for the unity of two beings. Thus, for Jesus, even more than for the author of Genesis it seems, sexual desire cannot be reduced to its procreative function, nor to its social function which allows the creation of a new familial entity (Gen. 2:24); it reveals something about the very essence of man, who exists only in relation to others.

The text of Genesis 2, to which the Gospel refers, is an admirable commentary on the risks and promises of this relationship with another. It shows how Man (Adam, the prototype of every man) recognizes in Woman (Eve, prototype of every woman) when she is presented to him by God, the one with whom an authentic relationship is possible (as opposed to the animals). " 'This at last is bone of my bones and flesh of my flesh!' " (Gen. 2:23). This amazed outcry contains the promise of a relationship, made possible by the recognition of similitude. But at the same time, his outcry betrays the ambiguity of a relationship founded on similarity only: only one of the partners of this first couple speaks, the woman remains silent during the whole scene. Here is an indication of the trap that relationship risks; one of the partners is in the process of reducing the other, of absorbing the other into himself: "bone of *my* bone, flesh of *my* flesh." Sexuality is the promise of authentic relationship, but only when both partners realize that each is indispensable to the other in their irreducible separateness.[8]

A third element can also be noticed in the text. Sexuality is described as the possibility (and also the consequence) of being uprooted from the infantile status and moving into adulthood: "Therefore a man leaves his father and mother and cleaves to his wife. . . ."

The movement of the man and woman towards each other affords this transition to the adult state and implies a breaking away from the preceding infantile state. Man and woman must leave the security of the family milieu to reconstitute, at their risk and peril, a new social and familial reality. The humanization of the man and woman by one another becomes possible less through a slow reciprocal maturation than by an initially painful uprooting.

But the reciprocal is equally true: sexuality, even if it allows for the uprooting from infantile dreams of security and dependence, is also, in its concrete manifestation, the consequence of this break. If the latter is not real on all levels, conscious and unconscious, sexuality can find itself redirected or blocked. How many couples have had this tragic experience!

Thus, biblical tradition situates sexuality within the global process of humanization where it plays an active and major role. In order for the break (leaving mother and father) to be possible, it is necessary that men and women have reached adulthood on the sexual plane, physiologically. This is a legitimate requirement of the sexuality which beckons men and women to uproot themselves from their original familial setting, which is incapable of a normal fulfillment of their desires. As the possibility of reaching adulthood, not only on the sexual but also on the social level, sexuality is also the consequence of this transition from one stage to another. If man and woman do not truly tear themselves away from their infantile dreams, then sexuality cannot permit a truly authentic relationship. That's what scriptural tradition wishes to show when it links the reality of the couple to the fact that the two partners really and totally share their existence with one another. "Sexuality in its fullness is a need to share the *condition* of the other, not only a brief sexual union but at every moment of the day, in a shared encounter of responsibilities, in a mutual enrichment and unfolding of self in the joy of living."[9]

Finally the gospel text records Jesus's commentary on the verses from Genesis: "Let no man put asunder what God has joined together!" This warning is at the same time a theological affirmation of extreme importance. Jesus recalls that the creative love of God Himself is found at the basis of the relationship which unites man and woman, a union in which sexuality functions as the sign and the locus. Sexuality is thus the token, the sign of the highest possible human vocation, that of being in relationship with God. Through it sexual life is called upon to signify, in the whole life of the human couple, the creative love of God. The failure of conjugal life is considered as the failure of God's creative handiwork, and as a sign of the more fundamental disturbance which affects the relation between God and men, between God and His people. This is why the sexual relationship can serve as a parable of God's relationship with His people in the Old Testament and of the relationship between Christ and the Church in the New Testament: the fact is, if sexuality becomes meaningful through the theological perspective in which scriptural tradition places it, it in turn clarifies the theological perspective itself, by furnishing a key to interpretation, i.e. God risks Himself before His people, before mankind, just as the fiancé before his fiancée.

And thus sexuality is affirmed by a theological meaning which it in turn enriches.

b) The Wonder and the Tragedy:
The Teaching of the Old Testament (O.T.)

There is, then, a definitive value placed on sexuality in the biblical tradition. But it is accompanied in the O.T. by the denunciation of the perversion to which it can fall prey. We must pause here to better understand what the Bible really wishes to make clear concerning the rapport between the recognition of otherness through sexuality and the recognition of the otherness of God through His Word. This constitutes, in my opinion, the decisive point of the scriptural teaching.

The Old Testament continually denounces any practice of sexuality that results in the loss of self in non-differentiation, in ecstasy. Because sexuality is a parable, it is a perversion to make it serve any experience which disqualifies word and lays claim to the immediacy of an encounter with the sacred, if not with God. This is why scriptural tradition, and especially that of the Old Testament, never ceases denouncing idolatrous sexuality which presents itself as the locus for instant experience of the divine, accompanied by loss of word. For God is not found in that place where man experiences loss of word, but rather is there where man understands the Word that is his foundation because it is other. Throughout the history of Israel, battle is waged against the orgiastic cults of the Canaanites with which Israel is faced; these cults link a perception of God to sexual orgasm, i.e. to the experience of a fusion with the undifferentiated by laying aside word, by a loss of consciousness of self. In this perspective, sexuality does not imply a personal relationship with another since the partner is here considered the mere occasion of an ineffable experience (which moreover is why the cults imply the institution of sacred prostitutes). Thus the concept of a divinity, which is considered as the whole in which man loses himself, carries with it a sexuality that abolishes, along with the Word, the personal value of the partners of the sexual act.

Therefore the Bible vigorously condemns this interpretation; what's at stake is the very concept of God. The God of the Bible is not the All in whom we lose ourselves, He is the All-Other whose Word speaks within each man and causes him to live and not die. He is the One in whom the gift of life originates, which belongs to us only so that we in turn can give it to another in the risk of encounter and love. Sexuality is an integral part of this gift—so much so that it becomes a parable of the relationship with the God who is All-Other, the Creator who binds Himself to us through the gift of the Word.

Thus the radical rejection of an ecstatic sexuality is primarily theological. That which is rejected is a theological perversion which misunderstands the otherness of God. The discovery of sexual practices where otherness was not acknowledged caused Israel to fully realize, after having entered Canaan, the theological opposition between itself and Canaanite religion (and later Greek religion). The history of Israel is marked by this twofold development: perceiving sexuality as the locus of a theological verification and having this very theology become the ultimate meaning of the relationship between a man and woman. For Israel, a "perverted" sexuality, one made sacred and aiming at non-differentiation, is a very clear indication of the rejection of the God of Word and of Promise. It is idolatry, that is, the cult of man founded on himself.

In opposition to this fascination with self, a battle must be waged for otherness, or what the Bible calls love. This love is not a feeling nor is it a reaching out to another so that a vacuum can be filled, but is first of all, and originally, the word of another which shatters the enchanted circle of self, and self-sufficiency. Love, as originating in God, is an unexpected call which disturbs the world of a man closed in on himself, upsets his order, his balance, his sleep (his death?). Therefore that kind of love is always linked to hope, because it is the affirmation of a possible life, of something that could happen.

It is this love, according to the scriptural tradition, which invests human sexuality with meaning. Man and woman become for one another the sign and bearer of word, of the word which arises unexpectedly like the unforseeable call of the Other, shattering the order of death at the very moment that it compels an admission of finiteness. In the most intimate relationship that can occur: man and woman know themselves to be messengers for one another of that which alone can give them life, that which escapes their lust as well as their fear. Otherness of the other, based on this ultimate otherness of the Word. Because of this, man and woman can live together, can become "one flesh" without absorbing each other, destroying each other, de-valuating each other, or victimizing each other. The battle of the sexes, which is the triumph of Fear, can be superseded by acknowledgement. Acknowledgement of one another by one another.

The risk and the gamble in sexuality was best of all expressed by the anonymous author of the ancient "yahwist" tradition in Genesis 2–3. The issue he tackles is the contradiction that constantly appears to place the reality of human existence (marked by precariousness, violence, suffering and death) in opposition to the benevolent will of God. In particular, why does Adam's awe-struck wonder upon discovering Eve always seem to be obscured by the animosity and violence which tragically link men and women? Why have those who were originally called to become "one flesh" become in reality master and slave? In a word, why did sexuality, the very thing which had been called to signify the wonder of life, become the expression of the tragedy of human existence?

The extraordinary myth of Genesis 2–3 is an attempted answer. This text must be examined, on one hand for its own sake, but on the other hand because it ultimately played a considerable role in traditional western morality, through the unfortunate and debatable exegesis of Augustine.

What is the meaning of the story that we traditionally, and incorrectly call "the Fall"?[10] It presents itself as the explanation for the presence of evil (cf. 3:14–19) in a world that was created good: man, having disobeyed God's order (2:16; 3:11), is punished by God and is deprived of his original bliss. This explanation is only in apparent conformity to the text; what really appears in the story, in a chronological succession, (there is an explanation before and after the "fall"), is the mythic expression of the coexistence in man of two conjoined realities: the vocation given by God to man that he should acknowledge that he is founded upon the Word which also creates him with limits (Gen. 2:16), and the refusal that man constantly makes vis-à-vis this acknowledgement. It is the connection between these two instances in the story that must be considered, not a time-sequence, i.e. two points in time of the life of the first man, but as the tension which, for the author, constitutes the dramatic aspect of all human existence, yesterday and today.

The turning point of these two instances (Gen. 3:1–5) is vitally important because it expresses, by means of the enigmatic figure of the snake, how dramatically man lacks authenticity and becomes lost when he deludes himself. The figure of the snake[11] somewhat objectifies this inner struggle and expresses the experience of the quasi-exteriority of temptation. With genial finesse the author shows how the foundational *command* of God (Gen. 2:16: "you may eat of all trees but one") which allowed man to exist as man, i.e. in a relationship of otherness with God and in a world received as gift, is transformed by the serpent into a *prohibition* that restricts his freedom: "You shall not eat of any tree of the garden. . ." (Gen. 3:1). And this is confirmed by verse 5; the serpent expresses the suspicion of man with regard to God: what if the limitation on man was really only a sign of God's fear and jealousy which sought to keep man in subjection? Of course this reveals man's hostility in refusing his humanity with its limitations, in order to seek to become like God (Gen. 3:5), to be all-powerful.

What is played out in the brief dialogue between the serpent and the woman is the image that man creates of God which in turn determines the image that he has of himself. If God be the one who hinders man from attaining freedom, the castrating father who maintains the child in a dependency relationship, then man must effectively violate the prohibition and kill this God to become man. But who says that this is who God is, except the voice of the serpent, that is to say the voice of the dream of non-limitation, of total power and total conquest? The text symbolically describes this next: the world is no longer received as gift but is seen as an object to covet ("So when the woman saw that the tree was good for food, and that it was a delight to the eyes, and that the tree was to be desired to make one wise. . . ." Gen. 3:6). That which qualified the world as gift (tree/command) is exactly what arouses covetousness.

On the level of sexuality the consequence is instant: the other, being different, becomes an object to lust after, or he becomes the subject who objectifies the other by his lust. Fear separates the man and woman, and nudity is felt to be shameful (Gen. 3:7; 2:25). The difference which structured the relationship of promised unity in 2:18–23, which allowed for joy in the encounter, becomes the consciousness of weakness and of threat. Otherness has changed its symbolic value from positive to negative. Henceforth everything must be done to minimize it. Thus to the false image of God (jealous God) corresponds a false image of the other sex, who is now seen as a threat. To the dread of God, now phantasmically imagined as a wicked Father, corresponds the fear of the other and also of self. That which demonstrates sexual otherness must now be hidden by clothes made of leaves. It is henceforth the sex of the other which becomes forbidden fruit and the same interplay of covetousness and fear will repeat itself ad infinitum. Sex itself is thus subtly made sacred and takes the place of the foundational limitation, i.e. sexuality, when it was really only there to point the way to the latter.

The rest of the story multiplies the indications of this change in the relationship. Because man constructs a negative image of God, he has no choice but to fear God (3:8). A new age has begun, where fear of God and of others dominates; "has begun" in mythic language means "begins over and over again," for man is that ambiguity who is beset at every moment by the question "Should I love or should I fear?"[12]

The consciousness of guilt described in v. 12–13 is also tied to the falsified image of God: the really guilty party is God (Gen. 3:12 ". . . the woman whom *thou gavest* to be with me . . .").

Just a word on what is described as divine sanction against human disobedience (3:16–19). First of all it should be noted that the condition of human existence, which is dramatic in so many ways, is interpreted not as a fatal and irremediable destiny but as the result of a transgression. Unhappiness belongs not to the category of essence but to the category of accident. What is foremost, i.e. what remains as the object of the permanent promise made to man, according to the yahwist editor, is the goodness of the will of God, the Creator, as expressed in Chapter 2. The unfortunate finiteness in which man is now trapped can always reverse itself by man's righteous acknowledgement of his limitations. If there is a drama of human existence it is in the fact that the case between man and woman and God is never closed and never without consequence. Every time that man imagines God as a tyrannical Father, he finds Him to be just that. Although the drama repeats itself continually, the author is not dissuaded from the hope that things will not always be this way; his recitation, in fact, culminates with the call given to Abraham (Gen. 12:1–3), which constitutes a veritable re-creation of mankind in the new covenant that God seals with the Father of nations. Thus a faith in God ("And he believed the Lord; and he reckoned it to him as righteousness" Gen. 15:6) which restores God's image in man is possible.

But this hope does not erase the harshness of the situation. Woman, described by the author as he sees her in Israelite society of the tenth century, is reduced to existing only in relation to her children, brought into the world through suffering, and to her husband in a relationship of desire/seduction and of domination (Gen. 3:16). This last issue is important: scriptural tradition recognizes that in the facts of the matter sexuality is lived out as a relationship of master/slave (cf. for example, 2 Samuel 13:1–15)—a dramatic impasse where woman is always the victim. The woman comes up against the violence of man, and the man in turn struggles against the violence of the earth (3:17–19). Man and woman are out of joint even in their day-to-day destiny: the woman is mother and slave of man, and man is the unhappy bread-winner, subjected to the law of harsh and painful toil, a slave of the earth.

To recapitulate: in the texts at the beginning of Genesis, the very ones that Jesus quotes, sexuality is described in turn

—as the locus for the joyful experiencing of the complimentariness of man and woman. "It is not good for man to be alone." The "goodness" of the union between man and woman reflects the goodness of creation, for sexuality is the sign of differentiation, of the otherness by which God reveals His own otherness. Thus in Gen. 2:23 the ability of man to speak (and not simply to name things as in 2:20) is described as the result of his encounter with the woman. Man cannot speak to God until he is revealed to himself through the otherness of the other (sex). This bespeaks the positive function of sexual desire in its acknowledgement of the other, i.e. the experience of one's limitations, because without the other, I cannot exist. (This is what the forbidden tree in the middle of the garden symbolizes, in the middle of the place designated for the encounter between man and woman.)

—as the locus of the unhappy experience of the violence of desire, resulting in the enslaving of one sex by the other. The principal locus of experiencing fear and shame, where the consciousness of difference is expressed by aggression. The woman is particularly in danger of not being able to live out her sexuality, except in enslavement to a man. The text qualifies this somewhat in recalling that the tragic aspect of woman's existence nevertheless issues forth in motherhood ("The man called his wife's name Eve because she was the mother of all living"

Gen. 3:20), by which woman is associated with God's own creation ("I have gotten a man with the help of the Lord" 4:1). But this point itself remains ambiguous, since it reduces woman to her role as mother; as woman she seems able to live out only the failure of her desire and is constantly scorned for that by the man: ". . . . your desire shall be for your husband and he shall rule over you" 3:16.

The theological importance of this text is the positioning of man between the promise (which is from the beginning, but is also far off on the horizon) and the realistic awareness of the drama which besets him. And above all, the text links the whole life of man and his sexuality to his attitude towards God, or the image of God he creates. Genesis 2 and 3 thus speak of sexuality in rigorous theological terms by showing that the real stakes in human existence, which are made obvious by the very ambiguities of sexuality, are essentially theological: what is your image of God? Luther, in his paradoxical genius, phrased the point quite well: "Adam's God is the one he believes him to be; he finds him to be as he imagines him in his heart. . . . This is why God says, if you imagine the right picture of me, you shall truly have me as a good God; if you do not rightly imagine me, I shall be an evil God; I will become for you what you believe me to be. If you believe I am a devil, then I shall seem that way, and the responsibility will not be mine."[13]

When man suspects God of being an evil God, then, in fact, man has to deal with an evil God! It is God the Judge whom Adam and Eve finally encounter because they choose Him to be so. At first God sanctions man's choice and departs, as witnessed in the whole history of Israel and even more in the teaching and person of Jesus; but He does so in order to do everything possible, including accepting the shame of death on the cross, so that man's interior image of Him could change. All the unhappiness of men, and all the unhappiness forced on man by other men, has its source in the image of God that man carries within, because that image directly determines his relationship to others. For consciousness of the otherness of others is bound up with the otherness of God. All that transpires is based on the meaning that man gives to otherness: it is the limitation which establishes one's very existence, or a threat that should be minimized at all cost, an unjust and intolerable restriction of one's desires?

Sexuality causes man to experience even in his very flesh what happens when he refuses the otherness of others (the sign of his refusal of God's Otherness); sexuality expresses, often in a cruel way, the fundamentally theological stakes of human existence. This is why sexuality is so often associated with sin, particularly, as we will see, in the western Augustinian tradition; this association unfortunately confused the revealer with the revealed, i.e. that which sexuality indicates was confused with the indication itself. Sexuality is not sinful in the scriptural tradition; rather, it reveals, through its drama, the risk of human existence; sin is idolatry, the adoration of a false image of God. This is the reason, as mentioned previously, that all the history of Israel is marked by the battle against religious idolatry which is so often expressed—by chance?—in sexual practices that reduce the otherness of God and of man.

c) You Are Your Body: The Teaching of Paul

The debate on the meaning of limitation and otherness reappears in an altogether different context at an altogether different time, when the apostle Paul steps in at Corinth to counsel against the confusion of freedom with licentiousness, and of spirituality with disdain for the body (1 Cor. 6:12–20). This text, which is crucial to an understanding of what scriptural anthropology really is, deserves much attention:

" 'All things are lawful for me,' but not all things are helpful. 'All things are lawful for me,' but I will not be enslaved by anything. 'Food is meant for the stomach and the stomach for food'—and God will destroy both one and the other. The body is not meant for immorality, but for the Lord, and the Lord for the body. And God raised up the Lord and will also raise us up by his power. Do you not know that your bodies are members of Christ? Shall I therefore take the members of Christ and make them members of a prostitute? Never! Do you not know that he who joins himself to a prostitute becomes one body with her? For, as it is written, 'The two shall become one.' But he who is united to the Lord becomes one spirit with him. Shun immorality. Every other sin which a man commits is outside the body; but the immoral man sins against his own body. Do you not know that your body is a temple of the Holy Spirit within you which you have from God? You are not your own; you were bought with a price. So glorify God in your body." (R.S.V.)

This text seems to be an answer (rather polemical) to a moral attitude apparently adopted by the Corinthians (cf. 1 Cor. 5:1). This attitude is somewhat resumed in the saying or quasi slogan of verse 12a: "All things are lawful." The Corinthians, manifesting through this a form of spirituality akin to gnosticism, would have relied on two arguments: the truly spiritual person can do whatever he wishes, because he is above ordinary contingencies (v. 12a); and, all that is of the flesh is of no account since it is destined for death, and only the spirit matters (v. 13a). These arguments justify a twofold affirmation of man's freedom: on one hand, with regard to ordinary moral laws, and on the other hand, with regard to the different taboos concerning food (probably of Jewish origin). In so doing, the Corinthians probably believed they were right in line with Pauline teaching on freedom. Paul is going to have to set things right.

"All is lawful" (12a): this phrase is a declaration of principle from the Corinthians themselves. Paul agrees with the concept: the freedom brought by the Gospel is to be limited neither by law nor by taboos. But he immediately interprets the saying by two qualifications which clarify its meaning: "not all things are helpful" (12a) and "but I will not be enslaved by anything" (v. 12b). The first qualification seems, because of the parallel with 1 Cor. 10:23, to be a reminder that liberty is to be applied to the service of edifying the community; "all is not helpful," that is, not helpful to the edifying of the community. Through this Paul dismisses any individualistic interpretation of freedom ("I am free to do whatever I please, without caring about anybody else"). The second qualification is very clear: what kind of liberty is it that ends in slavery? In slavery to sex, for example?

The following verse on food and the stomach could also have been meant by the apostle to contest the deep-rooted food taboos that are so abundant in Judaism. This problem comes up again later in chapter eight. But Paul rejects the parallel that the Corinthians were making when they would probably add something like: "and the body is for immorality as immorality is for the body, and God will destroy both one and the other." For even if the stomach and food are perishable, the body, on the other hand, is much more than just a flesh covering to be despised. Here Paul breaks with the body/soul dualism which is so traditional in Greek thinking. The body is not something I use, for I am a body, and the way I am a body is not irrelevant. Therefore Paul makes a contrast between "body for immorality" and "body for the Lord." In the first instance where the body is used, it becomes a thing and as such it ceases being truly a body. In the second instance the body becomes my mode of being while I acknowledge that what gives me meaning ("the *for* what I am made") does not belong to me (it's for "the Lord").

This explains the mention of the resurrection in the very next verse: if I am to be resurrected it is because I am mortal and only an act of God can snatch me out of the jaws of death. So then the body itself is the mode of acknowledging my limitation, as opposed to the Corinthian view that whatever is mortal is irrelevant and of no account, and that the real self escapes all limitations, being immortal in and of itself. The acknowledgement of limitations is intimately bound up with a positive acknowledgement of the body.

Furthermore, the body is our way of being in relation to others. Vis-á-vis others, verse 15 confirms that: our bodies are "members of Christ" (Christ Himself is compared to a body), which signifies that we are beings in relationship to one another and that none of us can claim to be free from our limitation. None of us is the whole, each of us has a radical need for others by whom we are completed. This immediately clarifies the whole meaning of our corporeal existence: it is to be in mutual relationship in the "mystery" of Christ (cf. Ephes. 5:32), i.e. in the inter-dict of Christ, the plane of invisible reality which is the Lord Christ by Whom we can live in a relationship of freedom, and not in one which merges the individuals.

This is why the person who uses his body as an instrument is deceived when he thinks, for example, that he is not engaging the totality of his person in a sexual relationship with a prostitute. What Paul highlights here (v. 15b–17) is not sexuality per se, but the instrumentalizing of sexuality by separating it from the order of being. The contrast is not being made between spirituality and sexuality but rather between the body-made-instrument, reduced to exterior appearance or genital functioning, and the body-made-spiritual, the sign of an ultimately mysterious presence because it finds its meaning in the Lord Himself. Again, this is the rationale for fleeing immorality because it is a negation of the body (at the very moment it believes itself to be fulfilling natural instincts!) insofar as it is a presence inhabited by the Spirit. We can readily see how this "Christ"-consciousness of the body lays the foundation for an ethic of sexuality. It is because the body is an icon of the Spirit that it cannot be made into an instrument and it is an illusion to think that it would be a neutral or inconsequential matter to engage the body in a relationship that is purely physical.

This is stated decisively in the admirable statement (v. 19) where Paul joins together exactly what the Corinthians were contrasting, i.e. the body and the spirit: "your body is the temple of the Holy Spirit within you, which you have from God." The body then has its ultimate significance in being inhabited by the presence of God. It is therefore the icon of God. There is thus a wondrous rapport between the visible (the body which I am) and the invisible (the being which inhabits this body and which comes from God); between the category of presence which alone gives meaning to the body and without which the body would be a mere organic opaqueness, and the category of absence; for the Spirit, in a certain way (like Christ in verse 15), is God insofar as he is absent (not apprehendable), insofar as he constitutes us as subject precisely because he himself is our true foundation while altogether eluding us.

Thus "I" am not until I cease identifying myself with my body and thus attain the symbolic reality as a subject, as defined by the word of the Other (Spirit) who gives me being while eluding me. This is why "you do not belong to yourselves" (v. 19b).

Here we have an altogether original perspective: faced with the Corinthian dualism which opposes the body (disdainful since it is mortal and limited) to the immortal soul/spirit, Paul recalls the Christological foundation of Christian anthropology. His stand can be encapsulated in these three points:

1) The body is not a thing or an instrument that man can use without really investing his whole being. The body is the person himself stamped with the limitations of his condition as creature and called into relationship and encounter with others. Sexuality is not a function comparable to the digestive function, but rather the expression of a body/person insofar as he is called into relationship.

2) Immorality is serious because it is a theo-anthropological perversion (even more than a moral one). It is a denial of the body as limitation and as a mode of presence which can only come by means of the other. As such it is a denial of the Lord, insofar as the body is the mysterious link which allows for relationship and is also the locus of the joining together of all the "members" in one single "body."

3) The body is the icon of God. Pitted against disdain for the body and the reduction of man to his body, Paul affirms that the choice is not between a non-incarnated spirituality and a body reduced to its organic opaqueness; the whole meaning of the body is to be a mode of presence inhabited by the Spirit of God.

3. Conclusion

How does the Bible speak about sexuality? Definitely as an ambiguous reality. It plays a major role in the ordering of the world, because it is inscribed in man himself so that he can, from that starting point which he is, organize all creation; it is the structuring principle of difference. But it can also constitute a dangerous factor that brings disorder whenever it transgresses the laws relative to differentiation. The Old Testament does not hide these dangers: sexuality can even lead to murderous violence, as told in the astonishing story of Judges 19–21, concerning the sexual violence of the inhabitants of Gibeah against the woman of the Levite from Ephraim (19:22–26). Since that incident transgressed the most sacred laws of hospitality, of heterosexuality, and of respect for the wife of one's neighbor, it led to a collective violence and quasi-destruction of almost the whole tribe of Benjamin.[1]

As a counterpoint, the exemplary couples among the Patriarchs demonstrate how sexuality, ordained as a benediction of God on life, becomes creative with regard to history and love. An initial line of thought becomes apparent which not only considers difference as the organizer of the world, but above all as the condition of possibility for an authentic relationship. That which limits man, since man is not woman nor woman man, is necessary so that there can be a union, a reciprocal recognition.

The initial anthropological reflection is elaborated in a decisive fashion in the yahwist account of Creation, which is later taken up, interpreted and confirmed by Jesus Himself. Gift of the Creator so that man can experience the very otherness of God, sexuality humanizes man[2] because it allows him to confront the structuring essence of limitation, to leave behind his dreams of total power and squarely meet the otherness of a unique other being. "That is why man shall leave his father and his mother. . . ."

Finally, these reflections on sexuality lead to a reflection on God. What the scriptural tradition actually discloses is that if sexuality is lived out as a means of challenge to otherness and to finiteness in a search for salvation through the non-differentiation of pleasure, it becomes the sign of a misunderstanding of God, and of an idolatrous practice. The sacredness that is exalted in the quest for pleasure is nothing but a divinized image of self. Thus the most serious risk that sexuality runs for man is denounced, that of a shutting in upon himself in the illusion of self-sufficiency: a belief that one is his own ground of being and that others have no meaning or function apart from the construction of his "self"; a refusal of the validity of the other who is immediately reduced to being only an instrument of pleasure. But to reject the other signifies in fact, according to scriptural tradition, a rejection of the God-Who-Is-Other, by a radical defiance with respect to His Word, which is the reality which does not proceed from the heart of man and which, in calling him, decentralizes him from himself to lead him into a creative relationship. Genesis 2–3 tells how, in deceiving himself about the meaning of the limitation that sexuality has stamped upon his body, man (Adam) deceives himself in the truth about God and makes Him out to be a tyrant; and it also tells how the man/woman relationship is immediately overwhelmed by violence, fear and hostility.

Thus the goodness of sexuality ("God saw that it was good") is linked to the acknowledgement of the otherness of God; and also to the positive understanding of limitation. The vital issue which man is called upon to discover, by the very fact that he was created a sexual being, concerns his rapport to otherness: is it seen as the limitation which allows for a creative relationship, or is it denounced as a threat to be opposed at all cost, an unjust and unbearable limitation placed upon sexual desire?

In asking this question it is clear, by the very meaning which scriptural tradition ascribes to the body, where the Bible stands. The body, a positive sign of limitation of the possibility of a relationship with others which does not fuse others, is not in fact "some thing" any more than sexuality is "some thing"; they are each the habitat of God, this Other who is in us, the Word which speaks us forth as much as we speak It forth.

III

Love and Institution: Scriptural Theology of Marriage

We have seen in the study of scriptural tradition how sexuality inscribes a limitation in man, which makes the acknowledgment of otherness in others possible. And how because of it, sexuality makes relationship possible. That is why sexuality in its positive significance is not to be separated, according to the Bible, from the couple through whom that significance is revealed, through whom it really becomes creative and through whom undifferentiated impulses become humanized. Scriptural tradition never speaks of sexuality per se except to denounce its potential of making man into an object. In other words, the distinction that has been made between the significance of sexuality and the significance of the marital couple should really be a relative one. And yet this distinction continues to be retained in the name of what seems to be the fundamental perspective of scriptural tradition—a perspective which is hardly explicit in the text but which is constantly taken for granted. In fact, we are struck by the tension throughout the biblical text between the calling and promise given to man and the fact of the actual social situation in which these must unfold. On the one hand, scriptural tradition does not hide the fact that there is a dimension and a depth to sexuality that marriage, in the way that it is always lived out, can never fully express; but on the other hand, it also asserts that in the faithful and continuing life shared by the couple there is a depth and a promise which instantly disqualifies the other possible ways of living out a sexual relationship. There is, then, a twofold reciprocal critique—one which is applied to the conjugal institution by sexuality and one applied to sexuality by the married couple. The ethical consequences of this twofold critique will be studied in the fifth chapter. For the moment, let us try to understand how the biblical tradition deals with marriage, and what theological meaning it posits to the marital institution when it finds its place in the plan of God for man.

The marital experience involves a mystery and a risk, which various traditions and biblical authors pondered over quite a bit. How does one understand the connection that marriage affords (but often hinders!) between love and institution, between desire and the appropriate time for it to be structured into a framework, between the impatience of fulfillment and the patience of a shared history? But everything being said here about marriage is also posited by the Bible concerning the relationship between God and His people, which is constantly in tension between the completion of a slowly unfolding history and the bursting forth of a hope and a love which are impatient to be fulfilled. This rapport between the relationship of man and woman and the relationship of God and his people is at the center of biblical theology. Its richness is to be found in examining first the Old Testament (O.T.) and then the New (N.T.).

1. Marriage According to the Old Testament

It is unnecessary to examine the elements of conjugal morality which are specific to Israel: they are of more concern to ethnology and history than to ethics for, with the exception of certain specific facts (which will be discussed later), they belong to the traditional sexual and marital customs of the Middle East.[1] I am more interested in perceiving Israel's theological consciousness in sexual and marital understanding and practice.

Marriage, like sexuality[2] is a gift from God the Creator: "Then the Lord God said, 'It is not good that the man should be alone. I will make him a helper fit for him.' " (Gen. 2:18).[3] The yahwist editor emphasizes the goodness of the gift, and even more so because in the rest of his account he describes with harsh realism what men have done with this gift: marital practice reflects instead a relationship of domination and rivalry between the man and the woman. "To the woman He said: . . . 'your desire shall be for your husband and he shall rule over you.' " (3:16)

But, as I already pointed out when discussing the words of Jesus on the man/woman relationship, to posit "in the beginning," at the origin of creation, as the old Hebrew author does, recalls the fundamental and foundational purpose of God. Despite the appearances, the text is not hearkening back to a golden age lost by man's transgression, but rather announces that the situation currently experienced by men and women is neither a fatalistic destiny nor the expression of the creative will of God. Marriage is a promise that God has not forgotten despite whatever facts seem to contradict that.

This conviction, that marriage is more than the experience of a sociological reality and that it carries a promise which men and women are called upon to discover and rejoice in, is attested to by the O.T. in countless instances. There is first of all (not in the chronological but in the theological and aesthetic sense) the wonderful Song of Solomon,[4] right in the middle of the O.T., the most lyrical of all celebrations of human love. The Song of Songs sings of the joy, the pleasure, the beauty of conjugal love. The dialogue between the bridegroom and the bride delighting in one another exalts physical beauty and sensual love:

—Behold you are beautiful my love; behold you are beautiful; your eyes are doves.

—Behold you are beautiful my beloved, truly lovely. Our couch is green. . . .

—As a lily among brambles, so is my love among the maidens.

—As an apple tree among the trees of the wood, so is my beloved among young men. With great delight I sat in his shadow, and his fruit

was sweet to my taste. He brought me to the banqueting house, and his banner over me was love; sustain me with raisins, refresh me with apples; for I am sick with love. (1:15–2:5)
—You have ravished my heart, my sister, my bride, you have ravished my heart with a glance of your eyes, with one jewel of your necklace. How sweet is your love, my sister, my bride! How much better is your love than wine, and the fragrance of your oils than any spice! Your hips distill nectar, my bride; honey and milk are under your tongue; the scent of your garments is like the scent of Lebanon. A garden locked is my sister, my bride, a garden locked, a fountain sealed. (4:9–12). . . . How graceful are your feet in sandals, o queenly maiden! Your rounded thighs are like jewels, the work of a master hand. Your navel[5] is a rounded bowl that never lacks mixed wine. Your belly is a heap of wheat, encircled with lillies. Your two breasts are like two fawns, twins of a gazelle. Your neck is like an ivory tower. . . . How fair and pleasant you are, o lovely one, delectable maiden! You are stately as a palm tree, and your breasts are like its clusters. I say I will climb the palm tree and lay hold of its branches. Oh, may your breasts be like clusters of the vine, and the scent of your breath like apples, and your kisses like the best wine. . . . (7:1–4a, 6–9a)
—Set me as a seal upon your heart, as a seal upon your arm; for love is strong as death, jealousy is cruel as the grave. Its flashes are flashes of fire, a most vehement flame. Many waters cannot quench love, neither can floods drown it. If a man offered for love all the wealth of his house, it would be utterly scorned. (8:6–7)

The conjugal love celebrated here is possible because it is free of any religious or utilitarian ends. Marriage is not the reenactment of the union of god and goddess destined to make the earth fruitful; neither is it the means of keeping one half (the feminine half) of humanity enslaved. It is given to the man and the woman in order for them to perceive therein a dimension of liberty, the gratuitousness and the joy of the love of God itself. Nothing is more striking in this respect than the way in which the Canticle reverses the very terms of the curse upon the woman which was quoted above (Gen. 3:16): amorous sexual desire can also signify authentic love, the joy of the gift of oneself: "I am my beloved's and his desire is for me" (Song of Sol. 7:11). Master/slave: the Old Testament is quite aware of the condition to which the male/female relationship can revert, but nevertheless does not consider that situation to be the last word. The last word comes from the Bridegroom and the Bride of the Song of Songs who acknowledge in their desire the liberating gift of God. A stupendous light flashes forth here: "Ancient Israel preferred to experience sex and sexuality in a spiritualized, human, and profane environment."[6]

The love between a man and a woman, now de-sacredized and re-turned to its full human signification, becomes for Israel the very image of the covenant between God and His people. Marriage, through the very promise attached to it, indicates the mystery of covenant, and in a "feed-back" effect, this symbolic usage of marriage leads to a considerable deepening of the spiritual and ethical significations of the marital institution. Israel, because of the God who chose her and who reveals Himself as totally different from other gods, de-sacredizes sexuality; sexuality, brought back to the human plane and freed from religious fear and utilitarianism, is recognized to be the locus of an amorous relationship between the man and the woman. This relationship in turn can then analogically signify that of God with His people (encounter, otherness, unfolding, shared life); and this symbol opens the door to a deepening of the ethical, spiritual and humanizing value of marriage.

The prophet Hosea, who exercised his ministry in the second half of the eighth century, was the first to use the image of a married couple to explain the intimacy of the link between Yahweh God and His people.[7] Jeremiah[8] and Ezekiel,[9] as well as deutero-Isaiah[10] take up the same image. This image affords at the same time a deepening of the meaning of covenant (berît in Hebrew) as well as of marriage, while highlighting what makes for an authentic relationship between a man and a woman. We find love (hesedh, i.e. kindness, affection, gentleness), faithfulness (emunah), and jealousy (qin'ah, i.e. jealous rivalry in regard to any other potential lover). All these terms become applied to the relationship—loving, faithful, jealous—of God with His people. There is one more important term:[11] ahābhāh, amorous desire:[12] " . . . (in) this concept we find that marriage—expressed in terms of 'ahābhāh (love), hesedh, and berîth—originated in a spontaneous feeling and desire, led on to a definite choice, and was regulated by a covenant and established in the loving faithfulness of hesedh."[13]

As a terrestrial reality and a creation of God, marriage in the O.T. is assigned an important symbolic function which in turn posits value in the elements of the relationship which constitutes it. Love, faithfulness, covenant, tenderness are offered to the man and woman as reminders and signs of a love, faithfulness, covenant, and tenderness which the whole history of Israel tells of and comes to acknowledge as having come from God Himself.

But this promise must confront real history! In other words, it is fleshed out in a social and cultural reality, in the habits and customs of the ancient East. I have already discussed the de-sacredizing which the theological consciousness of Israel performed vis-à-vis sexuality; in the realm of customs, however, the work of liberating the human significance of the marriage relationship is slower. It is quite obvious that at the outset, in the important context of blood ties within the tribe, marriage constitutes a link in the chain of the succession of generations which forms the tribe and ensures its continuity. Its primary value, then, becomes procreation, which is held in much more esteem than the quality of the encounter between the spouses or the faithfulness of their love.[14] Sexuality is the means by which the couple becomes involved in the creative and historical plan of God, i.e. through children. "From generation to generation" is an eminently biblical expression; so too the countless geneologies which irritate today's Bible reader who no longer senses their joyful and triumphant intonations. This is, moreover, why polygamy was allowed, as well as the replacement of the barren wife by the concubine whose duty was to give the couple a child (i.e. Hagar replacing Sarah with Abraham). But the line of thought which values procreation so highly becomes somewhat muted (but not done away with) in favor of the one previously mentioned which effectively constitutes the original and innovative contribution of Israel—what could be called the elective and affective theme. The growing importance of the values of relationship in marriage reinforces monogamy more and more; and so does a certain moral rigorism destined to protect marriage from the ravages of unsanctified sexuality. This tendency to moralism is already evident in the prophets who compare Israel's unfaithfulness to prostitution, and especially in post-exile Judaism which faced the moral freedom of the greco-oriental civilization. However, this tendency becomes more and more manifest until it reaches the point all over again where pregnancy and child-rearing are seen as the supreme dignity of conjugal union.[15] Thus the tension that occurs in the O.T. between "the patriarchal-geneological emphasis where descendancy wins over love and the prophetic-messianic emphasis where the wonders of love take preeminence over the obligation of serving the species"[16] is not resolved. It seems, however, that the O.T. itself does not entirely regard these two approaches as equal in value. The geneological side is presented as historical reality and the relationship-oriented side is presented as promise, a hope, a meaning to be discovered. I do not believe, once again, that it is purely accidental that the O.T. begins with a twofold description of the human couple: one according to God's creative plan (Gen. 2) and one according to historic reality (Gen. 3). That which is "in the beginning," the most "in the beginning", is the hope of the union where man and woman are enraptured with one another and enter into a covenant of love. This beginning is the promise whose meaning Israel has sought to make concrete and whose utopian force Israel has sought to verify all throughout its history.[17]

2. Marriage According to the New Testament

The New Testament demonstrates the effort of the young Christian community to translate into ethical terms the teaching of their Lord and Saviour, Jesus Christ—teaching which was received and practiced by that community in such a significant way. The attempt occurs in the midst of, and in confrontation with, Jewish culture on one hand, which holds true for the Judaeo-Christian tradition, and with Hellenistic culture on the other hand, as is shown in the pagan-Christian tradition which in the beginning was so influenced by the models of Hellenistic Judaism. Because of this we cannot approach the New Testament without carefully distinguishing the different types of Christian tradition and the different cultural settings which faced the young community.

a) The Teaching of Jesus

My starting point is the text already partially studied in relation to sexuality: Mark 10:1–10; cf. Matt. 19:1–8. I have already demonstrated the reference by Jesus to the foundational intention of God in creating man "male and female" and in calling them to a unity of flesh.[1] It should be noted here that this teaching was given in response to the question about divorce (presented as a snare by Jesus's adversaries). Whatever the formal character of the actual evangelical presentation,[2] we find an echo in this scene of a polemic discussion by Jesus directed against the casuistry of the doctors of the law. The text is less explicit in Mark's version where Jesus forces his interlocutors to admit that there is no commandment whatsoever in the law of Moses on divorce but only a permission, a concession to the hardness of the human heart. As for the commandment of God, it aims, rather, at the unity of the couple. But Mark had no understanding of the background of the debate concerning the true interpretation of Deuteronomy 24:1, whereas Matthew, due to his Jewish heritage, certainly did. That text was the object of lively discussion in Judaism during the time of Christ.[3] The rabbinical school of Shammai conceived of the authorization for repudiating one's wife in a strict and restrictive way, whereas the school of Hillel gave it a very broad interpretation.[4] What had originally been conceived of as a defense of the rights of the repudiated wife in the deuteronomic legislation—the bill of divorce allowed her to remarry and thus avoid being forced to beg or become a prostitute[5]—was transformed into a legal authorization to practice (at least for those who were financially able!) what could be called a successive polygamy. It is this hypocrisy, this fatal consequence of legalism, that Jesus primarily wishes to denounce. To respect the law of Moses is to respect what undergirds it, its foundation, i.e. the creative will of God. In both Matthew's and Mark's versions this point is clear: all the subtle distinctions of legalist interpretations are disqualified by the fundamental assertion that God had desired the human couple to be solidly united in love. That intention cannot be doubted. Through this, Jesus implicitly accuses his adversaries of betraying the law which they arrogantly claim to respect. For if Moses authorized the repudiation, it was forced by human wickedness[6] and not in order to allow a violation of God's own intention. The polemic is clear. But it would be a serious mistake to think that Jesus by His words was in His turn promulgating, now in a radical fashion, a law on marriage and divorce. Notice that Jesus does not criticize Moses, but rather only restores the intention of the text from Deuteronomy, thereby clarifying the social status of the law: it is a response to the unfortunate fact of human wickedness and its function is to deflect the catastrophic consequences that can come from the presence of evil in man and in society. Jesus does not denounce the law in its status, nor in its function. But He does challenge the turn-about effected by Jewish doctors who raise a contingent law to the status of a norm in God's will, when actually just the reverse is true. The law is necessary as a response to the necessity of evil; but it is not, as such, the expression of God's creative will. To confuse the two is what Jesus finds scandalous, especially since it becomes the basis of the most blatant hypocrisy, and, along with that, the basis of the enslavement of women!

Jesus wants to remind men of the plan of God, of His will which is also His promise. In the light of God's will, it becomes clear that any repudiation of the wife by the husband is sin, that is, not so much a moral wrong as a checkmate to God's plan, will, and promise. And to establish that fact is not to establish a new legalism which is harsher than its predecessor, but to place marriage in the context of the struggle between the divine promise and the hardness of the human heart. The stakes are moved from practical problems (where marriage is thought of as a "natural" reality and is therefore regulated in practice by a morality of "do's" and "don'ts") to a perspective where marriage is recognized as the place of man's and woman's apprehending of the promise and grace of God, but where it can also signify (and more cruelly than in any other realm of human existence) the refusal to believe in the creative and recreative grace of love, a closing-in upon oneself in fear and covetousness—in brief, a refusal of the other. This shift is of major importance, for it lifts marriage out of the purely juridical domain in order to reveal its theological significance. I will return to this crucial point shortly. But for now, notice what the Gospel of Matthew reports that the disciples said to Jesus after hearing his teaching on marriage: "If such is the case of a man with his wife, it is not expedient to marry" (Matt. 19:10). Matthew probably wishes to denounce the legalistic reaction that the church of his time seemed to have concerning these words of Jesus. If Jesus is to be a new legislator, harsher than his predecessors, then marriage effectively becomes a fearful ball-and-chain! However, Jesus is speaking not as a legislator but as a prophet who is revealing the theological dimension of marriage.

In confirmation of this last statement, witness the attitude of Jesus toward the men or women who have known failure or difficulty on the conjugal or sexual level:[7] it is marked by great compassion and a gentleness that He certainly did not manifest to the hypocrites (i.e. Matt. 23) or to the Temple merchants (Mark 11:15–19). Jesus is very severe (as were the prophets) to those who take on the promise of God whenever it suits them, but He is full of compassion for those whose failure brings them to the brink of despair. They are the ones who need to be told that where sins abounds, grace abounds even more; in the midst of the greatest distress the promise still holds true. And he who has seen the failure of his married life needs, more than anyone else, to be freed by the gospel from the guilt to which legalism condemns him. Freed from the despair of no longer being able to hope in love.

For, usually the failure continues to exist while the promise of God is scoffed at and forgotten, in this realm as in so many others. Jesus is aware of that, and even mentions it in the text concerning the Mosaic law. But He speaks of it again elsewhere: the evangelical tradition has maintained the trace, even several traces, of the words of Jesus concerning adultery.[8] One should recognize therein a direct echo of a teaching of Jesus. I will come back to the restrictive clause, "except in the case of *porneia*," which was introduced by Matthew (although not originating with him). Under slightly different form, this saying from Jesus has a very clear meaning: contrary to traditional interpretation, He likens repudiation to adultery. To put away the wife is to scoff at the hope the couple should embody; even more concretely, it is to betray the confidence that the wife had placed in her husband by agreeing to live with him; and last of all, it is to minimize the importance that God attaches to the marriage bond. If the repudiation is motivated by the desire for another woman, it can be nothing other than a hypocritical way of legally justifying adultery. But here again, the intention behind the statement must be clearly seen: this saying belongs to a group of polemical teachings by Jesus aimed against legalistic interpretation, and Jesus here denounces the practice which allows a repudiation that minimizes and disdains the strength of the marriage bond. "In his teaching on divorce, Jesus does *not* lay down a *law,* but rather reveals the *reality* of marriage, and does so precisely in opposition to any legal narrowing of the issues. . . . The demands made by marriage do of course become apparent when its reality is laid bare."[9] Whoever puts away his wife, even if in accordance with the law or even if to sanction the misconduct of his wife[10] commits adultery, that is, he destroys, by his own action, the unique bond of marriage. No interpretation, no casuistry whatsoever can here justify the blocking of the will of God; no repudiation can be blameless.

Facing the possibility of the failure that threatens a married couple, Jesus does not want people to delude themselves by distinguishing between "authorized" failures and "forbidden" failures. What threatens the unity of the couple is basically lust[11] which reduces the other to being an object of desire, and which denotes within the very core of a person the refusal of other as other. This is the very heart of the matter in the sexual and conjugal relationship: the struggle is not between "permitted" and "forbidden," but between lust, fear, and refusal—as opposed to acceptance of the other and discovery of the presence of a creative and forgiving love.

Having said this, it does not seem correct to deduce from the text the idea that Jesus strictly forbade divorce. Certainly every divorce indicates a failure and no juridical or moral quibbling can change that fact, but I do not see where Jesus ever thought that this failure was forbidden to believers. I use the expression "forbid a failure" on purpose to emphasize the absurdity of the problem. There are perhaps cases where, despite the efforts of one of the partners, or even of both, the conjugal bond is destroyed. "The words of Jesus stigmatize divorce as contrary to God's original will; but they do not presuppose the existence of a marital reality independent of the husband and wife. The will of God continues to exist and qualifies the disunion, but it does not maintain the union beyond its breakdown."[12] I will return to this difficult point when examining the way in which Matthew and Paul themselves have tried to take into account the "hardness of heart" in man all the while maintaining the theological meaning of the words of Jesus. Before that, however, a discussion of the very unusual and fascinating text already briefly alluded to is in order.

"The disciples said to him 'If such is the case of a man with his wife, it is not expedient to marry.' But he said to them 'Not all men receive this precept, but only those to whom it is given. For there are eunuchs who have been so from birth, and there are eunuchs who have been made eunuchs by men, and there are eunuchs who have made themselves eunuchs for the sake of the kingdom of heaven. He who is able to receive this let him receive it.' "[13]

From their legalistic perspective, the disciples felt this saying of Jesus on adultery was too severe. What Christ wants to have them understand is that from now on the presence of the kingdom makes it possible to live marriage as a grace, and not a merely natural state having human laws. The disciples of Christ can "understand that language." And to confirm this declaration, Jesus alludes to three situations which are in fact not "natural"; in addition to the two categories of eunuchs which were disqualified by Judaism because they constituted incapacity to contract a marraige and were thus seen as a curse,[14] Jesus posits a third category, one in which the renunciation of marriage is voluntary, "for the sake of the kingdom of heaven."[15] Thus both celibacy and marriage, because of the kingdom, cease being mere natural realities or destinies to be submitted to, and point to the grace which makes human freedom possible. It is freely chosen celibacy which guarantees that marriage is itself a free choice; it is marriage lived as grace calling for faithfulness that guarantees that celibacy is not a curse, but that it can be recognized by some as their vocation.

Thus, without idealizing the human condition in any way, Jesus invites man and woman to go beyond a natural or purely social perspective which accords with appearances only, in order to recognize the goodness of the bi-sexual creation and through it, the vocation that God gives to man and woman.

b) The Teaching of the Apostolic Tradition

How did the early Church interpret the teaching of Jesus? The answer is found primarily in Paul's letters, but the way in which the evangelists transmitted and interpreted the words of Jesus is also of interest.

1) The Evangelists

Luke has a tendency, in the realm of sexuality as well as with other moral questions, to radicalize the teaching of Jesus. Thus he is the only one to list marriage as one of the (inappropriate) excuses offered by those invited to the banquet (Luke 14:20). The *logion* on renunciation of self to follow Jesus takes on a radical form that is almost unbearable;[16] for instance, among the things that a man must hate in order to become a follower of Jesus is the love of his wife. The same idea occurs in 18:29 where Luke (once again the only one of the gospel-writers) mentions love of a wife in the list of elements that can be, if not must be, renounced "for the sake of the kingdom."[17] Finally, in Luke's version of the debate between Jesus and the Sadducees on resurrection (Luke 20:34–35), the evangelist uses a formula which is quite ambiguous and which could mean that to be judged worthy of the resurrection, one must have had neither a husband nor a wife.[18] It seems that we are at the beginning of a line of thought here which was very popular in the later Church history, a line followed by certain Christians who, in order to better testify to the innovation of the kingdom, believed themselves called to a rigorous sexual and conjugal asceticism.[19] The suspicion appears in this third gospel that perhaps marriage might be the real obstacle to a truly Christian life. Luke seems to typify a kind of attitude which characterized the late first-century pagan-Christian communities who were faced with the immorality of the Hellenistic world and influenced by its ascetic traditions.

Matthew, on the other hand (or rather his community), does not share these ascetic views, which are hardly Jewish. His interpretation of Jesus' teaching is conveyed in his addition of the restrictive clause in 5:32 and in 19:9—"except in the case of *porneia*"—to the saying of Jesus on repudiation and adultery. Why did he add this?[20] We could formulate the following hypothesis: quite early on, and especially in the heart of Judaeo-Christian communities, people must have made the sayings of Jesus a norm for the moral life of the Churches, which completed or rather interpreted ancient Mosaic Law. The gospel of Matthew is itself the result of such an attempt at interpretation. And if this attempt was made, it was because the communities with a Judaeo-Christian base like Matthew's risked, by their loyalty to the law of Israel, bringing the teaching of Jesus into the narrow confines of their traditional teaching. Matthew's intention is to show that Christ, the new Moses, has the authority to interpret the will of God anew ("You have heard that it was said to the men of old. . . . But I say to you. . . ." 5:21, 27, 31, 33) and through that interpretation to call men, and most especially his disciples, to a "righteousness" that exceeds that of the scribes and Pharisees (5:20).

But to immediately convert the teaching of Jesus into a commentary on the law that was comparable to that of the scribes and doctors of the law showed misunderstanding. With regard to marriage and divorce, that commentary would be particularly severe. Severed from its eschatological perspective in this way, the remarks by Jesus about the indissolubility of the married couple would become a legalistic declaration, i.e. abstract, juridical and guilt-forming for all those who experience a failure in this area; whereas, originally, Jesus was aiming at calling to mind the theological meaning and promise which accompany the reality of a couple and was denouncing the hypocrisy of legalism which violated the spirit of the law while claiming to hold to its letter. In a situation like this, where Jesus' words become law, what do you say to those who fail, who, for instance, find themselves victims of the adultery of their mates? What should happen when the couple is experiencing serious marital difficulties? To send them to Jesus' dictum without reminding them of the character of the promise, risks leading them into a definite condemnation, and to exclusion from the community, since it would really be sending them to an absolute law! My hypothesis is that the interpolation by Matthew aims at dealing with this difficulty by recalling the prophetic dimension of the words of Christ which would discourage a legalistic reading by placing it in a theological (and not moral) perspective.

Let me elaborate on this point. First of all, what does "except in the case of *porneia*" mean?[21] *Porneia* has several meanings: prostitution, unchastity, debauchery, adultery, misconduct. The brevity of Matthew's phrase makes a clear-cut and definite translation very difficult on the lexicographic level alone. Therefore the context of the discussion then current in Judaism and in early Christianity on the conditions allowing repudiation must be examined. Two main possibilities have been explored.

The first, initiated (if I am not mistaken) by Bonsirven and followed by Baltensweiler and Bonnard,[22] understands *porneia* in the context of the difficult relations between Jewish and pagan Christians in the early Church. One of the attempts to regulate these relations is recorded in Acts 15:20, 23–29: for the sake of peace, gentile Christians were told to "abstain from the pollutions of idols and from unchastity (*porneia,*) and from what is strangled and from blood," i.e. to respect certain prohibitions on some issues that were sensitive for the Jews. The *porneia* of the text in *Acts* would be evoking the prohibitions in Leviticus 18:6–18 concerning the impediments to marriage relative to consanguinity. The exegetes mentioned above hypothesize that Matthew had the same preoccupation and that he uses the word in order to instruct the gentile Christians that if they separate themselves from their wives in order to submit to this teaching, they are not committing adultery. Matthew, then, would be seeking to alleviate the problems arising from the conflict between Jesus' dictum forbidding all repudiation and the demand placed upon the gentile Christians by the Jewish Christians of not contracting marriages that are illegitimate under the Law (if it be the case) of separating from a wife under such conditions.

This hypothesis has received the acceptance of many exegetes. But it does not seem convincing. First of all, it is implausible to explain a text by another text that comes later and comes from a very different source. Moreover, it is not readily apparent why Matthew would risk modifying the text of one of the Lord's teachings to address himself to gentile Christians, who are not his main audience. The problem for Matthew is not a difficulty concerning a specific case of marital union contracted by former Gentiles, which is probably altogether exceptional, but to answer a question that is surely more anguished and unfortunately not so exceptional—that of the failure of a marital union within his own Judaeo-Christian community. Finally, why would Matthew be referring to the text of Leviticus 18, which lists the cases of illegitimate marriage, with an eye to preventing them, in a debate that concerns divorce? At the very least, this contorted and indirect argument should have deserved some additional explanations. Matthew, as we have seen, is so brief and concise that we can ask whether he does this purposely in order to posit some ambiguity therein, or whether he thinks that the expression is so clear for the readers that he need not explain it. If he feels the expression is clear, then we must take *porneia* in its most common meaning, i.e. sexual immorality, serious and willful misconduct.

For these reasons, the second line of interpretation, that of Hoffmann, Schillebeeckx, Leenhardt and others, is preferable; it does not seek an explanation elsewhere than in the text itself and its context. Is divorce permissible? This is the question that preoccupies the young Christian communities who are simultaneously aware of the authority of Moses (Deuteronomy 24:1) and the dictum of Jesus on repudiation-adultery. Considering that the question of divorce had already long been discussed in Judaism, it is more probable that Matthew uses *porneia* in the meaning it had in all the debates of the rabbinical schools, i.e. "immorality," "adultery," "sexual misconduct of the woman."[23] We must acknowledge with Schillebeeckx that ". . . Matthew was writing for Jewish Christians, (and) it seems clear that he was not thinking of the Greco-Roman custom (according to which the wife could also take the initiative) but of the Jewish custom (according to which only husbands could send their wives away because of unchastity)."[24]

From these remarks, two readings are possible. The first explains the text of Matthew 5:32 where, if *porneia* signifies "adultery" in the strict sense, the meaning becomes very clear: "every one who divorces his wife makes her an adulteress, except in the case where she has already committed adultery." Matthew, who wishes, in reporting the *logion* of Jesus, to warn the believers of the terrible responsibilities incurred by those who divorce their wives (they will literally be responsible for the adultery their wives will commit), takes pains to add that obviously this risk does not exist if the wife has already committed adultery on her own. For Matthew it would only be a question of raising a difficulty that the saying of Jesus could cause: no one can push another into adultery if adultery has already been committed! The dictum of Jesus, then, would not apply to those who are victims of the adultery of their mate, but only to those who would put away their wives for more insubstantial reasons.

From the springborad of this interpretation, the other text, Matthew 19:9 could be explained like this: even he who has justly put away his wife (since she committed adultery)[25] is not authorized by the Lord to remarry. The emphasis here would be on the prohibition of the separated mate to remarry. I will return to this point shortly.

Clearly this interpretation minimizes the value of the insertion by Matthew: the simple common-sense remark of 5:32 is found in 19:9 only to better highlight the universality of the principle of prohibiting remarriage to all separated or divorced people.

A second reading seems possible, which differs somewhat from the preceding one. My hypothesis is that Matthew (in 19:9) wishes to discourage a legalistic interpretation of the words of Jesus and for that reason he introduces this addition which seems to authorize divorce. How so? "What God has joined together let no man put asunder," said Christ with reference to God's original intention (19:6). This is as much as to say that man can effectively separate what God has united. Marital union can be destroyed! To postulate, with the scholastic tradition, that the indissolubility of marriage constitutes an objective bond, independent of the will and love of the partners, does not seem in conformity with the gospel. This is what Matthew seems to be saying; once one of the conjoined (in the Jewish setting it could only be the woman) evidently demonstrates by his conduct that he has broken the marital bond, it is only right to admit that fact without having to condemn the other partner to unhappiness, all in the name of an unmerciful legalistic exactitude. It is thus not contrary to the Lord's words to say that there are cases where the marital union is destroyed. But Matthew multiplies the precautions so that such a declaration does not open the door to the casuistic hypocrisy denounced by Jesus! On one hand, only the case of *porneia* is recognized here as authorizing divorce. Because of the context, this term must be taken in its strongest meaning: "*Porneia* does not indicate only adultery here, even if duly stated. The word itself . . . covers a broader area. It's a matter of a specific kind of misconduct, i.e. let's say in this context the continuous and deliberate conduct of a woman who has resisted all the equally continuous and deliberate efforts of her husband bent on turning her away from her deviation in order to save the marriage."[26]

Moreover, even the one who should be admitting that his marital life is destroyed should not feel himself authorized to remarry (19:9). Why? Essentially, so that the door to a possible pardon, an eventual reconciliation, would not be totally shut and to demonstrate a hope that yet exists despite the failure and death.[27]

This interpretation of Chapter 19 seems dictated by the other text (5:32) which likens repudiation (except in the case of *porneia* of one of the partners) to adultery. Why are the two similar? Because in divorcing his wife, the husband precipitates a crisis, renders it irreparable, solidifies objectively that which up until now was relational difficulty—briefly he proves that all hope is gone. Thus the marriage no longer belongs to the realm of the kingdom of God which comes as forgiveness and as life, but becomes relegated to the realm of the Law which judges and condemns. Whoever believes in the kingdom believes in the possible resurrection of that which sin meanwhile condemns to death.

Thus, for Matthew, consistent misconduct of the wife severs the marital tie and leads to the actual separation of the couple. Human will has succeeded in separating that which God had wished unified. But this does not free the believing partner from his responsibility; he must continue concretely to manifest his hope in the midst of failure, to continue to believe the promise which is attached to the existence of the couple by God and which can be resuscitated by repentance and reconciliation.

It seems, then, that Matthew tries both to contest this legalistic reading of the words of Jesus occurring in the Christian communities and at the same time seeks to avoid the trap of casuistry.[28] Being responsible for a community which would experience the "hardness of heart" of man, as did Israel and Moses before it, Matthew wishes vividly to maintain the critique of legalism established by Jesus: God does not "authorize" divorce by His Law, but on the contrary attaches His promise to the existence of a united couple. But neither does God desire the death of the sinner, but by the Law wishes to provide a breathing space, in spite of everything, where the hope for pardon and reconciliation can subsist. The whole ethical effort of the community would be to avoid the hypocrisy which toys with the rule and the promises, the prideful self-righteousness which thinks itself authorized to cast into the outer darkness those who have made a mistake; on the positive side, the ethic should recall the promise of God and provide a space for a possible life to those who are wounded by failure, who have been tempted by evil, who have been submerged by covetousness. This, I believe, is what Matthew tried to do.

2) The Apostle Paul

It is in his correspondence with the Corinthians that Paul was led to approach the problem of marriage (and especially in 1 Corinthians 7).[29] The context is very different from that which applied in the case of Jesus and the gospel writers. Here in the environment of Greek mentality, two dangers are imminent: immorality and asceticism. Immorality was almost a Corinthian specialty—there was a verb "korinthiazein," to live in Corinthian style, which evoked promises of libertine delight to the travelers who came to Corinth. Certain Christians seemed to react to this by practising a rather rigorous asceticism, justified by the dualism in Greek religious thought and by Christian eschatology which announced the end of all things. Paul had in a previous letter[30] congratulated the Corinthians for reacting against the moral dissipation of their fellow citizens[31] and had also vigorously protested against any kind of disdain for the body: "The body is not meant for immorality, but for the Lord, and the Lord for the body. . . . Do you not know that your body is the temple of the Holy Spirit within you, which you have of God? . . . So glorify God in your body" (1 Corinthians 6:13, 19–20). In the same letter, Paul aligned himself nevertheless with those who desired a rather strict moral discipline: "Do you not know that in a race all the runners compete, but only one receives the prize. So run that you may obtain it. Every athlete exercises control in all things. They do it to receive a perishable wreath, but we an imperishable. . . . I pommel my body and subdue it, lest after preaching to others I myself should be disqualified." (1 Corinthians 9: 24–27).

It seems that this teaching was so well received in Corinth that certain people concluded that it was in line with the normal ethical consequences of faith to renounce all sexual relations. In a letter to the apostle from the Corinthians asking him certain questions we read this sentence: "It is good for man not to touch a woman."[32] All of chapter 7 of 1 Corinthians constitutes a lengthy response to the different questions raised with regard to marriage and sexuality because of their ascetic tendencies.

Paul immediately challenges (in 7:1–6) an asceticism which, because of spiritual pride, clearly borders on unreality. "He who tries to become an angel becomes an animal"—Pascal's saying clearly illustrates Paul's commentary: to the couple who attempt a spiritualized and ascetic lifestyle, Paul recalls that each partner literally belongs to the other and cannot on his own decide to break the sexual union: "The husband should give to his wife her conjugal rights, and likewise the wife to her husband. For the wife does not rule over her own body, but the husband does; likewise the husband does not rule over his own body, but the wife does." (7: 3–4). The one concession the apostle makes is only valid if there is common consent: "Do not refuse one another except perhaps by agreement for a season, that you may devote yourselves to prayer; but then, come together again, lest Satan tempt you through lack of self-control." (7:5). And so to the married members of the community, Paul recalls that even the perspective of the kingdom that is close at hand (7:29,31) does not modify conjugal reality, whose meaning continues to be the locus of experiencing belonging to one another in a bond of mutual dependence (7:4). Aceticism is acceptable only if provisional and freely accepted by both partners.

Next, the apostle deals with a series of specific questions based on the central thesis that "each has his own special gift from God, one of one kind [marriage] and one of another [celibacy]" (7:7). Thus for Paul, as for Jesus, marriage and celibacy are vocations, gifts or "charisms" of God. Here we go beyond the natural plane (where Jewish thought was still centered) which makes celibacy a curse and marriage an obligation, to the vocational plane where the Gospel henceforth posits all human possibility. Man is not freed of contingencies through faith, but through faith he can live them out as a gift and promise from God. Thus marriage! This is why Paul advises the unmarried members of the community to remain in the state they are in, that is to say, to acknowledge their present state as a charism of God: "To the unmarried and widows I say that it is well for them to remain single as I do" (7:8). But if that seems impossible, then: "But if they cannot exercise self-control, they should marry; for it is better to marry than to be aflame with passion." (7:9). Such a statement lends itself to much equivocation: Paul seems to be recommending marriage as a lesser evil for those who do not have the strength to remain continent or celibate. It would be quite strange if in these two verses the apostle were really contradicting the thesis that he has just proclaimed in verse 7! Actually, Paul is saying something else, deriving from his realistic perspective: if someone cannot accept celibacy, let him recognize in this fact a call from God; if continence is impossible, why continue obstinately with it as though it represented a higher spiritual path? There is a diversity of gifts! It is right and good to marry, to accept the reality of it and make of it a vocation.[33] There is thus no devaluation of marriage in this text, as a certain traditional reading of the text has claimed, but rather an appeal to realism, without which there is no possibility of recognizing where one's vocation lies. The proof that Paul is in no way disdaining marriage is furnished in the following verse where he recalls Jesus' teaching: "To the married I give charge, not I but the Lord, that the wife should not separate from her husband (but if she does, let her remain single or else be reconciled to her husband)—and that the husband should not divorce his wife." (7:10–11). Not only does the new reality established by Christian faith not authorize separation, it also invites men and women not to despair of a possible reconciliation. This is exactly the same perspective found in the gospel writers and particularly in Matthew.

As to "mixed" marriages (where one of the partners is not a believer) they are regulated by the same perspective. The gospel cannot be the occasion of separation solely on the grounds that only one of the partners has accepted it. On the contrary, it is a hope for potential discovery together, for communal sanctification. The promise of sharing affixed to a marital union is such that one of the partners can sanctify the other by his/her very presence: ". . . I say, not the Lord, that if any brother has a wife who is an unbeliever, and she consents to live with him, he should not divorce her. If any woman has a husband who is an unbeliever, and he consents to live with her, she should not divorce him. For the unbelieving wife is consecrated[34] through her husband" (7:12–14a). The gospel cannot be a pretext for separation on the part of the believing partner. But the non-believing partner must have his freedom respected: "But if the unbelieving partner desires to separate, let it be so[35]; in such a case the brother or sister is not bound. For God has called us to peace. Wife, how do you know whether you will save your husband? Husband, how do you know whether you will save your wife?" (7:15–16). Respect for the liberty of the other and, again, realistic appreciation on the part of the apostle: no spiritual vanity, no false heroism.

After the parenthetical discussion (7:17–24) where Paul develops his thoughts on how important it is that no one submit to his situation as destiny, but should rather perceive his real vocation therein, the apostle returns to the Corinthians' questions; it is impressive to see Paul's humility as he confesses that on certain questions he can only give advice and not specific commands.

There is the case of the celibates (7:25). Celibates perhaps do well not to marry, not because celibacy is superior to marriage, but because of the difficulties of the times: "I think that in view of the impending distress it is well for a person to remain as he is. Are you bound to a wife? Do not seek to be free. Are you free from a wife? Do not seek marriage. But if you marry, you do not sin. Yet those who marry will have worldly troubles and I would spare you that" (7:26–28). In eschatological terms (where Paul situates Christian experience) the marriage state in fact is more difficult both because solidarity with regard to the partner and family may conflict with one's faithfulness to Christ—for example, in time of persecution; and because the concrete concern for the other spouse leaves the married man or woman less free and available than the celibate. It is clear that in this whole passage (7:29–35) Paul reveals his own preference; but he immediately qualifies his "apology" for celibacy by adding "I say this for your own benefit, not to lay any restraint upon you, but to promote good order and to secure your undivided devotion to the Lord" (7:35). Each person must discern how he can best respond to the Lord's call. If the Kingdom is not a flight from reality, it nonetheless requires an availability to its call and to its commands of breaking with certain things. How to respond realistically to this requirement is what Paul is trying to discern.

Taking up the question of engaged couples next, the apostle handles it with the same realism: "If any one thinks that he is not behaving properly toward his betrothed, if his passions are strong, and it has to be, let him do as he wishes; let them marry—it is no sin. But whoever is firmly established in his heart, being under no necessity but having his desire under control, and has determined this in his heart, to keep her as his betrothed, he will do well. So that he who marries his betrothed does well; and he who refrains from marriage will do better" (7:36–38). For the engaged couples, the principle previously announced that every one should "remain in the state in which he was called" (7:20) could have presented more of a trap than a vocation. Here again the temptation to spiritualized heroism—a kind of "sexless marriage"[36] —must be denounced, and reality lucidly appreciated: there is no sin in realizing that one is not cut out for celibacy. Moreover, before deciding to renounce marriage, one should think twice; Paul multiplies the precautions and requires above all that no force, exterior or interior, is exercised upon the person considering the issue.

Next, the apostle deals with the final question concerning widowers and widows: do they have the right to remarry? Isn't remarriage a distressing demonstration of a lack of spirituality? Paul gives this answer: "A wife is bound to her husband as long as he lives. If the husband dies, she is free to be married to whom she wishes, only in the Lord. But in my judgment she is happier if she remains as she is. And I think I have the Spirit of God" (7:39–40). Paul follows the same principle; legally there is no restriction to remarriage, but each one should consider where his own vocation lies; he thinks—but he adds it's a personal opinion—that widowhood is a better state than remarriage.

The whole of chapter 7 in 1 Corinthians is of particular importance in understanding how the discussion of a Christian marital ethic evolved. In Paul's response, we see a concrete approach, in its initial stage, which is built on three basic premises: the commandment of the Lord, serious confrontation with reality, and an eschatological perspective. The first, in a broad sense, represents an interpretation of the Law according to the words and person of Christ; it recalls the fundamental thrust of God's plan for man. God's intention is inscribed in a real situation and gives it meaning; it can never be the pretext to escape from the reality that is not to be abandoned but courageously changed. We can sense that Paul mistrusts any type of spirituality where ethical courage is replaced by spiritual smugness. For only this kind of courage can signal the innovation of the kingdom that is coming to dwell in the midst of men, whereas claims to spiritual superiority separate men and make them incapable of love. It is only too easy to dream of perfect obedience by neglecting to consider concrete reality. In contrast to this illusion, Paul recalls that we must know where God has really placed us so that He can invite us to be witnesses to an alternate possibility.[37] And finally, an eschatological perspective defines a framework for obedience and helps it avoid succumbing to the traps of conformity and legalism. This is why marriage is also a vocation.

Thus, Pauline thought on the marriage theme is based on a triple premise: first, the commandment of the Lord which reveals the hope as well as the requirement affixed to the man/woman relationship, i.e. the proclamation of grace in marriage; secondly, the personal and social reality where this hope and requirement are lived out; finally, the eschatological perspective which makes the so-called "natural" givens relative, in order to help man accede to the vocational dimension where this freedom can really be expressed. Sexuality no longer indicates fate or necessity, but the possible exercise of a freely chosen vocation.

3) Pauline Tradition

There are two other references to marriage in Paul's epistles: 1 Thessalonians 4:3–7 and Colossians 3:18ff.

The first text presents marriage as a possible way to live in holiness and to resist immorality, in particular by respecting the wife of one's "brother." Here is the little-known text: "For this is the will of God, your sanctification: that you abstain from immorality; that each one of you know how to take a wife[38] for himself in holiness and honor, not in the passion of lust like the heathen who do not know God; that no man transgress, and wrong his brother in this matter, because the Lord is an avenger in all these things, as we solemnly forewarned you. For God has not called us for uncleanness but in holiness."

The second text repeats a classical exhortation of ancient moral teaching: "Wives, be subject to your husbands, as is fitting in the Lord. Husbands, love your wives, and do not be harsh with them."

This last text is elaborated and commented on quite conclusively in Ephesians (5:21–33). This commentary is an excellent example of the way in which the Pauline tradition[39] followed the theological and ethical work of the apostle.[40] It is the first theological attempt at considering marriage in its application according to the innovation of the Gospel. This text, which constitutes the most developed theology on the question of marriage in the whole New Testament, is of great importance:[41] "Be subject to one another out of reverence for Christ. Wives, be subject to your husbands, as to the Lord. For the husband is the head of the wife as Christ is the head of the Church, his body, and is himself its Savior. As the Church is subject to Christ, so let wives also be subject in everything to their husbands. Husbands, love your wives, as Christ loved the Church and gave himself up for her, that he might sanctify her, having cleansed her by the washing of water with the word, that he might present the Church to himself in splendor, without spot or wrinkle or any such thing, that she might be holy and without blemish. Even so husbands should love their wives as their own bodies."7

On a first reading, this text does indeed justify, with the aid of theological or rather christological arguments, the necessity of the wife's submission to the husband; and it has been often interpreted in just that way. I believe that a more serious reading makes something else come forth in this text, something I would call the tension between a cultural assumption and a theological aim. To be more explicit, the tension between the traditional discourse of Jewish and Judaeo-Christian morality on marriage as opposed to a new language based on the innovation of the gospel, which seeks to express itself.

Here are some indications of this tension in the text:

—The phrase which introduces the passage in its entirety (verse 21) calls for the believers, *whoever they are,* to submit to one another "out of reverence for Christ," that is to say, out of respect for His will, out of love for Him. Now, this fundamental thesis, which no one can claim to escape, seems to be withdrawn abruptly in the next verse when the author addresses women: submission seems to be the woman's specialty, whereas the husband is exhorted to do the loving. Why should there be a particular kind of submission within a ruling that is applied to everyone? Why does the reciprocity of mutual submission in faith not apply to the conjugal domain? Insofar as they are Christians, the married couple is called to submit to one another; but insofar as they are married, then Christians seem to escape this ruling! The author thus juxtaposes two formulas, as if the domain of marriage were not included under the gospel rule. In the ensuing verses however, the author attempts a christological interpretation of the man/woman relationship.

—In verse 23, the author justifies the call for the wife's submission by the argument that ". . . the husband is the head of the wife . . ." This explanatory proposition, introduced by a "for" (oti), is immediately completed and interpreted by the comparison which follows, introduced by an "as" (ôs); he is a head, but not in any old way: "as Christ is the head of the Church," i.e. as "savior" (v.23), as He who gives Himself (v. 25), as a fiancé who leads his fiancée (v. 27). His comparison essentially transforms the preceding affirmation: it looked like a "natural" statement—the husband is the wife's head—but it turns out to be a christological declaration of the link between Christ and His Church, and this link is presented as the norm for judging the kind of link that should be between man and woman in the conjugal relationship. This is exactly what the text says further on when it explicitly makes the Christ-Church relationship the reference point for the conjugal relationship: "Even so—(as Christ loved the Church)—husbands should love their wives as their own bodies." The determinative factor is the Christ-Church relationship and not the "natural" affirmation of the superiority of the man over the woman.[42]

We can readily see, through the example of this text, how the gospel introduced into the human consciousness of that time a crucial factor which radically questions the "natural" (ie. cultural) assumptions, insofar as they present themselves as fate. The gospel reveals that they are nothing but the consequences of forced circumstances where love has no place.

But why, then, maintain a call for the submission of wives? Very simply, I believe that for a man of the first century, nourished by Jewish and Hellenistic traditions, such a submission is a self-evident and "natural" assumption, outside of which it would probably be impossible for him to consider the question of marriage. What is astonishing as well as important is not that the New Testament authors hold to a hierarchical model in speaking of man/woman relationships, but rather that they put it, as though in spite of themselves and as though constrained by the very reality of the gospel message, so radically in question.

In the context of the first century, any preaching which would have proclaimed an end to the submission of the wife, the abolition of all hierarchy, could not but seem totally unreal, having neither relevance nor merit;[43] Christian teaching on morality will try to include both the givens of reality and the innovation of the gospel. As we have said, reality, for the Christians of the first century, bears out the inferiority of the woman.[44] For all the authors of early Christianity, that's a basic assumption; to set oneself in opposition to it is either folly (cf. 1 Cor. 11:13ff.) or spiritual and utopian exaltation which so greatly anticipates ultimate reality that it neglects simple decency (as it was conceived of at that time). Such is the context of all early Christian thinking. But—and here is the new and decisive point—this reality, despite the weight conferred upon it, is not the ultimate assumption. A more profound point, which turns that one upside down, is the proclamation by the gospel which causes this reality to be viewed otherwise, i.e. as secretly indwelt by a hope[45] which makes the so-called natural givens relative. Thus in the domain of relationships between man and woman the hope is that it is possible for a man to "love his wife as his own body" (v. 28) as it will one day be possible, when a socio-cultural context can receive the true significance, for the wife to love her husband as her own body.

It is clear that in a cultural scheme which seemed self-evident to the Christians of the first century, i.e. man and woman are not equal, the theological insight of the author of Ephesians introduces an element which changes that meaning. In the short run, that theological element seems to reinforce the cultural scheme by justifying it. But it only seems that way: here the cultural given is no longer decisive, and no longer self-evident, because now the factor being emphasized is the "mystery"[46] of the unity of Christ and His Church which marriage is called to reflect. A theological task thus opens before us, which is to consider the possible meanings of this manifestation by marriage in the light of the meaning of the relationship between Christ and His Church. The author of the epistle attempts just that in his text when he reflects on what the love of Christ for his body (the Church) is, and from it deduces the exhortation to husbands to love their wives in the same way. The task to pursue is certainly not a mechanical repetition of biblical formulas on the wife's submission, as though our cultural, sociological and psychological context had not changed; but rather we must ask ourselves how in our changed context the "mystery" of the love of Christ for his Church can be signified today.

We have thus come to the heart of theological reflection on marriage: human love freed by the gospel from all kinds of conformity and from legalism, can signify the love of Christ for His Church. Theological reflection at this point consists in understanding the mystery of this love and of seeing how it connects with the reality of the marital existence of men and women in our time.

3. Conclusion

At the end of this study of the scriptural tradition, I will attempt a brief synthesis. The Old Testament is replete with a theology of marriage which emphasizes on one hand the meaning of marriage (which is to signify the relationship of God with His people) and on the other hand the promise or hope that is attached to marriage: an offer to the man and woman of the wonder of a love encounter (cf. Song of Songs). But even for all that, the burden of the actual condition of the marital institution, itself caught in social constraints that the Bible certainly is aware of, is not denied: the love encounter can at any moment be deflected and become a relationship of domination and a conflict of power; the project which creates life can become the bearer of death, through weariness, disdain, or misunderstanding. This is why the Old Testament finally proposes an understanding of marriage which is in tension between two contrary poles, both of which are indispensable: the promise, which in a certain way always challenges the institution—there is always something beyond the institutional conjugal reality that one hopes to discover—; and the institution which alone can give an actual creative meaning to sexuality—for outside of the institution, sexuality is nothing but disorder and violence.

Jesus, faced with a somewhat hypocritical and legalistic practice, reviews the terms of that tension: the compassionate close presence of God, as it is proclaimed in the preaching of the kingdom of God, finds itself testified to in the compassionate intimacy of man and woman who have been reconciled. The relationship between man and woman is recognized anew as the locus par excellence for the issuing forth of love. This is why adultery is condemned as the deliberate rejection of this acknowledgement and as a complete submission to the covetousness that brings death. The core of the law is recalled, not from a legalistic viewpoint, but to remind people of the extraordinary essence of that which occurs between a man and a woman, which is nothing less than the possibility of experiencing the nearness of God's love.

Ancient Christian tradition (the gospels and Paul) not only transmitted this teaching of the Lord, but also had to adapt it to the concrete reality of the life of the first communities. How does one, being sensitive to the contingent reality of those to whom the teaching is addressed, maintain the thrust of the Gospel without changing it into a new legalism? It is exciting to see how Matthew tried to resolve the question by speaking of the value of the forgiveness of failure, or how Paul responds by attempting what could be called eschatological realism in the face of marriage.

All these attempts, as diverse as they are, have in common the recognition (because of Jesus' teaching which echoes Genesis) that marriage is a vocation, i.e. a calling from God (and from this comes the possibility of renouncing that call in favor of another call from the same God). In other words, marriage is one of the ways that man and woman can act out the meaning of life. The author of Ephesians causes us to catch sight of this through his wondrous reflection on the theological mystery that is connected to marriage. That which must be finally realized in the relationship of a man and woman in marriage is something that belongs to the order of the kind of love Christ has for the Church, His body.

From this point on, a theological task arises, which is to see how, in different cultural contexts, this same mystery of love can and should be signified by a human couple engaged in the risk of faithfulness and freedom. The fourth chapter will discuss how this was done during the history of the Church, and in the fifth chapter, I will discuss how we in turn, given our present context, can attempt a response.

IV

Christianity and Sexuality: An Ambiguous History

Any research on the Christian ethic of sexuality can not bypass the history of the difficult and ambivalent relations of Christianity to sexuality, (unless it be frivolous or in bad faith). No one could ingenuously claim to go straight from the Bible to our time while ignoring, or pretending to ignore, the impact which this tradition has had on the consciousness or the unconsciousness of Christians in our day. This could only reveal presumption or childishness. Presumption, if we want to claim that we are our own beginning or to think that we ourselves are the initiators of Christianity; childishness, if we believe that shutting our eyes dispenses with reality! One cannot refute, whether we rejoice in it or denounce it, that our western morality largely flows from the past that belongs to Christian tradition. But it is equally true that more often than not we are unfamiliar with that tradition and that we rarely attempt to place it in its real intentions and in its confrontations within the theology of a time very different from our own. Because of this, my fourth chapter tries to measure the real value of the Christian moral tradition and tries to understand, with supporting texts, how and why Christianity took a particular stand on sexuality, wherein was merged, at least from our contemporary viewpoint, the best and worst of things. I shall also examine why, on certain important points, Christian tradition distanced itself from the scriptural tradition, and to discern thereby what is at stake in the ethical interpretation which the Church has made and continues to make of its sources.

84

This intention summarizes my field of interest here: it is less a question of reporting the whole history of the rapport between Christianity and sexuality than of highlighting the major trends, particularly those that defined what we finally have come to call "Christian morality." The first category is composed of reflections by the Church Fathers in the second, third and fourth centuries. As members of ancient society, they sought to formulate a morality (they preferred to call it an "asceticism") whereby gnostic dualism would be repulsed and an eschatological tension be maintained. This patristic ethic will be taken up and elaborated with great precision by Augustine (too great, in fact), whose teaching clearly dominated all of medieval western morality. The Augustinian position represents a second category. The third concerns the Protestant Reformation, which in its deliberate return to scriptural sources for morality as well as for faith, develops a morality which is clearly at odds, particularly in the area of sexuality and marriage, with Catholic morality.

At the end of the sixteenth century, we can say that in its broad outlines, Christian morality in the West vis-à-vis sexuality and conjugality is constituted under two forms—Catholic and Protestant. I will define the characteristics of both in a concluding section. I have decided not to follow the evolution of these two moralities down into our modern era (from the seventeenth to the nineteenth centuries) because that development has not been influenced by any internal theological necessity but has been a reaction (positive or negative) to the general evolution of a society where the influence of the Church and of theology has been progressively diminishing. In fact, a close look reveals that the evolution altered nothing fundamental in the two moralities, but only accentuated, by emphasizing the difference, the essential characteristics of Catholic and Protestant morality. The models already set up in the course of history were not essentially affected by that evolution. Only in the twentieth century, more precisely in the mid-twentieth century, did certain Catholic moralists begin to discuss the validity of the foundations of traditional Catholic morality and did Protestant theology begin to question its links to bourgeois society with its moral ideals. This critical review has only just begun; it is certainly rich in promise, but it cannot be included in a chapter devoted to the history of the problem! Therefore, in my last chapter, I will try to deal with the necessity of reinterpreting scriptural and ethical tradition in a critique vis-à-vis the ideology of our contemporary culture.

1. The Early Church and Sexuality (Up to Ca. 250)

During this time the Church insists above all on the necessity for *moral discipline*. In so doing, the Church joins the ranks of a polemic tradition existing in Judaism as well as in Hellenism, which pronounces judgment on ancient customs (particularly sexual customs) that is often quite harsh. Thus the indictment of Paul against the immorality of pagans in Romans (1:18–32)[1] takes up the terms of the traditional polemic in Judaism against the idolatry of ancient religions and its dual consequence in the area of sexual morality: sex made sacred and homosexuality.[2]

In the New Testament, the denunciation of the ancient Greek world is frequent. Here, for example, is a list of sins which provoke indignation on the part of the author of the first epistle to Timothy who is faced with the moral situation of his day: ". . . the law is not laid down for the just but for the lawless and disobedient, for the ungodly and sinners, for the unholy and profane, for murderers of fathers and murderers of mothers, for manslayers, immoral persons, sodomites, kidnappers, liars, perjurers. . . ."[3]

In the midst of this kind of society, Christianity proclaimed itself the messenger of a religious morality which linked concrete practice to religious faith and sought thereby to express the cohesiveness of the Christian anthropological scheme.[4] Here are some examples from Christian texts of the end of the first and second centuries. In opposition to the popular practice of the *exposure of children,*[5] Justin writes: "Lest we molest anyone or commit sin ourselves, we have been taught that it is wicked to expose even newly-born children, first because we see that almost all those who are exposed (not only girls, but boys) are given over to prostitution. As your forefathers are said to have raised herds of oxen, or goats, or sheep, or grazing horses, you now raise children only for this same disgraceful purpose, for in every country there is a throng of females, hermaphrodites, and degenerates, ready for this evil practice. And you who should eradicate them from your land, instead accept wages, tribute, and taxes from them. Anyone who consorts with them, besides being guilty of a godless, impious and shameful action, may by some chance be guilty of intercourse with his own child, relative, or brother. . . . Still (another reason against this practice is) lest some of them would not be (discovered and) taken home, but die, and we would then be murderers."[6] Thus the exposing of children is denounced first of all because it encourages prostitution and immorality, and secondly because it is often equivalent to homicide. This link between respect for life and respect for the other is clearly evidenced in the *Didache*: "You shall not commit murder. You shall not commit adultery. You shall not corrupt boys. You shall not commit fornication. You shall not steal. You shall not practice magic. You shall not practice sorcery. You shall not kill an unborn child or murder a newborn infant."[7] The same teaching is found in the *Epistle of Barnabas* (19:4a,5d). Along with a very unusual exegesis of Leviticus (chap. 11), this epistle condemns sodomy, adultery, homosexuality and the practice of *fellatio.*[8] The same condemnation is perhaps found in the list of vices in the *Epistle of Clement of Rome to the Corinthians*: Christians should be ". . . fleeing from evil speech, and abominable and impure embraces." (30:1).

The Christian ideal exalts fidelity and purity in marriage. "Tell my sisters to love the Lord and to be satisfied with their husbands in the flesh and spirit. In the same way tell my brothers in the name of Jesus Christ to love their wives as the Lord does the Church. If anyone is able to persevere in chastity to the honor of the flesh of the Lord, let him do so in all humility. If he is boastful about it, he is lost. . . ."[9] The ideal of chastity must here be understood as the quest for a moral discipline capable of checking the current immorality. Thus Hermas sees himself commanded to "guard purity. Let it not enter your heart to think of another man's wife, nor about fornication, nor any such thing. If you do, you will commit a serious sin. Keep your wife in mind always and you will never fall into sin."[10] There is as yet no exaltation of the spiritual virtues of celibacy, but only concern for safeguarding a sexual ethic by and in marriage that respects, among other things, the person of the woman. And so Tertullian affirms: "So, we who are united in mind and soul have no hesitation about sharing what we have. Everything is in common among us—except our wives. In this matter—which is the only matter in which the rest of men practice partnership—we dissolve partnership. They not only usurp the marriage rights of their friends, but they even hand over their own rights to their friends with the greatest equanimity."[11] This text is important because it brings out the fundamental justification for the moral discipline called for by the Christians; it holds to an absolute distinction made between the relationship of man to things and the relationship between a man and his wife: the latter is structural and thus cannot be lived out according to the model for the former without fundamentally altering humanity.

In their insistence on the value of moral discipline, the first Christians met the expectation of a great number of their contemporaries.[12] Stoicism, which I shall come back to later, had already raised the ethical issue but its morality of moderation was not sufficient to respond to the most pressing questions. "One must admit that the Hellenistic and Roman world lived in the greatest sexual confusion. Nor did it find itself more 'liberated' or happier as a result. Certain societies outside of Europe that have perpetuated these customs (condemned on the surface) to this day certainly do not give the impression of having blossomed! We can well understand that the moral requirements of Christianity should have appeared as true liberation for those with sensitive consciences and for the victims of that kind of anarchy."[13] As an example, among many others, of this expectation and of the quest for a more exacting morality, here is an extract of ordinances of a private shrine founded at Philadelphia in Lydia in the first century B.C., dedicated to the goddess Agdistis: "Let men and women, slave and free, as they come to this shrine swear by all the gods that they will not knowingly devise any evil guile or harmful poison against man or woman; that they will neither know nor employ baneful spells; that they will neither themselves use nor recommend to others nor be accomplices in love charms, abortives, contraceptives, robbery, murder. ... No man shall have intercourse with any married woman other than his wife whether free nor slave, nor with any boy, nor with any virgin, nor advise another to do so, but if he shares another's guilty secret, he shall make public such an one. ... A married woman who is free must be chaste, and know the bed of no man but her husband: if she know another, she is not chaste but impure, infected with incestuous pollution and unworthy to venerate this god whose shrine is erected here. ... These commandments were set up by Agdistis the most holy guardian and mistress of this shrine. May she put good intentions in men and women. ..."[14]

Pliny the Younger, describing Christians in one of his letters to Trajan, particularly highlighted the moral discipline they submitted to: "... (they met) regularly before dawn on a fixed day to chant verses alternately among themselves in honour of Christ as if to a god, and also to bind themselves by oath, not for any criminal purpose, but to abstain from theft, robbery and adultery, to commit no breach of trust and not to deny a deposit when called upon to restore it."[15]

Meanwhile, the same dual struggle which was outlined in our study of Paul's teaching continues on within the church and becomes intensified. On one hand, certain ascetic excesses must be restrained and on the other, certain antinomian tendencies linked to Gnosticism must be repelled. The first Christian theologians (Clement of Alexandria, Irenaeus, Tertullian) are the witnesses and the actors in this struggle which will mark Christian moral tradition for many centuries.

Clement of Alexandria,[16] with regards to marriage and sexuality, fights against encratic movements on one hand and licentious gnostic sects on the other. The whole third *Stromata*[17] is devoted to this battle.

Encraticism is more of an extreme ascetic attitude than a philosophy of a particular sect;[18] Clement sees it as defended by Marcion and his disciples, by Tatian[19] and his movement, and by Julianus Cassianus[20] and his school. It strongly influenced certain apocryphal texts like the *Apocryphal Acts,* particularly the *Acts of John*[21] (second century) and the *Gospel of Thomas* (early third century). That influence is essentially defined as a rejection of marriage. The encratic arguments, judged from Clement's refutation, are as follows. First, marriage is sin because it is stained by the uncleanness that comes from sexual relation; it (therefore) discourages any spiritual relationship with God and only perfect chastity can signify the resurrection, and is the means whereby one can experience that reality even here on earth. Second, marriage belongs to the old order of reality, that of the Law, which has been abolished: "The Savior has transformed us and set us free of the error of the union of sexes."[22] Finally, since Christ was not married, chastity is part of the imitation of Jesus. The Encratites freely cite, as does Clement himself elsewhere, passages from the apocryphal *Gospel of the Egyptians,* a text which seems to have been authoritative in Alexandria. This text, or at least the fragments which have come down to us through Clement, link sexuality and procreation with the continuation of the reign of death. Marriage is thus in service to death[23] and the Kingdom is characterized by the abolition of sexual difference.[24] It is clear that encraticism displays a profound pessimism toward creation, a pessimism which naturally engenders disdain for the body since it is mortal and inhabited by desire and passion.

In the face of this asceticism, Clement defends the dignity of marriage. First of all, marriage is instituted by God. It is in no way the consequence of sin, and sexuality was willed by God for the propagation of the human race.[25] Moreover, marriage joins man to the creative work of God: "This is to share in God's own work of creation, and in such a work the seed ought not be wasted nor scattered thoughtlessly...."[26] Following Ephesians 5, Clement especially interprets marriage from the starting point of the bond that unites Christ to His Church. This battle for marriage is a battle for the positive affirmation of divine Creation; it becomes part of the broader debate on the meaning of Christian eschatology. The Encratites, like certain Gnostics who will be discussed later, set redemption in opposition to creation and sought to manifest the already active presence of the *eschaton* by their unworldly attitudes. This was carried to the point where they denied all value or goodness to creation and became more and more systematic (one thinks of Marcion) in their juxtaposition of creator-god to God-the-savior. Under these conditions, we can understand Clement's forceful insistence on the fact that marriage is in collaboration with the divine work of creation.[27] So now, the principal end of marriage can be nothing other than procreation. We can see how the concern to fight for the value of the order of creation led to an emphasis on the procreative function of marriage. Against those who scorned marriage for spiritual reasons, it was necessary, in line with I Timothy 4:3[28] and Hebrews 13:4,[29] to honor the marital institution and consider how an authentic spirituality could be lived out in it—which idea was not self-evident in the stoic and dualistic context that the Christians were living in. The problem seemed to be solved by insisting on the link of sexuality to procreation.

Clement meanwhile clashes with certain *gnostic groups* in Alexandria who have very unusual views[30] on marriage and sexual life.

First of all, there are the disciples of the Gnostic Basilides and his son Isidore, who were Alexandrians at the beginning of the second century. From what we can reconstruct of their doctrine, it seems that Basilides recommended to the disciples who could not live in total sexual abstinence—which was his ideal—that they practice free sex without scruples, as long as no domination or compulsion by amorous desire was allowed. He preaches a sort of indifference to sexuality, an indifference which can as easily end up in continence as in immorality. In a very characteristic proposition, possibly inspired by epicureanism, Basilides distinguishes between love and sexual desire: he condemns love as a sign of aspiration contrary to nature and as a revolt against the limitations that it imposes on man, and he exalts sexual desire as a sign of man's participation in the spermatic power of God. One must thus satisfy sexual instinct, which is in conformity with nature, and therefore moral, without becoming dominated by love. Sexual desire is good, but love, which disturbs *mystical agnosia*,[31] is not. Where Christianity defends the indissolubility of monogamous union and tries to promote the idea that the morality of that union is linked to the love between the partners, Gnosticism proscribes sexual promiscuity which abolishes all love and authorizes spermatic communion. Even if at the beginning Basilides may have had the lofty ideal of the total adhesion of man to nature, of man's complete immersion in a sort of primitive and innocent ignorance whence all passion would be abolished, it is readily apparent that his less scrupulous disciples would have conserved only the simplest and grossest elements of that doctrine and that the sect would have degenerated progressively into immorality, going as far perhaps as establishing a spermatic cult (cf. Irenaeus *Adv. Haer.* I,19).

Next (in *Strom.* III, ii), Clement calls to mind the sect of Carpocrates and his son Epiphanes. They preached total communism especially with regard to women: "God made all things for man to be common property. He brought female to be with male and in the same way united all animals. He thus showed righteousness to be a universal fairness and equality. But those who have been born in this way have denied the universality which is the corollary of their birth and say, 'Let him who has taken one woman keep her,' whereas all alike can have her, just as the other animals do."[32] Thus sexual desire is an original expression of God's will, and it is the Law, promulgated by the evil god of the Jews, which has disturbed the good order of things. According to Clement, the Carpocratians gathered together for sacred meals which ended in orgies; after the meal, ". . . they have intercourse where they will and with whom they will." (III, 2, PG8, 112).

Against all these movements (he further cites the Nicolaitans, the disciples of Prodicos, the Antitactes), Clement opposes an all-encompassing refutation which has bearing on two points: the meaning of freedom and the religious justification for morality.

As to the meaning of freedom, the debate on the gnostic position is not new;[33] the claim of absolute freedom (which is measured by significant transgressions against moral laws) is illusory; it is nothing but a theoretical justification for the concrete enslavement to instinctive drives. "We have learnt to recognize as freedom that which the Lord alone confers on us when he liberates us from lusts and desires and other passion."[34]

As to the second point, the battle is against moral indifference that the Gnostic extols (since he believes himself to be already in the perfection brought by salvation); the most effective weapon for this battle is a theology of creation which on one hand challenges any dualism between Old and New Testament, (evil creator-god of the Jews vs. the good-god of Jesus) and on the other hand assures the moral and theological value of natural law. We must pause to consider this point because its historical importance was so great in the future development of Christian morality. It was for pastoral and theological reasons that the first Christian theologians (especially Irenaeus and Clement of Alexandria) had recourse to the concept of natural law, because it seemed more effective than any other argument against Gnosticism. But in so doing they accepted a problematic attitude that was more stoic than biblical.[35] The concept of *nature* has three meanings for the Fathers at the end of the second century: a) a disposition is natural when inscribed in a process which is not contaminated by sin or by human error (for example, the sexual process is "natural" to the extent that it is analogous to the sowing of seed in a field); b) whatever animals do is "natural": here again is the conviction that the universal models that are useful to man can be found where man's sin is absent, i.e. in the animal kingdom; c) finally, nature is a structure belonging to the realm of the human body: we could say that the most evident function of a particular bodily organ is "natural" (the eye is made to see).[36] This recourse to stoic values sought to anchor morality in an objectivity no longer conferred by the Old Testament and disqualified by gnostic arguments. But instantly the accent was removed from the morality of a faithful and loving covenant between man and woman and placed upon a morality of objective principles (or so-claimed!) which ratified the dualism between spiritual love (agreed as belonging to the Christian vocation) and bodily, sexual love (excluded as not natural).

We can see how, in order to fight against the aberrations of certain gnostic propositions, Christian thinking made use of stoic arguments which allowed a defense of marriage, while meanwhile excluding bodily love and sexual desire. Clement declared that Christian law intended ". . . husbands to cohabit with their wives with self-control and only for the purpose of begetting children" (*Strom.* III, xi, 71); and that "to indulge in intercourse without intending children is to outrage nature" (*Paidagōgos* II, x, 95). As Noonan correctly remarks,[37] "in Clement this view was linked to his basic position that desire as such was evil. . . . It is the purposeful, nondesirous act of intercourse which he defends." Love is certainly not excluded between the partners, but it is a spiritual love which can really be expressed only by continence. "A man who marries for the sake of begetting children must practice continence so that it is not desire he feels for his wife, whom he ought to love . . ." (*Strom.* III, vii, 58). This kind of moderate asceticism[38] which Clement preaches concerning conjugal ethics is indicative of Christian ethics at the end of the second century; it is a question of defending the necessity for moral discipline without falling into the excesses of an acesticism that disdains the body, and thus disdains divine creation. The goal is to gain some distance from a society where the disregard for others is so often manifested in sexual license (slave-concubines, easy divorce, homosexuality, sodomy. . .), while simultaneously avoiding the creation of a Christian ghetto—but also to allow for the practice of an uncompromising morality. The ethical responsibility which the Christian has a duty to assume in and for the world must be taken even more seriously, since the world was created by God for all men so that they could enjoy His material and spiritual blessings. It is thus correct to take inspiration from what is best in the moral values of philosophers and sages who also fought against moral disorder and thus to enter resolutely into the mainstream of the moralizing on sexuality and marriage which was operative at this time in Roman society.[39]

We can see already why stoic ideas had such a great influence on Christian morality. There will be more than one opportunity of confirming that as we continue.

2. The Early Church and Conjugal Rights

The moral trend on this issue is similar to the Church's attitude toward the institution of marriage. Modern historians today by and large agree on the fact that early Christianity did not evidence any originality in the realm of laws, rites or customs concerning marriage. As the author of the *Letter to Diognetus* says: "They [Christians] marry like the rest of men and beget children, but they do not abandon the babies that are born."[1] Christians readily adopted Roman law and traditional pagan custom.[2] The celebration of marriage, as practiced in the Empire by Christians as well as by pagans, "was accompanied by various ceremonies . . . the later custom of . . . *usus* as a condition of matrimonial authority . . . disappeared in imperial Rome. Marriages were concluded at this time without any form of law, and merely by mutual consent, though in traditional circles, this was supplemented by the ancient religious customs. The two concrete elements necessary to make the marriage valid were the *consensus*, or mutual consent of both partners, and the *domum-ductio*, or leading of the wife to her husband's house. The *domum-ductio* and the community of the partners, the *individua vitae consuetudo*, together formed, at least for those who were not slaves, a . . . valid and lawful marriage. . . . In the Christian era, stated Justinian finally, the mutual consent of both partners was sufficient for a valid marriage without any further formalities: *nuptias non concubitus, sed consensus facit*; in other words, marriage was not brought about by *usus*, or actual sexual intercourse, but by the partners' mutual consent."[3]

There is no such thing during this whole period as a "religious marriage." Marriage remains essentially a familial and earthly affair, even if it is acknowledged as a gift from God. Anything to do with marital rights comes from civil legislation. The concern of the Church in the matter is neither juridical nor liturgical, but pastoral: marriage between Christians must be protected from harmful pagan influence. That is the thrust of two texts which have sometimes been interpreted (incorrectly) as an indication that the Church intervened from the very beginning in matrimonial jurisdiction. Ignatius of Antioch requests that when "men and women marry the union should be made with the consent of the bishop, so that the marriage may be according to the Lord";[4] Tertullian speaks of "that marriage which the Church arranges, the Sacrifice (of the Eucharist) strengthens, upon which the blessing sets a seal, at which angels are present as witnesses, and to which the Father gives His consent. For not even on earth do children marry properly and legally without their fathers' permission."[5] However, in both cases, the goal is to call to mind the spiritual link between the wedded couple and the community, which alone can guard that marriage in its spiritual richness and authenticity. So then, there is here a pastoral and spiritual concern which seeks to suffuse the earthly affair of marriage with a Christian spirit, but there is no juridical concern whatsoever.

Of course, certain concrete problems were quickly raised, such as divorce, the remarriage of widowers and widows, and the sensitive question of "mixed marriage" with non-Christians. Paul had already dealt with these problems and the early Church would take its inspiration chiefly from his teachings.

Here are some examples that concern *divorce*.[6] We read in Hermas's *The Shepherd*: " 'Sir,' I said, 'if a man has a wife who believes in the Lord and surprises her in adultery, does he commit sin if he lives with her?' — 'Before he finds out,' he said, 'he does not. But, if her husband knows the sin, and she does not repent, but persists in her fornication, he becomes guilty of her sin, so long as he lives with her, and an accomplice in her adultery.' — 'Sir,' I said, 'what then is he to do, if the wife continues in this passion?' — 'Let him divorce her,' he said, 'and remain single. But, if he divorces her and marries another woman, he himself commits adultery.' — 'But, if, sir,' I said, 'after the divorce the wife repents and wishes to return to her husband, will he refuse to receive her?' — 'No, indeed,' he said, 'If the husband does not receive her, he sins. He incurs great sin. The sinner who has repented must be received. However, not often, for there is only one repentance for the servants of God. To bring about her repentance, then, the husband should not marry. This is the course of action required for husband and wife.' "[7] We can see how the question presented itself in the middle of the second century: divorce was authorized, and even recommended so that one should not take part in error. But, as in the scriptural tradition, remarriage was not authorized, so that the door to forgiveness and reconciliation could remain open.

The same motive authorizing divorce is found in Tertullian: "You will find him (Christ) also, in whichever direction you will, taking forethought regarding marriage: while he will not have it dissolved, he forbids separation: and while he will not have it continue under stain he permits divorce."[8] Thus, once the marriage tie has been severed by the adultery of one of the partners, divorce only ratifies an existing fact, and as such is legitimate and so allows for remarriage.

These two examples are interesting in that they clearly manifest the pastoral concern of theological reflection; there was a concern to safeguard the dignity of marriage, which adultery precisely destroys, and a desire that those who experience failure in conjugal life should not be crushed by legalism.

Another problem, remarriage for widowers, is commented upon by Hermas: " 'Sir,' I said, 'If a wife or husband is deceased and either one of the survivors marries again, does he or she sin by marrying?' — 'There is no sin,' he said. 'But, anyone who remains single achieves greater honor for himself and great glory before the Lord. But, even in remarriage, there is no sin.' "[9] He expresses a point of view that is to become traditional: remarriage is allowed, it does not constitute sin, but the widower who can remain in that state follows a better path, that of continence and chastity.

Finally the question of *mixed marriages* is equally preoccupying. In Paul's teaching (I Corinthians 7:12–17), the Fathers see an opportunity for the Christian member of the pair to be a witness. But, probably judging from the experience of many couples, they fear the risk and the problems involved; the non-Christian partner can hinder his mate (by his demands) from living out the requirements of faith. This tension becomes more and more vigorously described by authors, as shown in the following choice example from Tertullian: "Her duties to the Lord she certainly cannot fulfill according to the demands of ecclesiastical discipline, since she has by her side a servant of Satan who will act as an agent of his master in obstructing the performance of Christian duties and devotions. Thus, for example, if a station is to be kept, her husband will make an early appointment with her to go to the baths; if a fast is to be observed, her husband will, that very day, prepare a feast; if it be necessary to go out on an errand of Christian charity, never are duties at home more urgent! Who, indeed, would permit his wife to go about the streets to the houses of strangers, calling at every hovel in town in order to visit the brethren? Who would be pleased to permit his wife to be taken from his side, when she is obliged to be present at evening devotions?"[10]

In general, the Christians aligned their juridical conception and their practice of marriage with those of the Roman world. There is one point however, where their Christian convictions led them away from adherence to common laws: the *marriage of slaves*.[11] No right protects or recognizes the marriage of slaves. The union of two slaves is neither *connubium* (fully legal marriage) nor *matrimonium* (marriage in the general sense), but rather only a *contubernium* (intimate relationship, concubinage). With no legal guarantees whatsoever, slave couples were at the mercy of their masters' discretion.[12] Very quickly, it seems, the Church afforded aid and protection to Christian slave couples and recognized the validity of these unions in her eyes. Pope Calixtus (217–222) acknowledged as licit and honorable what would be called "marriages of conscience" which were contracted without the knowledge of the civil authorities but with the bishop's approval. These marriages particularly involved the union of a free woman with a slave. The Church stood as guarantor and witness to this marriage just as a family would have in the case of a legal marriage.

To conclude: up until the middle of the third century, the ethical thinking of Christians on marriage and sexuality was essentially in defensive reaction against the quasi-obsessive and aberrant practices of certain hyper-ascetic Christians or against libertines. In a reaction against the moral eschatology of the latter group, i.e. their affirmation of an already actualized salvation which authorized transgressions of the moral laws of this condemned world (which has already been transcended), the Fathers wished to root ethics in a theology of creation (which allowed the theological justification for recourse to natural law). They indeed defended marriage, but insofar as it was ordained by natural law for procreation. As for conjugal love, it was described as a chaste respect for one's partner, which was more threatened by sexual desire than expressed by it.

On the other hand, the formal and juridical aspect of the problem was never really approached: the Christians essentially adopted the laws and customs of the Roman world.

3. The "Yes, but" of the Great Patristic Tradition in Regard to Marriage and Sexuality (Fourth and Fifth Centuries)

The most systematic thinking of the great moral theologians of the fourth and fifth centuries (Gregory of Nyssa, John Chrysostom, Ambrose, Jerome, Augustine) leads to two conclusions which will mark the Christian morality of marriage and sexuality for many centuries: 1) sexuality is completely separate from love; it is aligned with sin with which it secretly connives; 2) virginity is superior to marriage since the latter continually threatens to turn one away from God.

Let us examine these two affirmations more closely.

Ambrose writes: "For now (since the fall), although marriage is good, it includes something that makes even married people blush at themselves."[1] This quotation is typical: it affirms the goodness of marriage, but with some reservations, since marriage implies sexuality (which is felt to be shameful).

This feeling of shame which accompanies sexuality can be observed in Augustine's statement: " ... in all united pairs ... there has been a permanent necessity of avoiding the sight of man in any work of this kind (sexual intercourse), and thus acknowledging what caused inevitable shame, though a good thing would certainly cause no man to be ashamed."[2] To interpret the private, secret and intimate character of human sexuality by the single category of shame reveals the inability in patristic thought of conferring positive value on sexuality (other than procreation).

The subject of shame is explained by Augustine in a very interesting way; "The undeniable truth is that a man by his very nature is ashamed of sexual lust.[3] And he is rightly ashamed because there is here involved an inward rebellion which is a standing proof of the penalty which man is paying for his original rebellion against God. For, lust is a usurper, defying the power of the will and playing the tyrant with man's sexual organs. It is here that man's punishment particularly and most properly appears, because these are the organs by which that nature is reproduced which was so changed for the worse by its first great sin."[4] What causes shame is the discovery of the irrational power of the libido, which challenges the rational and free-will ideal of the self. If all of man's dignity lies in this rational capacity, one can only fear and repel this disturbing force: "Such lust does not merely invade the whole body and outward members; it takes such complete and passionate possession of the whole man, both physically and emotionally, that what results is the keenest of all pleasures on the level of sensation; and at the crisis of excitement, it practically paralyzes all power (*acies*) of deliberate thought (*quasivigilia cogitationis.*)"[5] It is clear that for the Fathers, this kind of loss of self in the sexual act was felt to be a humiliation and therefore was a denunciation of the secret complicity between sexuality and sin—the latter being interpreted as revolt, disorder, irrationality. From this vantage point, it is not surprisng to read this sentence from the great thinker of the West: "I have decided that there is nothing I should avoid so much as marriage. I know nothing which brings the manly mind down from the height more than a woman's caresses and that joining of bodies without which one cannot have a wife."[6]

Sexuality is evidently so linked to sin that the question of how to avoid its culpability takes on more and more interest! And naturally, we find arguments, which have been defended by tradition until now, on the value of procreation. But the perspective has changed slightly: where the theologians of the third century defended procreation in order to defend the theology of creation, now the Fathers of the fourth century see procreation as the excuse for exercising sexuality. As Jerome said, "The activities of marriage itself, if they are not modest and do not take place under the eyes of God as it were, so that the only intention is children, are filth and lust."[7]

This excuse became more and more relative, especially with the eastern theologians, who under Origen's influence, came to consider marriage and sexuality as consequences of original sin. But how can the texts in *Genesis* which state the contrary and affirm that God created man "male and female," thus as sexual beings, from the beginning be explained? Here is Theodoret's answer: "Foreseeing and foreknowing that Adam would be liable to death because of the violation of the command, He already fashioned a nature of this kind beforehand, and formed it into a male and female body. The reason, of course, was that this is the design of bodies that are mortal and need the procreation of children to conserve the race."[8] By this kind of exegetical sleight of hand, the principal notion in *Genesis* of the goodness of sexuality—the notion that it was given by God to man and to woman so that they could learn to recognize the call of God's own love—was swept aside completely.

In this patristic perspective, God desired, in creating man and woman, that they should live as angels, in virginity and chastity.[9]

If challenged, the theologians, at least the western theologians, would not say that sexuality is sin, but they would indeed emphasize its connection to sin—the signs being sexual desire, irrational instinct and pleasure. Had there been no sin, sexuality would have been pure love, free from all desire whatsoever. Sexuality would have existed—and on this point, western Augustinian theology differs from eastern theology (cf. above)—but it would have existed without libido; it would have been a sign of differentiation calling for a relationship that was purely voluntary and without concupiscence. Augustine attempted to describe it: " 'Increase and multiply and fill the earth.' Although it seems that this could not happen without the intercourse of a man and woman . . . still we may say that in mortal bodies there could have been another process in which, by the mere emotion of pious charity, with no concupiscence, that sign of corruption, children would be born."[10] "Who denies that marriage would have existed even if sin had not preceded it? But it was to have existed so that the reproductive members would be moved by the will, like the other members, not aroused by lust; or (not to burden you with sorrow about lust) they would not have been aroused by lust such as now exists, but by lust obedient to the will."[11]

Such a devaluation of sexuality must necessarily be accompanied by an exaltation of virginity. And this is the second line of thought in patristic teaching. As we have seen when discussing Clement of Alexandria, this element is already quite present in the Church of the second and third centuries[12] under deviant forms that Clement had to fight against.

However, it is especially in the fourth century that Christian theology develops systematic thinking on the value and dignity of virginity. A whole series of writings comes forth on this theme,[13] which aims at eulogizing virginity.

Virginity makes one divine, or as John Chrysostom says, it makes "mortals like unto angels." In the words of Ambrose, "A virgin marries God."

To better understand the rationale for this glorification of virginity, let us take the example of Gregory of Nyssa and his *Treatise on Virginity*.[14] Written in 371 by a man who, according to his own memoirs (cf. 3:1, 5–15) was himself married (even at the time of his bishopric), this treatise is very representative of the manner in which the Fathers of the fourth century approached these questions.

Gregory proposes first that virginity is a perfection that belongs to divine and incorporeal nature: "Virginity is exceptional and peculiar to the incorporeal nature, and, through the kindness of God, it has been granted to those whose life has been allotted through flesh and blood, in order that it may set human nature upright once more after it has been cast down by its passionate disposition, and guide it . . . to a contemplation of the things on high." (II,ii,5-10). For "purity alone is sufficient for receiving the presence and entrance of God" (II,ii,12). On the other hand, marriage is the proper state for those who cannot renounce passion: "However, the one who is stupid looks downwards and hands his soul over to the pleasures of the body . . . being alienated from the life of God . . . considering nothing else to be good than pleasing the body" (IV, v,l ff.). The "intelligible and immaterial contemplation of the beautiful" (V, 19) is incompatible with a subjection to "the afflictions that accompany mankind" (IV,viii,9). Certainly, marriage as such is not to be condemned, but it does become a risk for those who are in that state, i.e. the risk of forgetting the spiritual because of sensual pleasure (*hèdonè*) (IV,v,7) and of being dragged along by nature (IV, v, 8). Moreover, marriage "was contrived as a consolation for death" (XII,iv,23); it is thus a consequence of sin, a lesser evil which collaborates in the end with the reign of death because it constantly furnishes that kingdom with new occasions for triumph (XIV,2).

On the other hand, virginity "is stronger than death (by promising a spiritual fruitfulness which escapes death)" (XIV,3). He who practices virginity "reaps the choicest goods in the resurrection and in the present life. For if the life which is promised to the just by the Lord after the resurrection is similar to that of angels—and release from marriage is a peculiar characteristic of the angelic nature—he has already received some of the beauties of the promise . . ." (XIV,iv,13–18).

Of course one must practice the virtue in a temperate way, nor should one believe that avoiding shameful pleasures automatically safeguards a person from the attraction of the more subtle pleasures of honor or power (XVII,i,1). With great finesse, Gregory warns against the danger demonstrated by those "who, by reason of much fighting against pleasures, are somehow easily overcome by an opposite kind of weakness and spend their lives in grievances and irritations and malice . . ." (XVII,i,9-12). And there is always the fact that ". . . if you are longing for God to appear to you, why do you not listen to Moses who ordered the people to abstain from (the privileges of) marriage in order to be present at the appearance of God?" (XXIII,vii,36-39). To see God, one must be chaste and pure.

As we can see, the word "virginity" has a very broad meaning: *parthénia* means the uprightness of a body consecrated to God; absolute continence; exclusion of all moral error; virtuous life considered in its totality; the fullness of divine life communicated to man; a state of life in contrast to normal life; finally, one of God's own perfections. The warnings of Gregory against those who are excessive and who in the last analysis show themselves to be more obsessed with their bodies than freed from its needs, demonstrate clearly that, for him, virginity is altogether different from sexual abstinence alone; it's a whole way of life centered on seeking God. But, since sexuality is linked to passion, to the body, to pleasure (all negative terms), it is an obstacle to the contemplation of God. It must be renounced because it drags man downward, toward the material and the temporal. For isn't it linked to death, being "life in the flesh which death normally follows upon?" (XIII,3). For this reason, one should choose virginity, which is love for eternal and spiritual things, which uproots passion for carnal things; it is a quest for the incorruptible, an angelic life. It is a way of anticipating even here and now heavenly divine life. It is also a way of reversing the movement of Adam's sin—Adam, who was condemned to sexuality after his disobedience.

This kind of exaltation of virginity (while disqualifying marriage and sexuality) is classic in most of the texts cited above. The only exception, it seems to me, is in the *Symposium* by Methodius[15] where virginity is presented less as a return to the lost paradisiac state than as an ultimate step in the evolution of humanity according to God's plan: "It was a most extraordinary disposition that the plant of virginity was sent down to mankind from heaven. Hence too, it was not revealed to the first generation" (I,ii,16). "To begin with, they were to advance from brother-sister unions to marriage with wives from other families. Then they were to give up practicing, like brute beasts, multiple marriage (as though men were born merely for intercourse!). The next step was to take them from adultery; and the next to advance them to continence, and from continence to virginity. . . ." (I,ii,18).

This extraordinary (and very modern!) way of describing the progressive moralization of mankind does not devalue marriage since it is a step on the road to the highest morality; it is not, then, a result of the fall. And this viewpoint allows Methodius in a treatise exalting virginity, to describe the force and complexity of sexuality without seeking to disqualify it: ". . . this was perhaps the symbolism of that ecstatic sleep into which God put the first man, that it was to be a type of man's enchantment in love, when in his thirst for children he falls into a trance, lulled to sleep by the pleasures of procreation, in order that a new person, as I have said, might be formed in turn from the material that is drawn from his flesh and bone. For under the stimulation of intercourse, the body's harmony . . . is greatly disturbed, and all the marrow-like generative part of the blood, which is liquid bone, gathers from all parts of the body, curdled and worked into a foam, and then rushes through the generative organs into the living soil of the woman" (II,ii 31ff). And thus, one could write an apology for virginity—which is the thrust of the second discourse (cf. 7:49)—without necessarily disqualifying the material, corporeal and sexual world.

But this text, so vitally interesting because of its scientific imagination, is isolated. Gregory's position is the classic stance. We need not number the patristic texts which heavily insist on the inferiority of marriage while glorifying virginity. One main argument, which was already mentioned by Gregoy, reappears constantly: marriage turns one away from God. The next four examples prove the point.

First of all, Jerome: "Do you think that it is one and the same thing to spend days and nights in prayer and fastings, and to paint the face in anticipation of the arrival of a husband, to break step, to feign flattery? . . . Add to this the prattling of infants, the noisy clamoring of the whole household, the clinging of children to her neck, the computing of expenses, the preparing of budgets. Then there is the pounding of meats by a busy band of cooks; there is the chattering of a crowd of women weavers. In the meantime, she is told that her husband has arrived with friends. Like a swallow, she flies over the entire interior of the house, to see if the couch is properly arranged, if the floors have been swept, if the drinking bowls have been set in order, if the dinner has been prepared. Tell me, I ask you, where is there an opportunity to think of God in the midst of all this?"[16]

This pessimism (or realism) about marriage is common. Augustine says " . . . nothing seems more certain to me than that he was unwilling to reveal and explain in words that same tribulation of the flesh which he had predicted for those who chose marriage, in the suspicions of marital jealousy, in the bearing and the raising of children, in the fears and anguish of bereavement. For, what man is there who, when he has bound himself by the bonds of wedlock, is not torn and harrassed by these emotions?"[17] The same echo, the same description is found in John Chyrsostom: "It is an evil thing to wed a very poor wife, or a very rich one; for the former is injurious to the husband's means, the latter to his authority and independence. It is a grievous thing to have children, still more grievous not to have any; for in the latter case marriage has been to no purpose, in the former a bitter bondage has to be undergone. If a child is sick, it is the occasion of no small fear; if he dies an untimely death there is inconsolable grief; and at every stage of growth there are various anxieties on their account, and many fears and toils. . . . Is this then life, Theodore, when one's soul is distracted in so many directions, when a man has to serve so many, to live for so many, and never for himself?"[18] One should note in passing the high esteem John Chrysostom has for the woman whose only "usefulness" is to provide a lineage for her husband; the conjugal bond, already quite arduous, has no other meaning!

Ambrose sees the cares and the trials of marriage which turn one from God already symbolized in the sleep Adam was put into by God when

He took one of his ribs to fashion Eve: "What does the phrase 'deep sleep' signify? Does it not mean that when we contemplate a conjugal union we seem to be turning our eyes gradually (away from) the direction of God's kingdom? Do we not seem as we enter into a vision of this world, to partake a little of things divine, while we find our repose in the midst of what is secular and mundane?"[19] The encounter between man and woman is no longer compared to the love of Christ for His Church, as in the scriptural tradition (cf. Ephesians 5), but interpreted as the occasion of allowing oneself to be turned away from God, the one relationship which truly fulfills human destiny. Whereas the Scripture made of the male/female relationship a privileged place of experiencing otherness, and consequently, the sign of the human vocation to relationship with God, the Fathers, on the other hand, insist on the spiritual dangers in the male/female relationship, which tie man down to his material body and to temporal cares.

From this point on, what could possibly excuse, let alone justify, marriage? "Procreation and the education of the children are obviously the first excuse (and for many the only valid one). A concern to avoid even worse sexual impurity (adultery, fornication, etc.) or the fear of disrupting the fidelity which is indispensable to the survival of the marital institution are equally valid excuses: these are the three "goods" of marriage. More precisely, the evil that would come if these three goods were destroyed justify exercising sexuality, which is indispensable in their service; in brief, the lesser of two evils must be chosen."[20] Sexual practice is excused, although it nonetheless is an admission of spiritual weakness (if not error) because it is required for the procreation of children and for maintenance of marital fidelity. But, things become pushed to this point: "The wife will be saved if she engenders children who will remain virgins, i.e. if that which she has lost (virginity) is regained through her progeny, if the fall and corruption affixed to the root (of sex) is compensated for by the flower and the fruit."[21] This astonishing passage unabashedly avers that sexuality is so sinful that even procreation does not sufficiently excuse it and that the children who have been conceived must in some way expiate for the fault of the parents by themselves renouncing any practice of sexuality!

Such a perspective immediately risks heading into deviant forms of asceticism that lead closer to Gnosticism and Encraticism than to Christianity. But doesn't the exaltation of virginity risk leading, on the theological level, to disdain for the creation of God, and on the pastoral level, to the formation of an elite kind of Christianity that is cut off from the people? Augustine saw precisely these problems in his debate with the Manicheans.[22] If sexuality is condemned as sin, there can be no response to the attacks of the Manicheans against the theology of creation which is delineated by the Old Testament. The "be fruitful and multiply" of Genesis 1:28 must be upheld against the radical pessimism of the Manicheans. But to do that, any disdain of sexuality must necessarily cease; or, rather, it must be demonstrated that sexuality is linked, because of procreation, to the creative act of God Himself. This is a repetition of Clement's debate with the Gnostics. Like the Gnostics, the Manicheans scorned sexuality precisely because it had a procreative function; they urged those who could not altogether abstain, to at least avoid procreation, since it subjects a soul to the domination by matter: ". . . the unrighteous law of the Manicheans, in order to prevent their god, whom they bewail as confined in all seeds, from suffering still closer confinement in the womb, requires married people not on any account to have children—their great desire being to liberate their god."[23] It must be remembered that ". . . eternal law—that is, the will of God the Creator of all—for the preservation of the natural order, permits the indulgence of bodily appetite under the guidance of reason in sexual intercourse, not for the gratification of passion, but for the continuance of the race through the procreation of children."[24] Thus to preserve the theological value of sexuality, which is linked to the recognition of the value of creation, its procreative function is unilaterally emphasized, and that even more since the Gnostic and Manichean opponents devalue this function and seem to justify sexuality sometimes only by the satisfaction of desire. Everything, then, conspires to narrowly link sexuality to procreation in the discussion of Christian ethics.

Exaltation of virginity and a condescending acceptance of marriage (justified by procreation): these are the two fundamental thrusts in patristic teaching which will mark Christian practice and thought for many centuries. Eusebius of Cesarea summarizes it quite well: "Two states of life have been established in the Church of Christ, one of which is actually superior and goes beyond the normal capacity of man. . . . The other . . . permits a modest use of marriage and procreation of children."[25]

Why was the theological reflection in the early Church incapable of maintaining itself within the perspective of scriptural tradition? Why was sexuality never thought of in terms of tenderness or love? Why was marriage never described as the privileged locus of an existential experience of God's love? For, as we have seen, these very issues incorporate the sense and the meaning of the scriptural teaching on this area.

In order to answer these questions, a distinction must be made between what could be called the *external causes* of the patristic evolution—essentially, the influence of the ideology of ancient society on

Christianity and the *internal causes*—the interpretation of the gospel in theological (and particularly eschatological) categories that were insufficiently criticised.

The External Causes:

The influence of ancient society on Christianity is evidenced in at least four areas. The first is that of customs. In a clear reaction against a social setting where the breakdown of traditional societies had encouraged a great relaxation of moral standards (particularly in the sexual domain) and where consequently Christian authors constantly emphasized that the weak—the "little one," i.e. the children, slaves, women, were being sacrificed to the covetousness of the strong, the "great ones," Christianity defended the necessity of a moral discipline. The apparent "puritanism" of the early Christians is best understood as a reaction against a world where sexual practice was effectively often lived out in the mode of "murderous" violence. In this kind of atmosphere, the "test of procreative intentions seemed to many Christians, as it had to the pagan Stoics and to Jewish thinkers like Philo, the measure by which sexual promiscuity might be rationally criticized."[26] It should be repeated that this "puritan" reaction occurred not only on the part of Christians but also on the part of a whole strata of society at the turn of the second century. Christianity certainly reinforced this current of thought but it in no way created it. Having become the major religion, it allowed its extension to the whole population, uniting in one common development of morality both the aristocrats' need for respectability and the sexual conservatism of plebeian milieus.[27]

Thus, the moral context made even the possibility of thinking of sexuality in terms of affection and love quite difficult for the Christians. The *juridical* status of marriage, governed by Roman law, accentuated the difficulty; Roman law had established the procreation of children as the only goal of marriage—whence the custom at the end of a wedding for the father to read a declaration calling to mind that the engaged couple are marrying *liberorum procreandum causa* (in order to procreate children). There is no mention in the law, nor in customs, of the value of the affective bond which unites the pair, or of the reality of communion within the marital bond. On the juridical level, the marital institution leaves no room for love; it is essentially defined as a contract. As we have seen, the Christians had readily accepted this juridical situation; here again, the social influence greatly affected Christian thought and practice.

But even more central, I believe, is the influence of ancient man's *mentality.* Even if a critique of that mentality appears here and there among the theologians, as we will see further on, it is itself determined by the categories of ancient thought. This thought is marked especially in the first centuries of the Christian era, by a deep pessimism, clearly revealed in philosophical and religious thinking.[28] Thus the Stoic seeks to abolish his temporary character: "The essential part of man is the Logos, and the Logos is timeless. So the Stoic concentrates exclusively upon his Logos-being, thus rising superior to all obligations and denying himself any future. But in this repudiation of the future, he deprives the present and the past of their temporal character as well."[29] In a denial of temporality, salvation comes from making man equivalent to the divine law that is immanent in the universe. It is a negative ethic, where liberty consists in freeing oneself from whatever turns one aside from this equivalence where man saves himself by denying himself. We could certainly consider Stoicism as the most positive attempt at handling the deep pessimism of ancient man in some way, for its fruits are incontestable. But it structures itself completely into a framework where man perceives (and even feels) himself to be an exile in the world, a stranger to himself, having come from somewhere that is now forgotten, but for which he is nostalgic. The mystery religions, Gnosticism, popular astral religions, each express it in their own way; human destiny is a source of anguish, for man knows that he is the victim of strange forces, exterior and interior, that dominate him.

Even if Christianity reacted strongly against this tragic dualism by affirming the value and goodness of divine creation, it also at the same time quite "naturally" admitted that contingency and temporality could not express the divine.[30] Thus the contingency of marital existence cannot truly signify man's call to the divine, the spiritual, the eternal. As for sexuality, which is evidently a sign of our temporality in its irregularity, its instinctive force, its brutality, it is even more surely excluded from the "noble" part of man. This perspective prohibits ever discovering its humanizing value. The best people will renounce it; as for the others, let them consent to it only in order to avoid even greater disorder.

On another level, Christianity was not able to question one of the most significant points of Indo-European culture, i.e. the juxtaposition of marriage and passion-love. This subject has been admirably researched by Marcel Detienne[31] who shows that the mythic opposition of Adonis and Demeter actually evokes the opposition of amorous seduction and marriage. He shows in particular how society, by means of aromatic spices seeks to arouse passionate love at wedding time, but how, except for this brief time, society considers it antithetical to marriage. We can ask, along with J.L.Flandrin[32] whether or not this paradox constitutes a real social prohibition that aims at discouraging any spiritual and affective intimacy between the spouses which could threaten social unity and cohesion. The early Christians shared this conviction, even to the point of no longer hearing the radical biblical contestation of it.[33]

Finally we must reemphasize the considerable importance of the influence of *Stoicism* on the Christian *ethical discourse*.[34] Not only did the Christians find a very elaborate and lofty ethical system in the Stoics, they also shared with them the same criticism of current sexual customs. The theologicans, in their battle against the Gnostics, borrowed the concept of natural law from the Stoics, which allowed them to define an objective moral standard, as well as to give themselves a principle for an ethical interpretation of the theology of Creation. Furthermore, Stoicism had some reflections on the meaning and value of the couple that were already developed. It insisted on the quasi-biological unity of the man and woman,[35] all while affirming the social value of fidelity.[36] But Christianity also inherited from Stoicism its distrust of the imagination and of passion, both of which upset the equilibrium of the sage.[37] Pleasure is an enemy because it links one to ephemeral and deceptive things, and therefore one must maintain detachment even in affective relationships: "How, then, shall I become affectionate?—As a man of noble spirit, as one who is fortunate; for it is against all reason to be abject, or broken in spirit, or to depend on something other than yourself, or even to blame either God or man. I would have you become affectionate in such a way as to maintain at the same time all these rules; if, however, by virtue of this natural affection, whatever it is you call by that name, you are going to be a slave and miserable, it does not profit you to be affectionate."[38]

If tender affection can be considered weakness, how much more should one indeed guard against sexual desire! This is why one must be careful about love. "Any love for another's wife is scandalous; likewise too much love for one's spouse is adultery. The wise man should love his wife with his head (with discernment, *iudicis*), not with his heart (not with affection, *non affectu*). He should control his passions and not let himself be dragged along into intercourse. Nothing is more impure (*foedius*) than to love one's wife like a mistress. Surely those who claim to unite themselves to their wives to beget children for the good of the State or for the human race should at least imitate the animals and once their wives are pregnant, not destroy the offspring. Let them approach their wives as husbands and not as lovers." This surprising passage from Seneca has come down to us only through Jerome's respectful quoting of it. He precedes this quote with one from Sextus the Pythagorian[39] whose original text he corrects: "An adulterer is also he who is shamelessly immodest with his own wife." This quote becomes a formula that is closer to Seneca: "An adulterer is one who too passionately loves his wife."[40] This sentence will often be quoted, with complete approval, by Christian moralists up until the time of Gratian and Peter Lombard. We find an almost identical version of the saying in Augustine: "For he who is intemperate in marriage, what is he but the adulterer of his own wife."[41]

"The conclusion is inescapable. Christian moralists owe a large debt to philosophy, especially stoic philosophy . . . in the moral domain its influence (stoic philosophy) is primary and can be clearly discerned. Stoicism furnished Christianity with a series of concepts and theories; it dictated—even in the wording—its practical morality. These concepts are sometimes adapted or transposed, but Stoicism is everywhere discernable, and its overall place during the first centuries of the Church is very significant in all the questions that concern man."[42]

There is no doubt that these external causes carried significant weight in the evolution and development of Christian ethics. However, it is clear that they had that influence only because they were in fundamental agreement with Christianity itself. This point should be elaborated.

The Internal Causes

In the gospel there is a twofold manner of presenting the kingdom of God and of calling for its acceptance: on one hand, it is the presence of another world which can neither be perceived nor received without leaving one's own way of life behind; on the other hand, it is presented as the way which God, through Christ, and next through His disciples, takes to penetrate reality and "act" on it from within in order to bring about its ultimate fulfillment. These two elements—a break (or separation from the world) and the taking hold of present reality—are in the gospel. The whole issue consists in maintaining this twofold requirement and of understanding the reasons for it. The temptation is always to present only one of these aspects. Thus, if the accent is placed upon the break (with the world) the immediate consequence is that this world becomes a place of exile; if, on the contrary, the emphasis is unilaterally placed upon the responsibility of taking a firm hold of things here, the consequence is that any challenge or criticism about the way in which this responsibility is exercised is posited as proceeding from an evil intention. In the first case, the other world is posited as the real world, a someplace else; but then there is no longer any possibility of concretely signifying the reality of this world. The Kingdom becomes unutterable, inexpressible except through a dream, utopia, or wordless cry. In the second case, one leaves behind the eschatological and critical perspective of the Kingdom when applying oneself to a task or project and risks having it marked by covetousness more than by responsibility.

The question, then, revolves around the meaning of Christian eschatology. As the horizon of this world, simultaneously the goal or end of all accomplishments and the reversal of judgment, eschatology has bearing on all personal and social existence. If it calls for a separation, it is with the idea of recapturing the plan of God for man in its essence, as already attested to in the history of men.

How did the early Church understand and experience this eschatological tension? It certainly had a vivid consciousness that it was a witness to ancient society of another way of living. Although the primitive Church united concrete morality and spiritual reference, and called for moral discipline but only so that it would be a sign of submission to the requirement of love, i.e. an indication of willingness to incarnate the love of God here and now, the early Church instead progressively dissociated the two streams of morality[43] and spirituality. The battle against the gnostic movements played an important role in this. Because the Gnostics wanted to live an "already-realized-eschatology," and manifested that by transgressing common moral laws, it was necessary to insist on responsibility with regard to morality, i.e. to insist on discipline which is the refusal of disorder, and on facing concrete reality. All at once, the eschatological accent on separation was displaced onto the side of spirituality only; it is through spiritual life, as opposed to sensual or corporeal life, that the Christian can enjoy a real apprehension of the divine world, and can participate here and now in the eschatological work of beatitude.

The willingness to break (with the world) did not remain on the ethical level, but manifested itself more strongly than ever on the spiritual level. Morality, in reaction to the aberrations of certain Gnostics, became conformist and aligned itself with the highest values of the ethics of the Stoics. There was no doubt a desire in this on the part of the Church to be recognized and accepted by society, and not to appear as a destructive social factor. But all this took place as though eschatology was of no consequence whatsoever to morality, that it really was only a promise of another world, celestial and eternal, which man could only participate in down here by contemplation and prayer. Morality, then, remains entirely in the realm of this present world and is not in any way qualified by the *eschaton* of the Kingdom. Man connects with this *eschaton* by spirituality, and not by morality.[44] Morality belongs to provisional, contingent reality and is only needed to make a space for man which is sheltered from passions and wicked desires, so that man can devote himself to the only thing that's important: God. In this realm of contingent reality, everything can be regulated by reference to natural laws without ever suspecting that such laws might be cultural rather than natural, i.e. that they signify in reality a fixed social order.

This eschatological reference afforded no criticism of the type of society that existed in the Empire; on the contrary, it led the Church on many points to reinforce the dominant ideology of ancient society. In fact, by presenting itself as the voice of the other (eternal and celestial) world, Christian eschatology, as proclaimed by the Church, called for a separation indeed, but a purely spiritual separation, like the quest for the long-lost real world, which this one only shadows and reflects. The gospel, meanwhile, was speaking of another kind of separation—one which concerned the mode of relationship a man had with himself, with others, with the world, and with God. As Christ had lived it, it was accomplished by a critique of social ideology (religious in that case) and it proposed to the disciples another mode of community life, founded on other values. This critical dealing with reality was not imitated with the same enthusiasm in the following centuries. Why not? Essentially, I repeat, because of a misunderstanding of biblical eschatology. This misunderstanding was the source of a double morality in the Church, illustrated by its stand on virginity and marriage: there are those who can, through asceticism, anticipate the other world more directly and clearly and there are those who content themselves, due to a lack of spirituality, with general morality, described mostly in negative terms.

But the paradox is really only an apparent one: the groups with the strongest will to break with the "world" (for example, the anchorite movement and the first monastic communities) are in fact the very ones who reinforced the contemporary dominant ideology the most. They did so on two decisive counts: whereas Christ had proclaimed the possibility of new relationships between men and women because of the Kingdom, Christian asceticism reinforced the ancient disregard for women; whereas the Gospels and Paul had presented a new understanding to the Christians of their bodies, a new way of living, this same Christian asceticism tended to devalue, along with all ancient thinking, the corporal by juxtaposing it to the spiritual.

In a discussion of the first point, it is easy to verify the good intention of the Church when it uncritically adopted the dominant ideology of the age, even though the gospel gave it the means for a critique—I am referring to society's disdain for women.[45]

It is not necessary to recall at length the rigid subordination of woman to man in ancient society, Greek as well as Jewish. "It's a truism to say that man in Greek culture congratulated himself for being born human and not animal, man and not woman, Greek and not barbarian."[46] The same concept is found in Judaism: it is taken up by the liturgy of the synagogue and three times daily the Jew thanks God for not having made him a Gentile, a woman, or a slave.[47] Given this state of affairs, we can measure the revolutionary character of Paul's affirmation in Galatians 3:28: "There is neither Jew nor Greek, there is neither slave nor free, there is neither male nor female, for you are all one in Christ Jesus." This affirmation of the principle of equality, which did have some practical consequences in the first years of the Church's existence,[48] was never forgotten in following centuries; however, it remained for the most part an affirmation of principle, sufficiently there to oblige the Fathers to multiply explanations and interpretations which justified (sometimes in bad faith) the marginal position of woman in society; but it never brought the principle of the subordination of the woman into question.

When Augustine recalls that, according to Genesis, "human nature itself, which is complete in both sexes, has been made to the image of God, and he does not exclude the woman from being understood as the image of God,"[49] he openly affirms the dignity of woman before God, but he draws no social consequences from it that would modify woman's status. As Jean-Marie Aubert says, "we can summarize this traditional concept of woman by the words *equality* and *subordination*: equality in God's eyes and in terms of the possibility of perfection; subordination to man in terms of temporal, earthly work down here."[50] Such a separation between theological thinking and social practice is proof of the misunderstanding of eschatological meaning that was discussed above: there is no attempt to orient reality toward the eschatological kingdom, or to transform it with a view to fulfilling the sense of divine creation, but instead two separate worlds are postulated. In one, man and woman are fully equal, and in the other woman is entirely subordinated to man.

The influence of such a mentality could exercise itself without restraint since the critical function of the gospel was reserved purely for inner spirituality. Something of the gospel, of course, would cross over into Christian practice;[51] but in the end, the most influential thing for the longest time would be the theological justifications (although it would be better to call them ideological) which the Fathers multiplied in ratification of social reality, i.e. society's disdain for women. This disregard is translated into a refusal of the otherness of woman: the way in which she is different (sex, weakness, sensitivity) is exactly what is disqualified by the Fathers. And so for Augustine, only the masculine is specifically human; woman participates in being human only by having a soul. But she is definitely inferior in regard to her body—which is how the second account of creation (Genesis 2) is to be understood, where the distinction is made that man is created first and in the image of God whereas woman is created second and comes from the man.[52] With this kind of mentality, Christian theology showed itself incapable of going beyond the level of ideological justifications on this point;[53] it took up instead the most traditional interpretations, like, for example, that of the Jewish philosopher Philo: "For progress is indeed nothing else than the giving up of the female gender by changing into the male, since the female gender is material, passive, corporeal, and sense-perceptible, while the male is active, rational, incorporeal and more akin to mind and thought."[54]

Thus in spite of continual affirmations of principle, the Fathers of early Christianity did not acknowledge the otherness of the woman. The disqualification of feminine sexuality by patristic theology is indicative of this misunderstanding. Tertullian, for example, reduces the role of woman in procreation to that of a field which receives seed sown: "she brings neither sperm nor pneuma, nor substance for the embryo, but only nourishment for it, whereas the man produces pneuma and substance."[55] Man alone, then, is the source of the embryo, and he transmits the soul along with the flesh. "Finally . . . is it not a fact that in the moment of orgasm, when the generative fluid is ejected, do we not feel that we have parted with a portion of our soul? As a result, do we not feel weak and faint, along with a blurring of our sights? This, then, must be the seed of the soul which proceeds from the dripping of the soul, just as the fluid which carries the bodily seed is a species of droppings from the body."[56] A similar theory is found in Clement of Alexandria.[57]

The man thus furnishes all that is necessary to constitute a new being; the woman only receives the seed and nourishes it. Thus even in the area of generation, the woman is still dependent on man and subordinated to his creative force. Woman creates nothing, but receives everything, her role being only to bear the fruit of what she has received from the man.[58]

Consequently, anything that indicates active sexuality on the part of the woman appears as an abnormal and dangerous phenomenon. Once the woman does not accept being reduced to submissive passivity, she becomes a threat. Her apparent weakness covers up dangerous and mysterious powers which fascinate man and cause him to lose control and reason.[59] "Hurtful are women, my children; because, since they have no power or strength over the man, they act subtly through outward guise how they may draw him to themselves; and whom they cannot overcome (they draw) by craft."[60]

The only thing that remains to be done is to convince woman to accept the disqualification of her sexual otherness, to propose consecrated virginity as the best means of being liberated from submission to the man. Ambrose of Milan will use this argument frequently, which consists of denigrating marriage to cause virginity to appear as a liberation for the woman. Of course, from a certain point of view that was not false, but it is revealing that the Fathers presented liberation to the woman by her acceptance of that which denied her womanhood, in the rejection of what really seemed like an inexplicable otherness in the eyes of the Fathers.[61]

If woman hides that which designates her otherness in the eyes of man (cf. for example the importance in the Fathers of the discourse on modesty of conduct in women and the dangers of coquetry[62]), then could she perhaps be forgiven for being a woman; by denying herself she could attain a certain kind of recognition, entirely determined by her rapport with man.

In a certain way, a call for consecrated virginity affords, through the detour of a negation of sexuality, the discovery of something in the evangelical affirmation on the equality of man and woman in the presence of the Kingdom of God. It is a sure proof that Christ's and Paul's teachings have not been forgotten, but actually it succeeds in making the most of that teaching only by accentuating the subordination of the woman to masculine models of ancient society. In order to escape rigorous submission to man, as was the case in marriage, woman must accept and interiorize a totally androcentric vision of herself!

It seems established, then, that the disdain for woman is closely linked to an incapacity to conceive of sexuality in terms of positive value. Anything that recalls sexuality is by that fact disqualified; insofar as she has sexuality woman is disqualified. But keeping in mind the gospel teaching where there is no value differentiation between men and women, a second trend appears, parallel to the first, which exalts the the counter-values of the woman. Over against Eve—the tempting seductress by whom man loses himself in losing his liberty, his authority, his reason—Mary, virgin and mother, is raised up, symbol of unsexed love, of a gentle love that is wholly spiritual which no contingency threatens. The ground is now laid for the birth and development of the typical stand on woman in our western society, the stand which will be repeated throughout the Middle Ages under diverse forms: seductress or inspiration, Eve or Mary, a double image of the one same desire which bespeaks both the search for affectionate love and the impossibility of linking it to sexuality, because desire is firmly rooted in flesh.

The elements of the twofold stance, disdaining and exalting the woman, are easily seen in the Fathers of the fourth century. It is clear that this position reflects the desire of man, for only man has the right to speak about woman. In the case of the Fathers, the difficulty is increased: only men can speak about women and, what is more, celibate men (since the vast majority of them had chosen consecrated celibacy). Theology, from the third century on, and then more and more as time goes on, is the work of monks for whom women symbolize what they have renounced and who constantly threaten their special devotion to God. Without over-emphasizing this fact, it is necessary to at least recognize that it carried some amount of weight. Celibate monks whose experience with women was through sins in their youth (like Augustine and Jerome) or through maternal love (like John Chrysostom) are not particularly equipped to recognize women as the "other" whose otherness signifies the very otherness of God. For them, the otherness of woman signaled instead the otherness of the devil!

*   *   *

This ends the analysis of the patristic tradition. I have tried to draw out the major trends. It is indeed difficult to do justice to all the theologians of an era which is distant and foreign to us. Nevertheless, it may perhaps be safe to conclude that a study of patristic texts does seem to bring out the Church's difficulty in its attempt to maintain itself within the eschatological tension. In breaking with the basic assumptions of contemporary society on the spiritual level only, patristic theology failed to exercise any criticism of that society's dominant ideology. And on the contrary, its own theological presuppositions, on matters of sex and marriage, led Christian morality to reinforce some of the most debatable assumptions (judging by the Gospel norm) of ancient society: fear of sexuality, disdain for women, pessimistic dualism in anthropological matters, reinforcement of "natural" hierarchies.

In all fairness, it must also be acknowledged that the gospel was certainly not forgotten, and that even within this moral conformity it exercised a critique which during the Middle Ages ended in radically challenging the ancient model.

4. Saint Augustine and the Medieval Moral Tradition

Although Augustine has already been quoted several times, a special section is devoted to him as the master of medieval thought; for, through him, the Middle Ages was furnished with a framework of ethical reference in the area of sexuality and conjugality. Right up the the twelfth century, theologians, moralists and jurists systematically referred to him whenever discussing these ethical issues.[1] There are two reasons for this: Augustine expressed himself quite completely on these questions,[2] and he did so with a remarkable spirit of clarity, allowing him to present a genuine synthesis of the patristic theology of his time, leaving to his successors all the elements of an elaborated doctrine.

This synthesis hinges on three points: the link between sexuality and concupiscence, a description of the triple goal of marriage, and the beginnings of a reflection on the sacramentality of marriage. Since these three elements dominate medieval thinking, they should be briefly examined.

a) Sexuality and Concupiscence

Augustine is the first Christian theologian to have systematically analyzed the link between sexuality and sin.[3] Briefly, these are the elements of his analysis. Sexual diversity comes from God, as well as sexual union in its procreative aspect: "For God made the sexes. . . . But how could it possibly happen, that they who were to be united together . . . were not to move their bodies?"[4] On the other hand, that which comes not from God but from the devil is concupiscence, manifested by passion which, outside the control of reason, subjects genital organs to its empire. Incontrollable erection of the male organ whenever desire comes upon man is the sign of the irrationality of concupiscence, and a clear indication that it is evil. It is concupiscence "over which even marriage blushes, which glories in all these before-mentioned goods. For why is the especial work of parents withdrawn and hidden even from the eyes of their children except that it is impossible for them to be occupied in laudable procreation without shameful lusts? Because of this it was that even they were ashamed who first covered their nakedness . . . when . . . they felt their members disobedient to themselves."[5]

If there had not been a fall, sexuality would have been exempt from concupiscence: " . . . the seed would have issued from the human being by the quiet and normal obedience of his members to his will's command."[6] "That concupiscence . . . had no existence in the body during its life in paradise before the entrance of sin. . . . Without this concupiscence it was quite possible to effect the function of the wedded pair in the procreation of children: just as many a laborious work is accomplished by the compliant operation of our other limbs, without any lascivious heat; for they are simply moved by the direction of the will, not excited by the ardour of concupiscence (*aestu libidinis*)."[7]

Clearly, Augustine does not fall into the Manichean trap of confusing sexuality with sin. He firmly holds to the original goodness of sexuality. Even if there had been no "fall," Adam and Eve would have had intercourse for procreation, but without passion, that is, without the shame, without having their bodies affected in spite of themselves by "libido." Thus concupiscence is the consequence of original sin, and it forever marks sexuality with ambiguity, making it a threat wherein man is ceaselessly separated from himself, stripped of his reason and his control. Concupiscence manifests the state of enslavement to sin in which man finds himself. Thus in opposition of Manicheanism, Augustine maintains the goodness of procreative sexuality and in opposition to the Pelagians he maintains the force of concupiscence which links sexuality with sin. In so doing, he systematized and crystallized the intuitions of previous tradition which had effectively sought to avoid rejecting sexuality by focusing only on its bad aspect and to avoid misconstruing the tragic aspect of human existence, in which sexuality so often plays a death-dealing role. But in distinguishing as he does between a good sexuality (procreative) and a bad sexuality (concupiscent, passionate), Augustine plunged Christian ethics into the old stoic impasse whose difficulties we have seen. Moreover, when he interprets the "covetousness" in Romans 7:7, that sin reveals, only in terms of sexual concupiscence, Augustine considerably diminished the theological depth of Pauline anthropology. While Paul was evoking fundamental human idolatry (covetousness toward all things that can permit man to escape God), Augustine speaks only of sexual relations. As a result, all of Christian ethics became almost fixated upon sexuality as the very symbol of the idolatrous covetousness of man. From this point on and for many centuries, sexuality could not be spoken of without simultaneously evoking the thought of sin.

b) The Goals of Marriage

"These are all goods on account of which marriage is a good: offspring, fidelity, sacrament (*proles, fides, sacramentum*)."[8] This Augustinian formula is repeated through all of the Middle Ages. It is the necessary conclusion to the preceding propositions: since God willed the "human couple" before the fall, one must meditate on the meaning that God wished to confer on this privileged relationship where sexual difference

Procreation

could not be reduced to the functional role of procreation. Augustine refuses this reduction, and rightly comments that if it were only a question of ensuring the continuation of the species, marriage would not have been necessary. "You are entirely mistaken if you think that marriage was instituted to compensate for the departed dead through the succession of those who are born. Marriage was instituted so that through the chastity of women sons would be acknowledged by their fathers and fathers by their sons. It was indeed possible that men be born through random or unregulated intercourse, but there could not have been a bond of kinship between fathers and sons."[9]

Fidelity

Marriage allows for a major social experience, summarized by the term *fides* (pact of faithfulness). It is not only a means of socializing and regulating the anarchic impulses of the libido (*quod carnalis vel iuvenilis incontinentia . . . redigitur; De bono conjug.* III,iii), but it is also a possible means of experiencing what could be called the institutionalization of love. The pact of faithfulness guarantees life by permitting the existence of a locus where fathers and sons can recognize each other.

Evidently, the problem is that in this familial institution the values of socialization are dissociated from sexuality. It is not by chance that Augustine speaks only of the bond between fathers and sons here. Women are excluded from the familial and social acknowledgment. So then the pact of fidelity between a husband and wife makes possible a family, but it gives no meaning to the sexual relationship. So, if it happens that, in order to avoid a greater evil (like adultery for instance), the spouses have sexual relations with no intention of procreation, it would be as a concession to weakness and not as a conviction. Again this reveals the whole ambiguity of the matter: on one hand, the spouses are called upon to discover a social value in their conjugal relationship which goes beyond the procreative function, but at the same time this value is divorced from the sexual relationship which ever remains a lesser evil. Augustine, although he was more sensitive than others to the social dimension of the couple, was unable to conceive of the possibility that sexuality could hold tenderness, friendship, spirituality, and this lack of insight was very influential on later tradition.

c) Marriage as Sacramentum

Augustine sought to give Christian marriage its own theological status. This status, both juridical and spiritual, is expressed in the word *sacramentum*. "It is certainly not fecundity only, the fruit of which consists of offspring, nor chastity only, whose bond is fidelity, but also a certain sacramental bond in marriage which is recommended to believers in wedlock. Accordingly it is enjoined by the Apostle: 'Husbands, love your wives, even as Christ also loved the Church.' Of this bond the substance undoubtedly is this, that the man and the woman who are joined together in matrimony should remain inseparable as long as they live; and that it should be unlawful for one consort to be parted from the other except in the case of fornication. For this is the case of Christ and the Church; that, as a living one with a living one, they are forever united with no possibility of divorce or separation. And so complete is the observance of this bond in the city of our God, in His holy mountain—that is to say, in the Church of Christ—by all married believers who are undoubtedly members of Christ, that, although women marry, and men take wives, for the purpose of procreating children, it is never permitted one to put away even an unfruitful wife for the sake of having another to bear children. And whosoever does this is held to be guilty of adultery by the law of the Gospel, though not by this world's rule. . . . Thus between the conjugal pair, as long as they live, the nuptial bond has a permanent obligation, and can be cancelled neither by separation nor by union with another."[10]

Marriage, then, is *sacramentum* insofar as it allows a comparison of the union between man and woman with that of Christ and the Church. This third "good" is more vital than the other two (fruitfulness and faithfulness), for it establishes the indissolubility of the conjugal bond. Now the question remains as to whether or not this good is recognized and given to Christians only (because of their incorporation into the body of Christ through baptism) or if it applies to all couples. Augustine hesitates on this point. The passage just cited seems to lean to the first hypothesis, but elsewhere Augustine affirms that from the beginning, before the fall, marriage had a sacramental character as the mysterious prefiguration of the union of Christ and His Church; nevertheless, he is hesitant: "(in addition to faithfulness and offspring in marriage) a third good, which seems to me to be a sacrament (*aliquod sacramentum*) should exist in the married, above all in those who belong to the people of God, so that there be no divorce from a wife."[11]

Augustine, along with his time, seems to have hardened his position and to have considered all remarriage, even if between pagans, as adultery because of the indissolubility of marriage, its sacramental aspect.

But it remains nevertheless that the word *sacramentum* is somewhat indefinite with Augustine. It is only used to explain the rationale for the indissolubility of marriage. But marriage does not produce what it prefigures: it does not make the partners members of Christ—only baptism accomplishes that. So two themes overlap here: a juridical-ethical theme and a symbolic-religious theme. The first relies on the real meaning of the latin *sacramentum* (commitment, oath, juridical tie) which emphasizes the ethical imperative of the indissolubility of the marital bond. The second theme calls to mind the text in Ephesians 5:32, where the Greek *mystérion* is translated as *sacramentum* in the Latin versions of the New Testament; here the word evidently refers to the symbolism of the conjugal bond as a sign of the bond between Christ and the Church. This evokes the theological depth of the ethical reality of indissolubility. Augustine wished to go beyond the tenuousness of morality in basing indissolubility instead on a broader consciousness of the meaning of the marital relationship, on the awareness that analogically, it signifies the meaning of a love relationship and faithfulness between Christ and the Church. Even if the conjugal commitment is juridical, it is much more than juridical: it has a theological signification.

By reintegrating the profound viewpoint of Ephesians 5 with theological reflections on marriage, Augustine rescued the Christian ethic of marriage from a dull theologizing that viewed marriage only in its normal function. But it must also be noted that in so doing, he opened the door to a more objectifying conception of *sacramentum,* i.e. an objectively real bond that nothing can dissolve, in the name of which a very legalistic conception of marriage would finally be established. The introduction of *sacramentum* in the thinking on marriage certainly afforded a positive broadening of consciousness as to the implications of the male-female rapport, but it also led to a solidification of the juridical character of conjugal indissolubility, now made sacred.

The Middle Ages received the heritage of Augustine with great devotion. The next part of this chapter is devoted to the twofold juridical and theological problem that scholastic theology had to resolve as a result of Augustinian concepts: the validity of marriage and its sacramentality. But first, a few examples of how Augustinianism was taken up, and often caricatured, in later medieval reflections on sexuality.

*   *   *

Bishop Caesarius of Arles, the embodiment of the sixth century, endeavored throughout the troubled period of the great barbarian invasions, to maintain some moral standards in the Church. In his fight against concubinage, fornication and sexual disorders, he repeats (and solidifies even more) the Augustinian teaching on procreation as the single final goal of the marital sex act.[12]

Invoking Psalm 51:5 ("Behold, I was brought forth in iniquity, and in sin did my mother conceive me") and Exodus 19:15 ("Be ready by the third day [to meet God on Sinai]; do not go near a woman"), Caesarius emphasized the idea that all sexual relationship is sin.

At the end of the same century, Gregory the Great (Pope from 590–604) follows the same line, i.e. an Augustinianism that is reduced to a few major themes that constantly recur. For example, the link between sexuality and sin: "Because the first man fell from his state of innocence by sinning, he transmitted the punishment of sin to his children. For sexual appetite is the punishment of sin, and comes from the root of sin, so much so that no one is born into the world without its exercise."[13] The reduction of sin to sexuality is unreserved, and Augustine's subtle distinctions are forgotten. Married couples always sin when they have intercourse by the very fact that pleasure accompanies that act.[14] "But since even the lawful intercourse of the wedded cannot take place without the pleasure of the flesh, entrance into a sacred place should be abstained from, because the pleasure itself can by no means be without sin. For he had not been born of adultery or fornication, but of lawful wedlock who said, 'Behold I was conceived in iniquities and in my sin my mother brought me forth.' "[15]

As Noonan pointed out in his study of penitentials from the sixth to eleventh centuries, such a perspective resulted—in pastoral practice—in a condemnation of any form of sexual activity that did not specifically aim at procreation.

Peter Lombard, named bishop of Paris in 1159, expresses the traditional point of view quite well, taking up all the elements of the Augustinian elaboration which justify sexuality through the procreative intent: "original sin is transmitted by the act of generation, which act is preceded by concupiscence. The descendants of Adam are in their turn affected by concupiscence."[16] The result of this transmission of original sin and its consequences is the "law of deadly concupiscence in our members, without which no carnal union would be possible "; therefore, "coitus is reprehensible and evil unless excused by the bonds of marriage."[17]

In a similar manner, when the fourth Lateran Council (1215), against catharism, declares "Not only virgins and celibates, but also married people who please God by right faith and good conduct merit to arrive at eternal happiness,"[18] it is understood that the "good conduct" in question equals practicing sexuality with only procreative intention.

But from the twelfth century, powerful intellectual and spiritual mutations appear which are evidenced by certain movements outside the Church (for example, the courtly tradition and the catharic heresy) as well as by a new approach to a theology of the couple, love, and marriage (in particular by Abelard and Hugh of Saint Victor).

Peter Abelard (1079–1142) deserves particular mention because he knew how to transfer the elements of his century's new consciousness of love onto the theological and philosophical level; he had, through his relations with Heloise, experienced the human and spiritual values of it. Because of this he is recognized as one of the precursors of courtly love.[19] He defines a doctrine of pure love for God, of love for the perfection of God, which could go to the point of renouncing the happiness He promised to man. God should be loved precisely because He is God, and not because of what one might get from Him. Etienne Gilson has shown that this concept had been furnished to him by his love-relationship with Heloise: "The description of disinterested love that Abelard, turned theologian, proposes is that very same with which Heloise bitterly reproached him with never having understood when he pretended to love her. The Abelardian doctrine of Divine love amounts to this, that God is not to be loved as Abelard loved Heloise, but as Heloise loved Abelard."[20]

Accepting the loss of oneself by and through love is the very meaning of Heloise's obedience: "Not, however, by another, but by thee thyself, that thou who art alone in the cause of my grief may be alone in the grace of my comfort! For it is thou alone that canst make me sad, canst make me joyful or canst comfort me. And it is thou alone that owest me this great debt, and for this reason above all that I have at once performed all things that you didst order, till that when I could not offend thee in anything I had the strength to lose myself at thy behest."[21] There is a tragic aspect to love, a denial of self for the sake of the other which, beyond the framework of morality, unites and opposes human and divine love at the same time in one single cry. "But in the whole period of my life (God wot) I have ever feared to offend thee rather than God, I seek to please thee more than Him. Thy command brought me, not the love of God, to the habit of religion. See how unhappy a life I must lead, more wretched than all others, if I endure all these things here in vain having no hope of reward in the future."[22] Heloise speaks of Abelard like she does of God, while yet admitting, with the bitter lucidity that makes her letters so moving, that these two loves destroy one another.

Surely this is a singularly striking proof of the new sensibility which appears in the twelfth century, very close indeed to courtly love which exalts a love that is fully sexual (considered as the most concrete example of mutual love of man and woman!) and highly spiritual (since sexuality, when sexual activity is denied, is a call to a love that is completely sacrificial). This sensibility exalts the bond of love more highly than marriage: ". . . thou has not disdained to set forth sundry reasons by which I tried to dissuade them from our marriage, from an ill-starred bed; but wert silent to many, in which I preferred love to wedlock, freedom to a bond. I call God to witness, if *Augustus,* ruling over the whole world, were to deem me worthy of the honour of marriage, and to confirm the whole world to me, to be ruled by me for ever, dearer to me and of greater dignity would it seem to be called thy strumpet than his empress."[23] For marriage not only enslaves the philosopher and impedes him from freely applying himself to his intellectual tasks, but it also reduces love to a vested contract. "Nothing have I ever (God wot) required of thee save thyself, desiring thee purely, not what was thine. Not for the pledge of matrimony, nor for any dowry did I look, nor for my own passions or wishes but thine (as thou thyself knowest) was I zealous to gratify. And if the name of wife appears more sacred and more valid, sweeter to me is ever the word friend."[24] Heloise, furthermore, reproaches herself more for having consented to marry Abelard than for having been his mistress. For she thereby seemed to have contradicted her fundamental conviction of the value of simple disinterested, pure love. And so begins a critique of marriage in the name of love: " Question: Can true love exist between married people? Answer: We state and affirm, according to the tenor of those present, that love cannot extend its rights to two married people. For lovers are freely in mutual accord without constraint of necessity, whereas spouses are bound to the duty of a reciprocal submission of their wills and of not refusing anything to each other. May this judgment which we have pronounced with much deliberation, according to the opinion of a great number of Ladies, be for you a sure and indisputable truth. Adjudicated in the year 1174, the third day of the Calends of May."[25]

This critique of marriage is actually at the very core of *courtly eroticism*.[26] In its traditional perspective, marriage is primarily a contract which stringently subjects the wife to the desires of her "lord and master," reducing her to being merely the procreatrix of his children; marriage, then, cannot allow for a personal relationship between man and woman, but justifies only a functional relationship.

As opposed to the marital institution, courtly love appears as a vindication for the woman, a recognition of who she is, i.e. a person. The rejection, not of pleasure, but of sexual fulfillment in the "fin' amors" stems from this; woman is vindicated in her right to be a man's friend, which implies that the man accepts a reduction of his male power, a humbling of himself. "It is necessary, in the discovery of love, that the woman, freed from the threat of masculine omnipotence, be solicitous of the desire she arouses. It is thus necessary, in order to love, to renounce oneself and be noble and strong. . . . Paralleling feudal service, love becomes a service. Voluntary (or converted) humiliation abolishes the misogyny that would hinder love."[27]

The "couple" can only spring from a real recognition of the two partners, of their otherness, and from their mutual right to speak: the woman can also express her preference and pleasure.[28]

But this kind of couple—marginal by necessity since it is the counter-model to the contractual and hierarchical couple, is stamped with deadly ambiguity: it exalts erotic pleasure without being able to bring it to full term; by the technique of *asag* (lit. "putting to the test"),[29] it postulates that pleasure is never so pure and so great as when it is renounced while one is in a position to have consented to it. The prohibition against orgasm that *asag* presupposes signifies that one's desire is only finally fulfilled in death, and not in life. Only death can fulfill love. Time and history must be distanced from the game of love, that is, the child that signifies these contingencies; thus the child, which is the single justification for sexuality according to orthodox Catholic morality, is here totally negated. Along with the child, the assignment of love into the risk of a creative project is also denied.

It is as though, in this twelfth century so rich in so many kinds of renewals, the discourse of sex and marriage hesitates between two paths that are equally blockaded: a traditional morality, inspired by Augustine which links the male/female relationship to a social contract aimed at ensuring descendants to the family group and stability to social order; and courtly love which exalts love by tearing it away from the temporal reality of a conjugal couple to bestow it upon the marginal couple which consists of passionate and provisional lovers.

Thus love is opposed to marriage, because true love, (whether it be erotic love for the troubadours or mystical love for the theologians) can be nothing less than perfect, that is to say, eternal and non-contingent. The ideal Woman becomes the image of this Love which is elevated to the rank of essence: unreal, inaccessible woman, infinitely respectable and at the same time altogether unattainable.[30] Thus what courtly love had bestowed upon woman is cancelled out by making her vindication only an abstraction!

Wasn't it possible to think of the conjugal couple as capable of a love encounter? Wasn't is possible to go beyond the Augustinian position without falling into the "courtly" critique of marriage? Hugh of Saint Victor (1096-1141) is worthy of mention here, for he is the only one to consider marriage in terms of love.[31]

According to Hugh, the origin of marriage, or what constitutes its foundation, is the bond between a man and a woman:[32] marriage is first of all and essentially a conjugal community. This community was not abolished by the fall but it is threatened by a concupiscence which could possibly overshadow the friendship-love which unites the partners. Marriage is not primarily destined to allow procreation nor is it a remedy for concupiscence; it is primarily a community in service to the couple and their love. This is the sense in which it is sacramental, and Hugh rediscovers here the rich symbolism of Ephesians 5.

"Hugh is clear: he does not conceive of marriage as the institution for parenthood but as the institution for the tenderness and intimacy of the couple."[33] The important point is that love unites the married couple, and whatever leads to it or affirms it, including intercourse, is good. But sexual desire constantly risks shutting the couple up into egoism or violence, and therefore continent love is a more sure and noble path. The couple who can thus live in chaste love (an obvious parallel to courtly love) really know what love is, the sign in the life of man of the perfect and inaccessible love of God. Such a love is possible *within marriage*! This is undoubtedly Hugh's originality, for up until this point, in order to partake in perfect love, one had either to make vows of religious virginity or, as a courtly lover, to try to escape the extremely contingent bonds of marriage.

Hugh was thus rediscovering essential elements of the biblical strain and his reading of the texts in Genesis is not as whimsical as Marie-Odile Métral says.[34] For the first time, perhaps, a somewhat coherent theological attempt was made to consider marriage in terms of love and to associate sexuality with affection and friendship. Agapè-love was not opposed to eros-love! It must unfortunately be admitted that this attempt had no echo in subsequent moral theology. Why not? For two reasons, in my opinion: one historical and the other ideological. The ideological reason (which I will come back to in the comparison of Catholic and Protestant moralities) is rather obvious: to reestablish the human couple as being the "original man," as Hugh did, is to radically challenge the whole social and ecclesiastical structure founded on a strict hierarchy which postulates the superiority of the man over the woman and the superiority of the ecclesiastical celibate and virgin over the married (and incontinent) man of that time. To give woman personal value is to challenge the power of clerics who are justified precisely by the essential inferiority of woman!

As for the historical reason, it is connected to the appearance of the catharic heresy at that same era. Faced with a movement which recalled many elements of the old gnostic heresy, the Catholic Church naturally had recourse to classical arguments, which reinforced its long-standing distrust of sexuality. Catharism[35] is, in fact, a resurgence of gnostic dualism, by way of a Manicheanism that was reworked and corrected by Bogumil, a Bulgarian priest at the beginning of the tenth century. It took root in the West during the eleventh century and became a dangerous concurrent to the Catholic Church in the twelfth century. In the area of sexual morality, many elements noted in ancient Gnosticism resurface. The rigorous dualism which undergirds it results in a rejection of sexuality, especially insofar as it participates in the malignance of this world by procreation. There is only one sin: submission to the world, that is, attachment to the flesh. Sexual relations and sensual pleasure signify submission to the world. Thus any sexual activity whatsoever is sin, every marriage is lewd, *jurata fornicatio*. There are no distinctions in sexual activity, for it is all equally grievous; the Catholic distinction between sex authorized by procreation and perverse sex aiming only at pleasure is abolished. And, furthermore, procreation, to some extent, is a more serious sin than pleasure. Therefore pregnant women were not admitted into the catharic church.

But the simple faithful of the sect, who were not required to submit to the rigid ascetic prescriptions reserved for the "Perfect," very quickly deduced that since all sexual activity was equally wicked, the very notion of sexual perversion could be abandoned! Thus a double morality arose: "the sage, illuminated by the Spirit, denied himself the carnal act, but the believer, who had not evolved to such a total liberation, was supposed to obey his "natural" desire, and it mattered little if he sinned (in spite of himself and in spite of the Spirit) either in marriage or outside of marriage."[36] Once again, there is proof (for the paradox is only a surface one) that an absolute disdain for sexuality corresponds to very "permissive" morality in practice.

This explains the disregard of Cathari for marriage, which placed them in opposition to the Catholic Church. The Perfect is absolutely chaste; his nature is thereby changed and he resembles God Himself. He is free of the world, of contingency. On the other hand, no sacrament whatsoever is capable of making marriage innocent, of purifying it of the stain of physical love which condemns man to a submission to Satan. From this point on, what is required of the simple believers, who yet experience the disjunction of body and soul, is an adherence to the true doctrine; apart from that, whether they sin in or out of marriage is irrelevant. It is even probable that the Cathari were more lenient about a free union than about marriage, because marriage constituted a permanent wicked state whereas a free union could only be temporary, and therefore a lesser evil. Furthermore, marriage is fruitful in principle whereas free union could pass for a kind of sterile friendship or purification of passionate love. Love outside of marriage could partly escape evil and matter if it manifested at least the desire (if not the reality) of chastity.[37]

Without entering the complicated discussion on the rapport between catharism and *courtly love*[38] one can at least recognize the similar atmosphere in catharic heresy and the work of the troubadours. The shared insistence on continence gives rise to a new consciousness of love as purifying pain and a new consciousness of Woman—who moves from being the devil's bait to lure men into perdition to being Virgin Mother, protectress and inaccessible. For the troubadours and the best of the catharic believers, sexuality can be the locus of a spiritual experience. In any case, sexuality is no longer justified by procreation only. Whether it be through disdain for procreation and horror of submission to the evil world (as for the Cathari) or whether it be through the recognition of the value of the woman (as for the poets of courtly love), the dissociation of sexuality and procreation is important to notice. I will return to it later.

The Church, opposing the Cathari, affirmed, as it had before with the Gnostics, the goodness of divine creation. In its refusal of dualism, the Church recognizes the human and Christian values of sex within the framework of marriage. It denounces, and rightly so, the ambiguities of a dualism whose negative spirituality leaves the door wide open for moral indifference. But at the same time, by affirming the superiority of virginity, the Church supports a double morality that is equally ambivalent and which does not succeed (any more than its opponents did) in finding a correct rapport between spirituality and sexuality.

The catharic crisis, as well as the whole trend in the twelfth century which tried to reinvest value in human love by spiritualizing eroticism, would force the Catholic theology of marriage to take up and pursue its reflections on the sacramental value of the conjugal couple. And so the great scholastics of the thirteenth century would set themselves to the task of completing, nuancing, and correcting the traditional Augustinian doctrine.

Actually, the first signs of a new language were already appearing and manifesting a new consciousness whose values the Renaissance, the Reformation, and the Counter-Reformation would express. Some of these signs are:

1) Theologians discover the value of conjugal love: they are no longer satisfied to justify marriage by its social function of procreation, but discern (probably through the influence of courtly literature) that in male/female relationships something occurs which is neither in the order of (wicked) concupiscence nor in the order of procreative duty. However, this love is disquieting: it could be concurrent to that love which is owed to God alone: "Now amongst all relationships the conjugal tie does, more than any other, engross men's hearts. . . . Hence, they who are aiming at perfection must above all things avoid the bond of marriage. . . ."[39] If it can rival the love of God which leads to perfection, it must indeed be an extraordinary force! In their commentaries on Aristotle's ethics, both Albertus Magnus and Thomas Aquinas describe the

beauty of special friendship which is born between a man and his wife, a friendship based on sexual pleasure, the usefulness of creating a family together, and virtuous and reciprocal attachment. Bonaventure speaks of love and is amazed by it: ". . . there is something miraculous in the fact that a man finds an attraction, an appeal in a particular woman that he finds in no one but her."[40]

2) Another sign is the growing importance that medieval thinkers attribute to the education of children. It is not enough to bring children into the world; they must be educated, i.e. nourished morally and spiritually. And thus sexual relations cannot be justified in marriage by procreation alone; the married couple must assume all the consequences of that procreation. This argument is used by Thomas against fornication,[41] but it is also a way of giving value to the family setting and to the quality of the marital relationship. Conjugal love becomes the condition of the true education of children and by the same token the importance attributed to education reinvests value in the conjugal bond.[42]

3) Within the framework of Augustinian doctrine, theologians highlight the value of "conjugal duty." Up until this point, Paul's words— "The husband should give to his wife her conjugal rights, and likewise the wife to her husband" (1 Corinthians 7:3)—had been interpreted in a restrictive sense, as the authorization of a lesser evil. Reflections on conjugal fidelity (a sufficiently important value so that it is preferable to abstinence if abstinence pushes one of the partners to adultery) lead theologians to reflect on the purpose of the sexual act in a more subtle manner. All sexual activity cannot be justified solely by procreation because it can play an important role in conjugal fidelity.[43]

4) Along the same lines, and even more original, there is an attempt to restore value to pleasure. Under the influence of Aristotle, who defined pleasure not as an action in itself but as a subjective feeling which accompanied an action, theology, and particularly that of Thomas, ceases condemning pleasure as such. Henceforth pleasure is to be condemned only if it accompanies an indecent action. Conversely, it is recognized as good and desirable if it accompanies a good action.[44] With Augustine, as we have seen, sexual pleasure, since it is outside of reason's control, had been condemned per se, for it was the sign of concupiscence; in Paradise there was sexual activity but without "libido." This opinion is not shared by Albertus Magnus who thinks that Adam experienced pleasure in Paradise; and he adds that even if sexual relations recall original sin, it is not because they are accompanied by pleasure, but because the pleasure is not as great as it could have been: "I heartily concede that there would have been a greater and more genuine pleasure in the (sex) act at that time but it would have been under reason's control."[45]

Thomas shares the opinion of his former professor. His refusal to take on the Augustinian dualism of charity and cupidity leads him to see in all forms of love, even bodily love, something that shows forth the love of God.[46] Thus pleasure, willed by God, cannot be declared evil in itself. However it cannot be separated from the fidelity of the act that it accompanies; we cannot seek pleasure for its own sake. But if it be a licit act, as is the sexual union of the married couple desiring to procreate, it can in no way be condemned.

John T. Noonan[47] reports the arguments of an English theologian, Richard Middleton, who, in 1272, presented a defense of pleasure as a legitimate goal: pleasure, moderated by temperance, is part of the good that belongs to the sacrament of marriage. But it must be acknowledged that this point of view is isolated among medieval theologians. On the moral plane, Augustine remains the recognized authority.

5) Among the factors that contributed to a certain evolution of consciousness, as previously discussed, is the very distinct promotion of woman during the twelfth and thirteenth centuries. This phenomenon is of course reserved for the intellectual elite, but the impact of this new light on woman is striking and corresponds in the religious domain to the development of the Marian cult.[48]

In any case, women speak out[49] on sexuality, love and marriage, and express some thoughts and feelings which correspond very little to the rigid Augustinian traditions! There is an appeal for love, which by dint of customs and traditions, becomes more often than not a critique of marriage and a defense of adultery. As Evelyne Sullerot says so well: "The vigorous and constant revolt against marriage is a remarkable trait in the writings of women. Marriage imprisons them much more than men, and the disproportion in ages almost always is not in their favor. A young maiden is often handed over to an elderly man, or to an old man whom she hates. . ."[50]

This is a surprising kind of literature: women speak of themselves as subjects and their lovers as objects which they do away with at will! An expression like this, even if it is limited to a small elite, could not remain without influence on theological reflections, even that of celibate men! This is especially true since it did not come about by chance at that very moment of history: it exteriorized the expression of a slow but sure mutation that had been operating all along and to which Christianity, in spite of Augustinianism, was certainly not a stranger. The Christian discourse on marriage and sexuality, although in an apparently fixed state through Augustinian morality, was evolving and that evolution will be better perceived through an examination of how the questions of the validity and sacramentality of marriage were resolved in the Middle Ages.

5. The Evolution of Conjugal Rights from the Fourth Century to the End of the Middle Ages

As we saw in section two, Christians up until the third century adopted the laws and customs which regulated the conjugal and family questions in the Roman world.

Once it came out of hiding from the fourth century on, the Church was able to exercise a greater influence on laws which corresponded with its influence on morals. The collapse of the Western Empire conferred upon the Church (now the only stable juridical institution) a legal and moral importance that was considerable.

This reinforcement of the social importance of the Church is marked by the growth, from the fourth to the eleventh centuries, of a stronger emphasis on the ecclesiastical character of the celebration of marriage. The Church intervenes to recall that marriage, for Christians, has a religious and social significance. As Edward Schillebeeckx notes,[1] "increasing emphasis was placed on the church aspect of the marriage contract, without prejudice to its legal validity, by surrounding it with liturgical ceremonies." The bishop plays a more prominent role than in the first centuries and is more and more associated with marriage ceremonies.[2] The aim in these ceremonies is not to juridically validate marriage but to relegate onto a moral and religious plane any marriage contracted according to different national laws and customs. Therefore these ceremonies were not obligatory except for priests. One of the first detailed descriptions of a marriage liturgy has come down to us through the work of Paulinus of Nola (beginning of the fifth century): the ceremony is held at the church, the groom's father leads the couple to the altar where the bishop gives his blessing. The prayer is probably spontaneous, during which the couple's heads are covered by a veil that the bishop has stretched over them.[3]

It is important to note that all these rites remain absolutely optional. In the ninth century, Pope Nicholas I, in answer to a question from Bulgarian Christians, writes: "The Greeks, you say, insist that all these matrimonial rights are obligatory under pain of sin. We do not agree, especially since so many poor people cannot afford the expense. Only consent, exchanged according to law, is necessary. Conversely, if consent be the only element lacking, all the other rites and even conjugal union are without value."[4] This passage clearly shows the maintenance of the tradition which distinguishes between the validity of marriage, which is conferred according to Roman law by the mutual consent, and the religious ceremonies, which are personal testimonies, desirable, certainly, but not obligatory.

On the question of *divorce,* the Church which had now become official sought to reinforce the civil laws which prohibited it. With little success: the emperor increased the punishment meted out to adulterers, but divorce by simple mutual consent remained authorized, according to the tradition of Roman law.[5] Many Fathers loudly expressed their disapproval on this point—like Jerome who recognized with bitterness that "the laws of Caesar are different . . . from the laws of Christ"[6]—but the Church never tried to impose its laws on the State: the State was allowed to legislate, while the Church retained the right of calling the Christians to the imperatives of the gospel. Even within the Church, the most rigid position on divorce, defended by Jerome and Augustine, was not established in the West until the ninth century. Up until then, in the West as well as in the Eastern Churches, a more tolerant and pastoral attitude prevailed: "The right to remarry was not denied to the husband victimized by adultery or abandoned for no reason, according to Origen, Lactantius, Basil, or Chrysostom. They interpret Matthew's famous interpolation as support for this concession and liken adultery to the death of a spouse. That opinion becomes canonized in the East by the Council at Trullo in 692."[7]

In 395 Jerome wrote: "A husband may be an adulterer or a sodomite, he may be stained with every crime and may have been left by his wife because of his sins; yet he is still her husband and, so long as he lives, she may not marry another."[8] But in the middle of the eighth century Bishop Ekbert of York, a disciple of the Venerable Bede, translated the opinion received from the Church during the first millenium in this manner: "No one infringes on the Gospel of Paul with impunity; we are therefore against adultery completely. But we refuse to burden whomsoever, if it risks crushing him. We fearlessly proclaim the desires of the Lord. As for him whose weakness hinders him from fulfilling them (the Lord's desires), we prefer to leave judgment to God alone. Consequently, so that our silence be not encouragement to adulterers or that the devil who lures adulterers may not find his joy in them, we say to them 'What God has joined together, let no man put asunder.' But we add 'Let him who can, understand.' Often the experiences of life actually compel a violation of the law. What did David do when he was hungry (Mark 2:25–26)? We cannot accuse him of transgression. Thus, in difficult cases let us not be so definite: let us accept instead seeing our fixed notions jeopardized so that others may be saved."[9] It is regrettable that such an attitude was abandoned. Under the influence of the works of Augustine and Jerome which were enormously prestigious in the Middle Ages, the Carolingian theologians established an inflexible point of view in the Western Church, breaking with its own tradition[10] as well as with that of the Eastern Church. Here is a significant echo of that tradition: "He who cannot remain continent after the death of his first wife or who is separated from his wife for a valid reason like fornication, adultery or other cause, if he takes another wife (or if the wife takes another husband) Sacred Scripture does not condemn him nor exclude him from the Church or from life, but supports him because of his weakness. Not that he can have two wives, with the first one continuing a relationship with him, but if he truly be separated from the first wife, he may legally unite with another if the situation presents itself. For Sacred Scripture and Holy Mother Church take pity on him, especially if the man is otherwise pious and living according to the law of God."[11]

It was during the ninth century in the West that the situation evolved perceptibly. The juridical and cultural importance of the Church, since it seemed able to ensure a link with the prodigious past of the Roman Empire that the Carolingians were trying to restore, was henceforth very evident. Thus developed ecclesiastical legislation on marriage, which aimed at blocking incestuous marriages, "mixed" marriages (i.e. where one of the spouses was an "infidel" or a Jew), and forced marriages following abduction or rape. In order to avoid these cases, the publication of marriage, i.e. the celebration of marriage before the Church, became obligatory.

But it is the apocryphal writings of Pseudo-Isidore (ca. 845),[12] a collection[13] of False Capitularies (royal or conciliary decrees) and False Decretals (pontifical letters), which would modify the situation in a decisive way. Henceforth the nuptial blessing became canonically required and the civil forms of marriage were absorbed into ecclesiastical law. From that point on, the Church tended to add civil juridical forms to its jurisdiction.[14] However, one important note is that tradition was respected, i.e. the validity of marriage which throughout the Middle Ages never depended on the ecclesiastical celebration of marriage; the Church celebration was obligatory for Christians but it did not validate the marriage, which only the consent of the spouses could guarantee. It is the Council of Trent, in the sixteenth century, which finally mingled licitness and validity in one single obligation and declared civil marriage invalid.

From the eleventh century on, theological reflections concentrated on two problems, which were closely linked: the sacramentality of marriage and the validity of marriage.

"Since the church had in fact taken over complete jursdiction in matters of marriage, from the tenth to the eleventh century, she was faced in matrimonial lawsuits with the question as to what really constituted marriage as a valid contract between husband and wife. . . . The church discovered that it was a highly complex issue. . . . First there was the

Roman conception of the marriage of mutual consent—marriage by *consensus*. Then there was the Germanic, Frankish, Gothic, and Celtic *mundium* form of marriage in which the marriage contract was formally regarded as a handing over of the bride by her father to the marital control of the bridegroom. Finally, the very ancient idea that the marriage was not consummated until cohabitation and sexual intercourse had actually taken place played an important part in the minds of all peoples. The *domum-ductio,* or the solemn taking of the bride in procession to the bridegroom's house, was thus regarded both by the Greeks and the Romans and by the Western tribes as the consummation of the marriage contract. In the Middle Ages, these did not exist side by side as three distinct systems of law; they interacted upon each other."[15] From that time on, the debate concerned the rapport between the old Roman idea of mutual consent and the Germanic law which insisted on the importance of sexual union to validate the marriage. Already around 860, Hincmar, the archbishop of Reims, in response to Count Regimond's question, created a breach in the old Roman juridical tradition: "But I must tell you this: there is a valid marriage between people when the girl, who is asked for in marriage from the rightful authority—be it parents or tutors—, is properly engaged, duly equipped with a dowry, united in public nuptial ceremony in the bonds of marriage, becomes one body and one flesh with her husband, as it is written 'the two shall become one flesh'; notice, I did not say two, but one flesh."[16] Thus bodily union was recognized in the Frankish churches as necessary for the marriage to be completed; there must be cohabitation and sexual union for the mutual consent to constitute the "sacrament" of Christ and the Church.

The debate over Roman law, in full resurgence in the eleventh-century West, and the Germanic concept which linked the indissolubility of marriage to the accomplishment of the sexual act, continued on throughout the whole Middle Ages.[17] Two great schools opposed each other on this matter: the theologians of the French school (Hugh of Saint Victor, who died in 1141; Peter Lombard, who died in 1164) and the canonical writers of the school in Bologna (Gratian, who died ca. 1160). The first school continued in the old tradition: it is the consent which makes the marriage and not the promise to marry (*desponsatio*) or the consummation, i.e. sexual union. The second school distinguished between marriage "begun" (engagement, wedding, consent) and marriage "consummated" (sexual union and cohabitation). For the latter, only consummation creates the marriage because only that transforms the *sponsi* (the promised ones) into *conjuges*. While the French school insisted on the sacramental representation by marriage of the *love* of Christ for His Church, the canonical writers in Bologna emphasized the representation of the *union* of Christ with His Church by the physical union of the spouses.

The results of these discussions, summarized under the form of articles of law, are to be found in the Fourth Book of the *Decretals* of Gregory IX which is entirely devoted to marriage.[18] The importance of consent is immediately reaffirmed: "marriage is contracted only by consent" (I,1); as well as the importance of a free decision without which the marriage is invalid: "in marriage and espousal, there must be liberty, otherwise the promise is not binding" (I,29); and "no one can make a fiancée become a spouse by intercourse" (I,32). But at the same time it must be recognized, because of the issue of sexual impotence, that physical union constitutes the aim of marriage: "an impotence to perform intercourse is impotence to contract marriage, whether that impediment is from age or from nature" (XV,2); and "any natural impediment to intercourse, if not reparable by the art of medicine, impedes a marriage" (XV,3). He is concerned to avert clandestine marriages (cf. all of chapter III); to protect the spouses from the whims of parents: "a father may contract a marriage for his son if he is under age, but if he is not under age, the father can only do so with the son's consent" (II,1,cf. also I,11); and to affirm the church's right to control the juridical (and not only the liturgical) practice of marriage: "marriage cannot be contracted contrary to the interdict of the church or its judgment, because it alone has jurisdiction" (XVI,1); or "a man may not dismiss his wife, without ecclesiastical permission . . ." (XIX,3). Consider also the three important chapters on divorce (XIX,XX) and remarriage (XXI), both issues being subject to specific interdictions. In the discussion between theologians and jurists the debate on the validity of marriage could not be divorced from the issue of sacramentality, i.e. the debate on the value of the Christian tradition of marriage.

Augustine had closely connected his thoughts on *sacramentum* (the third good in marriage) to his pastoral concern for theologically establishing the indissolubility of the conjugal couple. Marriage, insofar as it is a "sacrament" or sign of the union between Christ and His Church, is indissoluble. This is precisely what the liturgical practice of the Church wished to emphasize by the benediction and the bestowal of the veil.[19] Through it, the Church called the faithful to discern in the terrestrial reality of marriage a spiritual truth which, aside from the moral requirement of indissolubility, recalled and signified the love of Christ for His Church.

From this point on, and because of the historical necessity of promoting marriage anew in opposition to the heretical movements of the twelfth century (which rejected marriage as a radical evil), scholastic theologians applied themselves to determine more precisely the nature of the mystery (Ephesians 5: *mystérion* in Greek, translated into Latin by *sacramentum*) that links Christ to the Church and which marriage signifies. The twelfth- and thirteenth-century theological reflections on the validity of marriage are divided into two camps on the question of sacramentality: some, like Anselm of Laon, believe that the the the sacrament is in the union of the bodies, that human sexual union symbolizes the union of Christ and the Church; others, like Hugh of Saint Victor, assert that the bond of love is the element that constitutes the marriage and the sacrament, the physical union depends on it but a marriage could be perfectly valid without sexual relations (like the marriage of Joseph and Mary!). An emphasis on union is an emphasis on love: in the end, the best theologians refused to choose, preferring instead a synthesis, and thus Thomas Aquinas defines marriage as "a certain joining together of husband and wife ordained to carnal intercourse, and a further consequent union between husband and wife. . . ."[20] What the spouses consent to is more than the sexual act; it's a whole life together, a unity of life which can exist without this act, but whose profound meaning is manifested in the conjugal sexual act. Sacramental grace, then, is not directly linked to the physical act but to the conjugal love which is actualized through it. The grace which is exercised in marriage makes of a specifically human community, a community of grace.

What such a theology highlights is the discovery that through the gospel the male/female relationship has its most profound signification revealed, its ultimate meaning: to signify the very love of Christ for His Church. This kind of theology affords an understanding of how the most human of acts can become the sign and the object of the most divine love.[21]

6. The Reformation and Protestantism

The Reformation was essentially a conflict over authority—in all areas, but primarily in the area of theology. Breaking with the oldest of traditions, Luther dared to affirm the primacy of Scripture over ecclesiastical magisterium. In the name of the Word of God, which he considered to be alive in the Bible, he questioned not only certain abuses of Roman power but even the very principle of that power. The consequences of this crisis were enormous, as we know. This was no less true in the area of morality since the challenge to Church authority was necessarily accompanied by a critique of its moral teachings and its claims to define the very details of the conduct of believers.

Certain facts, demonstrating the failure of the Church's teaching, caused that criticism to be even sharper. The more canon law tried to precisely elaborate regulations concerning marriage[1] the more it moved away from the real needs of a society that was trying to organize itself more autonomously. On two particular points the new lay spirit was in conflict with clerical authority: divorce and clandestine marriages. Sacramental theology, which had been superimposed little by little, led to almost insurmountable problems in these two areas when transposed to the level of civil law. Spouses, even though separated by the adultery of one partner, could not be divorced, because the indissolubility of the conjugal sacramental bond was absolute; the marriage bond had an objective reality that no one had the power to annul. Naturally, in practice the harshness of this kind of principle resulted in situations that were more immoral than those it was fighting against.[2] As for the second issue—how could clandestine marriages, contracted without the parents' consent and in the absence of a priest, be prohibited if the consent of the spouses is really the material cause in the conjugal sacrament? The union could not then be dissolved even if, under certain circumstances, things went as far as the excommunication of the spouses. Such were the difficulties that threatened a social order that had been founded on the quasi-absolute paternal authority, and constituted a ferment of anarchy for a society on its way to secularization, searching for new standards by which to establish its social and moral order.

There was another area that revealed the failure of the Church's teaching on sexuality: the customs of the clergy itself! The clergy at that time interpreted required celibacy as an obligation not to marry, but not as an obligation to renounce living with a woman. As we know, at the end of the fifteenth century, the great majority of priests were living with concubines. And this of course could not fail to provoke questions about the validity of the official theological stand which exalted the virtues of virginity and chastity. A choice had to be made: either authorize the marriage of ecclesiastics (the choice made by the Reformation) or restore moral discipline within the ranks of the clergy (the work of the Counter-Reformation).

In this context, it is clear that the crisis effected by Luther concerning the Church was going to appear to many as a possibility for liberation from the legalism and casuistry then in effect. The reception given to the Reformation by the urban bourgeois class was related to this ethical (and therefore spiritual) liberation, which appeared to many as the prerequisite for any attempt at "remoralizing" the social practice of the time. Countless voices at the end of the Middle Ages in fact protested against the presence of a clergy who had no well-defined professional activity; they were often described as social parasites who were ill-equipped for the role of moral guidance which had been delegated to them. Thus, in the minds of many, the demoralization of society was linked to the existence and status of the clergy.

The essential points of the Protestant perspective, outlined by men as different as Erasmus, Luther, Butzer, Zwingli, Calvin, Bèze,[3] can be summarized in these following four theses:

1) The Reformers aimed at freeing consciences from the yoke that canon law and pastoral practice had placed upon the believers, clerics as well as laymen.

2) The basic theological discussion concerned the relationship of marriage to the order of God's creation and ended in refusing to consider marriage as a sacrament.

3) The Christian doctrine of marriage, thus liberated from the canonical and theological constraints of ecclesiastical legislation, could once again play an important role (even a major one) in the social and ethical order. The underlying tone of Reformation teaching on this point came forth in the praise given to the beauty, dignity, and the deep-seated morality of the conjugal bond which is the foundation of all social life.

4) This kind of teaching was easily adaptable to the perspectives of the new western society which came about during the Renaissance. It tended towards flexibility by liberalizing divorce, and it reinforced social and economic structures by justifying a super-valuation of the family, now more tightly knit under the authority of the father as family head.

Let us briefly examine these four points.

1) In 1520, Luther, in his call *To the Christian Nobility of the German Nation,* had listed, among the propositions destined to favor the reform of the Church, freedom for the clergy to marry or not.[4] "You will find many a pious priest against whom nobody has anything to say except that he is weak and has come to shame with a woman. From the bottom

of their hearts both are of a mind to live together in lawful wedded love, if only they could do it with a clear conscience. But even though they both have to bear public shame, the two are certainly married in the sight of God. And I say that where they are so minded and live together, they should appeal anew to their conscience. Let the priest take and keep her as his lawful wedded wife, and live honestly with her as her husband, whether the pope likes it or not, whether it be against canon or human law. The salvation of your soul is more important than the observance of tyrannical, arbitrary, and wanton laws which are not necessary to salvation or commanded by God."[5]

"Let consciences be free" is the cry repeated a thousand times by Luther, and echoed by so many Christians (cleric and lay) who found in the rediscovered gospel the courage to break with a legalism that led to hypocrisy and guilt. "(And) Christ has granted to Christians a liberty which is above all laws of men":[6] here we have the boldness of a new liberty which so strongly marked the beginnings of the Reformation, along with a call to oppressed, "miserable consciences." Of course the time would quickly come when a morality would have to be constructed, a guideline to distinguish the do's and don'ts, but Luther's thrust would be sufficient forever to impede any return by Protestantism to a strict and contemptible casuistry in the realm of conjugal and sexual practice. "I would have nothing decided here on the mere authority of the popes and the bishops; but if two learned and good men agreed in the name of Christ and published their opinion in the spirit of Christ, I should prefer their judgment even to such councils as are assembled nowadays . . ."[7] Rejecting clerical casuistry, Luther appeals to individual conscience, enlightened and sanctified by the gospel; in some ways this defines the whole of Protestant morality!

"Christian or evangelical freedom, then, is a freedom of conscience which liberates the conscience from works. Not that no works are done but no faith is put in them."[8] Because of this, Luther undertakes a struggle against obligatory vows of celibacy and against the absolute prohibitions against divorce which in practice end in greater social disorder and in the personal despair of so many men and women.[9]

With Calvin,[10] typically, the struggle for the freedom of conscience takes on a more social and political aspect. With regard to divorce, he distinguishes between the will of God and the constraints upon political power which necessitate choosing the lesser of two evils. In contrast to an idealistic morality, which on the social plane can only lead to legalistic "tyranny" or to a loose and carefree attitude, Calvin proposes a realism which seeks to safeguard liberty: "It was the same as with the magistrate, who is constrained to bear many things which he does not approve; for we cannot so deal with mankind as to restrain all vices. It is indeed desirable, that no vice should be tolerated; but we must have a regard to what is possible (i.e. to consider what is possible in a given situation [author's note])."[11]

In virtue of the twofold principle of realism and of freedom of conscience, Calvin sanctions divorce in certain cases, as does Luther: "But if a comparison be made, Malachi says that it is a lighter crime to dismiss a wife than to marry many wives . . . for the husband . . . then not only deals unfaithfully with his wife to whom he is bound, but also forcibly detains her: thus his crime is doubled" (*idem*). In opposition to those who prohibit any remarriage of divorced people who are the victims of adultery, Calvin also writes: "Our impartial moderators bind them to perpetual celibacy. What if they need a wife? No help for it; they must just fret on and atone for another's crime with the destruction of their soul. Thus a Christian man will be forced either to cherish adultery and swallow the dishonor of an unchaste wife, or be cruelly subjected to perpetual disquietudes, if the gift of continence be not bestowed upon him. While they provide so ill for miserable consciences, shall we aid their inhuman tyranny by our assent?"[12] As to the ecclesiastical obligation of celibacy, he sees it as stemming from the same tyranny: "The prohibition, however, clearly shows how pestiferous all traditions are since this one has not only deprived the Church of fit and honest pastors, but has introduced a fearful sink of iniquity, and plunged many souls into the gulf of despair. Certainly, when marriage was interdicted to priests, it was done with impious tyranny, not only contrary to the word of God, but contrary to all justice. First, men had no title whatever to forbid what God had left free; secondly, it is too clear to make it necessary to give any lengthened proof that God has expressly provided in his Word that this liberty should not be infringed."[13]

Opposing the tyranny exercised on oppressed consciences, the Reformation points to an ethic of individual responsibility, which is capable of determining one's obedience to the gospel and of accepting earthly reality as a place for service to that gospel.

2) As we have seen, the whole juridical and moral construct of medieval Catholicism relied on the doctrine of the sacramentality of marriage. And to that doctrine was linked the rejection of divorce and the requirement of ecclesiastical celibacy. Actually, marriage had become gradually recognized as a sacrament partly in response to the diminished value that the religious exaltation of virginity and celibacy risked assigning to marriage in the West. This was clearly seen by the Reformers, who attacked both the ecclesiastical requirement of celibacy and the sacramentality of marriage. Erasmus,[14] in his *In Novum Testamentum Annotationes* of

1518,[15] had already inaugurated a very pointed criticism against the sacramentality of marriage. He developed three arguments which reappear in the writings of the Reformers and which form the core of the polemic against the Catholic doctrine of marriage-as-sacrament. The first argument is historical. Marriage as a sacrament is a new thing: it is unknown in patristic tradition, and when the Fathers speak of marriage they describe it as an image of the union of Christ and the Church: "The Fathers followed Paul in calling marriage a sacrament; by that, they meant that the union of man and woman, being a very close-knit friendship, represents the figure and a certain kind of image of the union of Christ with the Church, His spouse."[16] It is therefore not a sacrament in the scholastic sense of the word. The second argument concerns the precise nature of the sacrament. If a sacrament is a sign of God's grace which also confers grace, how can marriage, which scholastic tradition says is a remedy against concupiscence, be a sacrament? And if it is a sacrament, what bearing does that have on the free consent of the spouses? Finally, the third argument, which had by far the greatest success later on, is the scriptural argument. The classical interpretation was based on the Vulgate's translation of the Greek *mystérion* in Ephesians 5 by the Latin word *sacramentum*. This translation lends itself to serious misunderstandings, as Erasmus points out: "*Mystérion* must be translated as 'mystery' and not 'sacrament'; furthermore, the mystery refers to the union of Christ and the Church and not to marriage."[17] In this excellent exegesis, Erasmus notes that the word "mystery" does not designate a sacrament in the New Testament, but rather a secret and hidden reality (for example, Romans 11:25; 16:25; I Corinthians 2:7) concerning the work of God.

This critique by Erasmus was often echoed later. In 1520 Luther in *De captivitate babylonica* also rejects the sacramentality of marriage: "Christ and the Church are, therefore, a mystery, that is, a great and secret thing which can and ought to be represented in terms of marriage as a kind of outward allegory. But marriage ought not for that reason be called a sacrament. The heavens are a type of the apostles, as Psalm 19 declares; the sun is a type of Christ; the waters, of the peoples; but that does not make those things sacraments. . . ."[18] Marriage belongs to the natural order that is willed by God for all men: "Furthermore, since marriage has existed from the beginning of the world and is still found among unbelievers, there is no reason why it should be called a sacrament of the New Law and of the Church alone."[19]

In his *Institutes*, Calvin systematizes this critique (IV,xix, 34–36). Sensitive to the tragic history of men marked by sin (as all the Reformers were), he defines marriage as an order of creation prior to the fall, "that order of creation in which the eternal and inviolable appointment of God is strikingly displayed."[20] Marriage is even more necessary and beneficial in a world that is threatened by the disorder of sin: "Still marriage was not capable of being so far vitiated by the depravity of men, that the blessing which God had once sanctioned by His word should be utterly abolished and extinguished."[21]

This distinction between the order of creation and the order of redemption opens the way for constructive criticism of marriage-as-sacrament. Freed from the tutelage of canon law, marriage could rediscover its own ethical importance, as will be seen in section 3 which follows.

In concluding this point, it should be noted that among the Reformers, only Butzer refined this critique: even though he rejects the sacramental character of marriage, he nevertheless admits that it has the value of a sacramental sign when it is lived out in the faith and love of Christ. God's goal in instituting marriage is the total union of the man and woman. "In this verse (Genesis 2:23ff.), God shows what marriage is and why He instituted it. The communion of man and woman is such that in all things they are one flesh, i.e. one being, and that each of them has a willingness and desire to remain with the other more than with anyone else on earth."[22] This final end of marriage is fulfilled when the spouses live out their relationship as a sign of the union of Christ with the Church. Butzer did not wish the necessary process of de-sacredizing marriage to lead to a suppression of its spiritual (as well as moral) values. In 1557 he proposed this beautiful definition of marriage: "True marriage, as instituted by God . . . is a society and conjunction of man and woman, in which they are obliged to mutually communicate all things, divine and human, throughout their whole life and to live together in giving their bodies to one another whenever required or because of warm affection and genuine friendship."[23]

3) Why did the Reformers criticize the sacramentality of marriage? Apart from the reasons already stated, this was the only way to give marriage a morality of its own. Marriage involves first of all the liberty of two human beings who share the duty of creating a new community. The demand for individual liberty and responsibility which characterizes the beginning of the sixteenth century finds fertile ground here. The conviction in this case is the same for the Humanists as for the Reformers: the moral reformation of marriage occurs via a criticism of its juridical sacramental status. The grace *ex opere operato* of the sacrament must give way to the active and liberating grace of God, which stirs up the faith and the responsibility of the believer. Thus, another shift occurs in the understanding of the final end of marriage and because of it, of sexuality: no longer as a remedy for concupiscence, marriage becomes a means of exercising true charity and authentic spiritual chastity.

A new judgment is thus brought to bear on sexuality, as witnessed in the following quotations:

Against the anti-feminism of the medieval and patristic tradition, Luther declares: "So they concluded that woman is a necessary evil, and that no household can be without such an evil. These are the words of blind heathen, who are ignorant of the fact that man and woman are God's creation. They blaspheme his work, as if man and woman just came into being spontaneously!... In order that we may not proceed as blindly, but rather conduct ourselves in a Christian manner, hold fast first of all to this, that man and woman are the work of God. Keep a tight rein on your heart and your lips; do not criticize his work, or call that evil which he himself has called good."[24] He affirms the goodness of marriage and of sexuality, both willed by God: "God divided mankind into two classes, namely, male and female, or a he and a she. This was so pleasing to him that he himself called it a good creation. Therefore, each one of us must have the kind of body God has created for us.... Moreover, he wills to have his excellent handiwork honored as his divine creation, and not despised. The man is not to despise or scoff at the woman or her body, nor the woman the man."[25]

Although this new attitude on sexuality is prudent and discreet, it is nevertheless quite different from that of medieval theology, as proved by this passage from Calvin: "But that God should permit a bride to enjoy herself with her husband, affords no trifling proof of His indulgence. Assuredly, it cannot be but that the lust of the flesh must affect the connection of husband and wife with some amount of sin; yet God not only pardons it, but covers it with the veil of holy matrimony, lest that which was sinful in itself should be so imputed; nay, He spontaneously allows them to enjoy themselves. To this injunction corresponds Paul's statement: 'Let the husband render unto his wife due benevolence: and likewise also the wife unto the husband. Defraud ye not the other, except it be with consent'...."[26] The goodness of marriage is such that it can justify whatever could be "depraved" in sexuality. Fear of sexuality is not so easily surmounted, especially when it is reinforced by religious arguments. On this point, Calvin does not hesitate to denounce a diabolical scheme under "religious" appearance: "... he (Paul) knew how much influence a false appearance of sanctity has in beguiling devout minds, as we ourselves know from experience. For Satan dazzles us with an appearance of what is right, that we might be led to imagine that we are polluted by intercourse with our wives...."[27] The only means of fighting against the perversion of this human vocation is to recognize that sexuality is given to man so that he can experience love through it: "*But neither is the man without the woman. This is added* partly as a check upon men, that they may not insult ... women; and partly as a consolation to women, that they may not feel dissatisfied with being under subjection. The male sex (says Paul) has a distinction over the female sex, with this understanding, that they ought to be connected together by mutual benovolence, for the one cannot do without the other. If they be separated, they are like the mutilated members of a mangled body. Let them, therefore, be connected with each other by the bond of mutual duty."[28]

Giving this kind of value to marriage inverts the scale of medieval values: henceforth marriage is the order willed by God, and celibacy is an exception which is rarely acceptable: "I say these things in order that we may learn how honorable a thing it is to live in that estate which God has ordained. In it we find God's word and good pleasure, by which all the works, conduct, and sufferings of that estate become holy, godly, and precious so that Solomon even congratulates such a man and says in Proverbs 5:18: 'Rejoice in the wife of your youth' and again in Ecclesiastes 9:9: 'Enjoy life with the wife whom you love all the days of your vain life.' ... Conversely, we learn how wretched is the spiritual estate of monks and nuns by its very nature, for it lacks the word and pleasure of God."[29]

Calvin echoes this position: "If anyone imagines that it is to his advantage to be without a wife and so without further consideration decides to be celibate, he is very much in error. For God, who declared that it was good that the woman should be the helpmeet for man, will exact punishment for contempt of His ordinance. Men arrogate too much to themselves when they try to exempt themselves from their heavenly calling."[30]

From this point on, the Reformers continually reassert the dignity and the beauty of the marital bond: "... this great honor stems from the fact that God holds it in such high regard that He committed himself to it (symbolically) by the intermediary of His only-begotten Son and through Him united Himself to us."[31] Marriage, restored to the order of creation willed by God, must be defended not only against those who scorn or denigrate it, but against any attempt to make its moral values relative. For immorality is not only an offense to the love of God since He has made our bodies a temple of the Holy Spirit,[32] but also an attack against man and the right order he should establish in line with God's law: "For He has stamped His mark upon us, to indicate that we bear His resemblance, and doesn't this image lie partly in the fact that men do not let themselves go at every turn, whenever a man meets a woman, as a dog meets a female dog? But each one has his own match and finds therein companionship blessed by God and sanctioned by Him."[33]

4) Marriage, now de-sacredized (or should I say de-sacramentalized?), accrued extreme value within the order of social morality: the success of the family (and even more of society) hinged on its success. But, given this new perspective, it yet remained to structure marriage unto the legal level, and there was urgency on one point in particular: the validity of clandestine marriages contracted without the knowledge of the parents. According to canon law, which strictly adopted the Roman principle of "*consensus facit nuptias,*" these marriages were recognized as valid. The parents' consent was not a part of the essence of marriage. Such a position came into conflict with the needs of a society that was seeking a more open atmosphere (free from Church domination) and a more stable order. Giving marriage social importance meant fighting against clandestine marriages (which were valid according to canon law) because they threatened family order. Therefore the Reformers made this fight one of the favorite themes of their matrimonial doctrine.

Erasmus had already pointed out, with irony, that Christians (as opposed to Jews and pagans) could contract marriage very easily, but without being able to undo it![34] The Church had come to sanction hasty marriages, in bad conscience; it seemed to approve disorder and even anarchy, while preventing marriage from fulfilling its genuine social function. Therefore the authority of parents had to be restored, i.e. their consent required to validate their children's marriages.

Luther insisted on this point quite a bit. Marriage is a public event and should thus be ratified by witnesses. But even more crucial than witnesses is the parents' authorization. Thus a marriage is clandestine whenever it is celebrated without the parents' knowledge: this was the important point for the Reformers. The major scriptural argument used is that of obedience to parents: to go against the will of the parents is to disobey God. "There is a solemn commandment from God which says that children must honor their father and mother, and nature teaches us that children should undertake nothing that is not known to their parents so long as they are minors. Therefore no marriage can be founded in God when one scorns his parents and acts without their consent. This is the reason that Christian authorities must prohibit such unions."[35]

This point would be woven into the Genevan legislation on marriage by Calvin's *Ecclesiastical Ordinances of 1561*: "As for young people who have never been married, let none of them (be they sons or daughters) who have living fathers have the power to contract marriage without the authorization of their fathers, unless they have reached legal age, (20 for the son, 18 for the daughter); and if after reaching legal age, they obtain or ask their fathers for permission to marry, and if the fathers do nothing about it and that fact is known to the Consistory, after having called the fathers concerned and exhorted them to their duty, in such cases, it is legitimate to marry without the authority of the fathers. . . . If it occurs that two young people have contracted a marriage on their own through folly or levity, let them be punished and chastized; let such a marriage be rescinded (declared null) upon the request of those who have them under their charge."[36]

In principle this paternal authority is limited by law. And so at Geneva, these same ecclesiastical ordinances specify that: "no father [should] force his children into a marriage which seems good to him without their willingness and consent; let him or her who does not wish to accept the partner chosen by the father be excused, maintaining a humble and reverent attitude, without being punished by the father for such a refusal."[37]

But in reality,[38] the cases were rare, it seems, when paternal authority was discredited by the magistrate. Even if a consummation of the marriage (*copula carnalis*) had occurred, marriage could be annulled on request by the parents, according to the law as influenced by Calvin— which was not the case in the Lutheran countries. In the Germanic countries the trend would also be to reinforce parental authority, for example, by raising the "matrimonial age" which was 24 for the man and 20 for the woman (Strasbourg 1530) to 25 for both of them (Strasbourg 1565).

So, in general, the weakening of the authority of canon law in Protestant countries as influenced by the Reformation, was simultaneously accompanied by a strengthening of parental authority. As I have said, this new attitude fitted in with the needs of the new society. As proof of this, the very Catholic king of France, at the Council Trent,[39] called for a reform of cannon law condemning clandestine marriages, defined as (and the Council rejected this definition) those contracted without the consent of parents. The conjunction on this issue of political power and the Protestant position signifies an evolution of customs which posited a new and important responsibility to the family in the economic realm, as well as in the moral and educational realms.

This reinforcement of family order was undergirded by a hierarchical vision of relationships between men and women. The whole classical arsenal of arguments was taken up by the Reformers to affirm the rigid subordination of the wife to the husband in marriage. Luther very strongly affirms: ". . . it is necessary that the woman know and be convinced that man is higher and better than she is. For government and supremacy belong to man as head of the family and master of the household. . . . Consequently, in the conjugal state also, the woman must not only love her husband, but also be obedient and submissive; she must let herself be governed by him, reverence him, in brief, hold only to him and be directed by him; she must not only acknowledge the protection he affords her, but must remember, in seeing him, this example, and think of it: My husband is the image of the true and supreme head, Christ. . . ."[40] This interpretation of Ephesians 5 emphasizes the authority of Christ in His rapport with the Church. But Luther is aware that the text also speaks even more of Christ's love. This is why there is a tension in Luther's writings, as well as in Calvin's, between, on one hand, the affirmation of the primacy of love as the foundation of the marital bond—a love which implies the recognition of the spiritual equality of man and woman before God—and, on the other hand, the need for maintaining a hierarchial order within the couple. That tension between theological perspective and social requirement clearly appears in this passage from Calvin: "Woman is like a branch that has come from man; for she was taken from his substance, as we know. It is true that God did this in order to recommend the union that we should have together; for He could easily have formed Eve from the earth, as He did Adam; but He wished to take one side from man so that man would not have anything apart from the woman, but that he should recognize that God created us as one body and that we cannot be separated unless we go against His will. God took that into consideration, but . . . He nevertheless placed man over the woman."[41] Thus, in Protestant ethics, the desire to construct society based on a hierarchy that is able to resist the eruption of anarchy, is coupled with the concern for maintaining the theological affirmation of the primacy of the couple over the individual, and the primacy of the structural unity of the man and woman over the contingent reality of the wife's submission.

*   *   *

The Reformation was experienced by its proponents as a liberation movement. However, the Reformers, aware that the Church in its faithfulness to the Gospel must accept social responsibility, very quickly opposed radical revolutionaries (like the Anabaptists) who attempted to bypass the gradual evolution of mentalities and structures (because of the length of time required). An old debate! Given the two extremes of Catholic conservatism and Anabaptist utopianism, the Reformers tried to maintain a course between patiently coping with the weight of reality and impatiently and urgently proclaiming the rediscovered Gospel of justification by grace and of salvation by faith.

And so in the realm of sexual and conjugal ethics the Reformation opened the way for a new consciousness which represented a sharp break with the dominant ideology in the Middle Ages. The change was crucial (and full of potential) on at least three points. First of all, there was the break with the ancient Christian tradition which exalted celibacy as the royal road to salvation and obedience to God: the Reformation strongly asserted the primacy of marriage and thereby gave sexuality a new and positive status (even if its boundaries were carefully drawn!). Sexuality was recognized as the locus of the fundamental human experience of conjugality. Man does not exist independent of woman but is a partner in humanity, in a bond that is both emotional and social. "Man was created by God to be a creature of companionship," according to Calvin. And so—this is a major point—sexuality was no longer considered a priori as a fearful menace to guard against.

Next, and following logically, the Reformation took a stand on women quite different from that at the end of the Middle Ages. Woman, although rigidly subordinated to the husband, is seen neither as a demonical creature created to test the chastity of true believers, i.e. monks, nor as just a reproductive being charged with ensuring descendancy to her "lord and master";[42] she has co-responsibility with her husband for conjugal and family life. Examples of these "stalwart women" are not lacking in Protestant tradition (and even in American westerns!), especially in the traditions of the persecuted churches (whether Puritan or from the Cévennes region.)

Finally, restored to the created order, marriage became a matter of moral and social responsibility. What is lost as to the aspect of sacred mystery is regained in the awareness of what is relevant on the human moral and social level. It seems certain that the countries influenced by the Reformation were the first to attempt basing a social order on the family as the primary nucleus for all social life. This attempt at the moralization of society through the intermediary of the family is a characteristic of the Reformation. Through marriage, which is no longer deemed a remedy to concupiscence but recognized as an aid to human weakness, man can build mankind. It is important, then, that marriage and the family be protected by law.

It is at this juncture that the fact of institutional reality weighed most heavily on the attempt at renovating society. Through fear of the Anabaptist anarchy, the Reformers gave the Church a juridical power that constituted canon law.[43] They had fought against the meddlesome domination of canon law, but found themselves obliged to legislate that which fundamentally only belongs to the responsibility of each couple before God. Thus the Protestant canonical writers throughout the seventeenth century gradually returned to notions that existed before the Reformation: " . . . there was a very clear reaction near the end of the sixteenth century, which tended to discard the lay concept of the first reformers

and to accentuate the religious consequences of the fact that the institution of marriage was divine."[44] To structure a moral requirement into
a social and political context is quite difficult, as the Reformation Churches
came to see. Pierre Bels is undoubtedly right when he concludes his book
with this affirmation: " . . . the sixteenth century . . . is marked by an
accumulation of serious difficulties which left reformed law quite vulnerable. For instance, the initial doctrines that set the tone for Protestant
action and performance led to some inauspicious and harmful effects.
These doctrines, as part of a systematically critical and anti-juridical
viewpoint aiming at demolishing canon law and at attacking the Roman
Church, sought their justification along moral lines; marriage was thus
seen as a reformation of morals and not as an ensemble of juridical
mechanisms. This perspective affected the technical aspect of law, which
in turn presented insoluble problems."[45]

Thus, the essence of Protestant ethics in matters of sex and conjugality
has a twofold character. On one hand, there is a liberation vis-à-vis an
inquisition-like legalism in the sexual domain: "To the very extent that
the Protestants consider the issues of conjugal ethics to be the responsibility of each couple before God, the pastors, although married themselves, do not 'penetrate the mysteries of the conjugal sanctuary' and in
no way take on the role played by the Catholic celibate confessors with
regard to their penitents. Likewise, in opposition to the verbosity of the
theologians of the Roman Church, the Reformation theologians are extremely discreet on these matters."[46] But, along with this undeniable
freedom of conscience, there is a real juridical and social rigidity concerning conjugal questions in the reformed tradition. Therefore, (for
example) ecclesiastical control on the validity of marriage ends up being
more important in Protestant law than in the post-tridentine canon law:
"The direction of the evolution of the religious ceremony was exactly
inverse in the two faiths. The Catholic priest was deprived of active
intervention given to him by custom (to now become only a witness of
the marriage [author's note]). With the Protestants, the evolution developed logically and resulted in marriage being created only through the
religious ceremony and the preponderant action of the pastor."[47]

Freedom and responsibility were indeed restored to believers, but only
within the framework of a social order authenticated by the Church and
the bias of its ministers; this roughly summarizes the Protestant position.
On the social level, it fit into the effort to moralize society that was
undertaken by Christianity in the sixteenth century; what distinguishes
it from the parallel effort by Catholics is its sharper emphasis on personal
responsibility: it is henceforth the believer's conscience, more than the
exterior control of the Church (through confession), which ratifies what

is fitting and correct in moral attitudes on sexuality and conjugality. But that conscience, however, must be able to recognize and measure the social importance of a personal and conjugal practice of sexuality that is virtuous.

7. In the West There Are Henceforth Two Different Christian Ethics

The Reformation undeniably marked a break in the continuity of the history of Christian ethics. From the end of the sixteenth century on, two different moral systems develop in the West (partly because of their mutual polemic), becoming more precisely defined in later evolution, but with no change in essential characteristics. By a system of ethics, I mean not only the discourse developed vis-à-vis morality, but also the concrete practices and attitudes that accompany it.

From the seventeenth to the twentieth century, Catholic and Protestant ethics do indeed evolve in terms of formulation, but only in order to deal with questions springing from social practice that is more and more vividly marked by a secularization in science, in culture, in law, and finally in ethics. What is striking is that all through this evolution, the essential characteristics of the respective systems remain in place (undoubtedly with more rigidity in Catholicism than in Protestantism) with an equal constancy in affirmation of basic principles. These principles need to be more closely examined, and therefore this present synthesis will differ from my preceding sections: I will pay less attention to the historical internal evolutions than to their basic structural elements; for even today, to varying degrees, these basics mark the practice of Christian ethics (even if negatively).

Another fact justifies a synthesis-approach to this period: because of the confessional debate which led each side to harden its position, somewhat in order to highlight its uniqueness, certain stakes in Christian ethic became more obvious. Today, both of these Christian ethical systems are being equally submitted to criticism by modern secularization; in better perceiving the foundation of each system, we may better discern on what axis a Christian ethic of sexuality should really be established.[1]

In attempting to abstract a kind of typology of the two divergent systems,[2] I have chosen to pursue three classic questions in ethics: what kind of man is presupposed by any particular moral system?—in what name is man's moral obedience called for?—under what authority should he place himself to realize his moral goal?

a) Catholic Ethics[3]

Catholic ethics is based on a *hierarchical vision of man,* and that in two respects. Man is conceived as of two realities (body and soul) of differing quality; the soul is spiritual and immortal and the body is material and mortal.[4] There is, then, a hierarchy stamped into the very structure of man that goes from material/body (inferior) to spiritual/soul (superior). To this first hierarchy, static and unchanging, is added a second kind of hierarchy relating to man's destiny: as a natural being, man is called upon to go from a natural life to a supernatural one, which is a gift from God but already present in a certain way in what Bernard Häring calls (after Meister Eckhart) in a very significant way, "the center-point of the soul" or "the apex of the spirit."[5]

This hierarchical vision of the person signifies that whatever pertains to the natural order is only really fulfilled by its assumption into the supernatural. Such a point of view leads to this kind of definition of ethics: its objective is "the study of human action considered in its relation of conformity or non-conformity to the supernatural ends willed by God as binding on all men in their individual and social lives."[6] From that perspective, the standard that regulates moral life systematically posits precedence to the spiritual over the material, to intellectual over tangible, to contemplative over relational.

The result of this kind of perspective is obvious in the fact that Catholicism—this is true until Vatican II in any case—continued to practice what could be called a split-level morality: one for the people of the Church who must be taught essential principles of natural ethics and the necesssary minimum to stay in line with moral law, and an ethic for the elite of the Church (clergy, religious, monks . . .), for those who seek obedience to the ultimate requirements of the Christian absolute, in the exercise of self-denial, particularly in the sexual domain. The second ethic, of course, serves as the lighthouse, the ideal to the first; it indicates the possible progression toward the highest values. The first ethic affords a minimum framework for Christians as a whole who agree at least to the moral question.

The results with regard to sexuality are important. On one hand morality is reduced for the people in the Church to a few principles, applied with some flexibility, concerning the choice of a spouse, the obligation of a religious wedding, the stand against adultery, indissolubility, etc.; and on the other hand, in its most exacting expression, it conveys the negative image of sexuality as threat, danger, trial. Catholic ethics do not succeed in ascribing positive value to sexuality, i.e. associating it with love or seeing it as a locus for a positive experience of our corporealness, which is the condition for the possibility of a relationship of otherness and of love. Isn't the saint the one who renounces all sexual life, like the angels? On that level, Catholic ethics remain faithful to the patristic tradition: sexuality belongs to the order of impurity[7] having no justification other than procreation,[8] and in the logic of this hierarchical vision of man, marriage has a lesser value than celibacy: "If anyone says that the married state excels the state of virginity or celibacy, and that it is better and happier to be united in matrimony than to remain in virginity or celibacy, let him be anathema."[9] Supernatural life is better expressed by celibacy than by marriage, because celibacy allows someone to free himself, better than marriage does, from the "obstacle of matter" (Häring), from the weight of a flesh and a body imperfectly submitted to the spirit. Isn't sexuality an ever-threatening sign of this lack of submission? Also, even when the Catholic ethic posits value to marriage, it does not succeed in ridding itself completely of the attitude that sees the material as an obstacle to the spiritual, and the sexual as an obstacle to love.

If man is created for supernatural ends, only the Church in the last analysis (because it knows the plan of God) can really enlighten man as to what he needs to do to fulfill his destiny. Based on this, Catholicism always aims at universality, for the Magisterium must not only inform Christians as to what conforms to the requirements of the Gospel, but must also call to mind for all men (or at least for "all men of good will" to whom *Humanae Vitae* is addressed) what the fundamental principles of legitimate moral actions are. For there is only a difference in degree, and not in its basic foundation, between natural, rational ethics that any honest good man can recognize, and the ultimate aim of supernatural morality. This is the reason the Catholic Church expresses its concern for universality by recourse to the concept of *natural law* (which is so important for her). This notion plays such a major role in the ethical thinking of modern Catholicism that it is worthy of closer examination.

It is undeniably the strength of Catholicism never to have lost sight of the "ecumenical," universal responsibility which is incumbent on the Church: ". . . to designate a concurrence in the ethical rules and moral practices within the community of all men and to ensure the universal aim of moral principles amidst the variety of races, peoples, nations; to designate the essential continuities (of these principles) despite historical ruptures and ensure at least an objective regularity in the interplay of options and specific choices."[10] The Church's mission is to assure a recourse against totalitarian claims by the positivism of social sciences as well as by those who, for political and economic reasons, freely preach a morality that is "adapted" to circumstances. Whatever the difficulties of such a project, it is true that the Church cannot abandon this principle of universality without defaulting on its fundamental vocation; it has from the beginning refused the temptation to define itself (as have the Gnostics and apocalyptic groups) as an entity separate from the rest of men, as the ark of salvation which escapes the perdition wheriin the rest of mankind is mired. Because God the Savior is also God the Creator, and the Son became incarnated in the flesh of men and in their history, it is impossible not to seek to define the rapport between knowledge of the real and the significance that human liberty, informed by the gospel, confers on it. The Church, opposing the totalitarianism of positivism and the cowardice of submission to dominant ideology, must remember that man whom she defends and gives hope to has an objective reality.

But once this is recognized (which I will return to later), it must be noted that the natural law which manifests this design of universality is unusually vague in its application in Catholic ethics.[11] We have already seen that this notion was borrowed from Stoicism by the Fathers to counter the the gnostic disdain for creation. For them, it was a means of theologically defending the value of creation: the theological struggle was to maintain the incarnation of the Word of God at the heart of Christian thinking, so that neither the drama of human existence indicated by the Cross, nor its transfiguration through hope in the Resurrection would become void. Is it still the same today? I don't think so. In three ways, the concept of natural law fails to be in line with the theological intention of universality. First of all, the concept is used to affirm that morality can be the subject of science, of rational analysis, which all men of good will should recognize as valid, and yet at the same time current sciences (social sciences in particular) are denied the possibility of joining in with and confirming this rationality. It is as though the Church has a specific knowledge of reality, which, without owing anything to scientific research, discovers objective "real" nature on its own. But the dilemma becomes insurmountable: either it's a real science which is thus capable of answering the demands of all scientific research, or, if it's not a science but a philosophical or theological interpretation, it must in that case admit that any pronouncement it makes is risky, biased and partial! We can certainly understand that the Church does not wish to place itself at the mercy of the so-called objectivity of science (be it an exact or social science); but not so that it can, in its turn, claim an objectivity which can only be henceforth the mask for quasi-tautological authority. The serious consequence of this is that the critical task of theology, particularly with regard to totalitarian claims of certain scientific ideologies, becomes impossible; we are left with one totalitarian discourse opposing another totalitarian discourse, and the trial at Galilee continues!

In refusing critical discussion with modern science, Catholic ethics cannot maintain the concept of natural law except by depriving it of all rational coherence; and, therefore, of universal coherence. Why maintain it then? For the reason that it allows an even more dangerous fiction, i.e. the existence of a morality capable of being received by everyone everywhere, with no extenuating factors or contingencies. The illusion here seems to stem from defining universality in this case as similar to the universality of eternal principles and intangible standards; consequently there is no consideration given to the historical or cultural contingency except in a negative way. The Church speaks and its words ought to be suitable for everyone! But this takes no account of the importance of cultural differences, which become reduced to inconsequential phenomena. This is typical of all "imperialist" attitudes: any discourse by the powers-that-be is naturally universal. What was already no longer tolerable in the last few centuries at a time when European culture, despite its diversity, seemed to be the only horizon of the Church's discourse, has become, frankly, unacceptable today. The Church certainly can, but not at any cost, maintain a universal language for its faith confession, but when it tries to translate that meaning unto the moral level, it must reject a stand that can be all-encompassing only by becoming abstract. If ethics is precisely the attempt at taking reality seriously in all its diversity and clothing it with another presence, universality does not express itself in the abstraction and uniformity of a proposition, but in the quality of attention given by real men to specific circumstances, because of the gospel. No impartial observer would deny that most of the moral teachings decreed by Rome in the last century express a specific European political and social bias—and sometimes one that is purely Italian! Natural law is very cultural.

Universality cannot be expressed by one single morality. Here again, natural law runs the risk of masking, under a false objectivity, the claim of a particular culture to impose itself on all others. Relying on the eternal principles of natural law, Catholic morality does not succeed, or hardly does, in criticising its own assumptions and ends up developing a kind of moral positivism lacking spiritual depth. This last point explains the theological reason for the law's failure to lead to universality: Paul had understood that and denounced the law's hollow claim—which set itself up against God whom it should serve by presenting itself as the instrument of man's self-glorification. The recourse to natural law too often risks only being a means of rejecting any critical interpolation by the gospel.

As for the specific issue of sexualilty, an uncritical use of the concept of natural law resulted in giving value to the procreative function to the detriment of the symbolic function of sexuality. The solemn condemnations of contraceptives by Pius XI in *Casti connubi,* repeated with some qualifications by Paul VI in *Humanae vitae,* demonstrates that quite well. Sexuality, separated from those who live it, becomes a reality in and of itself, which is defined by its natural function, procreation: "But no reason, however grave, may be put forward by which anything intrinsically against nature may become conformable to nature and morally good. Since, therefore, the conjugal act is destined primarily by nature for the begetting of children, those who in exercising it deliberately frustrate its natural power and purpose sin against nature and commit a deed which is shameful and intrinsically vicious."[12] Creative freedom in the love of the human couple is absolutely left out. The only "honorable" thing is obedience to natural law, that is, to a practice of sexuality which disqualifies it from being the symbol of a loving union. In fact, the couple who does not desire more children is not condemned by Catholic morality if they renounce intercourse and live in chastity; on the other hand, they are shameful and intrinsically vicious if they use contraceptive methods. What is condemned is not a refusal of children but sexuality as a value of tenderness and love.[13] Once again, love is only love when it avoids sexuality as much as possible. And recourse to natural law seems finally to be a new way of discrediting sexuality, which is no longer recognized as a person's mode of being, but is only seen in its procreative function. Certainly Paul VI tries in *Humanae vitae* to correct this devaluation of sexuality somewhat by placing the two final ends of marriage on the same level: union of the spouses and procreation.[14] But the rest of his encyclical renews the prohibition on contraceptives and shows that the Catholic ethic continues, as I have said, to give priority to the procreative function in sexuality. All of this is based on the pretext of a natural law which actually expresses mostly the secular mistrust of sexuality in western Catholic tradition.[15]

Another characteristic should be mentioned: the importance of ecclesiastical magisterium in defining morality. The authority of the Church in matters of morality extends even to detailed regulation. The magisterium not only recalls general principles and standards deduced from the gospel but also defines in juridical terms the "do's" and "don'ts" and the detailed content of moral law. The movement towards an ecclesiastical framework for morality, begun in the Middle Ages, was clearly accentuated from the Council of Trent on. Thus, face to face with Protestantism, the Council reaffirmed (and solidified) the authority of the Church in matrimonial law: "If anyone says that matrimonial causes do not belong to ecclesiastical judges, let him be anathema."[16] Even if, as Eduard Schillebeeckx thinks,[17] this canon does not signify a denial of State authority, it carried a serious implication which gave the Catholic Church exclusive authority over marriage. On the other hand, that Council, in fighting against clandestine marriages, decreed that the legal ecclesiastical form would be necessary for the validity of the conjugal union, and that marriage between baptized Christians would be valid only when contracted before a curate (or priest delegated by him) and at least two witnesses.[18] Henceforth the problem of religious weddings vis-à-vis civil weddings became a burning topic of debate between the Catholic Church and modern European states.

The Church's desire to juridically control marriage was affirmed even more strongly when it was progressively contested by civil legislation. The French Revolution had subordinated the celebration of religious weddings to civil weddings and Pope Pius IX in the middle of the nineteenth century reaffirmed and strengthened the positions taken at Trent: ". . . No one is ignorant of, or can be ignorant of the fact that matrimony is truly and properly one of the seven sacraments of the evangelical law, instituted by Jesus Christ our Lord. It necessarily follows that: 1) among the faithful there cannot be a marriage which is not at the same time a sacrament; every other union between Christians outside of the sacrament, made in virtue of any civil law, is none other than disgraceful and base concubinage, repeatedly condemned by the Church; 2) the sacrament can never be separated from the marriage contract, and only the Church has the power to regulate those matters which pertain to matrimony."[19]

By likening civil marriage to concubinage, the catholic Church, in its desire to affirm its rights with regard to matrimonial legislation, broke with one of the oldest traditions in Christianity. It particularly manifested its desire to fight against the secularity of the State, which was a sign of the disastrous secularization of society in the Church's eyes. This last point seems to motivate the Catholic moral teaching at the present time. The Catholic Church has a systematically negative interpretation of the evolution of European society. Up until Vatican II, it saw secularization only as a secularism destroying religious values, and in secularity it saw an anti-clerical attitude. Of course, the modern evolution did take a position against Christianty (partly because of Catholicism's negative reactions), but the massive rejection of Catholic magisterium[20] confined Catholic morality to a defensive position. And this was all the more defensive since the gigantic effort at moralization undertaken since the Council of Trent (paralleled by a similar movement in the Reformation Churches) found itself contested as to its very foundation. The effort to define borders, to Christianize society via morality and general penetential practices ran up against the modern discourse—on freedom of conscience, on the secularity of schools, on moral and political pluralism. . . . Why? Because the attempt was marked by two unpardonable defects for the modern "enlightened" conscience. The first defect stems from the fact that this morality is imposed from outside by the pressure of a controlling structure, which thus appears as a major obstacle to the development of freedom. Secondly, this morality is associated with fear of sin, and of error, and consequently can only lead to legalism and conservatism.[21] The countless manuals of morality that appear from the beginning of the seventeenth century are all marked with an evident concern for pedagogy: the priests needed readily usable material for penetential practice. But pedagogy quickly leads to legalism especially when it resorts to the fear of error and the concern for not violating the law, i.e. staying in line with the commandments of the Church. The penitiential practice which becomes scrupulous, and even fastidious, in the sexual domain particularly, obviously reinforces the formalism of morality.[22] More and more, morality becomes objectivized into "duties that God imposes on us" as the *Cathéchisme à l'usage des Diocèses de France* of 1938 states; salvation is in terms of a scrupulous exercise of obedience, with God as the guarantor of those duties and also as the Judge who repays man according to his merits.

This effort at moralization was certainly not without fruit,[23] but at the same time it nourished a fundamental misunderstanding of Christianity and Christian ethics. Even today most criticisms made of Christian ethics find their basis and their arguments in this legalistic and authoritarian practice, which, in the sexual and conjugal domain, is more guilt-forming than liberating. And if there is a renewal today in Catholic ethics, it stems from the very sharp criticism of this practice.[24]

*   *   *

To conclude: the system of Catholic ethics that was formed (partly against Protestantism) in the course of our modern era has been founded on an ambiguous conception of man; man is invited to submit to natural laws on the one hand because these come indirectly from God and the Church authenticates and protects them, but on the other hand, man must place himself under other laws—those being supernatural. Man is not man until he consents to his state as a creature, in submission to the laws of Creation like all the other creatures; but yet man only fulfills himself by denying, in a certain way, his condition as a mortal and contingent creature so that he might anticipate by "asceticism" and spirituality the blessed immortality which is his real destiny.

In the domain of sexuality, this ambiguity comes forth in full force; should one submit to the natural law of procreation or renounce all sexual practice in deference to the supernatural love of God, which is not to be compared to human fleshly love? Which authority should be empahsized: the authority of natural law or of supernatural law? To remove this ambiguity, Catholic ethics had to split in two: for the layman, natural morality; for the clerics, supernatural law. But how can this distinction, which is hardly biblical and even hardly traditional, be justified? How can one support a distinction which is not really held to—since the supernatural and sacramental value of the marital bond is affirmed? And why was conjugal practice regulated only by recourse to natural laws (for example in regard to responsible motherhood)? On the other hand, if there is an emphasis (as was true with the Catholic pastorate right after the war) on the supernatural values of conjugal love to the point of relegating the procreative end to a secondary rank; and if, then, sexuality can also signify the love of God, how does one now justify ecclesiastical celibacy and the superiority of the ideal it represents? How does one allow the values of sexual morality to be defined by celibates, if their situation no longer *de jure* confers on them an ontological superiority and special authority?

All these questions are being asked by countless Catholics today, priests and laymen,[25] and they are indeed pressing questions.

b) Protestant Ethics[26]

The Reformation had placed the emphasis on the grace of God as the foundation of human existence, and consequently of ethics. Thus, for Calvin sanctification is the necessary result of justification.[27] From the beginning Protestants had strongly emphasized moral responsibility, even if it was not always understood in the same way. Thus the Reformers — and in the twentieth century the theologians of the dialectical school (Barth, Brunner, Bultmann) — understood responsibililty to be the capacity given to man by the vivifying grace of God to *respond* with love to the love of God, and described ethics as the response attempted by the man who allows himself to be moved by the Spirit of God: "Obeying the Law is thus not within our own power but is the work whose power comes from the Spirit to cleanse our hearts of corruption and softens them to obey righteousness. Therefore the practice of the Law for Christians is absolutely impossible outside of faith."[28]

At other times, especially under the influence of the *Aufklärung,* Protestant theologians emphasized man's moral responsibility before God as the fundamental characteristic of anthropology. Man is a moral being and ethics is not so much the result of faith as the royal road that leads to it. Influenced by Kant, himself descended from the Protestant pietistic stock, theology exalted moral responsibility as the very place for the experience of finiteness and freedom for man who is called freely to submit to moral law.[29] The essence of religion is in ethics. Such a position (which as we know was able to lead Protestant Churches to slip into moralism) is the result, perhaps a bit exaggerated but nonetheless true, of the vision of man, with strict reference to biblical tradition, that was defended by the Reformation. We need to pause on this important point.

"Our wisdom . . . consists almost entirely of two parts: the knowledge of God and of ourselves." Calvin's *Institutes of the Christian Religion* begins with this admirable formula where the structural link between theology and anthropology is immediately affirmed. If man can only know himself through his relation to God, it is primarily because he is God's *creature*. Everything hinges on this acknowledgement, without which man radically lacks authenticity and being. Man *per se* is never spoken about in Protestant tradition, but always man is called to acknowledge his true status as a creature of God. Ever since then body and soul—even though in previous western tradition they were spoken of as two distinct realities—no longer designate two separate entities (one essentially immortal and the other assigned to finiteness and sin) but designate two aspects of the one same man, a sinner called to salvation. The soul, no less than the body, is a creature of God: if man refuses to acknowledge God, it is his entire being—body, spirit and soul—that is consigned to death, and lacks authenticity. Inversely, the justified man becomes wholly "regenerate," as Calvin says, in soul, spirit and body. The drama of human existence does not occur in the tension between body and soul, between visible and invisible, but rather between sin and justification, between unbelief and faith.

This is why Protestantism, even when it exalts ethics to the point of almost dissolving religion, always links ethical responsibility to knowledge of God, on which it depends and to which it leads.[30] This emphasis on the fundamentally theological character of ethics is one of the essential characteristics of Protestant morality—but along with all the problems that arise because of the distrust of an anthropological analysis, the greatest risk is an idealistic morality. I will return to this point later. Nevertheless, in the most vital kind of Protestantism, i.e. Puritanism or German Pietism, a very strong and concrete attachment to Sacred Scripture kept morality from becoming too idealistic. But in all the different groups, the primary principle is for man to manifest his link with God via his moral attitude (along the lines of obedience with the Puritans and along the lines of affectivity with the Pietists).

On the level of sexual and conjugal ethics, the results of such an anthropological perspective were very important. The Reformation immediately gave great value to marriage, first of all because the Bible does, but also because it simultaneously discovered through biblical testimony another dimension of the body and sexuality. The distrust throughout Protestant history of consecrated celibates is not based on ecclesiastical reasons but on anthropological ones. God willed man to be a sexed creature and it is disregard for His will to consider sexuality as unimportant or even as an evil thing. That which is evil is not sexuality but rather the violence and lust (murderous for some) which it can express. The dividing line is not between sexuality and chastity, but between a sexuality of lust and a sexuality of love. In general, Protestant ethics mistrusts sexuality much less than Catholic ethics does. The issue is never sexuality per se (which is good since it is willed by the Creator) but rather that which it can signify. Will it express tenderness or lust, love or violence? If there is any distrust, it is in regard to what man himself (when he stops allowing himself to be transformed by the gospel) can make of sexuality: violence and disorder, destruction of family and society! Because of this, there is an opposition betwen the two kinds of love, which are classically designated as eros and agape. Eros is natural love, desire-love which values the other insofar as the other can contribute to the good of the subject. Agape, in the image of the love of God in Christ, is a gift of self, freely given with no ulterior motives.[31] It is necessary, then, constantly to purify sexuality of its natural eroticism and convert it to agape which comes from the Spirit of God Himself. It is immediately obvious that this kind of juxtaposition can become ambiguous: in actuality it often led to an idealistic ethic which was incapable, in the end, of giving meaning to erotic reality. A subtle dualism, which resulted in making believers guilty all over again in the face of desire and erotic pleasure, threatened to become established anew. Meanwhile, however, the other issue that this opposition highlighted is that sexual life is determined not by natural values that can be sanctified, but by a radical ethical choice which in the end concerns our relation to God. Agape is not simply the fulfillment of eros: it also restores its natural vitality. But such a transformation is impossible to man without the action and grace of God. And this is one of the central themes of Protestant ethics: it is the whole man, in his bodily and spiritual totality, which is to be transformed by the grace of God. Without this grace, there is no ethic because no tree that is planted incorrectly can bear fruit!

The second characteristic of Protestant ethics, it seems to me, is its search for biblical models allowing Christians to manifest the uniqueness of the life of faith. If natural law is referred to, and even often invoked in the seventeenth and eighteenth centuries, it is in order to recall that it is a gift from God the creator, and that it can only be known through Scripture.[32] The Bible is thus constantly referred to because of a conviction that to live as a Christian is not to be like everyone else but instead to separate oneself from everyone else's behavior. Even here this kind of attitude is not entirely free of ambiguity; it can easily lead to the well-known moral rigidity which seems to charaterize Protestantism so often to those on the outside, i.e. the Protestant's nervous tightening up which so often occurs when he is forced by his conscience to judge himself according to the opinion of others to discover whether he is different or not! But inversely, this concern can also manifest a real willingness to accept the eschatological tension which runs through the gospel, which challenges all attempts at restricting ethics to the self-satisfaction of a "duty accomplished."

Indeed, the same temptation which in ecclesiastical matters has so often led Protestantism into the formation of sects—where the "real" Christians gather together, who are different from the others because "really saved"—has often led in moral matters to the temptation of exemplarism. One must live an exemplary life in order to reach towards perfection and especially in order to be a model to a world which does not really know the Gospel. In this case, the risk is great (and has often occured in Protestantism) of having ethics become rigid and selective: it serves to separate the sheep from the goats! But it would be unfair not to see the positive aspect of this risk, which is to introduce the critical eschatological factor into the Church and into ethics itself by recalling that the Kingdom of God that is hoped for cannot become confused with either the Church, or with a life-style, or a society, or a culture.

The various Protestant Churches thus tried to draw out from the teachings of Scripture models which allowed them to maintain themselves in tension with the world. Ethics was considered as the serious meditation on the examples furnished by the history of Israel, the gospels and the life of the primitive Church. The acknowledgment of the Bible as a revealed text assures a paradigmatic character to everything it says. Not without a certain naïveté (which current Protestanism should no longer permit itself), the principle of the current relevance of the biblical text is posited in ethics as well as in theology. Given the lack of real critical reflection, at least up until the nineteenth century, there are no distinctions made between biblical teachings and the social and cultural context from which they are taken. The concept of historical distance will need some time to come to fruition in this area.[33]

In matters of sexual ethics, this desire to follow biblical teaching as closely as possible seems to me to have had two consequences. The first concerns the man/woman relationship, and the second the image of the family.

Rereading biblical texts carefully, especially those at the beginning of Genesis, the Protestant moralists discovered that the relationship between man and woman has first of all a structural value: everything else depends on the success of this relationship,—the destiny of individuals as well as of societies. The success of the human couple is first and foremost; the success of individuals and of society comes second and is determined by the success of the former. The model proposed by the

Bible carries a strict hierarchy in the couple, man being the head of the wife, and the woman owing him submission. But this hierarchy is conceived of as permitting the healthy accomplishment of the reciprocal duties to which the spouses must consent in order to ensure authenticity to their union and the well-being which is indispensible to social order as a whole. The couple is the archetype for all relationships, just as the family is the primary model for all social groups. In the words of a Puritan in an anonymous text from 1608: the husband/wife rapport is like "the major wheels in a clock which ensure the good functioning of all the other wheels."[34]

Starting from this consciousness of the importance and social responsibility of the couple, sensitivity can certainly unfold, and love can grow between spouses as well as so many other good consequences, but it can never go so far as to become the disorderly passion which ruins families and societies. Love becomes tenderness, respect, acceptance of the role that the Creator has ordained to each one within the couple, especially so that the hierarchical order in the couple never becomes the tyranny of man over woman. Here again the influence of the biblical texts is present: the submission of the wife to the husband is maintained along side of the affirmation of their fundamental unity in the plan of God.

Because the unity of the couple is the primary structure of human order as God has willed it, adultery is therefore a very serious matter. It undermines not only conjugal order but social order itself. But adultery does not express itself only in sexual infidelity; it can also slip into conjugal relationships themselves, especially if sensuality overshadows tenderness, and if sexuality is not purified by a respectful love for the spouse. But here again, Protestantism, because of its attention to the Bible, does not simply repeat what patristic tradition has said on these same themes; it is suspicious of the irrationality and disorder that sexuality can introduce into marriage, but it also speaks of its value when it is in service to affection and tenderness. To counter adultery, there is preaching, not of a heroic asceticism, but of concrete and attentive care for one another. William Gouge, a famous Puritan, wrote that the best remedy against adultery was for "the husband and wife to delight in each other, to preserve a pure and fervent love between themselves, by according each other the kindness and good-will which is guaranteed and sanctified by Sacred Scripture."[35] Since the man/woman relationship determines the future of individuals and of societies, it is necessary not only to protect this relationship against all that can threaten it from the outside, but to make plain, from within, its richness and meaning. Thus begins a reflection on the couple, which aims more and more at bringing out its value, by going beyond the traditional notion of procreation as the primary justification for conjugal life.[36]

The Reformers had already reinstated the authority of the husband and the father of the family. This continued in the Protestant conjugal ethics right up into the twentieth century. The authority of man is also exercised in the intellectual and religious realms: he should instruct his wife and explain the Bible to her. The biblical reference in this area was Ephesians 5, continually taken up and meditated on. A literal interpretation of this text defines a style of relationship where the superior party, in this case the husband, must constantly remember his duty to love his wife, and to guide her not as a slave, but as his own flesh. So the head of the family has a demanding vocation which includes an important spiritual aspect. The family is the basic cell-group, not only of society but also in the Church where the father is the minister and the pastor.[37]

The significance attached to the father is also the result of the specifically Protestant affirmation of the necessity of serving God in the secular world and of not withdrawing from it. Before the Reformation, the word "vocation" was never used to describe professional activity or a secular social status. Luther was the first to translate work and trade by *Beruf* (vocation). A vocation is no longer reserved for those who make religious vows, but belongs to all men wherever they are and however they are called to serve God. There are not two worlds, two states, two humanities, but one single world, created by God, and one single vocation: ". . . it matters little whether men be bourgeois, peasants, shoemakers, tailors, writers, cavalrymen, masters or servants, etc. For without these states of life . . . no city and no country can exist; none of these conditions are, in and of themselves, contrary to God and if anyone desires to serve God, he should not abandon his state and slip into a convent or monastery or go and form some kind of sect."[38] All of life in its many aspects (professional, familial, political) is called upon to become a place to praise the Lord, whenever man responds to his divine vocation. The result of this on the conjugal level is decisive and direct: marriage is not a concession to the weakness of those who are unable to enter into a religious vocation, but instead the very condition and means of a Christian vocation. The couple must recognize the call of the Gospel right where they are and in their very manner of life. This is why the emphasis in Protestant ethics is on personal responsibility much more than on obedience to laws decreed by the Church. The Church's role is not to take the spouses' place, but, through its ministers, to recall the gospel and the need for responsibility. Because of this there are no declarations as specific as those that the Roman magisterium multiplies on sexual and conjugal questions. There are no regulations of this kind in Protestantism. Anytime a Churchman is asked about the Protestant position on this or that moral area he answers by referring to the responsibility of Christians who are involved in that area.

The refusal of an elaborated position must be accompanied by a very strong interiorization of moral standards. That can be seen in the almost total absence of personal aural confession. Whereas the Catholic is called to judge himself according to detailed regulations of the Church, to confess his departures from that standard, and be pardoned by the very authority that defines these duties, the Protestant is called not to formal obedience but to judge for himself, in the face of the gospel's demands, what his obedience should be. In some ways, he never comes to an end of his soul-searching, and it is not within the jurisdiction of the Church or its ministers to release him from this soul-searching. Freed of casuistry, the Protestant nevertheless runs the risk of being hemmed in by a scrupulous morality and a scrupulous conscience.

The nature of Protestant ethics can be clearly demonstrated through two issues where Protestant and Catholic ethics differ!

1) Sexuality and Contraception

Whereas the Roman Catholic teaching forbids any recourse to contraceptives in the name of respecting natural law,[39] Protestant churches reacted positively very early on, to thinking and action concerning birth control at the turn of the twentieth century.[40] This happened for extremely significant theological reasons: the final end of marriage is not procreation first and foremost, but the unity of the spouses. Anything that encourages this unity is good. Now sexual abstinence, advocated by Catholic Churches as a means of regulation, cannot be in line with the goal of unity of the spouses, since, in a certain way, sexuality is discredited by being reduced to its procreative function. If, along with biblical testimony, it is recognized that sexuality can be the sign and the means of the spouses' unity—with the child as a sign resulting from that unity— it is right not to condemn the spouses to the fear of unwanted children each time they wish to be united in intercourse.

This is because "nature" cannot constitute a sufficient reference point here, and the will of God cannot be confused with the adventure of a sperm seeking to fertilize an egg! Protestant texts recall that conjugal life in all its aspects is a vocation and a responsibility, i.e. inscribing the existence of the spouses into a life-project where human intelligence and discernment collaborate in God's creation. "As evangelical Christians, we do not acknowledge so-called 'nature' as the supreme reference point, but rather God who delegated to man the power to dominate nature and who commanded and permitted him to form and transform nature so that community life would be possible to men."[41] Therefore the decision belongs to the spouses themselves; the Church is not meant to dictate their conduct, but should only recall the context in which their decision should be made: "We are looking for evangelical Christians a) to decide together, conscious of their responsibility before God, if and how they wish to "plan their family . . . b) [and] for spouses to seek together, in an attitude of mutual regard and after informed conjugal consultation, the method which would affect the equilibrium of the union of the couple the least."[42]

The answer by a Protestant theologian to a reporter is indicative of the fundamental option in Protestant ethics: "Should the Church ascribe to itself the right to legislate in this matter?" "No, The final decision is a matter between us and God. The Church can only point out reasons pro and con [and] . . . show under what circumstances it considers the use of these means to be permissible and even legitimate, and then to leave Christians to make a final decision in direct communion with their Lord."[43] In practice, Protestant couples have freely used contraceptives without feeling at any time that they were betraying their Christian or human vocation. This is why Protestant thinking has had so much difficulty understanding the Catholic position, as expressed again recently in the encyclical *Humanae vitae*. The question of contraception brings forward two different stands on sexuality, on the role of the Church, and on the ultimate reference point for moral action.

2) Abortion

The difference is not quite so clear in the question of abortion.[44] Although there is a similar rejection of abortion by Protestants and Catholics, that rejection stems from two very different mentalities and ethical approaches. Whereas Protestant Churches consider the surest means of fighting abortion to be the promotion of a responsible use of contraceptives, Catholicism censures both things equally: artificial contraceptives are considered abortive and abortion as a means of population control is condemned.[45]

Protestantism has refused to lump these two things together: "We should not confuse abortion and contraception. In the first case, a fertile egg is destroyed; in the second, fertilization is prevented. Abortion is an irreversible action, whereas contraception is a preventative action."[46] Contraception involves only the freedom of the two partners while abortion concerns the life of a third person as well. This is indeed why the approach to abortion cannot be the same as to contraception. The latter only involves the life of the couple whereas abortion raises the issue of man's right to destroy a life. Every life is a gift to man that should be welcomed and cared for. He cannot refuse this gift without an extremely serious reason. Therefore all the Protestant texts begin by recalling the extreme gravity of abortion.

But there again, the criteria is not an absolute law or principle but the awareness of the serious stake in the human situation, an awareness enlightened by the Word of God. If it must be recalled that man is never the absolute master of the life of another (even of an embryo), it must also be remembered that, according to the gospel, obedience to the Word of God is not obedience to principles but the acceptance of the concrete claims of the other with all his questions and difficulties. When distress engulfs a pregnant woman, what should we be most attentive to? Here again, Protestant ethics refuses to legislate but calls for all the concerned parties (mother, family, State) to pay strict attention to the facts and weigh the situation. Thus, when Swiss Catholic Bishops make a declaration on abortion, they make reference to the seriousness of an action which violently supresses a life, to the protection for the child threatened by the arbitrary power of adults, to the duty of the State to protect life—all excellent and necessary things. But they do not say one word about the tragic situation of the pregnant women, except to invite the State to furnish them welfare. The real distress of countless women driven to abortion is no longer noted or acknowledged. However, when the Council of Federation of Protestant Churches in Switzerland speaks on the same issue, it recalls that "pregnancy should be able to be accepted by the mother with joy. The parents should be prepared to fulfill their task as educators with love and devotion. However, experience and statistics show that not all mothers or couples are prepared to greet pregnancy this way. Moreover, the protection of a future life should not constitute an absolute principle in each case that arises. In certain circumstances, the assistance given to a woman in distress will prevail over all other considerations. An unwanted pregnancy can put a woman in insurmountable difficulty and plunge her into anguish and despair. In such a case, after a careful study of all the facts, an abortion can be justified as the only solution and be chosen responsibly."[47]

Abortion is not legitimized or prohibited according to principles, but according to a dual concern for the concrete situation of a fellow man and for the teaching in the Word of God. This absence of principles certainly has the disadvantage of allowing a diversity of opinions in Protestantism which sometimes leads to vagueness in interpretations of biblical teaching for particular circumstances. Often it leaves each Protestant alone to face an ultimately personal decision; but it is probably the vocation of Protestant ethics continually to point beyond itself to its foundation, which is limitless.

These two examples demonstrate, I believe, the pros and cons of Protestant ethics. Its most serious problem is its inability to formulate an ecclesiastical scheme except along the lines of the pietistic model of the *ecclesiola in ecclesia.* The temptation for the Protestant moralist is continually to refer people to their own individual conscience,[48] which risks leading people to align themselves with the dominant view. The personal ethical risk, after all, very often leads to trite conformity! This risk is even greater when community support defaults and when the Protestant moreover has neither the habit nor the desire to consult anyone else in making his decisions; and since today, consulting the Bible, which served for so long as an ethical paradigm, is not without serious problems. This is undoubtedly the trickiest point. Founded on the authority of Scripture, Protestant ethics cannot avoid facing all the problems raised by the new historical consciousness since the *Aufklärung.*[49] Henceforth the task of Protestant ethics is to begin by reflecting on the conditions and possibilities of interpreting Scripture.[50] In its own way, this book is an attempt to establish an ethical analysis on a serious hermeneutic, of confronting a critical reading of the text of Scripture with a critical reading of the current moral discourse. It is not up to me to say if this attempt has succeeded, but it is my conviction that there is no ethic possible, in the Protestant tradition at least, without this hermeneutical confrontation.

*   *   *

In the West there are two different Christian ethics. Here at the end of the twentieth century, faced with criticism directed at each of these ethical systems, and, moreover, faced with the secularization they suffer from, perhaps the time when we should reevaluate these divergencies has come. We could ask ourselves if Catholic ethics does not urgently need being pulled out of the quagmire where its concept of natural law has led it, by a serious confrontation, i.e. a theologically honest confrontation, with Scripture. Of course this also implies that in its very teaching, the Church would accept that it doesn't already know everything but would allow itself, through the Word of God present in the Scriptures and in the experience of the faithful, to be dispossessed of its hierarchical conception of authority which constantly transforms the liberating gospel into an ideology that justifies the Catholic system.

Likewise, we could ask if Protestant ethics is not urgently in need of liberation from its incorrigible individualistic idealism and its fundamental naïveté with regard to Scripture, through serious reflection, i.e. a theologically honest reflection, on the role and function of the Law and on its anthropological foundation. Of course this would also mean that Protestants must cease believing that everything begins and ends with their individual consciences, and must recognize the ecclesiastical dimension of ethics and the interpretations of previous traditions, which cannot be lightly dismissed except through pretentious vanity. Protestant churches must also realize that there is a way of referring to Scripture which risks being only a search for the justification of attitudes that in the last analysis are conformist. Some stubborn refusals of Catholicism should alert Protestants to the power that ecclesiastical authority can represent in ethical matters: isn't Catholicism in the end more courageous on certain points by refusing to align itself with certain modern values?

The time has come for a debate between western Christians on the validity of their ethical stands. I hope this chapter will in its own limited way, contribute to that.

8. Conclusion

What can we conclude at the end of this long (and yet brief and generalized) journey through history?[1] It can at least be said that Christian tradition demonstrates an ambiguous attitude towards sexuality: ". . . while admitting that in general, sexuality is good insofar as it is from God, Christian tradition had a long struggle to discover that it is perhaps not evil; throughout centuries, it juxtaposed two basic assumptions without being able to reconcile them, which did not have the same authority but seemed to carry the same weight: the radical goodness of sexuality and the radical evil (even if only venial) of sexual pleasure."[2] This is the best way to summarize the impression that is left by this study of history! In fact, the Christian tradition in this realm is the result of the conflict between the promises that biblical tradition presents "in the beginning" of the human adventure and the historical contingencies which always seem to call for a rigid control of sexuality. The biblical promise is sufficiently strong so that the meaning of sexuality always remains an open issue (a permanently unsettled issue all throughout the Church's history), but the reality is sufficiently impressive so that the ethical solutions proposed were stamped by fear and distrust.

The Christian tradition can be criticized on at least three points. Briefly (since I've already explained these points), Christianity showed itself incapable of thinking of sexuality in terms of love and because of that it was not able to give marriage, until perhaps recently, a truly positive value, and finally that it linked its teaching in this area to an exercise of power which led to a serious discreditation of Christian ethics.

The first point is striking, especially with the Church Fathers: a priori sexuality is ranked alongside the evil forces that inhabit man; it secretly plots with sin, and its violence and irrationality is feared. It was not thought of as possibly becoming, in love, the very sign of a real acceptance of the other, the action par excellence of tenderness. Christian education in this area is dominated by fear and is rarely motivated by the beauty of sexuality. Sensitive to the dramatic character of human existence which sexuality seems to express better than any other reality, Christian tradition never attains (or hardly ever) wondrous amazement in the face of this call of man towards woman, in the face of the pleasure which unites them and seals their union. All the biblical themes which tend in this direction seem forgotten. Undoubtedly this was because the incorrect reading of the texts at the beginning of Genesis prevailed, which interpreted the story of "Paradise Lost" as an irreversible destiny: man and woman are condemned to live out sexuality on earth with violence and domination. Certainly, there is a promise of another life, but only in the Kingdom to come, where it will be manifested precisely in the abolition of sexual contingencies. Paul's text, "There is neither Jew nor Greek, there is neither slave nor free, there is neither male nor female; for you are all one in Christ Jesus" (Gal 3:28), is read as an eschatological promise; in Christ, that is to say, in the Kingdom to come, all differences will be abolished beginning with (and particularly) sexual differences. Sexuality is thus the index of human misery. But Paul is not speaking of the future, but of the present, and he affirms that through faith in Christ, i.e. in the new historical space which faith creates, the three great human dividing lines (ethnic, economical-political, and sexual) can be abolished *insofar as they express alienation* between men. What is abolished in Christ is division insofar as it is hate, and not difference insofar as it is a relational condition. The age-old "curse" of Genesis 3:16, the objectivized expression of human experience, is thus overcome: man and woman can rediscover each other in a mode other than that of violence and domination, just as the Jew and Greek, and the slave and free can.

Christian tradition has a lot of difficulty in taking this promise seriously. It constantly relegates it into the future, or when it seeks to make it concrete here, it's through an abolition of sexuality. In this way, the exaltation of virginity is often justified by the affirmation that virginity is a quasi-angelic state, very close to the perfect state of the elect in Paradise. By denying their sexuality, men and women can better attain perfection. But this is in absolute contradiction to the meaning in the Bible! The Bible is certainly cognizant of all the dramatic violence that can be expressed through sexuality, but it never condemns sexuality, because it acknowledges sexuality as the best locus where a man and woman can experience the meaning of God's promise.

A devaluation of marriage obviously corresponds to this difficulty in associating sexuality with tenderness and acceptance of the other. If there is a long-standing polemic tradition vis-à-vis marriage, we certainly owe it to Christian tradition. The countless descriptions in the Church Fathers of the cares of the marital state are testimonies to this negative vision: marriage ultimately turns one away from God! And why? Not only because it means involvement with a great number of material and secular tasks, but particularly because it redirects towards a creature the love that is due to God alone. Here again, it must be stated that this departs from the biblical tradition. Whereas the biblical tradition calls for an understanding of the profound link which unites man to God, through the wonder of the force of love between a man and a woman, and conversely, an understanding the link between man and woman by reference to the bond of love that links God to His people, patristic and monastic tradition oppose the love for God to love for the creature: to love woman is no longer wholly to love God. The error here is once again theological. The God who is at issue here is conceived of as the Absolute who is beyond history and human contingency. We become united to Him by renouncing apparent reality. What a profound ignorance of the meaning of the Incarnation![3]

Anything that can be said after this to justify the conjugal institution will always stem from this negative foundation. But here again, the teaching of the most ancient biblical tradition will impede the Church from going to the ultimate point of opposing marriage to holiness; on the contrary, as we have seen, from Middle Ages on, there is a slow revaluation of marriage which results in a recognition of the sacramentality of the conjugal bond. But even there, the ambiguity continues in the Catholic Church when it affirmed the superiority of virginity over marriage at the Council of Trent (sixteenth century). The Reformation indeed marks a return to biblical tradition on this point, even if marriage is reinvested with value for political as well as theological reasons.

There is another point, finally, where it seems necessary to lay aside Christian tradition: the link between the teaching of "Christian" sexual morality and a certain kind of exercise of power by the Church.[4] Because sexuality was felt to be an ambiguous mystery, disturbing and yet rich with promise, it was the object of an ever-deepening control and interest. In the West, especially from the end of the Middle Ages on, it is through a discourse on sexuality that was more and more detailed that the Church expresses both its power and the manner in which it understands the exercise of that power. We cannot fail to see the connection between the growing hierarchical direction of the Catholic Church culminating in Vatican I and the development of a stand on sexuality and control of its practice. Likewise there is a rapport between the challenge to episcopal and papal power by the Reformation and its refusal of ecclesiastical celibacy. For to seek to reduce the mystery of sex at any cost, and thereby control it, as the Catholic Church had done, is clearly to express a desire for power, a refusal to accept the irreducibility of the mystery of the other. Once sexuality becomes an object and is separated from the totality of human endeavor to be catalogued into actions of "do's" and "don'ts," we can be sure that this is indicative of a reinforcement of the powers-that-be. The history of recent Christian tradition is a striking example of this: the more the discourse on sex was elaborated, the more it became really a question of the power of some to define for others what the good truly is, i.e. the permissible and the non-permissible. It is probably the link between the power of clerics and sexual morality which explains the violent rejection of the ethical teaching of the Church. Rightly so, I must honestly add, since nothing in biblical tradition justifies that link. It is necessary, in the name of the gospel and all of biblical tradition, to contest the claims of certain streams in Christianity to define and impose a sexual morality formulated according to principles that only a certain few have the privilege (the divine right?) to interpret.[5] Each time Christianity has approached sexual ethics this way, it has been less through a desire to teach ethics than through a concern to organize the exercise of power in a more rigorous fashion. The example of history had definitively taught us that the discourse on sex, more than on any other subject, can hide a discourse on (and a practice of) power.

This in no way signifes that any moral teaching is impossible but rather that anyone so engaged cannot avoid the instruction addressed to him by the gospel: every moralist should remember that Peter only received the responsibility of "feeding" his brothers, (John 21:15–17) after having had the bitter experience of his own renegade weakness! And the Church has too often forgotten the silence of Christ, tracing in the sand with his finger while the scribes and Pharisees denounced the adulterous woman; the gospel is not found in a denunciation of the law's guarantees, but in the simple words of Jesus to the woman: "Neither do I condemn you; go and do not sin again" (John 8:1-11).

Any moral teaching that is not rooted in that kind of compassion—in a sharing of common weakness and common sin—can only be the mask of a suspect desire for power. But, as biblical tradition clearly shows, it is also possible to illuminate the meaning of the great realities of existence without violence. From that point of view, the history of Christian tradition in sexual matters certainly does not hold only negative elements. I can draw three major lessons from its long history: Christianty followed the work of de-sacredizing sexuality that was begun in Israel; by reinstating sexuality on a human plane, it made its stakes and its drama more apparent; finally, it attempted, in its struggle against ancient dualism that was always ready to reintroduce itself into Christian thinking, to think of the body along the lines of kind of presence, as an icon of the Spirit. Yet today, these three propositions seem vitally important to me, in a social and cultural context which is witnessing the resurgence of very ancient demons. I will speak of this in my last chapter where I will discuss the significance that present-day Christianity can ascribe to sexuality.

V

Man and Woman: A Humanity to Be Created: Ethical Reflections

Having examined the sources and the history of the Christian ethic of sexuality and marriage, one further step is still necessary: a discussion of the possible significance that Christian faith could ascribe to the shared life of a man and woman. In such a discussion, it is imperative to keep in mind today's context (Chapter 1) and the basis for that significance (chapters 2 and 3), as well as tradition which is simultaneously a help and a hindrance (chapter 4). My procedure entails three stages: first, a resume of what could be called the Christian point of view on the human significance of sexuality. Second, an attempt to translate this specifically Christian approach to sexuality into ethical terms: how do we interpret the conviction that the human couple—as place of sexual encounter—does not really exist unless love overcomes lust and unless the acknowledgement of the mystery of the other overcomes the affirmation of self-sufficiency? Finally, I will discuss why, from this perspective, it seems urgent for Christian ethics to reconsider the meaning and value of eroticism.

1. The Human Significance of Sexuality: A Theological Interpretation

Sexuality is a human matter in Christianity (which is faithful to biblical tradition on this point) and not a divine force which propels man out of his mortal condition or, conversely, precipitates him into a demon-hell. Now de-sacredized, sex has to do with ... the other sex: it signifies otherness and one is compelled to take it seriously as the potential for all relationships. Sexual otherness and God's otherness are thus connected: just as a person cannot take possession of God, the All-Other who reveals Himself by hiding Himself (cf. I Kings 19:11-13), neither, then, can he reduce the other to himself without completely losing that other. A sexual relationship is not the fusion of two beings in an undifferentiated whole, but the relationship of two people whose mystery remains ultimately irreducible. This is a major point, because it explains why, from the Christian perspective, sexuality is always linked to the development of a relationship between two people, whose individual mystery is not dispelled in sexual union. Sexuality is not human unless it is structured into a situation, a project, an exchange, where the sexual aspect is only one of the elements. Any rejection of otherness, whether it be in reducing the other to a body offered either for one's pleasure, for a reproductive function, or for a possible experience of the sacred, is from that point on, a perversion.

Reinstated to the human dimension only, sexuality of course loses the tragic or fantastic grandeur which it has when it is linked to the impersonal cosmic forces of life and death that come upon man. Instead, it becomes an area where human responsibility is involved: how does one carry on a relationship with another and not fall short, when sexuality, insofar as it is an instinct, pressures a person to take no account of the other? Christianity, in its concern for this ethical aspect, has been made very aware of the risks that sexuality brings to bear in interpersonal relationships. It would be quite foolish or naïve to find fault with it; the most audacious defenders of sexual freedom do not go to the point of authorizing rape or sexual abuse of minors. There is a dramatic aspect to sexuality, an implicit violence, that no one can deny. But Christianity has refused to see this fatalistically,[1] and has explained it by recourse to the theological category of sin. In so doing, it has also refused to make it commonplace, by categorizing it, simply, as a problem of man's evil desire, be it personal or social. Sexuality reveals that man is grappling with a mysterious reality which inhabits him but which, however, he is responsible for, i.e. lust, the force of desire that can destroy or create, push aside a person or receive him. Christianity's originality, in taking up and interpreting the scriptural data, lies in simultaneously recognizing the violence of desire, the death-force which inhabits men, and yet refusing, by calling it sin, to make it a fatalistic force. For sin paradoxically implies an anterior state of innocence and the historical contingency of evil—in this case, the lust and violence which flows from it. Consequently, in the Christian perspective, sexuality, like Rousseau said of man, is "naturally good," but is always encountered and experienced as "depraved" in the normal operation of civilization and history. Sexuality is thus neither an ordinary hygienic function of sexual organs, a natural pleasure having no consequences, nor a tragic encounter with the forces of death and abjection; it is the gamble, the difficult choice, where the ambiguity of the existence of man, "destined" to be good but "inclined" towards evil,[2] is revealed better than anywhere else.

The obviously tragic and ambiguous aspect of human sexuality also explains why Christian tradition sought so desperately to understand the link between sexuality and spirituality—but also why it could not really succeed. On one hand it always had a tendency to contrast spirituality and sexuality; and on the other hand, in order to do away with dualism, it gave value to the body, since it was called to become the icon of the Spirit. This last point is very important because this is what prevented Christianity from becoming a "western hinduism" where the spiritual ideal is to flee any and all incarnation. For whoever says "body" also says "sexuality" even if his theological thinking objects to this identification. This is why Christian tradition, which seems to have a definite mistrust of sexuality, is nevertheless one of the religious traditions that has shown the most concern for sexuality by defending the nobility and grandeur of the body in spite of everything (and often in spite of itself)—by defending it as the place of a person's presence to himself, to others and to the world, and as the place of a spiritual experience. Therefore it is not by chance, nor is it disgraceful, if the language of Christian mystics is so often erotic. The fundamental stand in Christian tradition is to consider the body as an expression of the Spirit and as the visibility of the mysterious presence that inhabits it and is communicated through it.

This is also the way that the Christian stand on chastity (and in particular the patristic position) must be understood. Chastity is not really the negation of sexuality but rather its transfiguration, through a concern to prevent the body from presenting any fleshly obstacle to the being that inhabits it. As we have seen, this interpretation of chastity is rarer than the one where it is mixed with a fearful refusal of sexuality. But it does exist, and is perhaps one of the most original elements of Christian moral theology. What is at stake here is causing sexuality to emerge from non-differentiation, or from violence closed in on itself, in order to allow it to become a sign of a presence to another, a sign of a gift and of love.

"Starting with you, to say yes, to say yes to the world," says Eluard. The Christian would undoubtedly add that for him, this "you," by his very uniqueness and irreducibility and gift, also signifies another, namely God, whose love is recognized as the origin of all love and as the hope of avoiding the deadly snares of lust. Thus it is that the establishing and creative Word of God allows man to live out his sexuality as an acknowledgement of the other, this other who is so necessary and yet irreducible, a condition of his happiness and yet[3] a revealer of his own limitation and vulnerability.

This kind of theological interpretation opens the way for an ethic and I will discuss this shortly. However, I first want to add that in my opinion it was the desire to translate the richness of its interpretation of the body into ethical terms that led Christian ethics to be so interested in sexuality.

When someone denounces "the taboos of judaeo-christian morality," which is a popular thing to do today, he really seriously misconstrues the situation. For Christianity is not guilty of having denied sexuality, but perhaps, on the contrary, of having sought all possible means (even repressive ones) to interpret its ethical meaning. It can be blamed perhaps for failing in this attempt, but it cannot be accused of misunderstanding the importance of sexuality. Christianity, more than any other system, valued the richness of the human mystery of sexuality—which perhaps explains why it had so much trouble in translating its moral signification. But the undeniable difficulties previously discussed should not make us forget that Christian ethics is the first hearty attempt to structure the fascinating mystery of sexuality into concrete historical activity, i.e. marriage, the sacrament of love. To refuse the opposition of love to the marital institution but instead to link them together, is surely the greatest gamble undertaken by Christianity. The fact that many people today, no longer cognizant of its meaning, take exception to this gamble and loudly accuse the Church of having preached an oppressive morality should not cloud the fact that this gamble was truly one of the most powerful elements of fermentation in the transformation of ancient society and one of the contributing factors to the birth of western society.

2. The Couple Is the Long-Range Objective of Sexuality

The uniqueness of the Christian interpretation of sexuality is in its connection to the revelation of God in the work and person of Jesus of Nazareth. It is the Gospel's interpretation of the otherness of God, which the Old Testament had testified to in its own way, which gives meaning to the otherness that man experiences through sexuality. Sexual differentiation can be understood as the uncomfortable indication of human finiteness which must be supressed at all costs through violence, through denial, or through a loss of identity by merging with the Whole. But, conversely, the scriptural tradition designates this difference as the indication of the ultimate stakes in human existence by associating it with the experience of the Otherness of God. So then, either man recognizes otherness as a call to create a history, a world, with that other one whose ultimate mystery is respected, or he can refuse otherness by interpreting it as the negation of his own individual affirmation. The issue is quite the same in one's relationship with God as it is in one's relationships with others, and the sexual relationship is the most significant paradigm of that.

Biblical tradition translated the revelation of the otherness of God into ethical terms by affirming that it signified the antecedence of the couple over the individual as a sexual being. In Genesis 1, man is created as a couple, as part of a male/female relationship. In Genesis 2, Adam is really inscribed into the fundamental goodness of God's creation only when he receives Eve. What is "in the beginning," as Jesus says, is the couple. The image of God in which man was created can be understood as the presence within him of the desire for the other, an openess and incompleteness, a sign that man can be fulfilled only through encounter with the Other, through love of a particular other being. Strictly speaking, what is foremost is the relation of God with man, but the Bible adds that this relationship only becomes discernible to man through the analogy of the relationship of a man and woman. This is why, even when customs were not aligned with this scheme, the Bible makes monogamy the legitimate expression of the divine will and Christian ethics affirm that the couple is the objective or goal of sexuality. "Long-range objective," in that the antecedence of the couple over the individual is the foundational order and the foremost will of God and is also the order of His promise; what is fundamentally at stake, as the possible meaning of sexuality, despite the failures of human life (or through them), is the constitution of a lasting couple, created and recreated by love.

We must look more precisely at what the word *love* signifies in this instance. In ethics the task is clear: it consists in elucidating the meaning that love can have today in view of the fact that in the Christian perspective the love between a man and woman represents the very love of Christ for His Church. The author of the letter to the Ephesians tried to do this in his own socio-cultural context, and I in turn have tried to do it in mine, keeping in mind today's very different context, even if that consists only in the information on sexuality at our disposal.

The author of Ephesians had interpreted the love of Christ especially in terms of protective responsibility (cf. 5:25 ff.) and affectionate concern (cf. 5:29)—two themes that were profoundly innovative, let alone provocative, in the context of that time. I think we can enlarge on that perspective today and say that the human couple carries a threefold promise: that man and woman can be for each other the place of the actualization of freedom, of fidelity, of conjugality. But, consequently, there is the risk of a threefold failure: man and woman can become for each other the instance of a deadly experience of entrapment, of prevarication and alienation.

a) Fidelity

We can best understand the crux of the matter by approaching what is probably the most contested element of Christian morality today: fidelity. "I promise to be true to you, 'til death us do part' ": this is the promise exchanged on the wedding day.[1] Hypocritical promises, legalistic language, or speech that is insignificant because it is not consciously meant? The misunderstanding today on the meaning of fidelity is great. Let us try to see just what it is!

As a departure point for this discussion, let me say that in our society there are two contradictory discourses on fidelity which seem to correspond approximately to two separate generations. The first belongs to a society on the wane. Fidelity is conceived of and lived out as a *faithfulness to a past commitment*! "I promised something one day; fidelity means not questioning a promise, even if difficulties arise."

Whoever speaks in this way considers himself responsible for a certain order of things; he cooperates with that order by his commitment and maintains it by his fidelity. Thus marriage, even if it's not always rosy, deserves to be defended (insofar as it is an institution) by the fidelity of the spouses. I would say in this case that the content of fidelity is less important than its outward form; the emphasis is on institutional continuity more than on the quality of the relationship between the two people involved. In other words, one is more faithful to the past commitment than to the person to whom it was made. This concept, linked to a kind of society that is characterized by a need for *stability,* can also be found in feudal societies in the alliance between a lord and vassal, as well as in bourgeois society where fidelity is linked to property (and by extension the wife) which one has the exclusive right to "enjoy."

Because this perspective places the emphasis on continuity and stability, it tends to protect individuals from the risks involved in freedom. Or rather, freedom is very precisely ordered by the commitment itself: the commitment should be free, but once it has been made it substantially qualifies freedom. To be faithful is to be tied. The value in this kind of approach to fidelity is in the possibility of inscribing it within a social perspective. In a certain way, the individual submits himself to the needs of society. In return, he receives greater security. But the limitations of this concept are evident: it often tends towards hypocrisy, and a formal fidelity which hides actual infidelity (this is the whole mainspring of bourgeois drama!); furthermore, it often enters into conflict with the real needs of an individual and his development.

This explains why a new discussion which analyzes fidelity from a totally different angle is becoming more frequent. Fidelity is described in terms of *faithfulness to self,* of integrated growth and development for the individual. All human and social relationships are measured by this standard: does it encourage or hinder faithfulness to self? What is first in order of importance is the *freedom of the subject,* the freedom for the self, as well as for the partner (in marriage, for example). Commitment becomes a contract whose terms provide that the partners may modify the content according to circumstances. This represents a real change, as W. Ossipow has demonstrated so well, from a system based on the ideology of private property, which is stable and exclusive, to another system based on the capitalistic ideology of the free-flow of money. Just as people invest where the returns are the greatest, now people "invest" their desire where it can offer the best "returns," i.e. encourage personal growth the most. If the other becomes an obstacle to this personal development, it is best to leave them behind. This perspective can be summarized in this rather typical statement: "True faithfulness permits growth together and sometimes growth to the point of deciding to separate if separation is the only way to move successfully through the up-coming stages of growth."[2]

This concept of faithfulness, stemming from a very mobile society, does not link the present to the past, but links the past to the present. What has freely been decided in the past is now judged in the light of today's circumstances. This allows a person to adapt himself flexibly to the hazards in a personal evolution. The present becomes more important than the past and also more important than the future, which is also rigorously submitted to the potential value of the present. The risks of freedom are at their maximum in the present, since the couple is considered as the result (provisional perhaps) of two equal freedoms that are equally bound to follow after their own personal developments.

This perspective, which is that of so many couples today, married or not, should not be ridiculed. There is here, especially on the part of the woman, the right and just affirmation of the right to individual existence and the refusal to sacrifice one's life on the altar of moral or institutional principles. It also displays a desire to avoid the potential snare of hypocrisy within a formal relationship, and to reject make-believe and thereby commit an action with political significance which challenges, along with marriage, the very society behind it with its alienating constraints. Such a position is really the transposition (often dramatic in its results) of the ideology of capitalistic consumer society unto the moral plane. It often results in a perverse exaltation—perverse because it is absolute—of the individual's rights at the very moment when, in so doing, the individual accepts the most demanding and the most alienating imperatives of the current ideology. Furthermore, it expresses, even in the most incisive questions, man's inability in this consumer society to endure the real while maintaining the hope of a promise.

I believe there is an alternative, i.e. what could be called the gospel utopia of fidelity, based on the concepts of *project* and *limitation*. What are individuals committing themselves to when they declare their mutual intention of fidelity because of the gospel? There are several elements involved here:

—First of all, a shared desire to enter into a common project, considered to be sufficiently important so that the partners decide to commit themselves to each other in order to achieve their predetermined goal.

—In this perspective, the important word is "future," which becomes the potential for the fulfillment of the project. The past can certainly be of use in measuring the ground already covered, but it is no longer a determining factor, any more than the present is, for the present finds its meaning as the gateway to the future.

—Because of the predetermined goal or project, the partners therefore declare themselves ready to trust each other and be challenged, changed and transformed by each other, to better accomplish their plan. This leads to the creation of a history because each one renounces his present state in order to move forward, because of the other and through him, towards the realisation of their goal.

This definition can apply to other realms besides conjugal life, for example, religious life, one's relationship with God, God's relationship to His people; in the conjugal realm, it signifies that the two spouses consider themselves mutual witnesses of this project or goal, which, here, becomes the constituting factor of the couple. One becomes for the other the very meaning of the project, that which is aimed for and for which they commit and give themselves. More precisely, the conjugal partner is the very meaning of the project insofar as he is also himself linked and commited to the same history-to-be-made. In this perspective, then, the couple is neither the result of a past contract, nor a permanent confrontation of two freedoms who maintain autonomy, but a new reality, a "new person" that comes about through the exchange of two beings who mutually acknowledge each other as promise and limitation.

The other becomes a promise, because he is, as Paul the Apostle says, the other who gives meaning to my body (1 Corinthians 7:4; Ephesians 5:28). The other gives me meaning, not only because through him I am allowed to realize myself, but mostly and more importantly because the other is myself insofar as he/she is promise, project, just as I am the other in that same project. But in this perspective, the other is also my limitation, precisely because he/she incarnates the fact that what is indispensable to me is always what eludes me and does not belong to me. I cannot love the other without accepting the risk this commitment brings. The other is thus the sign, even when the relationship ends in failure, that I am not self-sufficient; I truly am, only through this risked relationship and through this gift, that is to say, through this dependence on the other to whom I bind myself so that he/she also presents me with his freedom so that our exchange becomes creative of another life, of a new person.[3]

In this perspective, the mutual commitment must be irreversible and with no guarantee apart from the other himself.[4] Fidelity, then, is neither faithfulness to self nor to a past commitment (even though these two elements are of course not totally absent); it is a reciprocal gift which is the very goal for which the commitment is undertaken. Now this gift is real only if it is total and unreserved (if the grain of wheat does not die. . . !). Whenever the gift is partial or limited, there is no longer a condition for the exchange I am speaking of. It is threatened by calculation and becomes an economic relationship where the partners lend themselves out but with reservation! The danger here lies in moving from the gospel perspective to an economic perspective.

This is why, from the gospel perspective, there can be no confusion between the conjugal relationship which is unique, privileged, particular, and other interpersonal relationships. The first is a total exchange, which is signified on one level by the exchange of bodies, and the reciprocal gift of two freedoms. Other relationships are an analogy of the first: other men and women are also the promise and the limitation of the two partners comprising the couple, but in a different way: they are the promise of valuation, of acknowledgment, but also the expression of limitation, because they remind the two partners specifically that they are no longer free with regard to gift of self, or life, but that they are already bound to each other.

b) Freedom

Now for the problem of *freedom*. What does freedom really mean in the life of those who have bound themselves together by a reciprocal gift and conjugal commitment? The gospel perspective does not separate freedom and faithfulness, contrary to the opinion of modern man, who today criticizes the requirement of faithfulness in the name of freedom. But is this the same kind of freedom? The freedom I am referring to finds its full revelation in the life and actions of Jesus Christ. What strikes a reader of the gospels is that Jesus never lived out freedom as though it consisted in abdicating all autonomy to submit to external law presented as the absolute standard. The freedom which finds its meaning in submitting to an absolute system external to oneself belongs to the pharisaical rabbis. Jesus sets Himself against it in the name of the requirement which through the law, to be sure, but rooted far beyond it, calls for the risk of love.

Furthermore, Jesus does not live out a freedom which bespeaks absolute autonomy, as though man were himself his own foundation. He does not present the problem of freedom in terms of do's and don'ts. He incarnates a life-style in freedom which in practice is truly liberating, i.e. a practice of relationship to others which always strives to liberate the other from his alienations. The freedom exercised by Christ in approaching man, while recognizing him for who he is (i.e. a wounded child of God who is called to the banquet in the Kingdom), has the effect of freeing man from being closed in on himself, whether that condition stems from others or from his own guilt in the matter. The freedom of Christ is liberating because it allows man to perceive his ultimate destiny, which is to be inhabited by the creative love of God: the healings performed by Christ are the signs of the re-creation which occurs within man when he consents to being loved.

If this is what liberty is, then it has a dual significance for the conjugal relationship. It is first of all liberation from one's fear with regard to others. We can ask ourselves, in this regard, whether speaking of freedom as if it were a sexual freedom to choose other partners besides the spouse does not actually express a real fear of truly deep relationship, which implies decentralization of self and a lucid recognition of the ambiguity which dwells in us. For other than momentary sharing, there is no authentic relationship except when fears have been appeased, but only a genuine and patient relationship allows this to happen.

But most of all, the freedom the Gospel refers to is the one that allows for liberation in the other of all that he carries with him. This is why the authentic couple necessarily inscribes itself in time and space—a time and space comprised of all that they have mutually allowed each other to discover about each other. The couple becomes the place, if I may say, of a practical exercise of liberation, in the sense that each permits the other to live in his own authenticity, which is both individual and conjoined, and to express his own richness in daily life. This is to say that freedom is first of all patient listening and fundamental trust: the mystery of the other finds its ultimate meaning in God, and is therefore irreducible (which forever prohibits an attempt to objectify him), but which must nevertheless be expressed in concrete life.

Thus the experience of being a couple allows each of the conjoined to know the freedom which is discovered through a liberating trust in each other. Here again, sexuality can express this trust which frees the other from his fears and his anguish, and allow him to express joy and tenderness, pleasure and play, even by means of his body. One lifetime is hardly long enough to explore this pathway to freedom! Freedom signifies the actual acknowledgment of the other, not in the static sense of who he is now, but in the dynamic sense of who he is called to become, through the progressive expression of all his potential talents. Freedom is therefore inseperable from the hope for the other and from the shared project. Freedom, defined in this way, is totally incompatible with a freedom which aligns itself with the demands made by desire and concludes that the other has no meaning other than to effect one's own growth or to stimulate one's own pleasure. The ethical risk of sexuality revolves around this: either it expresses and leads to reducing the other to a sexual function (whether it be for pleasure or for procreation is irrelevant, because in this perspective those two things are equal!) and signifies a desire to make the other into a thing, or else it allows an amazement and wonder before that which ever remains an irreducible mystery in the other and which erotic play never ceases enriching and celebrating.

This is why, from the Christian point of view, we can speak of an "asceticism" of conjugal life. Not in the sense of a voluntary limitation to intercourse which is meritorious in itself, but in the sense of the conjoineds' patient and reciprocal attention to that which inhabits them, i.e. a refusal to equate the depth of their existence to appearances. This is how conjugal life becomes the apprenticeship of a new outlook on a reality known to be inhabited by a presence; it is to build a world where eating becomes a communion, and making love celebrates the wonders of the love of God, where the gift of one's body signifies the gift of someone's vulnerability, the risk of a whole life given over, where the body itself becomes the sign of that which inhabits it and a means of communicating that to another and of celebrating it with him. Thus, the body (and when the other gives himself as he is, it becomes infinitely more than just the body) becomes the very place in love for the most spiritual, the most honest, the most "chaste" apprehending of the presence of the other. This symbolic function of the body is experienced in the instant when each one gives himself to the other, person/body, in the stripping away that nudity signifies, in the ultimate absence of any pretentions; this is where man and woman give each other life, and radiate a life to one another which is much greater than either of them.

We could say that the gamble of the couple involves allowing love to organize all of existence as a symbol, hinging on this rapport between flesh and spirit, where everything (including the most material things) is destined to signify this gift, but where, reciprocally, the spiritual is never separated from the flesh.

In this kind of concept of the human couple there is an implicit polemic against any reduction of the other to his body, or reduction of reality to the things which comprise it, or reduction of love to pleasure. To receive the discovery of this profound symbolic function of life, is to challenge the dominant ideology of our western society, i.e. the triple ideology of possessive force, material violence and commercial objectivizing.

As we can see, the "asceticism" I am referring to is not an inability to live life fully, nor is it a fear of sexual desire. It is the acknowledgement of the ultimate depth of beings, of their irreducibility in terms of what can be said about them. It is therefore an *endurance of reality,* an acceptance of who the other truly is, stripped of appearances, make-believe and idolatry. *Endure* means to allow time to reveal gradually the authenticity of the desire that dwells in us, through which a more profound truth is announced at the heart of daily reality. Sometimes impatience masquerades as a cry for freedom when really the cry is one of anguish at the necessary relinquishment of omnipotence and instantaneousness.

All this would only constitute a somewhat illusory idealism if this perspective were not solidly based on faith in the precedence of the Word which makes our own existence possible. "In the beginning was the Word" means that there is life only where it is received as a gift, and operates on the level of things and of bodies without being restricted or reduced to those levels. That something which is our foundation and precedes us is also the guarantee of our freedom and our existence.

Without this acknowledged precedence of the Word of God which makes our life a mystery and a gift, everything I have said about fidelity becomes odious moralizing and an impossible mission. For it is precisely because we are not our own foundation from the very beginning that freedom can be understood as the liberation by the gospel from murderous lust; the other, in fact, stops being a threat to our autonomy that must be swept aside, but becomes instead the sign of this otherness which is our foundation. From this point on, conjugal ethics is not an impossible (and therefore guilt-forming) ideal but a practice or exercise—(this is the meaning of the greek root for "asceticism")—of discernment, and thus of decentralization. The essence of freedom no longer lies in the autonomous existence of the subject to whom all things are subjected as servants (including the actual existence of others); freedom lies in the capacity for accepting otherness as the possible meaning of the conjugal project. This is the sense in which freedom and faithfulness are closely linked in the Christian perspective.

c) Conjugality

In speaking about the human couple, I have placed its existence under the twofold sign of freedom (i.e. liberation from fear and the risk of acknowledging the other) and of fidelity (i.e. the inscription of love in the temporality of a project that creates a history). But this alone does not constitute a married couple.

A man and a woman may have sexual relations and even live together without being married. This commonplace observation clearly points out that marriage, at least in our societies,[5] is constituted neither by sexual relations nor by a shared life. We could even, in fact, imagine a couple living out freedom and faithfulness as I have described them without being necessarily married. What western tradition calls mutual consent, even if it is a necessary element of marriage, is not sufficient to constitute a marriage. Marriage actually implies another dimension, i.e. the social space in which the couple lives—or, more precisely, a couple's actual taking account of that social dimension. There is a *marriage* when a man and woman freely decide to inscribe their love-relationship in social time and space, and when they confirm that decision by a public commitment to one another; and when, conversely, the social group they belong to (clan, tribe, city, nation) acknowledges them to be a couple and commits itself to their decision.

Let us examine the two aspects of this definition. I said that marriage is a *social commitment of the couple*. Their action acknowledges that marriage is essentially a social act. From the spouses' point of view it expresses their conviction that this most private and intimate human relationship, in order to be fruitful, should be structured into a time and a place, i.e. it should participate in a social project which reflects in some way, the personal project of the couple. The couple, which represents a richer potential than only the sharing of two individual existences, has a future which also concerns their social group as a whole. The child is the most obvious, but not the only, sign of this potential.

When they marry, a man and a woman declare—and that declaration should always be public—that the most personal part of their existence is inseparable from their social existence. In this sense marriage indicates a refusal to divide existence into heterogenous zones—private and public—since family, conjugal and sexual life, are inseparable from the society in which they occur and inseparable from the consequences that society's actions have on each one's personal life.

In other words, one recognizes in the public act of mutual commitment of the spouses, the affirmation (which is also the expression of their hope) that the uniqueness of the relationship between a man and a woman represents the potential example of living out the profound significance of all encounters and of all relationships. Not in a reductionist sense, as though nothing authentic can exist for the spouses outside of their reciprocal relationship, but in the sense of a gamble that this particular conjugal relationship can reveal the whole meaning of interpersonal relationships; that in this particular case, the plurality of all the other relationships can find a unifying focus in terms of meaning and value. It is the sexual love relationship which gives meaning to all the other relationships by permitting a unique and total experience of what relationship to another really is.

Thus marriage reveals the social character of love, or the social aspect of love. This is why I believe it is so significant that in all societies and cultures, under obviously diverse forms, marriage is publicly signified under the form of the spouses' mutual commitment in the presence of society.[6] The public act, whether it be regulated in all details as in ancient society, or whether it emphasize the freedom of the spouses as in modern society, is one of the two elements constituting marriage: in the presence of all others, two specific individuals define themselves as a new entity and separate themselves from the others, declaring that they have chosen each other and, from now on, they constitute a new cell in social life, a new family. Of course, depending on the society, the acknowledgment of the social aspect of marriage has received different interpretations. Generally, the history of the marital institution is above all (if not exclusively) that of a procreative function where the major issue is ensuring the survival of the group, and thus the personal desires of the individual are sacrificed to that cause. And yet something else is equally at stake: marriage is a social act not only because it ensures procreation, but because it also allows man and woman to accede *simultaneously* to social creativity, and this necessitates a conscious commitment on their part. This is why in many ancient societies (in Iran, Rome . . .) marriage escaped a total manipulation by families, and relied in part (and then more and more) on the consent of the future spouses. I will return to this point shortly. It is sufficient for now to notice that, through marriage, the most intimate aspect of existence is linked by a public act of commitment to the social responsibility of the spouses. In this respect, we can say that man and woman, by marrying, renounce marrying only for their own sakes.

If I insist on this point somewhat, it is because it risks being forgotten today in a society where, by an understandable reaction against the social manipulation of marriage, people have encouraged affective and elective values and the personal and free choice which alone permit love. Certainly we are not dealing with "marriage" in circumstances where consent is not required: that would belong to what I call the "infra-conjugal" realm, where partners have no right whatsoever to free consent.[7] But a recognition of the importance of free consent should not lead to forgetting the social dimension of marriage. No one can claim to marry in order to escape social responsibilities or to shelter his private life from the reach of society's oppression! That would be a contradiction in terms, since marriage, on the contrary, presupposes a desire to join personal existence and social existence into a single project. At the other end of the spectrum, is it possible, as some believe today, to reject the form of marriage while living out its social demands? This is obviously one of the debates of our time, but it is not possible to respond seriously to this without first approaching the other aspect in the marital institution, i.e. society's acknowledgement of the free consent of the spouses.

I believe that marriage is also the *commitment of society to the couple.*

As we have seen, one of the real signs of progress towards humanization was society's recognition of the fundamental importance of free consent. "*Nuptias non concubitus, sed consensus facit,*" as stated by Roman law. This formula acknowledges that marriage cannot be reduced to the status of a social act where only society's needs are expressed by ordering the life of man and woman for its own sake. Society, by being a *witness* to the marriage, acknowledges that marriage, even if it is oriented towards social goals and is indispensible to society's existence, does not belong to society as one of its possessions. Let me elaborate that point.

The public commitment of the spouses has society for its witness for two reasons: first, as we have seen, to manifest the spouses' responsible approach to social space and their desire to deliberately inscribe their conjugal and family life in that space; secondly, society is called upon to acknowledge the new status of the couple, i.e. to recognize a "couple" and not just two individuals who will live together. In so doing, society acknowledges that between itself and the individuals concerned, there now exists the new reality of this couple.

In committing itself to acknowledge the existence of this new entity, society implicitly renounces a concept of itself as the immediate or ultimate goal of individual life. The State, the nation, the community, do not constitute the goal of individual life: what is structural and primary is the couple, the social expression of the man/woman relationship. The State and society exist so that this primary relationship may exist, with the aim of encouraging its existence. This, at least, is what every social group seems to me to be affirming when it commits itself, as it does with regard to marriage, by some act of acknowledgement (ritual, symbol, law). This commitment emphasizes the importance, within the group itself, of this privileged relationship between a man and a woman. It also signifies, and for the same reasons, the group's concern to protect the conjugal entity.[8]

We could object to this reflection by saying that historical evidence proves that society's acknowledgement of marriage is oriented much more towards a reinforcement of social control on conjugal life, i.e. imposing standards and models on it, than to recognizing the structural primacy of marriage. The evidence appears conclusive. History multiplies the instances which prove that a hierarchical social model has been superimposed on the couple, i.e. that the man/woman relationship has been lived out as the master/slave relationship. We cannot really deny that the man/woman relationship "had recourse to the relationship of master and slave, for it is true that historically, and in a large number of cultures, it is man who is the master and enforces that status. A struggle for life and for possession of the world pits the sexes against each other and man establishes himself as master; the woman becomes a slave and a commodity for trade or abduction."[9] In fact, examples abound concerning virilocratic societies where the rapport of force and domination seem to reduce the man/woman relationship to the particular model of dominator/dominated. But I say "seem" because despite the overwhelming appearences of historical evidence, I am convinced that the man/woman relationship is a "dialectic on two levels" (Chirpaz) and that under the apparent domination of the master/slave dialectic, the man/woman dialectic has never really ceased being present. The reduction of the second dialectic to the first has never been total.[10] I also believe that the man/woman relationship subverted the master/slave relationship and impeded it from going the whole length of its hideous destiny.

Something irreducible, because structural, resisted and still resists the pigeonholing of the sexual and conjugal into the single categories of politics and economics, i.e. of power and possession. The public rituals and symbols marking the group's commitment to the newly-formed couple demonstrate the character of marriage which is ultimately not reducible to the social level alone, despite the appearances. Society realizes that its future depends on the way in which the problems of the relationship between man and woman are to be resolved. Everywhere and at all times, this issue was so crucial that it was necessary to ritualize its significance and symbolically to make its hazards and risks explicit. Of course, in so doing, society imposed a framework (often a rigid one) on conjugal life; but this fact is less important than the profound meaning behind this ritualizing: through it, society acknowledges that the man/woman relationship, in its ultimate uniqueness, belongs to an order that is other than purely social and that in spite of everything, it eludes social control. The importance of the sphere of intimacy, of secrecy, is to be carefully noted here: it signifies the irreducibility of the conjugal to the social. Now, if I understand it correctly, society's acknowledgment of marriage implies a recognition of this private sphere, since there is no known society that forces the spouses to have intercourse in public.[11] I consider this an important point, because it seems to indicate that societies have realized that the man/woman relationship was primary and foundational, the basis for all other possible relationships, the basis for all social life. And it does indeed seem that all societies up until now have considered their role with regard to the couple as that of offering them a well-defined and protected place, where man and woman can live out their sexuality, so that, through it, social life itself becomes possible.

All the ambivalence in marriage lies therein—in the social acknowledgement which continually risks being inverted by reducing the couple to conformity to a social model instead of recognizing in them the free source of all possible life. The history of the conjugal institution clearly manifests this ambivalence; in this sense it can be said that the "human couple" is still only a promise, something yet "to come," since our societies have only until now experienced inadequate sketches of that reality!

Having said all this, I can now add a nuance to my preliminary affirmation as to the essentially social character of marriage: marriage is indeed a social act but mostly because it expresses, in its very essence, the hope for a reconciled society—one where the goal of common life is not deadly rivalry but a vivid consciousness of the other and where life is not competition and slavery, but an acceptance that bears fruit.

The couple is the goal, the objective of sexuality: having come to the end of this section, let me summarize my position. It is based on the theological affirmation that sexual difference finds its meaning when it is placed in rapport to God's otherness, which is itself referred to by biblical testimony as the mystery of the love of God. On this basis, I have described the ethical risk in sexuality as being the movement from lust to love, that is to say, as the recognition that the couple is indeed what sexuality aims at. And we have seen that this couple could become the place of a threefold experience of love under the triple mode of fidelity, freedom and sociability.

The conjugal adventure allows man and woman to discover the real significance of otherness (I have spoken of freedom in this sense) and of facing the temporality of existence (this is the sense of a fidelity which experiences time not as a slow unfolding of what has been, but as the progressive discovery of the other and the completion of the project), and of interpreting social space as the place of the incarnation of love (which is what seems to me to characterize marriage).

Is it necessary to say that conjugal experience is often completely other than this? A whole other book would be needed to speak of the failures of conjugal life! We could, in particular, show why a fair number of couples do not succeed in understanding otherness, or in living temporality as a promise, or in structuring their affective life in a responsible fashion into social space. I could mention psychological, sociological, ideological, moral and spiritual reasons for these failures. But my purpose is not to enter the territory of marital or psychological counselors, who are themselves aware that in this realm there are only specific cases, and that problems cannot instantly be handled according to general rules! I have aimed at outlining the basis for a perspective of a Christian ethic of sexuality: but this could be misunderstood if I did not also add two important points.

a) This Christian perspective has no meaning if we separate it at any time from its theological foundation; it immediately and inevitably becomes an intolerable morality if we forget that it is the consequence— and not the condition!—of the acknowledgment of the otherness of God and the antecedence of His Word. In this sense, ethics is itself a grace, a road stretching out before man, a discovery of the wonders that already exist there. Without these theological roots, Christian ethics is nothing but a hollow tree that no longer has life.

b) To describe this kind of perspective is not to do away with failure, nor is it to make those who adhere to it partially or with difficulty feel guilty; it is, on the contrary, to recall that Christianity recognizes the positive side of failure, since it places the Cross of Christ at the center of its message, a failure if ever there was one. But that failure, however, signified the triumph of the love of God as it truly is: gift, vulnerability, risk. To speak of the couple as I have done, can awaken many memories and pains by presenting a magnificent ideal which seems so much more beautiful because it is inaccessible. But just the opposite is true: I am not discussing an ideal, but the rich potential which belongs to the existence of every human couple, the reality of the promise that God, according to the gospel, affixes to this relationship between man and woman. It's a question of outlining a perspective which qualifies our outlook, allowing it to perceive what is not evident (and is less and less evident in a society like ours), but which nevertheless we must patiently aim for and work at. Must I reiterate that all this does not do away with failures or the somewhat unfortunate choices that have been made? How can a person be committed to this ideal, this risky attempt, without encountering failure? There are some failures which reveal (better than success does) that which most deeply inhabits us, the something that resists the unbearable end of a relationship or a love, and resists the dwindling of gentle tenderness into insignificance.

If the couple is a humanity that is to be created, it is because it is and always will be a promised reality, prevailing over the essense of absurdity, violence and conflict. The promise is not a dream allowing escape from the harshness of reality, but a call to belief in the hope which is affixed to the human couple, to the gradual and patient acknowledgment of the other, which sometimes opens up unto wonder and which is often only conquered through confrontation. But is it otherwise in man's relationship with God?

d) Additional Note: And the Child?

If fidelity inscribes the life of the couple in a creative time and in a project, it is the child who best symbolizes its value. But we cannot confuse the issues: fidelity is not to be justified by children, since children symbolize the creativity of faithfulness and its stakes in life. The child symbolizes the point to which the symbolic function of the gift and exchange between man and woman goes: the point of allowing another life to come forth and grow.

If it is freedom that allows each of the partners to exist in his real condition as an individual and yet linked to another, the child most perfectly symbolizes the discovery that the ultimate foundation of life does not belong to us and that we can only indirectly signify it by love, gentleness, total openess, and finally, the child. He is the sign that genuine freedom leads to an acknowledgement that the ultimate reality of life does not belong to us, and that it is therefore useless to defend it by violence or by fear of the other.

If conjugality inscribes the life of a man and woman in an alliance (a genuine structure of social reality), here again, the child best symbolizes the sociability of love.[12]

Thus, on all three levels of this ethical approach, the child is the sign par excellence of love's creativity. I say "love's creativity" and not merely "creativity of the couple united sexually" for the child can also unfortunately be the victim of a loveless sexual reaction. I distinguish procreation, the natural end of sexuality, from creativity which belongs to the category of love. For the child of man, as opposed to an animal offspring, is not born "of flesh and blood" but of the spirit and the Word! He fills up the space created between the man and the woman by the mutual acknowledgement of their otherness.[13] He fills up that space as another being whose vulnerability and need immediately signify the risk of love and the need we have to recognize that life is only given when we decide not to keep it for ourselves only; he also signifies the profundity of desire which, beyond the pleasure that announces it, establishes in man and woman a courage to live which comes from beyond themselves.

It is thus clear that the child should not be the primary goal of the relationship between a man and a woman, and even less should he be its only justification. In order for the child to be, it is necessary that he symbolize the covenant exchanged between his parents. If his parents are only his progenitors, he does not truly exist. For the child can never create this link himself. At the most he can only negatively manifest its absence by the force of the death-wish which will inhabit him.

3. The Spiritual Value of Eroticism

The scriptural tradition always links the otherness of God to the vocation given to man to journey towards the encounter with this Other-God. Only those who displace themselves, who begin to travel that road, can hope to encounter the God who has put them in motion: Abraham, obliged to leave Ur, a land of possession, for Canaan, a land of promise; Moses and the Hebrew people leaving Egypt for the desert, a place of trials and revelations; David, Elijah, Jeremiah, constantly dislodged because of God. . . . The symbolic function of space also expresses a historical consciousness of God; God comes into time, He is the omega of the promise as well as its origin: and to know Him, it is necessary to resolutely inscribe oneself in time and space.[1] For God is not what is left over when we have made all reality disappear, but that to which reality owes all its existence and meaning.

This experience of the otherness of God determined, as we have seen, a specific understanding of sexuality, as the place par excellence of apprehending the otherness of others. But just as the otherness of God finds its meaning only in time and space, sexual difference only reveals the depth of the mystery of the other in the time and space of a long-lasting and faithful couple.

But this still doesn't tell us what place sexuality holds in the couple once it is formed, i.e. what role it can play, not only as a cause of the shared life of the conjoined, but also as the hoped for and sought for horizon of the conjugal existence. For sexuality surely is not a simple instinctive reality which totally yields its mystery whenever someone decides to exercise it: all couples know that it is also a reality to conquer, so that its fundamental darkness can become gradually lightened, revealing the transparency of persons.

The creativity of sexuality must be defended against a Puritanism which made sexually guilt-forming for so long, and against a modern accuser which, inversely, makes emotion and sentiment blameworthy, so that only sexual technique is valued and taken as an end in itself; it must be defended insofar as it is the hoped for horizon where a man and woman can experience the real significance of their bodies, their rootedness in the good creation of God, when they experience the nonconformity of their desires to rules and laws of present existence. In fact, it's erotic play that safeguards the couple from sinking into the formality of a relationship that is purely institutionalized and lacking in joy. But to speak of play is to risk causing the misunderstanding (so totally modern) of confusing eroticism with sexual technique. It's really something entirely different: technique objectivizes bodies and tends by that to reduce sexual otherness; whereas eroticism expresses the recognition of the liberating and creative value of that same otherness. It's a question of living out sexual difference as the possibility of inventive creativity that is capable of checking a deadly conformity to Sameness. It's a question of organizing—I will use the expression even if it leads to the misunderstanding of technical or political interpretation—the relation of two bodily presences who risk, at every moment through fear, refusing the adventure of their mutual acknowledgement. Eroticism in this case signifies the intention of pushing aside the banal order of things, and even more, of resisting the temptation to live out "the couple" as a refuge or remedy (for loneliness, for desire) for which one is ready to sacrifice and forego the risk of love.

It is clear that the man and woman who decide to form a couple desire simultaneously to structure their love into an order capable of supporting them in their personal project beyond the first thrusts of passion—in that project inscribed in a specific social space, but nevertheless acknowledged by others. Meanwhile, however, this order is full of a deadly menace for the couple: that of becoming a goal in and of itself, in the name of which each of the partners is called to sacrifice his or her creativity, or more precisely, the creativity of the couple itself. Security, first and foremost, and think of the rest later! But people who have somewhat higher ideals look with consternation at this spectacle of the conjugal couple trapped in conformity and habit, in "the obligation of expiating security by boredom and of choosing the monotony of the household versus the risks of instability."[2] Would it then be sheer utopia to speak of a couple who can conceive its security as being the feasibility of escaping from conformity that comes from love? Is it idealistic to think of a couple who structures their life according to a pattern where nothing is a closed issue, where the rule is never to engulf or contain the other, where each one would allow the other to come near without predetermining the other and limiting him to preconceived ideas of who he really is? But conjugal love has had bad press. It is stated, not without fear, that the modern ideal of marriage based on love is in a state of crisis: "As we know, marrying for love is a recent development; it is only recently that partners now freely choose each other, and with no consideration other than sentiment, marry each other on an 'I-love-you.' There was a good ideal behind this 'monogamy finally achieved' (Engels): an attempt to reconcile the earthly institution of marriage and the metaphysical vocation of love, i.e. the concurrence of two beings in the formation of one entity. What is happening, now that the external obstacles to a real loving contract have been removed and now that pas—sion, turbulent on principle, has become the principle for association?

Liberated love does not believe in distance. It commits itself constantly beyond what it knows and what it is capable of: the contemporary couple is the disaster engendered by this foolish risk."[3]

"Foolish risk," in fact, for those who cannot conceive that love ever inscribes itself in space and time or that it can ever make a projected existence fruitful. "Foolish risk" for those who only speak about it in terms of pleasure with no tomorrow—pure spontaneity with no goal in mind.[4]

But it is not sufficient to wager that there is still a future for love, that it can undergird the goal of a shared life; we must yet ask under what condition! How can sexual and erotic pleasure be creative of a life organized towards a global project, and not just destructive of all order, as the (Puritan) discourse on passion claims? Apologists are needed today less for the "disorder of love" than for a "new order of love"! To defend love in all its components, including of course pleasure and eroticism, as the possibility of ordering life, both personal and social: this task, which seems to be the very task of a Christian ethic, implies that we speak not only of the couple as the meaning of sexuality, but also of sexuality as a gift and promise made so that the human couple can exist and experience some of the joy promised by God to man and woman. It is thus not only legitimate but vital that we now try to discover the specific theological meaning of the *spiritual value of eroticism*.

Sexuality, as we have seen, is never simply instinct: it is the locus of the expression of desire—desire for the other as bodily presence. It impels a pursuit of the other because the other is also the promise of a pleasure, in this case, sexual pleasure. Pleasure, as we have seen, had a bad reputation in Christian moral tradition, where it was suspected of being part of the false values of this world to the detriment of God. As if certain great mystics did not find their pleasure in God Himself! It's true that pleasure is ambiguous to the extent that if it demands a partner, it is, in a certain way, in order to deny him as a person. Pleasure can actually present itself as an illusory affirmation of self in the face of death—as an attempt to protect oneself to the detriment of the other and even from the other—of whatever could recall the mortal destiny of all existence.[5] Pleasure is thus lived out as the reaffirmation of a power capable of checking insignificance and death, and of creating an imaginary refuge against the risk of life, against wounds and a wounded life. If Christian morality constantly mistrusted pleasure, it is because it saw in pleasure a temptation for man who consents too easily to it and refuses his mortal condition, a refusal which always ends up, as experience continually shows, in a negation of the other; for once I accept others, I accept evidence of my own limitation and thus of my death. Pleasure can thus also express itself by the negation of others, denied as persons, and objectivized into instruments of pleasure. Sadism is a tragic attempt to deny death, tragic because it can only issue forth in crime. This is what the Church, faithful to the best in its tradition,[6] tried to recall: pleasure can constantly transform the presence of the other into an object to manipulate, can idolize the real in order to enclose God in the closed-in world of self, and, finally, can engender death, thinking that life is being affirmed.

This criticism is fundamental even today, where confusion abounds between the principle of pleasure and the principle of reality, where pleasure is asserted to be without any limitation, whereas the pleasure principle, well understood, *is* the expression of this limit! Contemporary man is threatened by an unimaginable violence[7] because he demands the unlimited fulfillment of his desire. The quest for pleasure leads, then, to a refusal of all limitation, i.e. of all that indicates to man that he is not everything, but simply some-one in relationship with others.

The problem is that man cannot attain the depth of what he demands from pleasure without consenting to its limit, that is to say, without accepting the risk of suffering. For what man demands of pleasure is to permit him to affirm himself to be alive in spite of death, and to lift from him the weight of a daily routine, so that he can, like at festival time, abolish the determinism which sterilizes him from all sides. Now pleasure cannot be this sign of life unless man hears, through it, the call of another desire which is not silenced by a fulfilled need. It is necessary, then, to consent to the suffering of never being able to possess anything, not even his life, and especially not others, even when pleasure links one person to the other in a moment which seems to abolish all distance. One attains joy through the experience of pleasure once one no longer seeks to escape death through it and consents, because of it, to one's own vulnerability, to his own limit.

Let me emphasize this point: if pleasure can be "dangerous," to the extent that it could be only an expression of the anguish of death, or of resentment against the human condition, the refusal of pleasure is equally dangerous. For it is equivalent to claiming mastery of life: "In the name of a God, absolute Subject, representing in fact all the imaginary perfections of an *I* exalted to the ranks of divinity, a *person* avoids, in an unconscious and perverse manner the sudden appearance of a human subject."[8] One claims thus to avoid the risk of one's own vulnerability. Thus in the name of a pseudo-spirituality, one impedes man from attaining his authenticity, i.e. that which precisely does not belong to him but which he lives out when he consents to it: to recognize oneself as a "living man delivered over to the domination of death and, at the same time, to a desire to live eternally."[9] To refuse pleasure is to refuse vulnerability, which furthermore indicates the fact that the rejection always concerns the *body;* for if the Church readily condemns sexual or gastronomic pleasure, no one ever denounces intellectual or spiritual pleasure! This is because the body points to the precariousness of life, which is directly experienced, through the body, in sorrow, sickness, and old age. In this refusal of body by certain elements in the Christian tradition (cf. chapter 4), there is a reappearance of the old gnostic perversion which rejects creation and the status of being a creature, and which finds itself incapable of thinking positively about the body, including that of Christ "incarnated and crucified."

It is not a question of opposing an irresponsible exaltation of pleasure to an asceticism which negates all value in pleasure; in reality this opposition is altogether artificial since both instances are examples of the same rejection of the vulnerability of existence and the fact of death. My theological perspective locates the debate elsewhere, when it describes pleasure as the very sign of the vulnerability of human existence *and,* in spite of everything, of the gift of life. Pleasure is indeed the sign of vulnerability since it takes its meaning from its contrast, so fleeting and threatened, with the inescapable heaviness of time which leads to death. But it also revives and makes tangible to man the savor of life, which does not belong to him but is given to him by God. This relish for life, which pleasure points to, is the trace of a Word in man which is his foundation and which man does not possess. To recognize the otherness of this Word is to recognize that man must die to all his death-carrying and alienating fictions to attain the Resurrection.[10] Outside of this theological interpretation, which on this point is in conformity with the inspired intuitions of Freud on the "pleasure principle," pleasure risks being only the expression of a hollow and often violent quest for a kind of power over death which is to be obtained by rejecting all vulnerability and all openess to others.

If there is a theology of pleasure, it consists in closely relating the consciousness of vulnerability to the recognition of pleasure as the sign in man of a desire for life which he cannot satisfy, except by a renunciation of devising it himself and letting it, instead, be more deeply established in him through the presence of others.

We can experience the counter-proof of what I have said by recalling the dual impasse of narcissism and violence where sexual pleasure so often flounders, while wishing to affirm itself as not tied to the presence of others.

In narcissism, the presence of others is only sought to confirm to the subject the cogency or merits of his own existence. Others become the mirror where he contemplates his own image, the image he makes of himself. This narcissistic element, of course, exists in all human relationships. But sexuality can become the particular expression of this closing in on oneself, which really is the fear of the other, because the other can always refuse to reflect or return the image that the narcissist has made of himself. For the other is, by his very presence (and especially when he is truly another presence and not simply a reflection), an intolerable reminder of finiteness. The essential element of all narcissistic relationships is the refusal to be decentralized by others, of whom nothing more is asked than a confirmation, through the pleasure they afford, of the validity of the existence of the subject.

Because sexual pleasure, more than any other pleasure, makes man experience coincidence with his body and constitutes him as a body—whereas in exertion or work the body is instrumentalized—and because it reveals to man that he is really flesh, pleasure can close man in on himself in the self-contemplation of his body. In this perspective, others have no real existence, their otherness is denied.

Violence is another way of refusing otherness. In order for an encounter with another to be successful, it must calm whatever fears are instantly raised. The other is a promise of pleasure, of encounter, but he is also a threat. What if this other brings me unhappiness? Every human relationship carries a risk of death and a quest for recognition. If the other does not acknowledge me, in a certain way he kills me, by reducing me to nothingness; he objectivizes me, which authorizes him to use me like an object, or as a source of labor, or as an occasion for pleasure. This is already violence in its essence; the perverse behavior of the sadistic type only demonstrates these tendencies more fully: refusal of otherness and making the other into an object.

In the case of both narcissism and violence, sexual pleasure, in exalting itself against what seems to limit it, ultimately fails in its goal, i.e. the laying hold of life which checkmates death and all its harbingers. To give pleasure its rightful place is thus not possible unless we link it to the acknowledgment of the other as the meaning and the limitation of sexual desire. *Limitation* because the other signifies by his irreducible mystery that it is impossible for man to find fulfillment within himself and through himself; the other is that which always is lacking to me and whom I totally need, but who is necessary to me precisely because I cannot make him into my possession.

The other: limitation of my pleasure, but also the *meaning* it seeks. The other announces the possibility of a discovery, and the pleasure that draws me to him is the index of this possibility—tenuous and yet full of promise. But one cannot remain at the level of pleasure for long, or

mistake the index for the thing indicated: that which pleasure sumptu-
ously announces (to the point where the temptation of remaining on that
level is great!) is the richness of the life of the other and of his presence.
Isn't the meaning of sexual pleasure, through the mediation of the body,
to open someone to the inhabited presence of the other and discover his
face and his look?

This is expressed by the very action of desire, the *caress,*[11] desire's
translation into flesh. But a caress can signify two opposite attitudes. It
can, in touching the other's body, seek to take possession of that palpitating and warm object which promises pleasure: ". . . I can make the other
become flesh by my touch in order to appropriate that person for myself,
to make him my possession, available to my desire. The other changes
into flesh, into an erotic object. . . . There is no longer a person before
me, for I am only touching a body."[12] This is the reduction of the mystery
of the other to an objectified body.

But a caress can also bespeak the quest for the other as a person. In
this case, it can calm the other, draw him near, or call to him. Then it
is a *gentle love,* revealing to the other the reconciling intention of the
partner, the peace at the very center of the pleasure that tenderness
brings about. "Tenderness is not to be understood here as something
besides the sexual gesture, nor as something alongside it, but as that
which envelops the gesture and shines through it and inhabits it wholly."[13]
"Bodily" love is not to be set in opposition to "spiritual" love. The whole
issue revolves around knowing what motivates the sexual gesture and
whether or not the encounter of two bodies is also the acknowledgement
of two beings.

Pleasure, then, does not have only one significance: it can indicate the
refusal of limitation (as in the modern slogan "the right to pleasure"), but
it can also indicate, in accepted vulnerability, the encounter of that
which can truly nourish life and safeguard it, even its precariousness,
from being subverted by death. This taste for life, carried to a paroxysm
by sexual pleasure, also opens the man and woman to something else
that is spiritual. This "something else" could at first be categorized along
the lines of wonder. Something that does not belong to man comes to
him, it comes through the other but does not belong to him either, it
shatters the sphere of "usefulness" and ascribes gratuitousness and multiple meanings to the world: the world appears in its depth and fullness
without preliminaries or final end other than to bring joy to the one who
can, without being able to seize it, recognize it.

The wonder that pleasure opens up to is thus the welcome by the spirit
of the flesh-reality of existence at the very moment it is best attested to
consciously—received by the spirit, for in the love act, man and woman

find the richest source of their representations to the world. In the experience of love, which is both the encounter of bodies and the approach of the mystery of persons, which the union of bodies does not change, man and woman learn to celebrate the world in the fragile language of their flesh. Poets know this and describe the love of man and woman as the place where the world takes on meaning, where the sensual becomes the communion of man with things and a participation in their truth. The *Song of Solomon* had already sung of the love encounter as the place where the world becomes flesh, becomes beauty and life given to man and woman. The desire which draws man and woman towards each other transfigures the world: it also, like the flesh of man, becomes indwelt by fragility and life.

> I am my beloved's
>   and his desire is for me.
> Come, my beloved,
>   let us go forth into the fields,
>   and lodge in the village;
> let us go out early to the vineyards,
>   and see whether the vines have budded,
> whether the grape blossoms have opened
>   and the pomegranates are in bloom.
> There I will give you my love.
> The mandrakes give forth fragrance,
>   and over our doors[14] are all choice fruits,
> new as well as old,
>   which I have laid up for you, O my beloved.

In this text (Song of Solomon 7:11–14) nature is itself inhabited by the amorous desire of the lovers. Elsewhere, in an inversion of this, the body of the beloved becomes nature and world:

> "Your rounded thighs are like jewels,
>   the work of a master hand.
> Your navel is a rounded bowl
>   that never lacks mixed wine.
> Your belly is a heap of wheat,
>   encircled with lilies.
> Your two breasts are like two fawns,
>   twins of a gazelle.
> Your neck is like an ivory tower. . . .
> You are stately as a palm tree
>   and your breasts are like its clusters.
> I say I will climb the palm tree

and lay hold of its branches.
Oh, may your breasts be like clusters of the vine,
    and the scent of your breath like apples,
And your kisses like the best wine"...
                                (Song of Solomon 7:1b-4a; 7-9)

A text like this admirably illustrates what I call the spiritual value of *eroticism* because eroticism is first of all the song by which bodies celebrate the beauty of life. This beauty, of course, is somewhat concentrated in the body of the beloved, not primarily or essentially for aesthetic reasons, but because the body, offered in close proximity, signifies both the welcome afforded to desire and the tenderness of the gift, and because it opens up onto the very mystery of *life*, in testifying to the mystery of *one* particular life. Eroticism is thus the celebration of this very mystery, of the link that man perceives between his uniqueness and his limitation in the uniqueness of the sexual act, and his communion with the world and things. The body of the beloved becomes a world where the beauty of this gift is measured, and the world becomes body, vulnerable and palpitating, also inhabited by a presence.

This is why "to make love" (according to the popular expression) is always a poem, an act which organizes the world. This is also why there is an obvious link between a functional and technocratic vision of man's rapport with the world and the invasion of pornography. For pornography cannot celebrate the love act as gift and presence because there is neither gift nor presence anywhere to be found, neither in man nor in the world. Love becomes a function of instrumentalized bodies and pornography drowns in a deadly fascination with bodies that have no (indwelling) presence and leads only to nothingness.

On the contrary, "world, speech and flesh" bear witness to each other and become present to each other in the erotic celebration of love. The world: because it is in the world that human imagination takes root, which is the source of all "communicating" language (as opposed to utilitarian language) and because it is also in the world that man experiences his mortal fragility and his irrepressible taste for life. Speech: because it alone is capable of removing the opaqueness of need to make it comply with the fullness of desire. It is speech which at first calms fears and aggressions, and which ultimately celebrates the other as a gift that is forever irreducible, and which hinders sexuality from becoming quasi-sacredness, a false god which promises fulfillment and only gives the taste of death—speech which is rooted in the Word of God, the creative promise from God. And finally, flesh: the body of man insofar as it is inhabited by a presence; not flesh as a surface on which lust glides, but as the fragile palpitation of life, as the possible gift of that which in the eyes of the other, even more than in his body, reveals the unique mystery of a person.

In a very beautiful poem called "Hectares of the Sun," Jean Malrieu[15] has reunited the triple song from the world, speech and flesh to celebrate love. Here are two extracts from his profound and ardent celebration:[16]

> Today, everything is for you, only for you.
> I carry great armfuls of countryside to you.
> For you.
> Only for you.
> The colored fabric of fall leaves rippling as the wind
>   moves through the trees beneath the still line of the
>   mountains.
> For you.
> For no one else save you.
> The rough weather of desire, the mellow warmth, the
>   knife-edge of cold in the shadowed places.
>
> Oh, my open, demanding one, I must—and it's the only
>   law I know always bring new things for you.
> And just as in olden times, before setting out to find
>   new worlds, explorers came to the courts of kings
>   for audience,
> I came before you and found at your hands grace, and favor,
> And I hold fast, snorting with impatience at the end
>   of their tether, the paired horses of infinity.
>
> Every word in this poem addresses you.
>
> Before you,
> I am the one whom you know so well,
> A mortal man touched by the chill of death but still
>   desperately ignoring its shadow behind him,
> The man plumbed even to the depths of his dreams who
>   shelters in the past only to find himself at the
>   head of his own funeral procession.
> And a simpleton, too—stupid with happiness, over-
>   come with well-being—unable to speak his great joy.
>
> Before you,
> The warm ecstasy, like that of the hungry beast who
>   thrusts his soft muzzle into the sweet hay,
> The stubborn strength of new life locked in seed,
> The inexorable fidelity, like that of the stone-locked stream

that gushes forth to evaporate in a blaze of sun,
The wellspring
    like a glistening pool, brimful,
Your name
    kindling dead stone with ardor.

. . .

Oh! Press all nature to my belly so we may fill it with
    our warmth!
You are a wondrous maze of veins. The trees strip them-
    selves of leaves to better show where you await me,
The welcoming shore where supple thighs of light stretch
    themselves out on golden sands.
The fire is spreading. Catch it. Contain it. You know we
    are only beginning a long journey together.
You are the welcoming entry.
You are the way beyond the stars.
You are the shadow of the peach tree on the wall.
You are more and more naked to me, flesh to enflame my
    timeless battle against death.
Call out to me. I no longer have a name. Say that I am
    night, day. I have a thousand mouths to call out. I seek
    you, like a wise Priapus, in my heart-beat run, mortality
    riding on my back.
Are you the tree? I grasp the trunk with my legs and climb.
    A flight of doves bursts toward heaven. Spring is a
    falling petal. A high wind is blowing deep in
    the pine forest.
Don't move now.
Let me talk to you, my naked one, through teeth clenched
    tight with desire. We have become sculpted figures
    on an ancient tomb. The ocean swells.
    We give birth to islands. We sail beyond pleasure.
    I feel the lift of space beneath me, just as birds feel
    it at the moment when they fan out their wings
    and become the wind.
Flesh is native land to me. Your sultry perfume glides into
    my arms like a wind-fish,
Glides into my love so that finally I may know—my love-
    weapon white as a spill of new milk searching you out
    and laboring in your darkness—the full measure of
    your power, the blazing star-furnace hidden there.
Lovely Eve, you flee with the lithe, silken movement of
    rare, furred animals, the sky drawn in your wake. I

> want you as I crush you to me, and life, seminal
> essence, bonds us together.
> Sex suffuses all—a kiss, the skin, hair, flowers, sea
> creatures, the soft evening, cinched pouches,
> an edge of coal smoke on the air,
> Sexuality of remembrance,
> Of summer evenings beside the canal,
> The femaleness of water, the brotherhood of rainstorms,
> The smell of powder, of tar, of ships at anchor—the creaking
> of the floats as they rise and fall with the tide—

The whole world is summoned by the poet because only the world is vast enough to express the force of love. It becomes sex where man experiences the immensity of the impetus which flows through him. And how can someone tell of the profundity of desire unless he compares it to a tree, a flame, a bird, islands that are flown over, brilliant stars?

But this also bespeaks the vulnerability of the flesh of man who gathers all these songs but cannot retain any of them. "I have a thousand mouths to cry out. I seek you, like a wise Priapus, in my heartbeat run/mortality riding on my back." In love, the poet admits he is flesh ("Flesh is native land to me"), that is, earthy even more than earthly, giving speech to all the sounds of the world, and through it he becomes even more senritive to all the vulnerability of this song, speech which must consent to weakness and death at the very instant it loudly expresses an immense and irrepressible taste for life:

> Let's cry out love.
> So what if I should die of it!
> Let it catch us up in its fire-song like the insect
> who carries off the swallow!
> Let's cry out the good news
> Of death and of life
> Reconciled.

Because the other is and remains other even in a loving embrace, he (she) is both a harbor and a door: a place to anchor where everything—the whole world and our desire—takes on meaning, and an opening up into otherness, which is ultimately that of God.

Through sexuality, when it is a shared celebration, man and woman discover the stupendous force of the desire which indwells them and by which they share in the power of life which animates all things. Through it, they apprehend that real life is this gift which puts a person in communion with things and with people (and not the right that man ascribes to himself of subjecting the world and destroying it). There is thus, in human sexuality, a real contestation of the positivist and technical ideology but only when it is not in turn fashioned by the positivist and technical spirit! One of the biggest ethical stakes of our time is surely a restoration of the pleasure in erotic celebration to man by which the world becomes a place of communion fnr him. But everything is interconnected: in order to achieve that one must consent to vulnerability, so that the force of desire does not become a prideful and violent self-affirmation of rights over another, but participation in a gift that comes from elsewhere—from God!

Celebrated in this way, sexuality can certainly lead to a kind of pantheism which allows in advance the experience of the dissolution of personal consciousness into a total non-differentiation in nature. But to succumb to this temptation, it is necessary to deny that it is through encountering the mystery of the other, some specific woman or man, desired as he is (unique), that the celebration of the world has become communion with a gift, and not a subtle closing in on his own imagination. Pantheism is by definition an exclusion of otherness, of world, of others; it is thus clear that a pantheistic celebration of love or of eroticism does not succeed in really challenging the positivist ideology which it opposes. For there is only one road by which to seriously question the deadly inclination of modern man for power, which has led him to gradually disdain nature, the world and his own desire: to recognize the value of non-power, i.e. of weakness. The consequence of this in the domain of sexual ethics is to requestion the meaning of the love celebration by which man and woman testify to each other, and beyond each other, to the force of the gift of life given to man. How does a person consent to the force of this gift without perverting it into an affirmation of power?

All reflection on sexuality—at least from my theological perspective—must thus decide upon the meaning it will ascribe to pleasure and eroticism in an ethical system. A Christian ethic which is content merely to say that the couple is the long-range objective of sexuality risks forgetting why sexuality even has an objective! Refusing to determine the spiritual value of sexuality *would* inevitably give priority to the institutional order ' within the couple, who *would* then be reduced to being nothing but a means of channeling or socializing the violence of desire. It is clear, as we saw in the historical section of this book, that the use here of the conditional tense is a useless rhetorical precaution: this ethic has existed and was even dominant, since it presented itself as the only orthodox Christian ethic!

The age-old experience, and failures, of the Christian ethic should be a warning to us: it is a serious theological error to refuse to ascribe any spiritual value to pleasure. There would then be no possibility of demonstrating that an authentic spirituality of vulnerability and gift can undergird the erotic celebration of love. Sexual difference is not an unfortunate accident that healthy spirituality should erase: it is the very condition for discovering, in the pleasure it heralds, that all real life (real because desired and hoped for) comes from elsewhere, from the other. The Christian would see in the gift that the other makes of his incarnated presence, the sign of a life that has come from God, a life offered gratuitously, as it was on the Cross, this life maintained in spite of the omnipresence of death, as the Resurrection announces. In the experience of love, man and woman discover that their groundedness-in-flesh, their participation in the vital impulse that animates the world, their submission to the forces of instinct and desire—all these, far from testifying to a "fall" of the human into the infra-human, the material and the contingent, are the very condition for potential wonder, which ultimately constitues the most evident sign of man's vocation to be a "spokesman," i.e. he who can, because he is an inhabited body, carry the word of God to the world and the world to God. Woe to him who desires to escape his state, and refuse the limitation of his body; denying his vulnerability, he also denies the gift which in his fragility testifies to the grace of God.

But, of course, the recognition of the spiritual value of pleasure is inseparable from the recognition of the mystery of the other, which signifies, in particular, a rapport with the body of the other that is not dominated by lust. The body of the other is a sign, even in the erotic emotion which it arouses, that must be deciphered, a hope to be perceived, a gift to be received, briefly, a presence to be welcomed. In discussing it, the language of objective description (medical or physiological for example) is ridiculous: that can only describe an organism, when what has been encountered is a body.[17] To speak of it correctly, metaphors must be used to point to what lies "behind" the body, the "absence" which becomes present through it. The body of the other is always (and even more if it arouses desire) an ambiguous confirmation of a presence: "ambiguous" because this presence is here, in this place which is his body, but it is also, in a certain way, elsewhere, i.e. in me, to begin with, who must imagine him in order to go to meet him and next, in the other, insofar as he also points beyond himself to the Other Who is his foundation: God, or rather, as the Bible says, the breath of life (Genesis 2:7) of His Spirit.

The presence of the other in his body reiterates, in its own way, the vulnerability and the gift. Man is not the whole, he only exists through the other; but in all other things he can decipher, if he is willing, the presence of that which both exasperates and fulfills his desire of life. "Do you not know that your body is a temple of the Holy Spirit within you, which you have from God? You are not your own." (Paul, 1 Corinthians 6:19).

We must never leave the solid ground of biblical anthropology, for everything is tied together there. The consciousness of self is consciousness of a vulnerability inhabited by transcendence. Unwieldiness and grace! The wonder of a gift which makes itself fragility, human flesh and beauty, but also suffering; desire but also death. The amazing wonder of a freedom which becomes project, act, gesture, offering, for "the Word became flesh and dwelt among us" (John 1:14).

If the beauty of a young body can invoke, by the turbulence of desire it arouses in us, the irresistible power of the dream of beauty which animates all human creativity as a hymn to the unspeakable beauty of God, then the other beauty (more hidden) of the body of an old man, displayed in his face and his eyes, makes us see, in the affectionate emotion it arouses in us, the potential reconciliation of man with life. The labored gait of an elderly couple leaning on each other is as "erotic" (in the sense spoken of above) as the passionate impulse which thrusts the young man and the young woman towards each other in haste towards a nudity where their thirst will be heightened or appeased.

It's not a question of de-sexualizing love, but, on the contrary, of recognizing the real depth of desire, of marveling in the fact that it always inhabits us as long as we live in bodies, whatever kind of bodies they are. To let the entire depth of desire, its real depth, deepen itself in us is surely one of the most decisive stakes in the Christian spirituality of sexuality.

4. Conclusion

I have entitled this last chapter "Man and Woman: a Humanity to Be Created" in an attempt to point out the stakes involved in a Christian ethic of sexuality. That ethic tries to maintain two apparently contradictory basics of the problem: that which relates to responsibility and that which relates to the domain of wonder. The responsibility entails "creating humanity," starting from the desire which unites a man and a woman. I have described an ethical task, properly speaking, in the second part of this chapter by the three words "fidelity, freedom and conjugality." The wonder concerns the fact that humanity is first presented as a couple, with an emphasis on the verbal adjective "presented." Ethics becomes acknowledgment, welcome and grace. But there is no priority in this list; it is not necessary first to welcome the gift of the other in order to be enabled to humanize it; or conversely, it is not necessary to labor, all things considered, in order to merit the gift and the wonder. Each one comes with the other: responsibility and wonder. At the same time. Always together hand in hand.

It is necessary for desire to become life—human life. Therefore, it is necessary that it be socialized. Marriage, which desires to inscribe the creative force of desire in time and space, expresses responsibility. The child is the most obvious result of this inscription of desire into a creative project. But not the only result; as I have said, marriage also creates the possibility of permitting what I have called an exercise of liberation and of shared creation, founded on mutual confidence, given and received. It also implies a confrontation with reality, with its solidity and real weight, which compels discovering the other as he really is in his own reality, apart from and beyond dreams, appearances, and idolatries. Proof of reality, purification of the imaginary, to allow the other to come forth in his authenticity.

There is thus an ethical responsibility in the desire of not escaping reality and, better, of inscribing oneself into it: to incarnate love in reality so that it can become a creative force, a project of humanity. This is one of the favorite themes of Protestant ethics which always highlights the social function of the conjugal couple, and uses it as the example of the fundamental structure of every social relationship.

In a society like ours, Christians, faced with the agression of popular anti-conjugal ideology, can be tempted to fall back into a less ambitious conception of the couple, where the couple becomes a "private affair" with no social significance. But that would be to abandon completely the Christian perspective, according to which the struggle for fidelity, for freedom, and for conjugality of the couple in marriage is also a struggle for a certain kind of society. The current discrediting of marriage, far from being a sign of contestation, seems rather to me to be an indication of the interiorization of standards of the dominant economic and technocratic ideology. It also manifests elsewhere that a whole generation is unable to think of itself in terms of historical project or of inscribing itself in the temporality for which it affirmed it was responsible. In this sense, there is a crisis in civilization; and in this context, the ethical commitment of Christians in this realm should be clear. To marry and to stay faithful to the project of freedom is to contest a social order that wants to appear liberal and progressive in the so-called private domain so that it might better reinforce—in the political, social, and economic domain—controls destined to allow more efficient productivity. This dualism really signifies that the man/woman relationship is no longer considered the original and structuring pattern, as the biblical tradition affirms. What is now original and structuring is the relation of man to the things he produces; this is the reality that all other realities should submit to, including the man/woman relationship. Thus the economic model imposes itself even on the so-called private zone (which is not really so private!) of emotional and sexual relationships.

Choosing priorities cannot be avoided: one must either commit oneself to the conjugal project as I have outlined it, and through that, refuse priority to the economic model; or else one must let himself be dominated by this economic model, which sooner or later ends in a crisis for the conjugal relationship. For commitment to the priority of the man/woman relationship, recognized as the fundamental structure of all social relationships, has immediate consequences: it leads to the rejection of a society given over to the fate imposed by economic productivity in the name of which, for example, an environment is imposed on families which makes emotional and social life impossible, and which forces man and woman to work-schedules and displacements that destroy all creativity, including conjugal creativity, and which reduces man and woman, and even their desire, to the rank of consumer products. It also leads to a refusal of the social order where the woman is excluded from responsibility because she has no access to economic leverage, and further, to the refusal of political programs which leave only a choice between defense of individualism, incapable of thinking out the particulars of the man/woman relationship, and the promotion of a collectivism which tries to reduce totally the creative possibility of the couple, who represent a constant danger to its totalitarian claims.

Everything is inter-related: if ethical responsibility works to actualize the promise addressed to the human couple, it must lead to taking the social context in which the project is to be inscribed seriously. Does the social context allow for this actualization or not? We cannot claim to be inscribed, in the ethical Christian perspective concerning the couple, without asking about the political consequences, in the broad sense of the term, of this choice.

There is something here to frighten the most courageous, unless, at the same time, one remembers that which I have called wonder. We should also wonder that desire is so difficult to socialize. It is similar to God, in that nothing, no theology, no Church, can domesticate it for its own use and profit! Desire is then the horizon of the couple—hopefully the place where man and woman can renew their very life, their taste for living and fighting, playing and creating. The serious Protestant should here make way for the irreverential fantasy! Ethical responsibility should be contested as well as animated by the love-game: contested as to its spirit of seriousness and its potential claim to self-sufficiency; and animated in its protest against the technical-economic ideology that is popular today. Every game presupposes certain rules, and in this case the rules are imposed by ethical responsibility. But the pleasure comes precisely from the players' ability to push the rules back to their limit in order to arrive at the point of no longer sensing their presence, and thus to create a new lightness and freedom, like the wire under the tight-rope walker: need denied by elegance, obligation transformed to trampoline.

In the love-game the spouses experience the non-conformity of their desires to the rules and actual laws of social existence; there is a surplus which reveals the potential richness of existence, which thrusts aside the boundaries of ethical commitment and avoids its being trapped in formalism. Playful freedom of a poem, for nothing else than to bespeak joy and, through it, the ultimate call of man and woman to freedom and happiness.

Epilogue:
The Dual Battle
In Christian Ethics

Have I succeeded in making my hope for a renewal of
Christian ethical thinking plausible? What about my conviction that
Christian ethics can still present worthy proposals in the sexual and
conjugal domain which can challenge actual social behavior? If we do
not wish this hope and this conviction to become pious vows, they must
now begin to be inscribed in reality, that is to say, battle fronts must be
chosen. There is an urgent need for Christian ethics to understand who
the adversaries are: because battle fronts change location, and it's always
ridiculous to see an army fighting in areas that have long been deserted
by the adversaries. Christian ethics has often been in the position of
fighting adversaries that have long ago disappeared.[1] Therefore, I want
to clearly indicate where, in my opinion, the battle for the renewal of a
Christian ethic really lies.

There is first of all a negative battle, and even a doubly negative one.
To begin with (and as the condition for the ability to fight all the rest!),
there is the issue Christian ethics should work out with itself, or more
precisely, with its own tradition. The growing distance which separates
Christians today from the moral traditions of their Churches should be
neither accepted fatalistically nor exalted as the opportunity for emanci-
pation from old, out-worn ideas; it should be the object of a serious
critical analysis, without antagonism but also without weakness. It must
in particular be admitted that if the distance is largely due to the sclerosis
of the moral tradition, to its inability to really take stock of new

questions, it is also due to a misunderstanding of the debates that occurred within that tradition. Churches today too often are satisfied to repeat popular slogans about the "taboos of the Judaeo-Christian morality" as though through this excess of guilt at having formerly been so puritan, they may now be pardoned! It is important first of all to be informed about this tradition and its content, and next, to choose a critical method for the sorting out required of the weighty past of Christian ethics. That method cannot, without considerable risk, be modern man's point of view (who is, as such, really only a purely ideological abstraction!). Christian tradition should only be judged by what it claims to be a witness to and a continuator of, i.e. the scriptural tradition which is its foundation and nourishes it. The critical method (via scriptural tradition) is sharper in its criticism than many other denunciations often heavily ideological which are addressed by contemporary thinking to Christianity.

We must return to the scriptural tradition to discover the criteria to evaluate subsequent Christian tradition and to discern how the fundamental goal of what is called the "gospel utopia" was inscribed during the course of history, how it revealed itself in and lost itself in the cultural and social reality of the time.

If the scriptural tradition is to be taken as the standard, we should not forget, as we have seen, that this tradition is itself as much *norma normata* as *norma normans*; it also testifies to an internal debate between what could be called its utopian pole and its realistic pole. The first never ceases claiming to be the very meaning of God's creation, the total acknowledgement of the otherness of man and woman, and the second recalls that no one can live outside an institutional reality (which imposes standards which it claims to be absolute). From the beginning to the end of the Bible, we can sense the tension between a promise, a goal which concerns the complete explanation of the analogy that is proposed between the relationship of God to human beings and that of man with woman (not on a hierarchical mode but on that of the acknowledgment of difference) and a social cultural reality that imposes its codes, especially that of the "natural" superiority of man over woman. But it is precisely this debate which should serve as a critical instrument to evaluate how Christian tradition itself took up the challenge.

This struggle in Christian ethics against its own tradition certainly aims at restoring access to its original source, but also of putting it on guard against idealism: today, no less than yesterday, it is not easy to propose a style of life which, on one hand, is held out by the utopian aspect of the Gospel and on the other hand, is practical, i.e. structured into human reality (and not just in moral treatises!) and capable of enlarging the boundaries in a liberating and creative way. For Christian ethics to criticise its own history signifies that it is aware of the risks of a project which tries to be both realistic and utopian. And it means to discover that the failures of this tradition are not due to the evil intentions or the imbecility of its ancestors, but rather to the difficulty inherent in a project that includes a critical hope and is inscribed in reality.

It is nevertheless clear that the surest way of ruining the future for Christian ethics is to refuse the self-criticism which is obviously demanded by the gospel message itself! To quote André Mandouze: " . . . most Christians err (because of a certain catechesis) in confusing the gospel of freedom of Jesus Christ with the puritan dogmatism which claims, in a sacrilegious way, to be from Him. If so many Christians today have a tendency to keep what they call the 'institution' at arm's length, it is because they have discovered . . . that they have been swindled."[2]

I said that the battle in Christian ethics today was a dual one. In fact, there also needs to be a confrontation with what I have described as the sexology standard (cf. pp. 13–18). I will not repeat what I said there except to highlight one element which seems to me to make this battle important: I believe that the "technical-sexological" discourse, which is attempting to impose its new moral imperalism everywhere, results in a profound demoralization of sexuality. The "sinless morality" triumphantly announced by Dr. Hesnard was quickly followed by an "amoral sexuality," i.e. a sexuality with no goal, or rather with no goal besides its own "success," symbolized by orgasm. An amoral sexuality which is supposed to be a liberated sexuality, is really a sexuality that refuses confrontation with the law of reality, and sets itself up as "pure" desire, i.e. not-fulfilled. But whenever it is fulfilled in the encounter with another (which can only mortally challenge the autonomy of desire) it loses itself. This is undoubtedly why there is so much anguish today about sexuality, and it's easy to see why: anguish arises because its reality would be necessarily perceived as aggressive since reality is always the other (man or woman) whose mystery, far from being the very condition of authenticity of the relationship, becomes that which unmistakably shatters the fantasy of omnipresence and destroys the desire for unlimited pleasure.[3]

Amoral sexuality—this is a curious reappearance of the old inability to ascribe meaning to sexuality which characterized the patristic period: sexuality caused fear and had to be excluded from the ethical field, being confined to the edges of the infra-human. In the same way today, even though the rapport is completely inverted, sexuality is again marginalized, but now, towards the top, if I can put it that way; it becomes as such the whole meaning of man and so absolute that it would only be compromised or lost if it were forced to bend to the requirements of an ethic! Formerly, man feared that sexual desire would drag him downwards, towards infra-moral animality; now man seems to fear that ethics would consign him to some kind of infra-sexual bog where he would no longer be master of his own desire. This wish for mastery is also marked by the strange claim in sexology of gathering all the dimensions of love into one single science. As if knowing everything about sex (but which sex?) safeguards against the risks of love!

To a certain extent it's the same battle that must be waged against a Puritanism that constantly reappears in the field of Christian ethics, and against the sexologist discourse that is prevalent today: both proceed from the same inability to think of otherness in terms of creative irreducibility. We must work against the objectifying of sexuality to restore the meaning of vulnerability and of gift, so that the otherness of the other will be accepted not as a distance to be reduced at all costs (including the price of pornographic exhibition, of scientific objectification, or of moral terrorism) but as the very possibility of a shared creativity in this open space which a recognized and respected difference constitutes.[4]

Any ethic, or in any case any "Christian" ethic, should begin and end with this absolute respect for persons in their truth and mystery, in their creativity and their vulnerability. It becomes necessary to affirm, in the face of the pedantic claims of popular discourses, the importance of not-knowing, that is to say, of an irreducibility of the other to being confined to any a priori preconceptions. Or to an a priori morality! Man and woman need more than ever to invent, to create their shared existence; Christians need, among themselves, to discover it as the possible place of their discovery of the love of Christ. There is no a priori here other than the precedence of love over law, of gift over responsibility. The ethical responsibility is how to recognize the gift and inscribe it in reality. Linked no doubt to a society where the possibilities it offers to the couples and the hindrances it sets before them must be measured, this responsibility nevertheless remains *personal* (which does not mean individual!); it is rooted in an acknowledgment which cannot be *social* (any nostalgia for a moral Christian order must be reminded of this), because it concerns the very convictions at the heart of the choices of existence. In this case, "personal" signifies, according to the perspective of biblical anthropology, the person that man and woman are called to become together. And so, we return to the major point: recognition of otherness (which does not signify indifference); it only has meaning in the stringent dialogue which accepts distance but refuses to transform it into a barrier; it signifies the quest with the other, acknowledged as such, of that which can make this distance an inhabited space. I firmly maintain, because of the biblical testimony, that the human couple is the first place of the humanization of persons, and through them of societies. But I do object to individualism, especially under its phallic form where man is man/male in all things, as well as to the "sociologizing" which claims to submit the personal components to the determinisms of social standards. It is no longer necessary to attend the grand evening of the social revolution in order for a new ethic of conjugality to become possible; that future is to be played out from now on in the relationship of man/woman; it depends on our ability and our willingness to let the other approach us with his word.

My attempt here can only conclude with an admission and a call: the admission is that the roots of my reflections are marked by an evident limitation, that of belonging to a man, who, if he wants to take his call to the acknowledgment of otherness seriously, should now leave room for another discourse, i.e. by woman. And from this thought proceeds the call with which it seems right to end this book: the call to women, especially theologians, to tell how they foresee the future of a Christian ethic of sexuality; to tell how they enter this battle and what the central theological themes of the acknowledgment of otherness signifies for them.[5]

Geneva, (February) –August, 1978

Excursus:
Note on Homosexuality

I said in the Introduction that this project would not be a work of sexology or a casuistic treatise in any way—which is why I did not discuss the countless specific questions that sexual life presents. My main interest was in the ethical stakes and not in the way that any one person expresses them in his life. For on that level, everything is a matter of individual freedom and interpersonal dialogue.

I will make one very brief exception for the homosexual question[1] because this issue presents two difficult questions to Christian morality that test its credibility. These two questions are referred to in the following quotation from Marc Oraison: "We have a spontaneous tendency, in a kind of unreflective reaction, to *judge* homosexuals. But I had to face facts: there *can* be a relationship between homosexuals, even a transitory one, where there is a genuine friendship, genuine *charity* (I have to use the word) . . . It is not difficult to judge: it's *impossible*."[2]

First question: It is impossible to judge, according to Oraison, in the name of an approach to homosexuality and homosexuals that is clearly deduced from the gospel. Biblical tradition judges homosexuality—and quite severely! Even if the texts are not numerous,[3] they are extremely explicit: homosexuality is an "abomination" for the legislators of *Leviticus*; Paul sees it as the clearest consequence of pagan idolatry. Aren't we caught here between two unreconcilable requirements: that of listening to brothers, without a priori judgment (which does not condemn but tries to understand what is trying to be said through the particular existence of others) and that of a theological and anthropological truth, in the name of which standards of behavior and ethical judgments become possible and necessary?

215

Second question: Experience proves, even if it is rare, that a homosexual encounter can lead to genuine friendship, a genuine charity. In other words, something of the love whose total meaning and significance was revealed by Christ can be translated into the homosexual relationship. Now the whole scriptural tradition links the discovery of the otherness of God and of His love to the acceptance of sexual difference. The encounter with the Other is structurally linked to the acknowledgment of one's limitation and of the irreducibility of others—which is experienced in the heterosexual relationship. Isn't there an absolute opposition in perspective here?

Let us briefly examine these two questions.

1) The Bible condemns homosexuality for two fundamental reasons whose importance cannot be minimized. The *first* is that homosexuality arises from the impurity which, according to the priestly tradition, indicates a return to original chaos which the creative act of God had repelled. Uncleanness is a mixing of that which should remain separate; it is also the refusal of differences and the triumph of non-differentiation, i.e. disorder. Now sexual difference, as we have seen, crowns the creative action of God: the creation of the world culminates in the creation of man as man-and-woman. The couple thus experiences in their flesh the order of differentiation which structures the world. Man, in acknowledging that he exists only through the acceptance of the difference of the other, to whom his own difference refers, consents to the order of the world and consents to be some-one, limited and situated, and not to be the whole. To repeat what I said at the conclusion of my study on Leviticus (pp.38–9): as a key to the whole order of differentiation which structures the world, sexuality should be lived out by the man and woman as the very meaning of all differentiation, that is, recognized as a call to a relationship that is organizational and creative, like a call to arms against the constant threat of disorder and chaos, whose most insidious form is the confusion of the sexes.

This is why homosexuality which is a quest for sameness and a refusal of difference, is consent to chaos, according to biblical tradition, a refusal to enter the creative and organizing scheme of God, and of course, a refusal to accept the procreative consequences of sexuality.

The *second reason* shows that the scriptural tradition's rejection of homosexuality has nothing to do with phallic disdain. On the contrary: whatever claim of tenderness, vulnerability and weakness there is in homosexuality is equally defended by the biblical tradition against the possessive violence of a sexuality without love. In opposition to a fratricidal society where the males oppose each other violently but unite in the same disdain for woman (a society with a clear homosexual tendency!), the Bible announces a promise of a brotherly society where man and woman will know how to accept each other and respect each other. But it is clear that this goal of reconciliation is not founded on a rejection of difference but rather on a real and deep acceptance of it. The homosexual protests against a society where masculine and feminine roles are narrowly defined and contrasted; in his own way, to be sure, he reacts against the violence that such an opposition of the sexes creates and maintains; but he accomplishes his protest by ultimately succumbing to the same fears that he is denouncing. Homosexuality is less the result of the fear of difference than a means of surmounting it and destroying it. This, at least, is the way the Bible speaks of it, for example in the admirable and tragic character, Jonathan,[4] David's close friend. In trying to shatter the hellish circle of fratricidal hate that encloses Saul (with regard to David, who is the hated and fascinating rival) Jonathan saves David by sacrificing himself. His "man-love," if not homosexual love, for David is a radical protest against the violence that Saul exercises with regard to David. But this protest can only end in death, as though, by loving David as himself ("for he loved him as he loved his own soul" 1 Samuel 20:17) Jonathan abolished himself, lost in the distressing fascination with sameness.

Clearly the judgment of biblical tradition concerns not only homosexuality but all the forms of violence or disdain that sexuality can spawn. I should even add that to the extent that homosexuals are rejected because of their marginality even by strangers—by these "others" to whom (especially if they have been wounded by life) the Bible vows an especial brotherly concern—they are less the target of biblical judgment than certain heterosexuals whose violence and scorn are accompanied by a good conscience. But it is no less true that on the level of ethical choices, homosexuality is described as leading to a radical impasse: a road that only leads to death.

But the gospel has taught us that death is not the last word. . . And I do not see by what authority one could say that the power of the Resurrection will be ineffective for homosexuals. It is thus true, as Oraison said, that it is not up to us to judge homosexuals in terms of a preemptory condemnation which would claim to exclude them from God's grace. But it is equally true that it would be wrong, and even contemptuous, to hide from them that their experience is marked by a radical and tragic weakness. This is why I like Oraison's conclusion: "Through faith in Christ, heterosexuals *know* that they are walking through time in the ambivalent experience of a radical *insufficiency*; homosexuals *know* that they participate in this *same* walk by an even more radical experience of lack, and that they are not separate from it."[5]

2) And this brings us logically to the *second question*. When Paul condemns homosexuality (Romans 1:26-27), he does not do so in the name of moral law but according to a theological argument, in the prime sense of the term: homosexuality is the "normal" consequence of idolatry (cf. Romans 1:25-26: " . . . they exchanged the truth about God for a lie and worshiped and served the creature rather than the Creator. . . . For this reason God gave them up to dishonorable passions"). It is the furthest point of movement which, however, has many other consequences (cf. 29-32) which consist in substituting the creature for the Creator, that is to say, to succumb to the fascination of self-sufficiency. Homosexuality illustrates in a particularly striking way the confusion that follows upon a refusal of the "truth of God." The rejection of God's otherness and the refusal of otherness of others are particularly evident here.

But here again, it would be too convenient, and more than questionable, to reserve this judgment only for homosexuals. Paul uses them as an especially striking example and shows that homosexuality, because of the ultimate questions it raises, clearly reveals the choices of a society. But he doesn't shoot all his arrows at homosexuality (as in 1 Corinthians 6:9 and 1 Timothy 1:10, when homosexuality is listed along with other vices that are denounced); finally, we can see that the overview of Paul's presentation in Romans 1:18-3:30 aims at establishing the universality of sin and especially of showing that salvation does not depend on moral merits or on social or religious origins: the Good News, the Gospel, the power of God for salvation is offered to whomsoever believes in Him, to the Jew first, and then the Greek (Romans 1:16).

To whomsoever believes, heterosexual and homosexual. We all need to discover, through faith, that love, in the vulnerability and weakness of our bodies, makes its way into us as presence-of-the-Other who makes us live because we can only consent to Him without being able to possess Him.

Theses

1/1 All research on *human* sexuality is research on the symbolic language whereby men continue, under diverse forms, to control and socialize the sexual mystery.

/2 Sexuality is the domain par excellence of rules. For human societies cannot freely consent to sexual instinct since, as opposed to animals, man cannot regulate it naturally; but neither can they renounce it without jeopardizing their own existence.

/3 Sexuality is dangerous because of its potential for violence which can subvert social order by arousing mimetic rivalry. Therefore its practice must be ritualized in order to deflect that potential violence away from the group or towards forms of useful and productive activity.

/4 Human sexuality, which is where nature and society intersect, is irreducible in its essence to clear language; it cannot be socialized except by a strict regulation which introduces it into a productive cycle, where the long-term product appears preferable to immediate satisfaction. This leads to masculine and feminine roles being defined.

/5 But sexuality bespeaks the fact that sexual desire, like life, is richer than the order that socializes it. If it is always necessary to control it, it is also necessary to allow times and places (festivals and rituals) where its disorder can be acknowledged and controlled.

/6 In our secularized society, the symbolic control of sexuality is always tight, although in a different way than in ancient societies: scientific authority, or whatever fills that role in social imagination, is charged with ensuring that control.

/7 The new sexual morality being proposed is characterized by these two values: the duty to say everything about sexuality (to lift it out from under ancient oppressions) and the requirement for sexual success which gives a religious dimension that is quasi-eschatological to the activism of pleasure. "Salvation" lies in successful orgasm.

/8 We must ask whether this new ethic of pleasure, which claims to be liberating, is really only the ideological expression of liberal capitalistic society.

2/1 In seeking the *significance of human sexuality,* biology and physiology are interrogated. The results are disappointing since it is quite difficult to distinguish what is natural from what is cultural. At the most, biology recognizes a difference between the sexes but without being able to bring a value judgment to bear on those facts.

/2 Biology can explain (without justifying it) why man attributed certain functions to himself at the beginning which established his social superiority over woman: muscular strength and aggression due to hormones.

/3 The first way of ascribing meaning to sexuality was to make it sacred. Thus man simultaneously bespeaks his fear of violence that sexuality can lead to, and his acknowledgment of the value of a reality by means of which he can organize the world, i.e. through differentiation.

/4 Then, when man emphasizes his difference in relation to nature (in Greece as in Israel), he simultaneously de-sacredizes sexuality. Man—because of his transcendent freedom or because of his vocation to the Word—tends to align sexuality with animality or consider it insignificant because it too obviously roots man in contingent reality. Sexuality thus becomes dissociated from the positive project of life that man can assign to himself.

/5 As a reaction to this in the West, negativity confers an evil prestige to sexuality and makes it the symbol of the libertine's revolt.

/6 The dominant ideal of sexuality in our modern western societies integrates it into the stable and faithful order of the conjugal couple. Sexuality is considered humanized when it allows for a free, mature, creative relationship that is integrated into the whole existence of the couple.

/7 That ideal is challenged today by the facts (cf. the weakness of the conjugal institution, frequent divorce, "trial marriages"), and by the flexibility of the models proposed.

/8 Analytic theory shows that the law of language gives meaning to sexuality, that is to say, establishes it as the possible locus of experiencing otherness and limitation, and as the potential for alliance with another.

/9 Thus sexuality cannot be, without perversion, the locus of abolishing limit or difference. Only when limitation is accepted is a reciprocal relationship possible. Similarly, sexuality only becomes human when it makes room for the acceptance of the irreducibility of the other. The humanizaion of sexuality occurs through consenting to limit (I am not the whole) and by a rejection of violence.

II

1/1 Sexuality, in the *biblical tradition* too, is the locus of an ambiguous and therefore dangerous experience. This ambiguity is highlighted in the most ancient traditions by a whole series of prohibitions aimed at protecting society and at promoting positive significance to sexuality, allowing it to be integrated into a constructive project. The *priestly tradition* preserved countless notations of these prohibitions especially in Leviticus.

/2 Leviticus situates sexuality in a list of regulations concerning clean and unclean. Sexuality is unclean whenever it challenges the order willed by God that organizes the world, i.e. whenever it threatens to go beyond certain boundaries or to erase or remove differences.

/3 The order of the world, as God willed it and as celebrated by the priestly tradition in Genesis 1, culminates in the creation of man "in the image of God." Instantly created man-and-woman, man is thus stamped in his very being with a sign of differentiation. Sexuality, then, is not an unfortunate accident but rather the high point of God's creative action; man is other than the world and other than animals in that sexual difference becomes the experience of the promise affixed to the order of differentiation.

/4 Sexuality, as key to the order of differentiation which structures the world, should be lived out as the very meaning of all difference, i.e. recognized as a call to a creating and organizing relationship and as a call to battle the threat of disorder and chaos.

/5 The promise of fruitfulness attached to sexuality confirms the fact that difference can be creative. Thus, man participates in the work of God the Creator and takes dominion over the earth by organizing it.

/6 The *Yahwist* and *Elohist* traditions emphasize the fact that sexuality participates in the creative work of God only if it is acknowledged to be preceded by the Word which is its foundation (man is not his own origin) and ordained to battle against idolatry (sexual desire is the sign of finiteness and not of a quest for immortality). This is the beginning of a theological approach to sexuality.

2/1 Questioned about divorce, *Jesus* recalls that the standard for all nations is the original will of God. He comments on verses from the two Creation accounts (Matthew 19:4–6) and this commentary constitutes the basis for any Christian approach to sexuality.

/2 This commentary brings forth four points: sexuality is a gift from God; its goal is the humanization of man and woman in their mutual encounter; this humanization presupposes a break with infantile dependency status; finally, it is called to signify the creative love of God.

/3 The Old Testament, along with its positive appreciation of sexuality, warns against an idolatrous practice of sexuality which promises an experience of the divine. This warning attests to the link the Bible makes between the acknowledgment of the otherness of others and the acknowledgment of the otherness of God.

/4 In the texts at the beginning of Genesis (2–3), sexuality is approached and described in two different ways:

a) as the place of the happy experience of the complimentariness of man and woman. "It is not good for man to be alone." The "goodness" of the union between man and woman is related to the goodness of creation, for sexuality is the sign of difference, through which God reveals His own otherness. Thus, in Genesis 2:23, man's capacity for speech (and not simply his capacity to name things as in 2:20) occurs as the result of his encounter with the woman. Man cannot speak to God until he is revealed to himself via the otherness of the other (sex). This points to the positive function of sexual desire when it is an acknowledgement of the other, that is to say, an experience of one's own limitation since without the other one does not truly exist. (This is symbolized by the forbidden tree in the middle of the garden, in the middle of the space assigned to the encounter between man and woman.)

b) as the place of the unhappy experience of the violence of desire, leading to the enslavement of one sex by the other. It is also the place par excellence of experiencing fear and shame, where the consciousness of difference is expressed by aggression. Woman is particularly in danger of not being able to live out her sexuality except as an enslavement to man. This is qualified somewhat by the reminder in the text that the tragic aspect of woman's existence does, in spite of everything, result in motherhood (Genesis 3:20: "Eve. . .was the mother of all living") which links her to the very creation of God (Genesis 4:1: "I have gotten a man with the help of the Lord"). But even this remark remains ambiguous because it reduces woman to her role as mother; as woman she seems able to live only the failure of her desire and as such is continually scorned by man: "your desire shall be for your husband and he shall lord it over you" (Genesis 3:16).

/5 In an entirely different cultural context, *Paul,* faced with the Corinthian dualism which opposed the body (which is disdained because it is mortal and limited) to the immortal soul/spirit, recalls the Christological foundation of Christian anthropology:

The body is not a thing or an instrument that man can use without really being personally involved. The body is the person of the man marked by the limit of his condition as a creature and called to a relationship and an encounter with others. Sexuality is not a bodily function comparable to alimentation, but the expression of the body/person insofar as he is called to relationship.

/6 Immorality is serious because it's a theo-anthropological perversion (rather than a moral one). It denies the body as a limitation and as a presence which can only come to him through the other. As such, it is a rejection of the Lord insofar as He is the mysterious link which allows relationship and a locus of gathering together all the "members" into a single "body."

/7 The body is the icon of God. Paul, comdemning disdain for the body *and* the reduction of man to his body, affirms that the choice is not between an unincarnated spirituality and a body reduced to its organic density: the whole meaning of the body is to be a presence indwelt by the Spirit of God.

III

1/1 In the Old Testament, marriage, like sexuality, is a gift from God (Genesis 2:18) and it is the object of a promise. The Song of Solomon sings of its wonders: conjugal love (along with sexual desire) is given to man and woman so that they can perceive therein a dimension of liberty, of gratuitousness and of joy of the very love of God. Love is possible in marriage because marriage is freed by the Word from any religious ends (it is not a reiteration of the god and goddess uniting to make the earth fruitful) and is not reduced to its social function (channeling sexuality, dividing up the women, procreating children).

/2 Marriage, an earthly reality and creation of God, is assigned, in the Old Testament, an important symbolic function which, conversely, gives value to the relational elements that constitute it. Love, faithfulness, covenant and tenderness are offered to man and woman as reminders and signs of a love, faithfulness, covenant and tenderness which the history of Israel records and professes to have come from God.

/3 The elective-affective interpretation of marriage constitutes Israel's specific contribution. But it is never separated from another interpretation which gives priority to the procreative function of marriage and subordinates the value of the conjugal bond to its fruitfulness. There is a tension in the Old Testament between the perspective where descendancy is more important than love and one where love is more important than the obligation of serving the species.

2/1 *Jesus'* teaching removes the problem of marriage from the legalistic realm where, considered as a "natural" reality, it is to be regulated by a morality of "do's" and "don'ts," and submits it to prophetic challenge. Marriage is revealed to have definite stakes: either it's recognized as the place where man and woman apprehend the promise and grace of God, or it becomes the expression of a refusal of the creative force of love, the sign of the deadly violence of lust.

/2 Lust is what most essentially threatens the couple. In comparing repudiation to adultery, Jesus challenges the casuistry of His time which justified violence perpetrated against the weak (in this case, woman) and which covers up the real reason for marital failure: the refusal that lust sets up against love. Jesus refuses to give any justification for divorce, although realizing that it does exist.

/3 Jesus rescues marriage from being only a "natural" necessity. In refusing to marry, Jesus institutes celibacy as a possible vocation and thereby gives marriage a value. Because of the Kingdom, both celibacy and marriage cease being natural realities, or destinies to be submitted to in order to refer both vocations to the grace which makes human freedom possible. In the gospel perspective, celibacy and marriage confirm each other's vocational character.

/4 The *apostolic tradition* deals with the question of how to integrate the Master's teaching into the life of the first-century communities. Luke emphasizes the need for ascetics. Matthew, responsible for a community that would experience, like Israel, the "hardness of the human heart," maintains Jesus' criticism of legalism; God does not "authorize" divorce but neither does he desire the death of the sinner. Jesus' words indicate a rejection of any legalism in conjugal matters; but in order to avoid the emergence of a new law arising out of this rejection, Matthew introduces a phrase authorizing divorce in the case of *porneia.*

/5 Paul's ethical thinking on marriage touches on three points; the commandment of the Lord revealing the requirement and the promise accompanying the man/woman relationship; next, the personal and social context where the requirements and the promise are lived out; finally, the eschatological perspective which makes the so-called "natural" given relative. Sexuality and marriage are no longer fatal destinies or necessities but indicate a possibility of a freely chosen vocation.

/6 The author of Ephesians introduces the critical aspect of the gospel into a cultural scheme that seems unquestionable to the Christians of the first century (i.e. man is superior to woman). The result is a challenge to that scheme in terms of its "naturalness," or irreversible destiny. The gospel reveals that this scheme, in fact, is really the consequence of a prevailing situation where love has no place. The analogy of the love of Christ for the Church, His body, is given as an analogy to the relationship of love between a man and a woman in marriage. This is the foundational principle for the theological interpretation of marriage.

IV

1/1 *Up until around 200* the Christian Church insists on the need for a moral discipline in regard to sexuality. It accomplishes this with the help of arguments drawn from Jewish and Stoic moral traditions in response to the strong expectation of the ancient world. The Christian ideal exalts fidelity and chastity in marriage. That ideal carries a concern to safeguard a sexual ethic which respects the most vulnerable people, i.e. children, slaves and especially women.

/2   The first Christian theologians (Clement of Alexandria, Irenaeus, Tertullian) reveal that a dual struggle develops within the Church. On one hand there is a struggle against an exaggerated asceticism (which rejects all sexuality) and there are calls for a defense of the value of marriage. Marriage, instituted by God, associates men to the work of creation. To defend marriage is to defend the value of creation. In this situation, the accent is strongly placed on the procreative function of marriage.

/3   There is an equal need to fight against the antinomianism proclaimed by the Gnostics who taught that man is above common laws and can never sin, no matter what he does. In that situation, there must be a reminder that real freedom is detachment from a domination by passion and that moral indifference disdains the laws of God the creator. The argument of natural law, borrowed from the Stoics, is used in this case. Recourse to this argument, in the face of gnostic aberrations, allows a defense of marriage, but one which excludes bodily love and sexual desire: here again, marriage is justified by procreation.

2/1 During the same period, the ancient Church tries to attain a general *discipline* with regard to marriage. It authorizes divorce in the case of adultery of one of the parties, but requires divorced people to remain single and thus leave the door open for a possible reconciliation with the guilty party. Remarriage of widowers and widows is permissible, although not recommended; as for mixed marriage with non-Christians, they are pastoral (and not juridical) concerns. Finally, the Church departs from the practice of the time by recognizing the validity of the marriage of slaves.

3/1 The most systematic thinking of the great *moral theologians of the fourth and fifth centuries* (especially Gregory of Nyssa, Ambrose, John Chrysostom, Jerome and Augustine) results in two conclusions that will stamp Christian ethics for many centuries. The first postulates that sexuality is totally separate from love and is aligned with sin. In fact, sexual desire, irrational instinct and pleasure are all signs of sexuality's link to sin.

/2 The second conclusion is that virginity is superior to marriage because it is the rejection of all sexual activity, i.e. of an action that turns one away from God. Virginity makes one divine and makes man similar to angels, whereas man's relationship with woman carries serious spiritual dangers by anchoring him to his carnal body and cares of this world. Only procreation and a concern to avoid even greater impurity justify marriage.

/3 *The causes of this evolution* are external and internal. The actual causes consist in the strong influence of ancient society on Christianity in four areas: morals (Christianity takes on the Puritan reaction which marked ancient society at the end of the first century); Roman law, which did not leave room for love in the conjugal institution; a profound pessimism about the world, man and history; finally, ethics, where Christianity took up almost the whole stoic discourse on sexuality and marriage.

/4 The internal causes stem from the real difficulty of maintaining the gospel tension between the need to separate from the world in order to receive the kingdom and the need to take charge of reality and structure into it the signs of God's plan for man. The ancient Church highly spiritualized the separation from the world in postulating that the real world was elsewhere and was attained by asceticism and a negation of contingencies; this led to approaching present reality by a somewhat distant participation in the regulations of this world. Christian spirituality is eschatological but Christian ethics is conformist.

/5 A good example of the theological ambivalence is found in the discourse on *women*: on one hand, it affirms the theoretical (i.e. eschatological) equality of woman to man but it defends the social and ecclesiastical subordination of woman to man. In the eternal Kingdom, sexuality will be abolished and with it the basis which justifies the strict subordination of women. Sexual difference is thought of in terms of sin.

4/1 The western ethical tradition was deeply marked by Augustinian thinking. All through the *Middle Ages,* ethical reflection occurs within the framework defined by Augustine. Three themes in particular are continually repeated. The first concerns the link between sexuality and sin. Augustine had defined the goodness of procreative sexuality (against the Manicheans) but his emphasis (against the Pelagians) that concupiscence is the consequence of the "fall" led western theology to make sexuality the very symbol of the covetous idolatry of man and the symbol of sin.

/2 The second theme concerns the final ends of marriage: children, the pact of fidelity (*fides*), and the stability of the union. Marriage's goals then are procreation, but also the structuring of the desire (that leads to the creation of family) into the stable and faithful institution.

/3 The third theme is the definition of the theological signification of marriage as *sacramentum*. It is a symbol of Christ's union with His Church. But Augustine still hesitated on the implications of the sacramentality of marriage: is it acknowledged and given only to believers, or is it an objective fact that concerns all couples? Theology becomes mixed with juridical aspects, and reflections on the profoundity of the conjugal bond lead to a reinforcement of the social prohibitions against divorce.

/4 Augustinianism in the High Middle Ages is often caricatured: sexuality has become sin, and even an intention of exercising it only for procreation does not remove its sinful character. Original sin is transmitted through sexuality because of concupiscence.

/5 In the twelfth century, serious spiritual and intellectual mutations begin to occur. Peter Abelard, with his theology of pure love (close to "courtly" sentiment) exalts love over against marriage; Hugh of Saint Victor attempts an approach to marriage as the institution of love and intimacy. A whole philosophical current attempts to restore value to human love by spiritualizing eroticism. This current, combined with the catharic crisis which marks a return of gnostic dualism, forces moral theology to rethink and to correct Augustinian doctrine in the thirteenth century.

/6 Thus scholastic theology integrates new elements into classical doctrine: a recognition of the value of conjugal love as friendship and affection; the importance of the education of children, which gives value to the familial setting; a recognition of the emotional value of intercourse. Two more points signal a departure by medieval theology from Augustinian doctrine: pleasure is no longer condemned per se (Aristotle wins over Stoicism!) and disdain for woman undergoes a modification (the importance of Mary).

5/1 The evolution of *marriage law* confirms the transformation of feeling and thought that was occurring in the theological realm. At first, from the fourth to the eleventh centuries, the evolution had led to a marked reinforcement of the Church's control of marriage. This compelled the canon-law writers to clarify two important points. The first concerns the validity of marriage: is it the spouses' consent or sexual intercourse which validates the marriage?

/2 The question of validity raised the issue of the sacramentality of marriage. A serious approach to sexuality led some to believe that the sacrament was in the union of the bodies while others believed that the love between the spouses instituted the sacrament. Thomas defines marriage by this synthesis: "a certain joining together of husband and wife ordained to carnal intercourse and a further consequent union between husband and wife." Sacramental grace is linked to conjugal love, which includes sexual union. Thus, there is a distinct evolution in medieval theology which rediscovers many elements of the realism in Scripture.

6/1 The essential elements of *Protestant doctrine* elaborated by men as different as Erasmus, Luther, Butzer, Zwingli, Calvin and Bèze, can be summarized into four points. The Reformers' first goal is the liberation of conscience (for clerics as well as laymen) from the heavy yoke of canon law and pastoral practice. Therefore they fight against the absolute prohibition of divorce which had led both to greater social disorder than the disorder it aimed to prevent and to despair for so many men and women. Likewise, they oppose the ecclesiastical requirement of celibacy.

/2 The fundamental theological discussion revolves around the rapport of marriage with the order of God's creation; it results in a rejection of the concept of marriage-as-sacrament, since marriage belongs to the natural order willed by God for all men.

/3 The Christian doctrine of marriage, now freed from its strict confinement by canonical legislation, can play an important, and even major, role in the social and ethical order. The tone of Reformation teaching on this point is found in the praise given to the beauty, dignity and profound morality of the conjugal bond, which is the foundation for all social life. Sexuality becomes the object of a sympathetic reevaluation. The scale of values which had dominated ever since the patristic period becomes inverted: marriage is now the order willed by God, the standard, and celibacy becomes an exception which is barely acceptable.

/4 Such an approach was easily acceptable because of the perspectives of the new western society that had come forth during the Renaissance. It favored flexibility by liberalizing divorce and it reinforced social and economic structures by justifying a super-valuation of the family, now closely knit together under the authority of the father.

/5 The further evolution of Protestant Churches demonstrates something that essentially remained from the initial thrust of the Reformers: the acknowledgment of the couple on the social, ecclesial, moral and spiritual plane, as responsible before God for their specific vocation. Along with their (married) pastors, Protestants realize that their conjugal life is not a matter for Church control but is their personal responsibility before God. On the other hand, as far as the control of the validity of marriage goes, there is a return to a clerical perspective and a constitution of canon law that gives the pastor a significant social role.

7/1 A comparison of the *two ethical systems in the West since the seventeenth century* reveals some significant differences in the realm of sexual ethics. Catholic ethics remains faithful to patristic tradition: sexuality is justified only by procreation and marriage is inferior to celibacy. Protestant ethics affirms that sexuality cannot be bad because God created man as a sexed being: what is evil is the lust which can make it unnatural.

/2 Catholic ethics essentially uses the concept of natural law as a reference point, and because of it prohibits any artificial contraception. Protestant ethics looks for its ethical models in the Bible, which leads it to confer a fundamental importance on the conjugal couple and a fundamental social value on marriage. Within the couple, the subordination of the wife to the husband remains unchanged.

/3 Catholic morality is defined, and often in great detail, by the ecclesiastical magisterium: boundaries are set, lines are drawn, especially for sexual morality, by clerical authority—which leads to sharp conflict with modern states on the issue of jurisdiction. On the other hand, Protestant morality assigns the responsibility for ethical decisions to individual consciences; it is up to the spouses, enlightened by the gospel, to decide how they will live their conjugality. Because of the strong interiorization of standards this entails, the danger here is the development of a scrupulous morality.

/4 The two examples of contraception and abortion reveal the practical differences in the two orientations of Christian ethics in the West.

V

1/1 *Sexuality,* in Christian theology, is neither the ordinary hygienic functioning of sexual organs, nor a natural pleasure with no consequences, nor a tragic confrontation with the forces of death and abjection; it is a gamble, a difficult ethical choice, where the ambiguity of the existence of man, "destined" to be good but "inclined" to evil (Kant), is best revealed. The dramatic and ambiguous character of human sexuality explains why Christian tradition desperately sought to understand the link between sexuality and spirituality. The ethical stakes, as revealed in Scripture, center on whether sexuality emerges from non-differentiation or from violence closed in upon itself so that it might become the sign of presence to others, the sign of a gift and a love.

2/1 Biblical tradition translates the revelation of the Otherness of God into ethical terms by affirming that it signifies the *antecedence of the couple* over the sexed individual. Therefore the couple is the long-range objective of sexuality, because man and woman, created in God's image are called to live out their sexual difference as an experience of otherness, i.e. called to live out their sexuality as holding a rich promise of a life created and recreated by Love.

/2 If, then, the love of man and woman is a sign of the love of God, the *ethical task* is to define how this sign can be concretely translated into the project of the human couple today (just as the author of Ephesians did for his period in translating the love of Christ for His Church in terms of protective responsibility and affectionate care). I believe that the human couple carries a triple promise: being the place for the effectuation of fidelity, freedom and conjugality.

/3 *Fidelity,* based on an acknowledgment of the love of God the creator, is not primarily faithfulness to a past commitment, nor is it faithfulness to the needs of personal growth and development. It is faithfulness to the project mutually decided upon, i.e. the ongoing creation of the conjugal couple. The partners, in the name of this project commit themselves to trust each other and to be challenged, changed and transformed by one another. There is thus the creation of a history since each one renounces his current status in order to move forward, because of and through the other, toward a fulfillment of their projected goal.

/4 In this perspective, fidelity implies that the two spouses are both promise and limit for each other, as well as the meaning of the project and the challenge to the illusion of self-sufficiency. The mutual commitment of the spouses, in the image of the irreversible commitment by God to men through Jesus Christ, must also be irreversible, having the other partner as its guarantee.

/5 *Freedom,* which the couple is called to live out, is in the image of the freedom lived out by Christ which results practically in the liberation of others, and therefore is above all mutual liberation. On one hand it consists in appeasing paralyzing fears and on the other hand in making possible the expression of the rich potential within the other. Freedom is lived out as an exercise in listening and trusting. The other must be allowed to approach as he is and must not be reduced to the flesh-density of his body.

/6 Freedom, like liberating mutual trust, implies an endurance of reality, the acceptance of the other as he really is, with appearances stripped away. To endure here means allowing time gradually to reveal the authenticity of the desire which indwells us, and through which a more profound truth is revealed at the heart of daily life. It is thus the contrary of what is normally called "sexual liberation."

/7 *Conjugality* signifies that man and woman not only live together but that they determine to inscribe their love relationship into a time and into a social space; they confirm this decision by committing themselves to one another publicly; in response, the social group they belong to acknowledges them as a couple and commits itself to them.

/8 Theologically this signifies two things. First of all, love has a social dimension: as the commandment of Christ shows, love is not an intimate feeling but a commandment, i.e. a required service and responsibility. Secondly, this signifies that society, by instituting marriage and protecting it, renounces a concept of itself as the immediate and ultimate end of individual life. The conjugal couple is the fundamental structure of society which structures the couple less than it is structured by the couple. The ethical task here is to ensure that this rapport does not become inverted and that the couple is not reduced to conforming to a social model; society must recognize that the couple is the source of all possible life.

3/1 Sexuality is a reality to be conquered by the couple so that its fundamental darkness can become transparent to the presence of person. But it must also be conquered so that man and woman can experience the reality of their rootedness-in-flesh and can experience, as an inventive game, the non-conformity of their desires to the rules and laws which threaten their existence with formality and habit.

/2 The creative force of sexual desire can be expressed by erotic play. But it can also be perverted into violence. If Christian morality always distrusted pleasure, it is because it can be sought after as an affirmation of one's desire to escape limitation and the risk of suffering—and this becomes a refusal of the other who is denied as a person and made into an instrument of pleasure.

/3 But this danger, which is quite real today because of the ideology of unlimited pleasure, should not consign us to a position that was too often defended by a Christian pseudo-spirituality: the rejection of pleasure. For such a rejection is also an affirmation of the desire to escape the precariousness of existence.

/4 Once man can consent to limits and accept himself as mortal, he can experience through pleasure a call and a gift of life which always subverts death and insignificance. It revives and makes tangible a savor for life for man, precisely because life does not belong to him but comes to him from elsewhere, from God. This savor for life which pleasure confirms is the trace of a Word in man which is his foundation and which he does not possess. Outside of this theological interpretation, pleasure risks being only the expression of a quest, and often a violent quest, for imaginary power over death.

/5 Sexual pleasure leads man and woman to a consciousness of the profundity of their existence, which belongs to the spiritual order. In the experience of love, which is both the encounter of bodies and the approach of the mystery of persons when bodily union does not change, man and woman can discover that the spirit is not truly received until the bodily flesh of existence is not denied but celebrated. The other is both the body close at hand and the irreducible mystery of a presence. Thus man and woman can celebrate, through the fragile language of their bodies, the mystery of the world and of God.

/6 An authentic spirituality of vulnerability and of gift can therefore undergrid the erotic celebration of love. But the acknowledgment of the spiritual value of pleasure is inseparable from the acknowledgment of the mystery of the other which is signified in particular by a rapport to the body of the other that is not dominated by lust. The body of the other is a sign that must be deciphered, a hope to be perceived, a gift to be accepted, a presence to be welcomed.

Notes

Translator's note: English editions have been used for the quotations in this text whenever possible. Therefore, any footnote with a foreign title indicates that the translation was done for this book. Abbreviations used in quoting the Church Fathers are fully explained in the bibliography.

CHAPTER I.   Section 1.

[1]Although this book was originally published in English, this preface accompanies only the French edition on p. 20. Original edition: Mary Tew Douglas, *Purity and Danger* (London: Routledge & Kegan Paul, 1966).

[2]Helmut Schelsky, *Sociologie de la sexualité,* (Paris, 1966), Coll. Idées 103, p. 15.

[3]Sigmund Freud, *Civilization and Its Discontents,* in *The Standard Edition of the Complete Psychological Works of Sigmund Freud,* trans. by James Strachey (London, 1961) Vol. XXI, pp. 96–97.

[4]The thesis which I have recourse to here is René Girard's, defended in *Violence and the Sacred* (French edition, 1972) and elaborated in *Des choses cachées depuis la fondation du monde* (1978) (cf. p. 85, p. 96).

[5]Helmut Schelsky, *op. cit.,* p. 129.

[6]On rape: Susan Griffin, *Le viol, crime américain par excellence,* (Montreal, 1972); Susan Brownmiller, *Against our Will: Men, Women, and Rape* (New York: Simon and Schuster, 1975); Marie-Odile Fargier, *Le viol,* (Paris, 1976); Andra Medea, Kathleen Thompson, *Against Rape* (New York: Farrar, Straus and Giroux, 1974); Ph. Robert, Th. Lambert, C. Faugeron, *Image du viol collectif et reconstruction d'object,* (Genèvé 1976), coll. "Déviance et société."

[7]Cf. René Girard (books cited) on the necessity for societies to keep violence (in its destructive effects) at arm's length, through regulating it by a unanimous act of violence via a scapegoat; and on the manner in which this unanimous act of transgression lays the foundation for prohibition.

[8]Georges Bataille, *Death and Sensuality* (New York: Walker and Company, 1962), p. 41. This whole book is extremely important in the analysis of other prohibitions which surround sexuality, especially insofar as it is linked to a consciousness of death.

[9]Augustine, *De civ. Dei,* XIV, xx, 40, *FC,* Vol. XIV, p. 395.

[10]François Chirpaz, "Sexualité, morale et poétique. Approche philosophique," *Lumière et Vie* 97, 1970, p. 85 ff.

[11]In this issue, the analyses of everyday language used by women to denounce "le sexisme ordinaire"—which is the title from a news report in *Temps Modernes* —are very revealing.

[12]Excellent presentation of the problem in Helmut Schelsky, *op. cit.,* pp. 23–42.

[13]"It can be verified that a chosen pattern of sexual behaviour in any given era is established (among multiple hereditary tendencies) for the role of the sexes, and that there also exists in each society a subsidiary division of that behaviour based on social class, educational level, or religion, and sometimes on clans or attitudes in that area." Helmut Schelsky, *op. cit.,* p. 38.

[14]A good example of this is "La Revue internationale des rapports humains" *Union,* which, every month under the respected direction of doctors (in sexology, psychology, psycho-pedagogy. . .), teaches one how to make love correctly, how to rid oneself of prejudices and taboos which have taken a heavy toll, to recognize the beauty of one's fantasies. With 275,000 copies printed, the September 1977 issue, for example, increased the testimonies concerning all kinds of sexual practices, each one accompanied by "scientific" commentaries aimed at ensuring the normality of these practices, in the name of sincerity on one hand (being of service to and participating in the great endeavor of liberation) and in the name of sexual "success" on the other hand, as measured by the intensity of pleasure.

[15]Like this one, in the same issue of *Union,* which I leave to the reader's appreciation: "The woman's legs crossed over the small of the back of her partner indicate to him the cadence of desired penetration. . . ." The "cadence of penetration"—What elegant terms. . . ! On the absurdity of the new Diafoirus of sex, cf. Pascal Bruckner and Alain Finkielkraut, *Le nouveau désordre amoureux* (Paris, 1977).

[16]Wilhelm Reich, *The Sexual Revolution,* trans. by Theodore P. Wolfe (New York: Farrar, Straus and Giroux, 1945).

[17]*Ibid.,* p. 267.

[18]David G. Cooper, *The Grammar of Living* (New York: Pantheon Books, 1974).

[19]Such is the manner in which David Cooper in his "Manifesto of Orgasm" invites his readers to an asceticism, to rituals and to a mystical religious experience. Likewise sexologists in popular magazines play exactly the same role as the clergy in the Catholic Church—they celebrate the sacramental liturgy of sex and judge the conformity of the faithful to dogma and morality.

[20]It is significant that Reich always denounces the opposition between nature and culture.

[21]Cf. F. Laplantine, "Les idéologies contemporaines du plaisir," *Lumière et vie,* 114, 1973, "Le plaisir," pp. 41–64.

[22]I have elaborated this point in *Bull, C.P.E.* (18e année, 1966, 2-3), "Sexualité et morale," pp. 5-17.

[23]With the assistance of an unedited analysis by W. Ossipow.

CHAPTER I.   Section 2.

[1]François Chirpaz, *Le corps* (Paris, 1969^2), coll. "Initiation philosophique" 50, p. 66.

[2]Cf. Geneviève Texier, "Sexualité feminine et maternité," *Esprit,* 1970/11, "La sexualité" pp. 1921-29. Abel Jeannière, *The Anthropology of Sex,* trans. by Julie Kernan (New York: Harper & Row, 1964), pp. 77-107; Annie Leclerc, *Parole de femme* (Paris 1974), pp. 78-86.

[3]There is another moment in life which is preceded by a long waiting—the moment when a life is extinguished. Perhaps it is not by chance that women have traditionally been the ones to sit at the bedside of the dying.

[4]Nicole Fatio in an unedited text.

[5]François Chirpaz, "Dimensions de la sexualité," *Etudes* (March 1969), p. 414.

[6]As Annie Leclerc clearly states: "They (men) have invented a whole sexuality through silence of our part. If we (women) invent our own, then they will have to rethink all of theirs." *Parole de femme.* (Paris, 1974), p. 53. This very beautiful book is a forceful and illuminating meditation on the experience a woman has of her own body. A real body and a symbolic body must simultaneously be invented by means of a newly liberated and established speech.

[7]Odette Thibault, in the conclusion of the first part of a collective work, *Le fait feminin,* edited by Evelyne Sullerot (Paris 1978), p. 218. Words underlined by the author.

[8]Moustafa Safouan, *La sexualité feminine dans la doctrine freudienne* (Paris 1976), p. 131 ff. Words underlined by author.

[9]Jeannière, *op. cit.,* p. 66.

[10]With incomparable force, Euripides demonstrates this in *Bacchae.* Cf. René Girard, *Violence and the Sacred, op. cit.,* pp. 126-142).

[11]Moliere, *Don Juan,* Act I, scene 2, trans. by George Graveley (New York: Oxford University Press, 1956), pp. 37-38.

[12]A recent sociological survey in Geneva of couples married within the last two years showed that the three values which best expressed the aspirations of these men and women were *equality, fidelity,* and *permanence.* Unedited document at the University of Geneva, CETEL, research group on the family.

[13]Cf. J. Kellerhals, "Couple et famille; ambiguités et tensions contemporaines," *Bull. CPE* 29, (1977), 5-6, "La famille," pp. 17-37.

[14]On the ambiguities and the contradictions of actual social practices in the area under discussion, cf. the article by J. Kellerhals, "Ambiguités sociales de la sexualité" in *Sexologie* (1970-73), edited by W. Geisendorf and W. Pasini (Geneva 1974), pp. 5-9.

[15]Cf. Jacques Lacan, *The Function of Language in Psychoanalysis,* trans. with notes by Anthony Wilden (Baltimore: John Hopkins University Press, 1968), p. 45 ff.

[16]D. Vasse, *L'ombilic et la voix* (Paris 1974), p. 111.

[17]"The subject disentangles himself from his imaginary and mirror indentification with things at the very moment he understands and takes up speech. . . .This speech is the one which names him (by the voice of another) as well as the one by which he names himself, things, and others." Vasse, *op. cit.,* p. 114 ff.

[18]Françoise Dolto, Preface to P. David, *Psychanalyse et famille* (Paris 1976), p. 12.

[19]Vasse, *op. cit.,* p. 129: cf, also P. David, *op. cit.* p. 114.

[20]D. Vasse, "L'ordre symbolique et la Loi," *Bull. Centre Th. More* 2 (1974), No. 7, p. 22.

[21]P. David, *op. cit.,* p. 118.

CHAPTER II.

[1]I use the singular (*the* Word of God) not to presuppose a facile concordance among the diverse traditions which constitute the Old and New Testament (which contain differences and tensions that will be discussed later) but to emphasize the fact that all these traditions seek to account for (even in their very diversity) the manner in which human language can express, and under what conditions, the revelatory Word of God.

CHAPTER II   Section 1.

[1]For a presentation of this tradition as a whole, cf. Gerhard von Rad, *Old Testament Theology* trans. by D.M.G. Stalker (Edinburgh: Oliver and Boyd, 1962), Vol. I, "The Theology of Israel's Historical Traditions". pp. 243–79.

[2]On this question, consult the excellent book by Mary Tew Douglas *op. cit.,* especially Chapter III on "The Abominations of Leviticus."

[3]". . . .(alimentary) rules (are) an *a posteriori* generalization of their habits. Cloven-hoofed, cud-chewing ungulates are the model of the proper kind of food for a pastoralist. If they must eat wild game, they can eat wild game that shares these distinctive characters and is therefore of the same general species. This is a kind of casuistry which permits scope for hunting antelope and wild goats and wild sheep. Everything would be quite straightforward were it not that the legal mind has seen fit to give ruling on some borderline cases. Some animals seem to be ruminant, such as the hare and the hyrax (or rock badger), whose constant grinding of their teeth was held to be cud-chewing. But they are definitely not cloven-hoofed and so are excluded by name." Douglas, *op. cit.* pp. 54–55.

[4]On man's longstanding distress about the body's apertures and about the non-enclosure of the body, cf. Vasse *op. cit.* We even find a prohibition concerning excrement, cf. Deut 23: 13–15.

[5]According to the text (Lev. 18: 26-28), These "abominations" defile the land, and the land takes its revenge by "vomiting out" its inhabitants. The land itself resists confusion by expelling those who sow disorder.

⁶The same thing is seen in Lev. 19: 35 ff. Likewise in Lev. 21: 16–23, those who are not physically whole cannot enter the priesthood: cleanness in this instance is the absence of physical defects. Of course the concept of holiness, in Leviticus itself, has a comparable moral significance (cf. 19: 9–18 on the respect for one's neighbor), but it is derived from the basic concept of holiness as an absence of confusion or mixture. Cf. also Deut. 22:5 against transvestism.

⁷Eliane Amado Lévy-Valensi, *Le grand désarroi aux racines de l'énigme homosexuelle* (Paris 1973), pp. 91 ff.

⁸The priestly recitation of the long geneological lists (eg. Gen. 5:1–32; 10: 1–32; 11: 10–32) intends to show the uninterrupted continuity of the history of their ancestors.

⁹On the diverse traditions that together make up the Pentateuch, see "Introduction au Pentateuque" in *Traduction Oecumenique de la Bible* (TOB) (O.T., pp. 31–36) or the excellent popularization by Jacques Briend, *Une lecture du Pentateuque,* Cahiers Evangile 15 (Paris 1976).

¹⁰An example of this reciprocal gift is included in the Yahwist tradition in the love of Isaac and Rebecca (Gen. 24).

CHAPTER II.   Section 2.

¹"You have heard that it was said, You shall not commit adultery. But I say unto you that every one who looks at a woman lustfully has already committed adultery with her in his heart." (Matt. 5:27–28, spoken in the context of the warnings in the Sermon on the Mount regarding what can destroy a relationship with one's neighbor, Matt. 5:21–48.).

²The difference with which Jesus speaks about money should be noted—Jesus brings much more of a negative judgment on it: the "Mammon" of unrighteousness (Luke 16:9) is a rival of God Himself (Matt. 6:24 and Luke 16:13); one must throw off its yoke to enter into the Kingdom (Matt. 19:23 ff). This should give cause for reflection to the bourgeois and puritanical societies which loudly condemn sex but consider wealth as the very sign of heavenly blessing!

³I shall not at this time discuss verses 1–3 and 7–9 of Matt. 19; they shall be analyzed in detail later in the discussion on marriage and divorce.

⁴Gen. 1:1–2: 4, which belongs to the "priestly" tradition, (6th century), as we have seen.

⁵Gen. 2:5–3: 24 which belongs to the "yahwist" tradition, the oldest tradition (10th century).

⁶On the theological importance of sexual differentiation, cf. Karl Barth, *Church Dogmatics* III, 1, trans. by Edwards, Bussey and Knight, (Edinburgh: T.&.T. Clark, 1958), p. 185 ff., 288 ff.

⁷George Crespy, "The Grace of Marriage" in *Marriage and Christian Tradition,* with Paul Evdokimov and Christian Duquoc, trans. by Sr. Agnes Cunningham (Techny, Illinois: Divine Word Publications, 1968), p. 13 ff.

⁸In the text, the failure to acknowledge otherness finds confirmation in the refusal to accept human limitation (the forbidden tree in the middle of the garden). This refusal signifies a refusal of God: the consequence is the fratricide by Cain, another radical refusal of otherness. I will return to this point later.

[9]Crespy, *op. cit.,* p. 19.

[10]For a more complete exegesis, consult: Paul Humbert, *Etudes sur le récit du paradis et de la chute dans la Genése.* (Neuchâtel, 1940); Franz J. Leenhardt, "La situation de l'homme dans la Genèse" in *Dans Menschenbild im Lichte des Evangeliums,* Festschrift f. E. Brunner (Zurich, 1950), pp. 1–29; Gerhard von Rad, *op. cit.*; Norbert Lohfink, "The Story of the Fall," *The Christian Meaning of the Old Testament,* trans. by R.A. Wilson (Milwaukee: The Bruce Publishing Company, 1968), pp. 52–67. P. Grelot, "Homme, qui es-tu? Les onze premiers chapitres de la Genèse," *Cahiers Evangile* 4 (Paris, 1973).

[11]Why a snake? Because of the cultural and religious traditions that are the author's sources, cf. note "w" in *TOB, AT,* p. 48.

[12]"...it is sin that is the nothingness of vanity. Thereby the possibility arises of interpreting the two states of innocence and sin no longer as successive, but as superimposed; sin does not follow innocence, but, in the *Instant,* loses it." Paul Ricoeur, *The Symbolism of Evil,* trans. by Emerson Buchanan (Boston: Beacon Press, 1969), p. 251.

[13]Martin Luther, Sermon on Matt. 8:13, June 18, 1534. *Weimarer Ausgabe* 37, p. 451ff.

[14]For a study of this text, consult the following commentaries (cf. Bibliography for Chapter II and III) and monographs: Herrade Mehl-Koehnlein, *L'homme selon l'apôtre Paul,* Cahier théol. 28 (Neuchâtel 1951); John A.T. Robinson, *The Body: a Study in Pauline Theology* (Chicago: H. Regnery Co., 1952); Walter Schmithals, *Die Gnosis in Korinth. Eine Untersuchung zu den Korintherbriefen* (Gottingen: Vandenhoeck & Ruprecht, 1956); J. Murphy O'Connor, *L'existence chrétienne selon saint Paul* (Paris 1974).

CHAPTER II. Section 3.

[1]Cf. also the accounts about Sodom in Genesis 19 and the rape of Dinah, Jacob's daughter, which was punished by the massacre at Sichem in Genesis 34. Deuteronomy is aware of the ever-threatening violence that can accompany sexuality and tries to guard the life of the people against it on certain points: 22:13–23, laws on virginity, adultery, and rape; 24:1–4 laws protecting the repudiated wife.

[2]And does not, as the puritan moralists of all ages say, lower man to animal nature.

CHAPTER III. Section 1.

[1]The bibliography is enormous. These seem to me to be the most important for an overview of the whole topic: Roland de Vaux, *Ancient Israel: Its Life and Institutions,* trans. by John McHugh (New York: McGraw Hill, 1961), pp. 24–53; Raphael Patai, *Sex and Family in the Bible and the Middle East* (Garden City, New York: Doubleday, 1959); Hendrick Van Oyen, *Ethique de l'Ancien Testament,* trans. by E. de Peyer (Genève, 1974) (German edition 1967), pp. 120–125, pp. 164–171.

[2]I have analyzed the texts at the beginning of Genesis in Chapter II, pp. 45–52.

[3]For the history of this interpretation, cf. Marie de Mérode, "Une aide qui lui corresponde: l'exégèse de Gn. 2: 18–24, dans les écrits de l'Ancien Testament, du judaïsme et du Nouveau Testament;" *Revue théol. de Louvain,* VIII, (1977), pp. 329–352.

[4]Cf. Daniel Lys, *Le plus beau chant de la creation* (Paris: Les Editions du Cerf, 1968), Lectio divina 51. This excellent commentary on the Song of Songs has an extremely useful bibliography.

[5]Daniel Lys translates this word as "ton sexe."

[6]Eduard Schillebeeckx, *Marriage: Secular Reality and Saving Mystery,* trans. by N.D. Smith (London: Sheed and Ward, 1965), Vol. I., p. 58; cf. also the pertinent remarks by Lys, *op. cit,* pp. 50–55.

[7]Especially chapters 1–3. For a commentary on these chapters, cf. Schillebeeckx, *op. cit.,* pp 65–76, and Edmond Jacob, *Osée (Commentaire de l'Ancien Testament XIa)* (Neuchâtel: Delachaux et Niestlé, 1965), pp. 18–38.

[8]*Jeremiah* 3:1–5; 31:1–4, 21–22.

[9]*Ezekiel* 16:1–63; 23:1–49.

[10]Cf. *Isaiah* 54:1–17.

[11]Cf. Edmond Jacob, *Theology of the Old Testament,* trans. by Arthur W. Heathcote and Philip J. Allcock (London: Hodder & Stoughton, 1958), pp. 108–114.

[12]This term, which indicates that only man can take the initiative to love according to the customs of the ancient east, designates man's love for woman and never woman's for man (note one exception: 1 Sam. 18:20 "Saul's daughter Michal loved David"). I will return to this point when discussing the texts in Paul that seem to reserve love for the husband and leaves submission to the wife.

[13]Schillebeeckx, *op. cit.,* p. 104.

[14]Even though, as we have seen, this element is not absent in the most ancient traditions of Israel, i.e. Jacob's love for Rachel. On the role of polygamy in Israel, cf. Patai, *op. cit.,* pp. 32–47; and van Oyen, *op. cit.,* p. 168.

[15]van Oyen, *op. cit.,* p. 168: "Facing deregulated life-styles obsessed by sensuousness, Israel makes an effort to keep its distance from sexual license, which gave rise in later Judaism to extreme requirements (which were perpetuated in Roman Catholic casuistry). Since erotic and sexual play was excluded as much as possible, conjugal love and its legitimate fulfillment attain supreme dignity in begetting children."

[16]According to André Dumas.

[17]I have developed these thoughts in "Chance et ambiguïté de la famille selon l'Evangile," *Bull, CPE* 29, (1977), No. 5–6, special edition on "La famille", pp. 38–47.

CHAPTER III.   Section 2.

[1]"Have you not read that he who made them from the beginning made them male and female, and said, 'For this reason a man shall leave his father and mother and be joined to his wife, and the two shall become one?' So they are no longer two but one." (Matt. 19:4–6a).

[2]Cf. Rudolf Bultmann, *The History of the Synoptic Tradition,* trans. by John Marsh (New York: Harper & Row, 1963), p. 39 and p. 333. I do not share, however, Bultmann's scepticism as to the community origin of these texts; I believe the text reports an original teaching from Jesus, although adapted to the needs of the community.

[3]On this issue, cf. Herman Leberecht Strack, and Paul Billerbeck, *Kommentar zum NT aus Talmud und Midrasch* (Munchen: C.H. Neck'she, 1969), Vol. I. p. 313 ff. (The abbreviation "Str.-B." will refer to this work); Abraham Cohen, *Everyman's Talmud,* Intro. by Boaz Cohen (New York: E.P. Dutton, 1949), pp. 159–170.

[4]Around 135 A.D., Rabbi Akiva taught that it was sufficient to see a woman more beautiful than one's wife in order to have the right to repudiate the wife. Josephus notes, in his autobiography (See 426): "At this period, I divorced my wife, being displeased at her behavior. She had borne me three children, of whom two died. . . ." in *Josephus,* trans. by H. St. J. Thackeray (Cambridge: Harvard University Press, 1956), Vol. I, p. 157.

[5]Cf. Franz J. Leenhardt, "Les femmes aussi. . . . A propos du billet de repudiation," *R.T.P.* (1969), 1, pp. 31–40.

[6]"They said to him, 'Why then did Moses command one to give a certificate of divorce, and to put her away?' He said to them, 'For your hardness of heart Moses allowed you to divorce your wives, but from the beginning it was not so.' " (*Matt.* 19:7–8)

[7]See, for example, in Matt. 21:31–32, on harlots as examples of faith: Luke 7:36–50 where Jesus presents to Simon the Pharisee a woman, known to be a sinner, as an example; she immediately recognized Jesus for who He was; John 8:1–11; the adulterous woman whom Jesus refuses to condemn.

[8]

Matt. 5:32	Mark 10:11–12	Luke 16:18	Matt. 19:9
. . . everyone who divorces his wife except on the ground of unchastity, makes her an adulteress; and whoever marries a divorced woman commits adultery.	Whoever divorces his wife and marries another, commits adultery against her and if she divorces her husband and marries another, she commits adultery.	Every one who divorces his wife and marries another commits adultery, and he who marries a woman divorced from her husband commits adultery.	Whoever divorces his wife except for unchastity and marries another commits adultery.

[9]Paul Hoffmann, "Jesus' saying about Divorce and Its Interpretation," *Concilium* (New York: Herder and Herder, 1970), Vol. 55, p. 64.

[10]If we interpret Matt. 5:32 this way, along with Leenhardt.

[11]"You have heard that it was said, 'You shall not commit adultery.' But I say to you that everyone who looks at a woman lustfully has already commited adultery with her in his heart." (Matt. 5:27–28). Jesus shows here a position far removed from legalism which can only judge completed actions. He intends to

nullify legalism on one hand and to reveal the infinite demands of love on the other hand; no one can pretend that something does not fall under this demand for there are no exempt areas.

[12]Leenhardt, *op. cit.,* p. 40.

[13]Only Matthew records this saying (19:10–12), but its very unusualness seems to be a guarantee of its authenticity; it is not clear what would have induced him to invent such a teaching which cuts across Jewish tradition. An extremely careful exegete like Herbert Braun sees an authentic *Logion* of Jesus in these words. Cf. *Spätjüdisch-häretischer and frühchristlicher Radikalismus. Jesus von Nazareth und die essenische Qumransekte* (Tübingen: J.C.B. Mohr: 1957), Vol. II, p. 112, n. 3 and p. 113, n. 1.

[14]On the situation of eunuchs in Judaism, cf. Str.-B. I, p. 805 ff. and Joachim Jeremias, *Jerusalem in the Time of Jesus,* trans. by F.H. & C.H. Cave (Philadelphia: Fortress Press, 1969), pp. 343–344.

[15]Jesus is perhaps thinking of Essenes who practiced celibacy and continence, cf. C. Daniel, "Esséniens et eunuques," *Revue de Qumran* (6, 1968), p. 353 ff. But it seems unwarranted to say that Jesus did not have his own disciples in mind (or Himself!), as does ₂Pierre Bonnard, *L'evangile selon saint Matthieu CNT* I (Neuchâtel-Paris 1970) p. 284 and p. 446 ff; the expression "for the sake of the Kingdom" points very specifically to the disciples of Christ.

[16]Luke 14:25–27. The same *Logion* is recorded in Matthew (10:37–38) in a less harsh form.

[17]Compare the same text in Matthew 19:29 and Mark 10:29.

[18]Luke 20:34–35: "The sons of this age marry and are given in marriage (lit.: marry and are espoused); but those who are accounted worthy to attain to that age and to the resurrection from the dead neither marry nor are given in marriage (lit.: neither marry nor are espoused)." In Matthew, the text reads: "For in the resurrection they neither marry nor are given in marriage" (22:30).

[19]From the second century on, some like Julius Cassianus will quote these texts in defense of a rigorous asceticism that goes to the point of castration. Cf. Clement of Alexandria, *Stromateis,* III.

[20]All exegetes agree that Matthew 5:32 and 19:9 are additions by Matthew. There would have been no reason for the other evangelists to leave out this word from Jesus which would have been so useful to regulate certain community problems, and thus we can readily understand why Matthew introduced it into the Lord's teaching.

[21]On this question, cf. Joseph Bonsirven, *Le divorce dans le Nouveau Testament* (Paris-Tournai, 1948); Jacques Dupont, *Mariage et divorce dans l'Evangile* (Bruges 1959): Bonnard, *op. cit.,* p. 282 ff.; Schillebeeckx, *op. cit.,* p. 203 ff.; Jean-Claude Margot, "L'indissolubilité du mariage selon le N.T.," *R.T.P.* (1967, 6), p. 387 ff.; Heinrich Baltensweiler, *Die Ehe im N.T.* (Zürich-Stuttgart 1967), p. 88 ff; Hoffmann, *op. cit.,* pp. 57–61.

[22]And also by the TOB which unfortunately "standardizes" this interpretation by translating "except in the case of an illegitimate union." A very typical example of the secondary discourse of exegetes replacing the text and doing away with its difficult ambiguities. What if they had been intended by the author?!

23Cf. Dupont, *op. cit.,* p. 29, p. 84.

24Schillebeeckx, *op. cit.,* pp. 217–218.

25This is how the term "except in the case of *porneia*" should be understood; in that case, the man who repudiates his wife cannot be categorized with those who repudiate their wives illegitimately.

26Leenhardt, art. cited, p. 26. The quote relates specifically to an exegesis of Matt. 5:32, but seemed to apply equally well to Matt. 19:9.

27The same idea appears in Hermas, a Christian author of the first half of the second century: " 'But if, sir', I said, 'after the divorce the wife repents and wishes to return to her husband will he refuse to receive her?' 'No, indeed,' he said. 'If the husband does not receive her, he sins. He incurs a great sin. The sinner who has repented must be received. However, not often, for there is only one repentance for the servants of God. To bring about her repentance, then, the husband should not marry. This is the course of action required for husband and wife.' " *The Shepherd,* Mand, IV, 7–8 *F.C.,* Vol. I, p. 264.

28In my opinion, this is why he does not define the meaning of *porneia* more precisely; he was referring to the case of an obvious failure in conjugal life without entering the difficult task of describing all the cases which would justify repudiation.

29The best modern commentaries on 1 Corinthians are, in my opinion: Johannes Weiss, *Der erste Korintherbrief* (Göttingen: Vanderhoeck & Ruprecht, 1910); Archibald Robertson, Alfred Plummer, *A Critical and Exegetical Commentary on the First Epistle of Saint Paul to the Corinthians,* 2nd edition (Edinburgh: T.&T. Clark, 1954): Ernest B. Allo, *Saint Paul: Premier Epitre aux Corinthiens,* 2^e ed. (Paris: J. Gabalda, 1934); Adolf von Schlatter, *Paulus der Bote Jesu* (1934); J. Hering *CNT,* VII (1949); Hanz Lietzmann-Werner, G. Kümmel, *An der Korinthen I–II* (Tübingen: J.C.B. Mohr, 1969); Charles K. Barrett, *A Commentary on the First Epistle to the Corinthians*$_2$ (London: Adam & Charles Black, 1968); Heinz D. Wendland *N.D.T.* 7, (1968); Hans Conzelmann, *a Commentary on the First Epistle to the Corinthians* (Philadelphia: Fortress Press, 1975).

30I am following the theory that the two letters to the Corinthians are actually a collection of several letters or fragments from Paul grouped together posthumously. According to that theory, the passage I am referring to (1 Cor. 6:12–20) is part of a grouping of two letters; whereas, Chapter 7, which I will examine next, belongs to a third letter.

31And perhaps of certain Christians who, under the pretext of Christian freedom ("All is permitted" seems to have been their ruling precept, cf. 1 Cor. 6:12) declare themselves above moral law.

32The ambiguity of the introductory sentence creates some difficulty in interpretation: "Now concerning the matters about which you wrote. It is well for a man not to touch a woman." The second sentence can be the content of what the Corinthians had written—which is my theory—or can be the apostle's introductory sentence for what follows; however, the ensuing development of thought as a whole makes the second theory unlikely. Cf. 1 Cor. 7:1.

33The expression "to be aflame," as used here, designates metaphorically the force of desire, "the fires of passion"—unless Paul has in mind the fire of Gehenna which awaits those who believed themselves strong enough to live in continence but end up steeped in immorality (cf. M.L. Barre "To Marry or to Burn: pyrosthai in *I Cor.* 7:9," *CBQ* 36, 1974 p. 193–202). In some ways, it's irrelevant; the main point is that Paul, by this expressive image, wishes to fight against an irritating spirituality that dispenses with objective reality and creates, on its own, the stipulations of God's gift!

[34]"And then, when in v. 14, he so forcibly emphasizes the fact that the unbelieving partner will be consecrated by the believer, his words reveal the existence in Corinth of a particular prejudice: fear of being made unholy by the intercourse with one's pagan marriage partner. Paul argues against this, reasoning that Christ has brought us freedom. The Christian party to such a marriage does not fall prey to the 'evil-world-powers'; rather, he consecrates his pagan partner, bringing her into the dimension of God's love." Hoffmann, *op. cit.,* p. 62. On this problem, cf. also Joseph Blinzer, "Zur Auslegung von I Cor. 7:14," *Neutestamentliche Aufsätze* (München 1963), pp. 32–41. Hans Conzelmann, *op. cit.,* pp. 119–125.

[35]This is the basis for the "pauline privilege" in canon law: the pope may authorize a convert to Christianity to leave his pagan spouse if that spouse is unwilling to accept the partner's conversion.

[36]This resembles the later situation in the church of *virgines subintroductae*: young girls desiring celibacy put themselves under the protection of a reliable man with whom they lived. It is easy to imagine the ambivalence of such a situation. Cf. Cyprien, *Epistolae,* IV, iv; John Chrysostom *Contra eos qui Subintroductas habent.*

[37]The same realism undergirds Paul's thinking on political power and the Christian's responsibility in that area. Cf. Eric Fuchs, G. Rist, "Realité du politique et obéissance de la foi. Remarques sur Rom. 13:1–7," *Bull CPE,* Genève 21 (1969) No. 1, p. 42 ff.

[38]Literally: ". . .to possess the vessel of himself." The "vessel" can designate the body, and by extension, the spouse, "vessel of her husband" (cf. 1 Cor, 7:4).

[39]Along with the majority of critics, I believe the letter to the Ephesians to belong to the post-apostolic generation (end of the first century). The letter is strongly marked by Pauline thought; the epistle to the Ephesians is a long exhortative commentary of the letter to the Colossians (authentically Paul's). The letter to the Ephesians belongs to what some historians call "The Pauline school."

[40]The same cannot be said for two other texts that are also commentaries on the Pauline exhortation in Colossians, i.e. Titus 2:4–5 and 1 Peter 3:1–7, which interpret Pauline thought in a restrictive sense: the wife's submission is a quasi-natural given and her activities are entirely regulated to the family and home. From this point on, the Christian woman is occupied strictly with children and the home. . . . This was a return to the traditional Jewish and Hellenistic situation; Paul's teachings allowing women to exercise a ministry of prophecy in the community (cf. 1 Cor. 11:5) are forgotten. The only point remembered was the apostle's "famous" sentence that "the women should keep silent in the churches"; this verse set itself against a kind of liturgical anarchy and invoked woman's submission, but without closing the door on the possibility (as stated by the apostle) that the Spirit of God could express Himself through a woman for the edification of the community (11:5).

⁴¹For a detailed study of this text, consult the following commentaries on Ephesians: Thomas K. Abbott, *A Critical and Exegetical Commentary on the Epistles to the Ephesians and to the Colossians* (Edinburgh: T.&.T. Clark, 1946); E. Haupt (*KEK*, 1902); Adolf von Schlatter (Erläuterungen, 1936); E.F. Scott (Moffat, 1948); H. Rendtorff (*NTD*, 1949); Martin Dibelius, *An die Kolosser, Epheser, An Philemon* (Tübingen: J.C.B. Mohr, 1927); Charles Masson, *l'Epître de Saint Paul aux Ephésiens* (Paris: Delachaux & Niestlé, 1957); Heinrich Schlier (1965); Joachim Gnilka *Der Epheserbrief* (Herders T.K., 1971); Martin Barth *The Broken Wall: A Study of the Epistle to the Ephesians* (London: Collins, 1960).

⁴²We find here the echo of Paul's text on women and veils, where Paul also recalled that the husband is head of the wife (11:3) and did so rather strongly (cf. 11:7,8,9). This makes his contrasting affirmation introduced in the middle of this development (11:11) so much more surprising: "Nevertheless, in the Lord woman is not independent of man nor man of woman. . . ." It's as though, in spite of himself, in spite of his desire to safeguard the hierarchy that seems right and natural to him, Paul had to affirm, constrained by the gospel itself, that the deep significance of the man/woman relationship is "in the Lord," that is, in accord with His basic will—full and free reciprocity excluding all hierarchy!

⁴³Or on the contrary, libertine and immoral—as demonstrated by later Christian sects like the Gnostics who proclaim the end of traditional structures of marriage or of the couple, but only in order to authorize sexual license—hardly signifying the meaning of the love of Christ!

⁴⁴According to Jewish tradition, which was in line with ancient eastern concepts, love (*ahabah*) is always the feeling of the stronger for the weaker; it can only refer to man who takes the initiative vis-à-vis the woman and not to the woman who can only consent to his overtures. This is why women are not invited to "love their husbands": that thought would be improper or stupid. Cf. Schillebeeckx, *op. cit.*, p. 104; Edmond Jacob, *Theology of the Old Testament, op. cit.*, pp. 108–114; van Oyen, *op. cit.*, pp. 97–101.

⁴⁵We are reminded of Paul's text: "For the Creation waits with eager longing for the revelation of the sons of God; for the creation was subjected to futility, not of its own will but by the will of him who subjected it in hope. . . . We know that the whole creation has been groaning in travail together until now." (Rom. 8:19–22).

⁴⁶"In Paul, a 'mystery,' mystērion, in conjunction with the Hebrew sôdh, means a hidden divine decree which is revealed in a veiled manner in the course of time. A 'mystery' or 'secret,' is therefore something revealed by God in the history of salvation. . . ." Schillebeeckx, *op. cit.*, p. 164.

CHAPTER IV.   Section 1.

¹"Therefore God gave them up in the lusts of their hearts to impurity, to the dishonoring of their bodies among themselves, because they exchanged the truth about God for a lie and worshiped and served the creature rather than the Creator. . . . For this reason God gave them up to dishonorable passions. Their

women exchanged natural relations for unnatural, and the men likewise gave up natural relations with women and were consummated with passion for one another, men committing shameless acts with men and receiving in their own persons the due penalty for their error" (Rom. 1:24–27).

[2]Erich Klostermann, "Die adäquate Vergeltung in Röm. 1:22–29, ZNW (1933) has demonstrated that this genre of indictment was known in Hellenistic Judaism. Cf. also Joachim Jeremias "Zu Rom. 1:22–32," ZNW (1954). On Judaism at the time of the birth of Christianity: Emil Schürer, A History of the Jewish People in the Time of Jesus Christ. 2nd rev. (Edinburgh: T.&T. Clark 1897–98); and George F. Moore, Judaism in the First Centuries of the Christian Era (Cambridge: Harvard University Press, 1927–1930).

[3]1 Tim. 1:9–10. Similar lists are found in 2 Tim. 3:2–4; Titus 3:3; 1 Peter 4:3.

[4]On the way in which Christianity took up certain moral requirements and radicalized ethics in a totally different way, cf. Alfred Darby Nock, Early Gentile Christianity and Its Hellenistic Background (New York: Harper Torchbooks, 1962), especially pp. 7–23.

[5]The exposure of children in a public place shortly after birth is well known in literature of the Hellenistic period (cf. Gustave Glotz, Etudes sociales et juridiques sur l'antiquité grecque [Paris: Hachette et Cie, 1906], pp. 187–227) where it is attested to as the classical means of population control. "A son is reared even if the family is poor; a daughter is exposed even if the family is rich" (Poseidippos, Hermaphroditos, fragment 11). The majority of exposed children were taken to become slaves. The exposition of children was still widely practiced in the period of the empire (cf. Letter 65 and 66 from Pliny to Trajan). Cf. Claude Vatin, Recherches sur le mariage et la condition de la femme mariée à l'époque hellénistique (Paris 1970), p. 234 ff.

[6]Justin, Apologia I, 27–29, FC, Vol. VI, pp. 62–63.

[7]Didache, II, ii, FC, Vol. I, p. 172. Cf. Jean Paul Audet, La Didachè: Instructions des apôtres, (Paris: J. Gabalda, 1958), p. 228 ff. and pp. 286–289.

[8]"Furthermore, Thou shalt not 'eat the hare either.' (Lev. 11:6). Why? You shall not become, he means, a corrupter of boys, nor shall ye become like such persons. For the hare gains a passage in the body each year, and every year it lives, it has that many passages. Nor shalt thou 'eat the hyena.' You shall not, he means, become an adulterer or fornicator, nor become like such persons. Why? Because this animal changes its nature every year and becomes now male, now female. Moreover he hates the weasel (Moses in Lev. 11:29), and rightly so. You shall not, he means, become like those men who, we are told, work iniquity with their mouth in their uncleanness nor shall you associate with impure women who work iniquity with their mouth. For this animal conceives by the mouth." Letter of Barnabas, X, 6–8, FC, Vol I., p. 207.

[9]Ignatius of Antioch, To Polycarp VI, 1–2, FC, Vol. I, p. 126.

[10]Hermas, The Sheperd, Mand, IV, i, 1, FC, Vol. I, p. 263.

[11]Tertullian, Apologia, XXXIX, 11–12, FC, Vol. X, pp. 99–100. This text can be compared to the following passage from Diogenes Laertius: "It is also their doctrine (the Stoics) that amongst the wise there should be a community of wives with free choice of partners, as Zeno says in his Republic and Chrysippus in his

treatise *On Government.* Under such circumstances we shall feel paternal affection for all the children alike, and there will be an end of the jealousies arising from adultery." *Lives of Eminent Philosophers,* VII, 131, trans. by R.D. Hicks (Cambridge: Harvard University Press, 1950), Vol II, p. 235.

[12]Paul Veyne, in his article "La famille et l'amour sous le Haut-Empire romain" (*Annales, E.S.C.* 33 1978, 1, pp. 35–63), shows that sexual and conjugal morality is in full evolution at the turn of the second century in Rome. This very interesting article sets forth the following thesis: "Between the time of Cicero and the century of the Antonines, a major event transpired that is not well known: a metamorphosis in sexual and conjugal relationships. At the end of this metamorphosis, pagan sexual morality becomes identical to the future Christian morality of marriage. This transformation was accomplished independent of all Christian influence" (p. 35). In response, I would say, that even if there were a conjunction between the Christian contribution and the moral transformation from pagan origins (and that therefore Christianity is certainly not the only factor in this moral metamorphosis), one could not affirm without being dogmatic (and Paul Veyne's article is not exempt from dogmatism) that Christianity had no effect on the evolution of morality in the Empire. It should be noted, however, that here we have a specialist in Roman History who would have us believe that Christianity had no effect on the victory at the heart of the Empire of what the whole world calls the "taboos of Judaeo-Christian morality"!

[13]Gabriel Germain, *Epictète et la spiritualité stoïcienne* (Paris: Editions du Seuil, 1964), p. 129.

[14]Quoted in Nock, *op. cit.,* p. 20–21. Nock goes on to say that it would be a mistake to think these moral requirements represent an isolated example: "In reality they are a striking illustration of a widespread change of moral outlook"; p. 22.

[15]Pliny, *Letters and Panegyricus,* X, xcvi, 7, trans. by Betty Radice (Cambridge: Harvard University Press, 1969), p. 289.

[16]The whole field of conjugal ethics has been authoritatively studied by J. P. Broudehoux, *Mariage et famille chez Clément d'Alexandrie* (Paris: Beauchesne et ses Fils, 1970).

[17]*Stromateis* III, trans. by Henry Chadwick in *Alexandrian Christianity* (Philadelphia; Westminster Press, 1954), Vol, II, pp. 40–93. Quotations will be taken from this edition.

[18]As P. Batiffol has written, encratism is "a spirit spread throughout the Church itself in the second century," *Etudes d'histoire et de théologie positive* (Paris 1968[8]) p. 53.

[19]Author of a work entitled *On Perfection According to the Saviour,* the thesis of which was that marriage was really only corruption and fornication; this is according to Clement *Stromateis* III, xii.

[20]His book *Concerning Continence and Celibacy* proposed castration as the ideal. Cf. Clement, *Stromateis* III, xiii.

[21]For example, this passage from *Acts of John,* 113: "O thou who hast kept me until this hour for thyself and untouched by union with a woman: who when in my youth I desired to marry didst appear unto me and say to me: John, I have

need of thee: who didst prepare for me also a sickness of the body: who when for the third time I would marry didst forthwith prevent me, and then at the third hour of the day saidst unto me on the sea: John, if thou hadst not been mine, I would have suffered thee to marry: who for two years didst blind me (or afflict mine eyes), and grant me to mourn and entreat thee: who in the third year didst open the eyes of my mind and also grant me my visible eyes: who when I saw clearly didst ordain that it should be grievous to me to look upon a woman: who didst save me from the temporal fantasy and lead me unto that which endureth always: who didst rid me of the foul madness that is in the flesh:.... Now therefore Lord, whereas I have accomplished the dispensation wherewith I was entrusted, account thou me worthy of thy rest, and grant me that end in thee which is salvation unspeakable and unutterable." In the *Apocryphal New Testament,* trans. by Montague Rhodes James, (Oxford: Clarendon Press, 1924, p 269.

[22]Julius Cassianus, according to Clement, *Stromateis,* III, xiii.

[23]Salome asks Jesus when man will cease to exist; Jesus answers that man will continue as long as women give birth to children; cf. *Stromateis,* III, ix, 64, p. 70.

[24]"When Salome asked when she would know the answer to her questions, the Lord said, When you trample on the robe of shame, and when the two shall be one, and the male with the female, and there is neither male nor female." Quoted by Clement in *Stromateis,* III, xiii, 92, in *op. cit.,* p. 83. The same idea is found in the *Gospel of Thomas.* "When you make the two one, and when you make the inside as the outside, and the outside as the inside, and the upper side as the lower, and when you make the male and the female into a single one, that the male be not male and the female not female;...then you shall enter (the Kingdom)," *Gospel of Thomas,* v. 22, in *New Testament Apocrypha I,* ed. Willhem Schneemelcher. trans. by Robert McL. Wilson (Philadelphia, 1963), p. 92.

[25]Clement, *Pedagōgos,* II, x, 83, *FC,* Vol. 23, p. 164 ff.

[26]*Ibid.,* II, x, 91, p. 170.

[27]Cf. Bourdehoux, *op. cit.,* p. 85 ff.

[28]"...some will depart from the faith by giving heed to deceitful spirits and doctrines of demons, through the pretensions of liars whose consciences are seared, who forbid marriage and enjoin abstinence from foods..."

[29]"Let marriage be held in honor among all, and let the marriage bed be undefiled; for God will judge the immoral and adulterous."

[30]On the licentious gnostic sects, cf. Hans Leisegang *Die Gnosis* (Stuttgart: A. Kröner, 1955); Robert M. Grant, *Gnosticism and Early Christianity,* rev. ed. (New York: Harper & Row, 1966); Werner Foerster, Ernest Haenchen, Martin Krause, *Die Gnosis* (Zürich: Artemis Verlag, 1969); as for Church Fathers, cf. Irenaeus *Adv. Haer I,* passim, Clement of Alexandria, *Strom.* III, and Epiphanius, *Panarion* XXIV–XXVII, PG 41, coll. 307–378.

[31]Hans Leisegang proposes quite similar parallels in certain expressions by Jakob Boehme and Meister Eckhart (*op. cit.,* p. 164 ff).

[32]Quoted from Epiphanes, *Concerning Righteousness* in Clement, *Stromateis,* III, ii, 8, *op. cit.,* pp. 43–44.

[33]Cf. Rom. 6:15; 1 Cor. 5:1–8; Gal. 5:13; 1 Pet. 2:16, 2 Pet. 2:19.

[34]Clement, *Stromateis,* III, v, 44, in *op. cit.,* p. 60.

[35]Michel Spanneut, *Le stoïcisme des Pères de l'Eglise* (Paris 1969[2]). Patristica Sorboniensa I, pp. 252–257.

[36]The reader can refer to further material on this point in John T. Noonan, Jr., *Contraception: A History of Its Treatment by the Catholic Theologians and Canonists* (New York: New American Library, 1965), p. 99 ff.

[37]*Ibid.* pp. 101–102.

[38]This is André Mehat's expression, *Etude sur les Stromates de Clément d'Alexandrie* (Paris; Editions de Seuil, 1966), p. 509 ff.

[39]Cf. Paul Veyne, art. cited, *Annales.*

CHAPTER IV.   Section 2.

[1]*Letter to Diognetus,* V, vi, *FC,* Vol. I, p. 361 (epistle at the end of the second century).

[2]On this point, cf. Schillebeeckx, *op. cit.,* Vol. II, pp. 3–18, and his helpful bibliography; cf. also Pierre Grimal, *The Civilization of Rome,* trans. by W. S. Maguiness (London: Allen & Unwin, 1963), Chapt. III, "Life and Customs."

[3]Schillebeeckx, *op. cit.,* Vol II, pp. 13–14.

[4]Ignatius of Antioch, *To Polycarp,* V, ii. *FC,* Vol. I, p. 126; for an interpretation of this text, cf. Korbinian Ritzer, *Le mariage dans les eglises chrétiennes du Ier au XIe siècle* (Paris: Editions du Cerf, 1970), pp. 81–84.

[5]Tertullian, *Ad uxorem,* II, ix, in *A.C.W.,* Vol. XIII, p. 35. Specialists like Ritzer and Schillebeeckx interpret this text as a reminder that the marriage of baptized people is ecclesiastic; its Christian and ecclesiastical character is reinforced by the fact that the spouses take part in liturgical celebration and pray together at home. The angels of God are the witnesses and guardians of this conjugal life. This is the kind of marriage the Heavenly Father approves of.

[6]Cf. P. Nautin, "Divorce et remariage dans la tradition latine," *Rech, Sc. Rel.* 62 (1974), p. 7–54 (a very well-informed article). It should be remembered that divorce in first century Rome was extremely easy: ". . .since marriage was neither a public nor a juridical action, nothing was easier than repudiating a spouse: one word was enough, and it was not even necessary to inform the spouse of the repudiation, which was not a solemn act." Veyne, art. cited, *Annales,* p. 42.

[7]Hermas, *The Shepherd,* Mand. IV, i, 4–8, *FC.* Vol. I, p. 264.

[8]Tertullian, *Adversus Marcionem,* IV, xxxiv, 7, trans. by Ernest Evans (Oxford, the Clarendon Press, 1972), Vol. II, p. 453.

[9]Hermas, *The Shepherd,* Mand, IV, iv, 1b–2, *FC,* Vol. I, p. 267.

[10]Tertullian, *Ad uxorem,* II, iv, in *op. cit.,* p. 29.

[11]Cf. R.C. Gerest, "Quand les chrétiens ne se marient pas à l'église: histoire des cinq premiers siècles," *Lumière et Vie,* 82 (1967), pp. 24–27.

[12]*Ibid.* p. 25 (note 51): "It was still current practice in the first centuries of our era for masters to set aside young slaves for prostitution and to regard those who were not in any established union as being in a more flexible position than the others."

CHAPTER IV.   Section 3.

[1]Ambrose of Milan, *Exhort. virgin,* VI, xxxvi, PL 16, 362.

[2]Augustine, *De nupt. et concup.,* II, xxi, *N–PNF,* Vol. V, p. 297; cf. *De civit. Dei,* XIV, xviii, 41, *FC,* Vol. XIV, pp. 391–392.

[3]Augustine's use of this concept signifies the sexual instinct as linked to sexual pleasure and desire which are not under reason's control. Cf. *De civit. Dei,* XIV, xv, 37, *FC,* Vol. XIV, p. 384 ff.

[4]Augustine, *De civit. Dei,* XIV, xx, 44, *FC.* Vol XIV, p. 395.

[5]*Ibid.,* XIV, xvi, 38, p. 388.

[6]Augustine, *Soliloquia* I, x, 17, *FC,* Vol, V, p. 365. Augustine, recently converted, was 33 when he wrote this.

[7]Jerome, *Comm. in ep. ad. Gal.* III, v, 21, *PL* 26, p. 415.

[8]Theodoret of Cyrus *Quest. in Genesium,* ch. 3, qu. 37, PG 80, 135.

[9]There is, however, an exception (the only one that I know of!). It comes by chance from the lay theologian Lactantius, who wrote in *The Divine Institutes,* VI, xxiii: "When God invented the plan of the two sexes, He placed in them the desire of each other and joy in union. So he put in bodies the most ardent desire of all living things, so that they might rush most avidly into these emotions and be able by this means to propagate and increase their kind. This desire and longing is found more vehement and more keen in man, either because He wished the number of men to be greater, or because He gave the power to man alone, so that it might be to His praise and glory in refraining from pleasures and in self-restraint. That adversary of ours knows how great is the force of this desire. . .and puts in illicit desires so that the foreign ones contaminate those which are proper, which it is all right to have without any fault. . . ."—in *FC,* Vol. XLIX, p. 457. This is a unique testimony which puts sexual pleasure and desire on the side of God and aligns sin with adultery, rather than with sexuality. Written between 304 and 313, this text has no echo in later tradition.

[10]Augustine, *De Gen ad lit.,* III, xxi, 33; *Oeuvres,* Vol. XLVIII, p. 264–265.

[11]Augustine, *Contra Julianum,* IV, xi, 57, *FC,* Vol. XXXV, p. 214.

[12]As is shown in this quote from Psuedo-Clement: "God. . .has declared that it (celibacy) is 'better than sons and daughters,' and that He will give to virgins a notable place in the house of God, which is something 'better than sons and daughters,' and better than the place of those who have passed a wedded life in sanctity, and whose 'bed has not been defiled.' For God will give to virgins the kingdom of heaven, as to the holy angels, by reason of this great and noble profession." *Epistola I ad Virgines,* IV, in *ANF.,* Vol VIII, p. 56; cf. Justin (I *Apol.* XXIX), the story of the young Christian who asks the prefect for permission to make himself a eunuch.

[13]These are the most important works: *The Symposium* by Methodius; *De virginitate* by Basil of Ankara; another by Gregory of Nyssa; and *De virg.,* and *Letters* (on virginity) by (or attributed to) Basil of Caeserea; *Exhort. Virg.* by Ambrose of Milan; *Contra Helvidius* by Jerome; *De sanc. virg.* by Augustine.

[14]Gregory of Nyssa, *De virginitate, FC,* Vol. LVIII, pp. 3–79.

[15]Methodius, *The Symposium,* trans. by Herbert Musurillo (Westminster, Maryland: The Newman Press, 1958).

[16]Jerome, *De Perpetua Virginitate B. Mariae*, XX, *FC*, Vol. LIII, pp. 40–41.

[17]Augustine, *De Sancta virginitate*, XVI, *FC*, Vol. 27, p. 159.

[18]John Chrysostom, *Paraenesis add Theodorum Lapsum*, II, v, *N–PNF*, Vol. IX, p. 115.

[19]Ambrose, *De paradiso*, XI, *FC*, Vol. 42, p. 328.

[20]Jean-Marie Pohier, preface to Kerns, *Les chrétiens, le mariage*...p. 13. The original edition: Joseph Kerns, *The Theology of Marriage* (New York: Sheed and Ward, 1964).

[21]Jerome, *Adversus Jovinianum*, I, xxvii, PL 23, p. 260.

[22]On Manicheanism, consult Henri Charles Puech, *Le manichéisme: son fondateur, sa doctrine* (Paris: Civilisations du Sud, 1949); François Decret, *Mani et la tradition manichéenne*, (Paris 1974). On St. Augustine and the Manicheans in regard to questions of sexual ethic, cf. Noonan, *op. cit.*, pp. 137–175.

[23]Augustine, *Contra Faustum*, XXII, xxx, *N–PNF*, Vol. IV, p. 284.

[24]*Ibid.*

[25]Eusebius, *Ad Marinum*, PG 22, 1107.

[26]Noonan, *op. cit.*, p. 101.

[27]Paul Veyne's article already quoted (*Annales*) sheds important light on this question. But I prefer the more subtle analysis of Henri Irenée Marrou, *Décadence romaine ou antiquité tardive?: IIIe–VIe Siecle* (Paris: Editions du Seuil, 1977); cf., for example, pp. 21–32 which describe the difficulties that Christianity had in significantly modifying ancient morals, especially in the area of entertainment.

[28]Marrou's book listed above offers many proofs of the surprising symbiosis between Christianity and the spirit of roman antiquity of the third and fourth centuries.

[29]Rudolf Bultmann, *Primitive Christianity in Its Contemporary Setting*, trans. by Rev. R.H. Fuller (New York: Meridian Books, 1956), p. 144.

[30]This was more and more readily admitted especially when the philosophical influence of Neoplatonic dualism supplanted stoic influence on theology in the middle of the third century.

[31]Marcel Detienne. *The Gardens of Adonis*, trans. by Janet Lloyd, intro. by J.P. Vernant (Atlantic Highlands, N.J.: Humanities Press, 1977).

[32]J.L. Flandrin, *Annales, E.S.C.*, 27 (1972), p. 1366.

[33]For instance, the *Song of Solomon* which could be accepted and understood only when interpreted allegorically.

[34]I am speaking of the ethical domain, for on the strictly theological level, the dominant influence in the middle of the third century was Neoplatonic, as we have seen from the example of Gregory of Nyssa.

[35]Stobaeus reports that the Stoics would say that whereas "Other friendships and affections resemble mixtures by juxtaposition—vegetables or other analogous objects—the affection of the husband and wife is comparable to a total fusion, like water and wine," *Florilegium* LXVII, 25.

[36]Cf. Epictetus, *The Discourses*, II, iv, 1–11, trans. by W.A. Oldfather (Cambridge: Harvard University Press, 1946), Vol. I, pp.233–237.

[37]"—Can we properly have confidence, then, in something that is insecure?—No.—Pleasure contains no element of security, does it?—No.—Away with it, then, and throw it out of the balance, and drive it far away from the region of things good," Epictetus, II, xi, 20–21, in *op. cit.,* p. 289; cf. II, xviii, 18, pp. 333–335.

[38]Epictetus, III, xxiv, 58–59, in *op. cit.,* Vol. II, pp. 203–205.

[39]"Sextus was probably, in fact, a Christian philosopher who, between 180 and 210, had reworked an ancient set of gnomic sayings. . ." Noonan, *op. cit.,* footnote # 23, p. 106.

[40]Jerome, *Adv. Jov.* I, xlix, PL 23, 281.

[41]Augustine, *Contra Jul.* II, vii, 20, *FC,* Vol. XXXV, p. 81.

[42]Spanneut, *op. cit.,* p. 266. What this author says about the Fathers of the second and third centuries describes the situation in the fourth century in the ethical domain equally well.

[43]The term itself is absent in patristic language. The Fathers speak of "asceticism."

[44]To repeat, this dissociation will be accentuated in the third century and even more later, when Christian thinking becomes more directly inspired by Neoplatonism. Cf. Etienne Gilson, "Le christianisme et la tradition philosophique," *Rev. des Sc. Ph. et Rel.* 2, 1941–42, pp. 249–266.

[45]Cf. Johannes Leipoldt, *Die Frau in der antiken Welt und im Urchristentum* (Leipzig: Koehler & Amelang, 1955); F. Quere-Jaulmes, *La Femme. Les grands textes des Pères de l'Eglise* (Paris, 1968); Jean-Marie Aubert, *La Femme. Antiféminisme et christianisme* (Paris, 1975); Elisabeth S. Fiorenza, "Le rôle des femmes dans le mouvement chrétien primitif" *Concilium* 111, 1976, pp. 13–25; Klaus Thraede, *Aerger mit der Freiheit. Die Bedeutung von Frauen in Theorie und Praxis der Alten Kirche.* This is the first part of the work by Gerta Scharffenorth and Thraede, "*Freunde in Christus werden. . . .*" *Die Beziehungen von Mann und Frau als Frage an Theologie und Kirche,* Gelnhausen/Berlin et Stein/Mfr. 1977, pp. 31–182.

[46]Elisabeth S. Fiorenza, art. cited, p. 17. It must also be shown that a more positive tradition existed, that "a feminist tradition fought against the misogynist tradition" (F. Quere), and that the defense of women by Plato (i.e. *Laws VII,* 804–806; VII, 833–839) tempered the narrow-minded sexism of Aristotle (cf. *Politics* I, 1254b, 1260a; VI, 1323).

[47]Abraham Cohen, *op. cit.,* p. 159.

[48]"Women were not marginal figures at the heart of the movement; they exercised a leading role as apostles, prophets, missionaries." Fiorenza, art. cited, p. 18; cf. also U. Ruegg, "Marthe et Marie," *Bull CPE,* 22, (1970), 6–7, pp. 19–36.

[49]Augustine, *De trinitate,* XII, vii, 10, *FC,* Vol. XLV, p. 352.

[50]Jean-Marie Aubert, *op. cit.,* p. 58.

[51]Which is clearly shown by France Quere-Jaulmes, *op. cit.,* pp. 18–38.

[52]Cf. Kari E. Borresen, *Subordination and Equivalence: The Nature and Role of Women in Augustine and Thomas Aquinas* (Washington, D.C.: University Press of America, 1981). There is also an article by this Catholic theologian on this same topic in *Concilium* III, 1976, p. 27–39.

[53]This is even rooted in language itself: in Greek as in Latin, the word designating *virtue* comes from the same root word for man: *andreia* from *aner* and *virtus* from *vir*.

[54]Philo, Supplement II, *Questions and Answers on Exodus 1:8*, trans, by Ralph Marcus (London: William Heinemann Ltd., 1943), pp. 15–16; cf. Richard Arthur Baer, *Philo's Use of the Categories of Male and Female* (Leiden: E.J. Brill, 1970).

[55]Spanneut, *op. cit.*, p. 181.

[56]Tertullian, *De Anima*, XXVII, vi, *FC*, Vol. X, p. 244.

[57]Clement, *Stomateis III*, xii, in *op. cit.*, p. 76 ff.

[58]This physiological theory (from Stoicism) will be taken up by Christian tradition from Augustine to Thomas, and even after them.

[59]There is a very nice illustration of this in the way in which Philo recounts how Balaam counsels Balak to make the daughters of his people seduce the sons of Israel, cf. *Vita Mosis* I, 295–299. As a prisoner of the desire aroused by woman, man loses all faculty to judge or defend himself.

[60]*The Testament of the Twelve Patriarchs*, Bk. I (The Testament of Reuben), trans. by Robert Sinker, in *ANF*, Vol. VIII, p. 10.

[61]Jean-Marie Aubert quotes these theories from the historian H. Leclercq: "He [Ambrose] does not go as far as Tertullian and speak of the pregnant woman's nausea, dangling breasts and small screaming children. (*Tertullian, De monogamia, XVI*); but it is Tertullian's spirit which breathes in him and inspires him to a kind of disgust for the laws and mysteries of [feminine] nature," *op. cit.*, p. 194, note #80.

[62]As for instance, among many others, Tertullian *De cultu feminarum, FC*, Vol. XL; Clement of Alexandria, *Pedagōgos* III; Gregory of Nazianzen *Carmina moralia*; Cyprien, *De habitu virginum*.

CHAPTER IV.   Section 4.

[1]The recent publication of a study by Huguette Taviani "Le mariage dans l' héresie de l'An Mil," in *Annales E.S.C.* 32 (1977), p. 1074–1089, convinced me that I should qualify this judgment. Even if Augustine is the main authority, the influence of Greek patristic thinking cannot be neglected; as we have seen, this thinking interpreted sexuality as the consequence of the fall and valued virginity as the paradisic state of perfect nature, i.e. non-sexed. "Gerard of Cambray (the bishop in charge of interrogating the heretics who denied marriage at Arras in 1025) is thus an heir of pre-augustinian and neoplatonic thought which was still present in the schools familiar with the teachings of Herik and Remy of Auxerre, themselves disciples of John Scotus. . . . The Carolingian theory of marriage is not a single unified theory. At the end of the 9th century John Scotus had reconnected neoplatonism and Greek Fathers, and his influence was still enormous in the 10th and beginning of the 11th centuries in Laon, Auxerre and Chartres." (p. 1082ff.). If these theologians defended marriage in the face of heretics (who, under the influence of encratic apocryphal texts, i.e. *Acts of Andrew, of Paul, Passio Sanctae Theclae,* made virginity the necessary condition for a return to God), they did not defend it by recalling, in augustinian style, that

marriage was willed by God before the fall, but by invoking its necessity vis-à-vis maintaining a social hierarchical order. "The rule constituting the spiritual anthropology of *Ecclesia* is actually the discrimination of *orders (discretio ordinis)*, which frames the whole discourse of Gerard of Cambray. To the hierarchy of values which places married-continent-virgin in ascending order on the road to beautitude, corresponds the distinction between a man of his century (*vir saecularis*) to whom marriage is reserved, and a man of the church (*vir ecclesiasticus*) who must abstain from marriage. . . . (To) impose on all laymen a continent state, which is the option pertaining to clerical or monastic status, disturbs *Ecclesia* as much as the fact of justifying marriage for clerics" (p. 1080). Marriage, a result of sin and a concession to the weakness of human nature, is thus not justified apart from procreation except by the social order which it allows and signifies.

²These are the major texts: *De bono conjugali; De Genesi ad litteram; De bono viduitatis; De conjugiis adulterinis; De nuptiis et concupiscentia.* Equally important developments on sexual and conjugal ethics are found in *Contra Faustum Manichaeum, De civitate Dei* and *Contra Julianum haeresis pelaginae defens.*

³Clement of Alexandria had already associated concupiscence and original sin, but that point of view had not been taken up by later eastern theologians, who do not ascribe a specifically sexual meaning to original sin; cf. Noonan *op. cit.,* p. 179 ff.

⁴Augustine, *De nuptiis et concupiscentia,* II, xxxi, 53, in *N-PNF,* Vol. V, p. 305.

⁵*Ibid.,* II, v, 14, p. 288.

⁶*Ibid.,* II, viii, 20, p. 290.

⁷*Ibid.,* II, xiii, 26, p. 293.

⁸Augustine, *De bono conjugali,* XXIV, xxxii, *FC,* Vol. XXVII, p. 48.

⁹Augustine, *Op. Imperf. contra Jul.,* VI, 30, *PL* 45, 1582.

¹⁰Augustine, *De Nuptiis et concupiscentia,* I, x, 11, p. 268.

¹¹Augustine, *Contra Julianum,* V, xii, 46, *FC,* Vol. XXXV, p. 288.

¹²Saint Caesarius of Arles, *Sermons* 42, 5; 43,5; 44,3–6; in *FC,* Vol. XXXI. On Caesarius, cf. Cyrille Vogel, *Césaire d'Arles* (Paris, 1964).

¹³Gregory the Great, *In 7 Pen. Ps.,* Ps 4:7, *PL* 79, 586.

¹⁴Gregory the Great, *Liber Regulae Pastorales* III, xxvii, *ACW,* Vol. XL, pp. 186–192.

¹⁵Gregory the Great, *Epistolae,* XI, lxiv, in *N—PNF,* Vol. XIII, p. 79. Some authors consider this letter apocryphal; in any case, it has been held since the 8th century to represent Gregory's teaching and, as such, did influence the whole Middle Ages.

¹⁶Peter Lombard, *Sentences,* II, xxx, 8, *PL* 1972, 722; cf. also II, xxx, 4; II, xxxi, 2–4, 7.

¹⁷*Ibid.,* IV, xxvi, 2, *PL* 192–909.

¹⁸*De Fide Cath,* Chapt. 1, *D.B.* 430.

¹⁹"When we look for the source of the courtly conception of love, we must not forget to reserve an important place for Peter Abelard. . . . We know from his own account that he composed and sang a large number of songs in honour of Heloise." Etienne Gilson, *The Mystical Theology of Saint Bernard,* trans. by

A.H.C. Downes (New York: Sheed and Ward, 1940), p. 158. Abelard explains this in Chapter VI of *The Calamities of Abelard* in *The Letters of Abelard and Heloise*, trans. by C.K. Scott Moncrieff (New York: Alfred A. Knopf, 1926), p. 11 ff.

[20]Gilson, *op. cit.*, pp. 162–163.

[21]*Letter II of Heloise to Abelard* in *op. cit.*, p. 57.

[22]*Ibid.*, Letter IV, p. 83.

[23]*Ibid.*, Letter II, p. 57.

[24]*Ibid.*

[25]Marie de Champagne, daughter of Eleanor of Aquitaine, text quoted by Evelyne Sullerot, *Histoire et mythologie de l'amour. Huit siècles d'écrits feminins.* (Paris 1974), p. 59.

[26]There is an excellent presentation in the work of Marie-Odile Métral, *Le mariage. Les hésitation de l'Occident*, (Paris, 1977), pp. 113–145; cf. also René Nelli, *L'érotique des troubadours* (Toulouse: E. Privat, 1963).

[27]Métral, *op. cit.*, p. 129.

[28]As in the example of this text by Marie de France (around 1170)

> "She wished to see her friend often,
> And her joy is to have him
> Whenever her Sire departs
> And night and day and early and late
> She has him at her beck and call.

[29]An extreme erotic technique which excludes intercourse.

[30]In 1140 at Lyon, the Canons established a feast to the Immaculate Conception: ideal christianized woman is obviously the Virgin Mary, who gives life without having to lower herself to conjugality.

[31]I owe my awareness of this little-known attempt to Métral, *op. cit.*, pp. 147–177.

[32]Hugh of Saint Victor's works to be read: *The Sacraments* (*PL* 176, I, 8, 12, 314 ff.; II, 11, 1–13, pp. 479–510) and *Letter on the Virginity of the Blessed Mary* (*PL* 176, pp. 857–876).

[33]Métral, *op. cit.*, p. 151.

[34]*Ibid.*

[35]On catharism and sexual morality, cf. Arno Borst, *Die Katharen* (Stuttgart: Hiersemann, 1953); René Nelli, *Le phénomène Cathare* (Paris: Presses universitaires de France, 1964) pp. 72–100; Denis de Rougemont, *Love in the Western World,* trans. by Montgomery Belgion, rev. and aug. ed. (New York: Pantheon, 1956), pp. 71–81 and passim. (Despite the attacks by specialists on this book, I continue to believe it to be one of the most illuminating books on the subject.) As for the rare catharic texts that have been preserved, they may be found in Ch. Thouzeillier, *Une somme anti-cathare. Le "Liber contra Manicheos" de Durand de Huesca* (Louvain, 1964); this historian also edited *Liber de duobus principiis* (Paris, 1973) (SC 198).

[36]Nelli, *op. cit.,* p. 78.

[37]On the way in which sexuality and marriage could be lived out in a catharic milieu, consult the excellent book by Emmanuel Ladurie Le Roy, *Montaillou, village occitan de 1294 à 1324,* Biblioth. des histoires (Paris 1976), esp. pp. 255–299.

[38]I agree with Arno Borst; he notes that in southern France, countless Cathari hid themselves as troubadours and that the singers of love are often also the preachers of renouncement. René Nelli says that there are about twenty or so troubadours that can be proved to have been Cathari (among them, de Guilhem du Durfort, Piere Vidal, Raimon de Miravel). Borst adds, however, that it is less through literary details than through the overall situation that Cathari and troubadours are linked. For one thing, many troubadours were vehement enemies of the Cathari. What the two groups have in common is a participation in the same Provençal culture where the whole mystique of chaste love (linked to the cult of the Virgin and to convent reform) was developed.

[39]St. Thomas Aquinas, *De perf. vitae spir.* VIII, trans. by Rev. Procter (St. Louis: B. Herder, 1903), p. 27.

[40]Bonaventure, *Sent.* IV, xxxvi, 2,2, *Opera omnia,* Vol. IV, p. 797.

[41]"Hence it is that in the human race, the male has a natural solicitude for the certainty of offspring, because on him devolves the upbringing of the child; and this certainly would cease if the union of sexes were indeterminate." Thomas Aquinas, *Summa Theologica,* II—II, Q. 154,2, edition of Fathers of the English Dominican Province (New York: Benziger Brothers, Inc., 1948), Vol. II, p. 1816.

[42]On affection for children during the Middle Ages in a peasant milieu, consult E. Ladurie Le Roy, *op. cit.,* pp. 300–321.

[43]Thomas Aquinas, *Summa Theologica,* Suppl. qu. 49.4, in *op. cit.,* Vol. III, pp. 2739–2740.

[44]*Ibid.,* Suppl. qu. 49.6 in *op. cit.,* p. 2742: ". . . pleasure in a good action is good, and in an evil action, evil; wherefore, as the marriage act is not evil in itself, neither will it be always a mortal sin to seek pleasure therein."

[45]Albertus Magnus, *In 4 Sent.,* d 26, a 7.

[46]Cf. Pierre Rousselot, *Pour l'histoire du problème de l'amour au Moyen Age* (Münster: Aschendorffsche Buchhandlung, 1908), p. 35.

[47]Noonan, *op. cit.,* p. 355.

[48]According to the theory of Reto R. Bezzola, *Les origines et la formation de la littérature courtoise en Occident,* 2e partie, T. II (Paris 1966), at the beginning of the courtly tradition, William IX of Aquitaine tried to thwart the preaching of the theologian Robert d'Abrissel who was defending the valuation of woman according to gospel standards. The courtly tradition would be an answer, via a secular mystique, to religious promotion of the woman. If Bezzola is right, it would be by means of theology that woman, from the 12th century on, would be called to rediscover her specific vocation.

[49]Sullerot, *op. cit.,* pp. 47–69.

[50]*Ibid.,* p. 52. The work of E. LeRoy Ladurie confirms this viewpoint, cf. *op. cit.,* pp. 273–278.

CHAPTER IV.   Section 5.

[1]Schillebeeckx, *op. cit.,* Vol. II, p. 39.

[2]The history of the evolution of liturgies is notably described by Korbinian Ritzer, *Le mariage dans les églises chrétiennes du 1er au XIe siecle* (Paris: Editions du cerf, 1970).

[3]Ritzer, *op. cit.,* p. 244 ff. It is interesting to note that Paulinus of Nola is describing here the marriage of Julian of Eclannum, Augustine's future pelagian adversary.

[4]*PL* 119,980.

[5]On these questions, consult Henri Crouzel, *L'église primitive face au divorce* (Paris: Beauchesne, 1971).

[6]Jerome, *Epistolae* LXXVII, iii, *N—PNF,* Vol. VI, p. 158.

[7]R.C. Gerest, art. cited, pp. 20–21.

[8]Jerome, *Epistolae* LV, iii, *N—PNF,* Vol. VI, p. 110.

[9]*PL* 99, 1153.

[10]P. Nautin has remarkably demonstrated this in an article in *R.S.C.* 62, 1974/1, pp. 7–54: "Divorce et remariage dans la tradition de l'Eglise latine." Here is his conclusion: "It was only in the second half of the 9th century that the doctrine of Augustine and Jerome triumphed. This was the result of the renewal in theological studies which marked the beginning of the Carolingian era. This change, which set aside the text of Matt 19:9, was not brought about by pastoral necessities but was the work of theologians who, I might add, thought that Augustine represented the whole Christian tradition."

[11]Epiphanius of Salamis, *Panarion* LIX,4, *PG* 41, p. 1024 ff.

[12]On these texts, cf. Willibald M. Ploechl, *Geschichte des Kirchenrechts* (Wein: Herold, 1960), Vol. I, p. 447 ff. and Ritzer, *op. cit.,* pp. 340–354.

[13]"One of the biggest falsifications of history, and also one of the most successful," as A. Bride says in *Catholicisme,* art. "Isidoriens (Faux)."

[14]Ritzer, *op. cit.,* p. 347: "From then on, the conclusion of a wedding would take place before the Church tribunal, but at the same time, the juridical civil forms were to be included in the sacred domain of the liturgy. . . . However, toward the middle of the 9th century, things had not yet come to that point: the conclusion of a legal marriage was still regarded as within the jurisdiction of common legal rights."

[15]Schillebeeckx, *op. cit.,* Vol. II, pp. 74–75.

[16]Hincmar, Letter XXII (around 860) "On the Marriage of Stephen to the Daughter of Count Regimond," *PL* 126, 132 ff.

[17]Jean Dauvillien, *Le Mariage dans le droit canonique de l'Eglise, depuis le Décret de Gratien (1140) jusqu'à la mort de Clement V (1314)* (Paris: Recueil Sirey, 1933).

[18]This collection, requested by the pope so as to put the various canon laws in order, is the work of Raymond of Pennafort who worked on it from 1227 to 1241: cf. A. Villien "Article Décrétales," *Dictionnaire de Théologie catholique,* IV, 1911, col. 206–212; Ploechl, *op. cit.,* Vol. II, pp. 477–481.

[19]The veil originally covered the couple, and later only the bride as a sign of

her consecration to Christ with her husband as His representative, the "image of Christ." For a study on the evolution of this liturgical ritual, cf. Schillebeeckx, *op. cit.,* Vol. II. pp. 96–108.

[20]Thomas Aquinas, *Summa Theologicae,* Supp. qu. 48.1, in *op. cit.,* p. 2735.

[21]From this perspective, there is nothing that the reformed theological tradition can accept; cf. R. Grimm, "Indissolubilité et sacramentalité du mariage chrétien," *RTP* (1967), VI, pp. 404–418. I will return to this point in the next chapter in my presentation of the critique of protestant theologians with regard to the marriage-sacrament.

CHAPTER IV.   Section 6.

[1]There is an excellent résumé of this in François Lebrun, *La vie conjugale sous l'Ancien Régime* (Paris: A. Colin, 1975), pp. 9–13.

[2]Anthony Meray's *La Vie au temps des libres prêcheurs ou les devanciers de Luther et de Rabelais; croyances, usages et moeurs intimes des XIVe, XVe et XVIe siècles* (Paris: A. Claudin, 1878) speaks of the ways in which the severity of these principles could be sidestepped.

[3]Cf. François Wendel, *Le mariage à Strasbourg à l'époque de la Réforme, 1520–1692* (Strasbourg, 1928): André Biéler, *L'homme et la femme dans la morale calviniste* (Genève: Labor et Fides, 1963); R. Stauffenegger, *Le mariage à Genève vers 1600* (Paris, 1968); Pierre Bels, *Le mariage des protestants français jusqu'en 1685* (Paris: Librairie générale de droit et de jurisprudence, 1968).

[4]These are the major works by Luther on marriage:

— *Treatise on Good Works* (sixth commandment), 1520, in *LW,* Vol. XLIV. (The abbreviation *LW* will refer to the edition: *Luther's Works,* Philadelphia: Muhlenberg Press, 1962.)

— *The Babylonian Captivity of Church,* 1520, in *LW,* Vol. XXXVI.

— *Estate of Marriage,* 1522, *LW,* Vol. XLV.

— *Catechism* (sixth commandment), 1529.

— *Von Ehesachen,* 1530.

— *Sermon on Monday after Quasimodo for the Marriage of Caspar Cruciger,* 1536.

A good synthesis, among many others, of Luther's teaching in this area: O. Lähteenmäki, *Sexus und Ehe bei Luther* (Turku, 1955) Schriften des Luther-Agricola Ges. 10.

[5]Luther, *To the Christian Nobility of the German Nation Concerning the Reform of the Christian Estate, LW,* Vol XLIV, p. 177.

[6]Luther, *The Babylonian Captivity of the Church, LW,* Vol. XXXVI, pp. 98–99.

[7]*Ibid.,* p. 106.

[8]Luther, *Judgment of Martin Luther on Monastic Vows* (1521), *LW,* Vol. XLIV, p.298.

[9]On the problem of divorce, cf. Luther, *Estate of Marriage, LW,* Vol. XLV, pp. 3–35.

¹⁰Calvin's major texts on marriage are found in *Institutes of the Christian Religion,* trans. by Henry Beveridge (Grand Rapids, Mich.: William B. Eerdmanns, 1966), in 2 Vols.; II,viii, 41–44 (commentary on the seventh commandment), in Eerdmann's Vol. I, pp. 348–350; IV, xii, 23–28 (against the celibacy of priests), in Vol. II, pp.468–471; IV, xiii, 3 (on the vow of celibacy) in Vol. II, pp. 474–476; IV, xix, 34–37 (marriage and sacrament) in Vol. II, pp. 646–649. cf. also Calvin, *Textes choisis,* edited by C. Gagnebin and K. Barth (Paris-Fribourg, 1948), pp. 196–216 for some excellent passages on the body, lewdness, marriage, and conjugal love.

¹¹Calvin, "Commentary on Malachi," (Mal. 2:16) in *Commentaries on the Twelve Minor Prophets* (Edinburgh: Calvin Translation Society, 1849), Vol V, p. 559. (The abbreviation *CTS* will hereafter refer to the volumes in this series.)

¹²Calvin, *The True Method of Reforming the Church,* in *Tracts, CTS,* Vol III, pp.301–302.

¹³Calvin, *ICR,* IV,xii,23 in *op. cit.,* p. 468.

¹⁴Cf. L.-E. Halkin, "Erasme et le célibat sacerodotal," *RHPR,* 57 (1977), pp. 497–511.

¹⁵Written at a time when Erasmus was still close to the position of the reformation movement. Later, in 1526, especially in his treatise *Christiani matrimonii institutio,* he returns to strict orthodox Catholic positions.

¹⁶Erasmus, *In Novum Testamentum Annotationes,* (1 Cor. 7:39) in *Opera Omnia,* Vol. VI, p. 192.

¹⁷*Ibid.,* (Ephes. 5:32), p. 855.

¹⁸Luther, *The Babylonian Captivity of the Church, LW,* Vol. XXXVI, p.95.

¹⁹*Ibid.,* p. 92.

²⁰Calvin, "Commentary on I Timothy" (1 Tim. 2:13), *Commentaries to Timothy, Titus and Philemon, CTS,* Vol.XLIII, p. 69.

²¹Calvin, (Gen. 2:18), *Commentaries on the First Book of Moses called Genesis, CTS,* Vol. I, p. 130.

²²Martin Butzer, *Von der Ehe* (1534), text prepared and translated by Wendel, *op. cit.,* p. 46.

²³Martin Butzer, *De Regno Christi* (1550).

²⁴Luther, *Estate of Marriage, LW,* Vol. XLV, pp. 36–37.

²⁵*Ibid.,* p.17.

²⁶Calvin (Deut. 24:5), *Commentaries on the Last Four Books of Moses, CTS,* Vol. III, p.84.

²⁷Calvin, (1 Cor. 7:5), *Commentary on the Epistles of Paul the Apostle to the Corinthians, CTS,* Vol. I, p. 226.

²⁸*Ibid.,* (1 Cor. 11:11), pp.359–360.

²⁹Luther, *Estate of Marriage, LW* Vol. XLV, p.40.

³⁰Calvin, (Matt. 19:10), *A Harmony of the Gospels,* trans. by T.H.L.Parker (Edinburgh: Saint Andrew Press, 1972), Vol. II, p. 249.

³¹Luther, *Sermon for the Marriage of Caspar Cruciger.*

³²"If we abhor immorality, it is because of the principle that our bodies are temples of the Holy Spirit." *Fourth Sermon on the Epistle to the Corinthians* (10:8–9), *Opera Calvini,* Vol. XLIX, p. 624.

[33]*Ibid.,* p. 625.

[34]Bels, op. cit., pp. 57–62.

[35]Martin Butzer, *Von der Ehe* (1532).

[36]Calvin, *Opera Calvini,* Vol. X, p. 105.

[37]*Ibid.,* p. 106.

[38]On this point, cf. Wendel, *op. cit.,* pp. 103–107 and Bels, *op. cit.,* pp. 135–140 and 163–173.

[39]His demands were inspired by the Edict of Henry II (1556) on the marriage of children which strongly reinforced parental authority. Cf. Isambert, *Receuil des anciennes lois françaises,* Vol. XIII, pp. 469–471. Quoted by J.L. Handrin, *op. cit.,* p. 42 ff. (Who incorrectly dates the Edict at 1566—probably because of a printing error).

[40]Luther, *Sermon for the Marriage of Caspar Cruciger.*

[41]Calvin, *Twelfth Sermon on the Epistle to the Corinthians,* (1 Cor. 11:4–10), *Opera Calvini,* Vol. XLIX, p. 729.

[42]". . . . Moses intended to note some equality (between man and woman [author's note]). And hence is refuted the error of some who think that the woman was formed only for the sake of propagation . . . as if she had been given to him only for the companion of his chamber, and not rather that she might be the inseparable associate of his life." Calvin, (Gen. 2:18), *Commentary on the First Book of Moses Called Genesis, CTS,* Vol. I, p. 131.

[43]On this question consult Wendel, *op. cit.,* and Bels, *op. cit.*

[44]Wendel, *op. cit.,* p. 59.

[45]Bels, *op. cit.,* p. 249 ff.

[46]Lebrun, *op. cit.,* p. 89.

[47]Wendel, *op. cit.,* p. 123.

CHAPTER IV.   Section 7.

[1]I must frankly add that one of the factors that dissuaded me from a detailed historical analysis of the Catholic and Protestant ethical systems from the end of the 16th to the beginning of the 20th century was my inability to manage an unbelievable abundance of information which would demand not only several years of intensive work but also a spirit of synthesis of exceptional quality! Perhaps Michel Foucault, who has announced his intention of publishing a six volume *Histoire de la Sexualité* will have the means of accomplishing such a feat. The first volume appeared in France in 1976; American edition: *History of Sexuality,* trans. by Robert Hurley (New York: Pantheon Books, 1978).

[2]On these divergencies, it is profitable to consult Roger Mehl, *Ethique catholique et éthique protestante* (Neuchâtel-Paris, 1970), Cahiers theol. 61.

[3]Let me repeat that when I say "Catholic ethics" and "Protestant ethics," I mean the denominational ethics as they developed, through a mutual polemic, from the 17th to the 20th centuries, i.e. a very general typology which does not take into account important current reinvestigations.

[4]Cf. B. Bartmann, *Précis de théologie dogmatique* (Mulhouse-Paris, 1951[7]) Vol. I, pp. 301–309.

[5]Bernard Häring, *The Law of Christ: Moral Theology for Priests and Laity,* trans. by Edwin G. Kaiser (Westminster, Md.: Newman Press, 1961–1966), Vol. II p. 355 ff. (Translator's Note: Although these expressions were not translated in the English edition, this is the section in which the concepts are found.)

[6]Dublanchy, "art. Morale," *Dictionnaire de théologie catholique* (Paris, 1929), Vol X, 2, col. 2398.

[7]Here is an example of how a Catholic—P. de Boisdeffre—describes the education he received and the atmosphere in a Catholic family at the beginning of the century: "Sex was impure but mostly unknown. Preachers inveighed against lewdness, but no one spoke about it at home. The word was taboo, it burned on people's lips.... In the eyes of the Church, the perfect man was sexless.... Theological dictionaries treated chastity (*castitas*) at great length but it was never a positive virtue. Chastity was a blank page, absence of desire, of all emotion. To be chaste meant to abstain and to avoid all 'occasion of sin,' to repress all desire. To be perfect, chastity should be *total*: that of the religious. Qualified as *imperfect*—and for good reason—conjugal chastity was handled with bare mention and with evident embarrassment; coitus (modestly qualified as an act of flesh) was allowed only for procreation. Sexual desire had a sinful connotation. In a general way, the body was a dirty rag." *La foi des anciens jours et celle des temps nouveaux* (Paris, 1977), p. 31 ff., as well as pp. 26–39.

[8]Even *Humanae vitae,* which, although showing some progress on this point by situating sexuality within the perspective of the couple as a unity and of love, says that "...an act of mutual love, which is detrimental to the faculty of propagating life, which God the Creator of all has implanted in it according to special laws, is in contradiction to both the divine plan ... and the will of the Author of human life." Paul VI, *Humanae vitae* (July 25, 1968), trans. by Odile M. Lebard in *Offical Catholic Teachings* (Wilmington, N.C.: McGrath Publishing Co., 1978), p. 337.

[9]Council of Trent, *De sacramento matrimonii,* can. 10, in *Canons and Decrees of the Council of Trent,* trans. by H.J. Schroeder (St. Louis: B. Herder Book Co., 1941), p. 182; Denz. 980.

[10]René Simon, "La déclaration romaine sur la sexualité et la loi naturelle," *La Croix,* Feb. 4, 1976.

[11]I have analyzed the way in which this concept has been used in the "Declaration on Certain Questions of Sexual Ethics," published at the end of 1975 by the Congregation for the Doctrine of Faith, in "Comment faire de l'éthique aujourd'hui?" art. published in *Choisir,* No. 196, April 1976.

[12]Pius XI, *Casti connubii,* in *Official Catholic Teachings op. cit.,* p. 41.

[13]On this point the moral teaching of the Magisterium, even after the rich insights of Scholasticism, returned to a strict Augustinianism, and even to Stoicism.

[14]"...the inseparable connection, willed by God and unable to be broken by man on his own initiative, between the two meanings of the conjugal act: the unitive meaning and the procreative meaning. Indeed, by its intimate structure, the conjugal act, while most closely uniting husband and wife, capacitates them for the generation of new lives, according to laws inscribed in the very being of man and woman." Paul VI, *Humanae vitae,* 12, in *op. cit.,* p. 336.

260 SEXUAL DESIRE AND LOVE

¹⁵The "Declaration on Certain Questions of Sexual Ethics," published at the end of 1975 by the Congregation for the Doctrine of Faith, shows in an almost caricatured fashion that this distrust is still present.

¹⁶Council of Trent, *De sacramento matrimonii,* can. 12, in *op. cit.,* p. 182; Denz. 982.

¹⁷Schillebeeckx, *op. cit.,* Vol II, p. 170.

¹⁸Decree *Tametsi,* November 1563, in *The Sources of Catholic Doctrine,* trans. by Roy J. Deferrari (St. Louis B. Herder Book Co., 1957), pp. 300–301; Denz. 990 ff.

¹⁹Pius IX, allocution of September 27, 1852, in *Papal Teachings,* "Matrimony," trans. by Michael J. Byrnes (Boston: Daughters of Saint Paul, 1963), p. 110; Denz. 1640.

²⁰A perfect example of this can be read in the *Syllabus* of Pius IX: cf. Denz. 1701–1780.

²¹S. Pinckaers. *Le renouveau de la morale* (Tournai and Paris, 1964): a study on an ethic faithful to its sources and to its present mission.

²²Foucault, *op. cit.,* pp. 20–21: "This scheme for transforming sex into a discourse had been devised long before in an ascetic and monastic setting. The seventeenth century had made it a rule for everyone. . . . The Christian pastoral prescribed as a fundamental duty the task of passing everything having to do with sex through the endless mill of speech."

²³Cf. Jean Delumeau, *Le christianisme, va-t-il mourir?* (Paris: Hachette, 1977), especially pp. 87–113 and 190–207, on the positive and negative effects of "the gigantic effort at religious acculturation" attempted by both Reformations as early as the sixteenth century.

²⁴To list only a few recent examples of this Catholic renewal, I would draw attention to René Simon, *Fonder la morale; dialectique de la foi et de la raison practique* (Paris: Editions du Seuil, 1974); Jean-Marie Aubert, *Vivre en chrétien au XXᵉ siècle,* Vol I, *Le sel de la Terre* (Mulhouse, 1976); C.J. Pinto de Oliveira, *La crise du choix moral dans la civilisation technique* (Fribourg, Paris, 1977).

²⁵Cf. J. Puyo, P. van Eersel, *Voyage à l'intérieur de l'Eglise catholique* (Paris, 1977), pp. 343–370 ("Querelles autour du mariage").

²⁶By "Protestantism," I mean the religious movement descended from and demanding the Reformation in the 16th century. All the Protestant churches, in spite of their great diversity, have maintained a common and deep attachment to the Bible as the primary authority in matters of faith and morals. That attachment was sometimes colored by a certain moral rigorism (for example in English Puritanism) and American Puritanism in the 17th century and sometimes mixed with religious sentimentalism, as in German Pietism in the 18th century or later in the Anglo-Saxon "revival" movements), but it nevertheless always remained fundamental. From the very beginning, it also preserved an obvious distrust of authoritarianism of the Church. Freedom of conscience, moral demands and the value of personal religious experience: roughly described, these are the characteristic fundamentals of Protestantism.

²⁷". . .regeneration or sanctification. . .(:) two aspects of it . . . are inseparable and linked together by penitence: mortification of the old man, and participation

in new life. The one and the other proceed directly from union with Christ." François Wendel, *Calvin: The Origin and Development of His Religious Thought,* trans. by Philip Mairet (New York: Harper & Row, 1963), p.242.

[28]Calvin, *A Brief Christian Instruction* (1536–1537).

[29]For Kant, all religions ask the question about how God desires to be honored; the only response worthy of God, he adds, is unconditionally to obey the moral law which is His law. In this undertaking, it is foolish to count on divine grace, for each man must, as the gospel says, use his "talent": even if man does not succeed in perfectly imitating the ideal symbolized by the Son of God, the sincerity of his conversion and of his intention is sufficient, plus the suffering inherent in the renunciation of the old man. This is the meaning, according to Kant, of the justification by grace which is acquired only by a personal and persevering effort. Cf. *Religion Within the Limits of Reason Alone,* trans. by T. Greene and H. Hudson (New York: Harper & Row, 1934).

[30]"Morality thus leads ineluctably to religion, through which it extends itself to the idea of a powerful moral Lawgiver, outside of mankind, for Whose will that is the final end (of creation) which at the same time can and ought to be man's final end." Kant, "Preface to the First Edition," in *op. cit.,* pp. 5–6.

[31]The opposition of these two loves has been systematized in Anders Nygren's classic, *Agape and Eros: A Study of the Christian Idea of Love,* trans. by A. G. Herbert (New York, Macmillan Co., 1937–1939).

[32]Of course, this is no longer true of the rationalistic Protestant moralists who, in the 17th and 18th centuries, tried to define a natural morality, founded on a very vague theism. With one of them, Hugo Grotius (1583–1645), the abandonment of reformation theology is obvious; in returning to Thomas, he declares that there would be a valid natural law "even if it were granted that God does not exist" (*Epistola* 154, quoted by Vernon Joseph Bourke, *History of Ethics* [Garden City, New York: Doubleday & Co., Inc., 1968], p. 152). Man is conceived of here as a rational being who is in dire need of being enlightened, and even of being restricted by law, but who is not in need of being saved, justified and recreated by God's grace. This juridical rationalistic movement is not part of Protestantism. Nevertheless, it is true that in the heart of Protestantism a whole undercurrent develops which, faced with the question of the basis for social and juridical ethics, returns to the traditional concept of natural law. On the other end of the scale, there were those (Puritans and Pietists) who sought to establish ethics on the law of God according to the Scriptures and constantly ran the risk of falling into the Anabaptist type of "illuminism." Protestantism experienced the hard fact that no one can go straight from Scripture to political and social reality; it is obviously necessary to think out the foundations of these things. To answer via the rationality of natural laws is assuredly too succinct, but it is interesting to note that Protestant ethics, especially when directly confronted with the problems of juridical organization of society (in Holland, in Germany, and in the Anglo-Saxon countries) also had recourse to natural rational law. Even if these moralists broke repeatedly with the central doctrine of the Reformation, i.e. justification, it must be acknowledged that there is an indicator here of a real difficulty in the classical Protestant position.

[33]On this question, cf. P. Gisel, *Vérité et histoire, la théologie dans la modernité* (Paris-Genève, 1977), pp. 49–53.

[34]Quoted by R.V. Schnucker, "La position puritaine à l'egards de l'adultère," *Annales E.S.C.* 27 (1972), pp. 1379–88 (cf. p. 1381).

[35]*Of Domestical Duties*, quoted by Schnucker, art. cited, p. 1388.

[36]Thus in German Pietism (for example, that of Nikolaus von Zinzendorf), new thinking on chastity, described as sexuality lived out in love, goes hand in hand with the recognition of the positive importance of sexual exchange in the couple. On this point, cf. P. Tanner, *Die Ehe im Pietismus* (Zürich, 1952) and G. Beyreuther, *Sexual Theorien im Pietismus* (München, 1963).

[37]This is particularly true for the Puritan movements; cf. Edmund S. Morgan, *The Puritan Family: Religion and Domestic Relations in Seventeenth-Century New England*, rev. ed. (New York: Harper & Row, 1966); Herbert Wallace Schneider, *The Puritan Mind* (New York: H. Holt and Company, 1930); John Demos, *A Little Commonwealth: Family Life in Plymouth Colony* (New York: Oxford University Press, 1978).

[38]Luther, *Psalm CXVII.*

[39]"Similarly excluded is every action which, either in anticipation of the conjugal act, or in its accomplishment, or in the development of its natural consequences, proposes, whether as an end or as a means, to render procreation impossible." Paul VI *Humanae vitae*, 14, in *op. cit.*, p.338.

[40]In 1930 the Conference of Anglican Bishops at Lambeth recognized that Christians can legitimately use other methods of controlling fertility besides total abstinence. For a complete study on Protestant positions taken, consult the important work by André Dumas, *Le controle des naissances. Opinions protestantes* (Paris, 1965). One of the latest texts published by a Church is that of the Federation of Protestant Churches in France, entitled *La sexualité; Pour une réflexion chrétienne* (Paris, 1975); on contraception, cf. sect. 42–51, "La liberté de la procréation."

[41]*Oui à la régulation des naissances.* Position-paper by the Council of the Federation of Protestant Churches in Switzerland (Berne, 1968), pts. 3 and 4.

[42]*Ibid.,*

[43]Jacques de Senarclens, *La vie protestante* (May 18, 1956).

[44]For more details on this Protestant view, cf. J. ten Doornkaat, *Le problème de l'avortement. Respectons la vie*: report edited in the name of the Federation of Protestant Churches in Switzerland, 1952; Robert Grimm, *L'avortement. Pour une décision responsable* (Lausanne, 1972); *La sexualité. Pour une réflexion chrétienne* (Paris, 1975), sect. 86–94; "Interruption de grossesse. Réflexions pour une solution légale et humaine plus juste.": text prepared by the medical group at the Centre Protestant d'Etudes in Geneva, *Bull. CPE* (1975), No. 8.

[45]". . . we must once again declare that the direct interruption of the generative process already begun, and above all, directly willed and procured abortion, even if for therapeutic reasons, are to be absolutely excluded as licit means of regulating birth." Paul VI, *Humanae vitae*, 14, in *op. cit.*, p. 337.

[46]Grimm. *op. cit.*, p. 35.

[47]*L'interruption de grossesse. Pour une décision responsable.* (Berne, 1972).

[48]"... *the starry heavens above and the moral law within* ..." says the inscription that Kant's friends wrote on his tombstone, quoting from the end of the *Critique of Practical Reason.*

[49]Except for certain "fundamentalist" groups who continue to claim obedience to the Word of God, that is, to the literal text of the Bible. This is pure illusion, since these very fundamentalists chose certain texts in the Bible rather than others, and thereby chose *an* interpretation of Scripture. Their naïveté (!?) is in believing that their interpretation is identical to the very Word of God.

[50]On this important question, cf. Gisel, *op. cit.*

CHAPTER IV. Section 8.

[1]Even more brief and general, since I have not mentioned the tradition of the Eastern Churches, except for the patristic period. For fuller information on this point, cf. Paul Evdokimov, *La femme et la salut du monde* (Paris, 1958); *Sacrement de l'amour. Le mystère conjugal à la lumière de la tradition orthodoxe* (Paris, 1962): "Conjugal Priesthood. The Theology of Marriage" in Crespy, Evdokimov, Duquoc, in *op. cit.,* pp. 67–105.

[2]Jacques-Marie Pohier, preface to the French edition of Joseph E. Kerns, *Christians, the Theology of Marriage* (New York: Sheed and Ward, 1964); French edition 1966, p. 14.

[3]A whole current of spirituality in the Eastern churches, especially around John Climacus, in particular, seems to have thought out the rapport that links human love and divine love, physical eros and spiritual eros. Cf. C. Yannaras, *La métaphysique du corps chez saint Jean Climaque,* soon to be published.

[4]And not only by the church! Cf. Foucault, *op. cit.*

[5]I am not thinking only of certain Catholic circles, like the one that produced the recent "Declaration on Certain Questions of Sexual Ethics," but also of certain fundamentalist Protestant groups who continually brandish "the authority of the Word of God" to defend the power they ascribe to themselves of interpreting the Bible in a certain way.

CHAPTER V. Section 1.

[1]But true in Greek tragedy, eg. the *Bacchae* of Euripides.

[2]According to Kant's formula in the first part of *Religion Within the Limits of Reason Alone* ("Concerning the Indwelling of the Evil Principle with the Good, or, On the Radical Evil in Human Nature"); cf. Ricoeur, *op. cit.,* p.233.

[3]Unless the texts should say "*because* it is the revealer ...!"

CHAPTER V. Section 2.

[1]According to the formula in most of the wedding liturgies.

[2]B. Besret, *De Commencement en Commencement* (Paris, 1976), p. 159.

[3]The gift and the exchange are symbolized in the space where the child, physically born, will become a person. The child, through his own otherness, is thus the sign of the specific reality of the couple.

[4]In the image of the irreversible commitment God made to man through Jesus Christ, which is also signified by the love of Christ for the Church.

[5]In primitive societies and generally in all societies that are rigidly controlled, even if sexual relations outside marriage are permitted, a shared life without marriage is much less permissible. But this does not invalidate my theory, because the strength of the link to society is the dominant factor here; for it is this link which seems to me to constitute one of the two essential factors in the conjugal institution.

[6]Cf. Liseron Vincent Doucet-Bon, *Le mariage dans les civilisations anciennes* (Paris: A. Michel, 1975); Lucy P. Mair, *Marriage* (Baltimore: Penguin Books, 1971).

[7]It should be noted that the evolution of societies does not necessarily mean forward progress: ancient Greece for example, had a matrimonial system that was freer and more respectful of affective and elective values (cf. Homer) than classical Greece (cf. Plato, Aristophanes, Xenophon). It is probably scorn for women that is the cause of this regression—scorn which becomes scorn for heterosexual affection and an exaltation of masculine virtues and . . . of homosexuality. Such departures into the "infra-conjugal" threaten all societies, including modern ones; we need only think of the Nazi society, for instance.

[8]Once again, I would refer the reader to studies by historians on ancient societies where the rituals that socialize marriage are accompanied by the acknowledgment of the transcendence of marriage in relation to that socialization (even if that only occurs because sexuality is involved!); cf. Vincent Doucet-Bon, *op. cit.*; Mair, *op. cit.*; Schillebeeckx, *op. cit.*, which contains a complete bibliography on the celebration of marriage in the ancient world (Vol. II, pp. 218–219) and in western European tribes (Vol, II, pp. 219–220).

[9]François Chirpaz, "Dimensions de la sexualité," *Etudes* (March 1969), p. 422.

[10]One must be careful in using historical sources since the majority of them comes from the masculine part of humanity. And the public or external discussion of the area of sexuality and conjugality (which represents the major part of the texts preserved by history) is of necessity masked and indirect!

[11]It is interesting to note that in all societies (that I am aware of), there is a marked contrast between the public time of marriage and the private moment (of intercourse). The feast, the noise, the shouts, the relatives. . . cease at the entryway to the bedroom (or comparable place).

[12]The new conjugal practice which seems to be occuring in our country demonstrates this quite well: first, people live together for a certain amount of time and marry only when pregnancy occurs or when conception becomes desirable. Sexual relation and a shared life are thus no longer considered to be in need of social ratification; but the child, on the other hand, can only be born in an agreement of mutual recognition (between the couple and society). This is precisely the time when people discover the rapport between conjugality and sociability.

[13]An acknowledgment which signifies that the woman decides to renounce a child-fetish, libidinal and narcissistic possession of the man, and that the man decides to renounce the imaginary omnipotence of the penis. Cf. P. David, *op. cit,*. p. 169.

CHAPTER V. Section 3.

[1]On this point, cf. the excellent work by Jacques-Marie Pohier, *Quand je dis Dieu* (Paris, 1977), especially pp. 13–48.

[2]Bruckner-Finkielkraut, *op. cit.,* p.139.

[3]*Ibid.,* p. 141.

[4]It seems very significant to me that the "new moralists," Bruckner and Finkielkraut, who with biting irony denounce the popular sexologist ideology with the avowed intention of writing an apology for the "disorder of love," can write over 300 pages on sexuality and love without once mentioning, even in passing, that which (until further notice) is the normal fruit of love, i.e. children. This betrays a massive refusal of the temporality of love; love is a passion or pleasure for two (or for three, four, ten or more) which has no other goal than a loss of self into the present. There is no other project—something constantly (and foolishly!) referred to by these authors as in need of order (the unpardonable sin!).

[5]Let me immediately add that there is a way of denying pleasure (because of the fear of vulnerability it reveals) which leads in the same direction: aren't the Puritan and Don Juan really brothers?

[6]Of course there is also a condemnation of pleasure in the Church which proceeds from less defensible justifications, i.e. from an obsessive morality, constructed as a system of self-protection and as a narcissistic defense of self—another way of conveying death while claiming to escape it! Not to mention what I spoke of above, i.e. the link between an oppressive ethic of sexuality and a more than suspect penchant for power—which is the way that institutions have of refusing mortal precariousness.

[7]Which reaches even to children, who are without moral defense, let alone legal defense, against the sadistic desires of adults, as shown in the shocking report by M. G. Landes, "Pornographie: les montreurs d'enfants" in the *Nouvel Observateur* (Nov. 28, 1977), pp. 120–170. Compare this to Pasolini's last film *Salo, ou les 120 jours de Sodome.*

[8]D. Vasse "Le plaisir et la joie," *Lumière et Vie,* 114 (1973), "*Le plaisir,*" p. 99 (underlined by the author).

[9]*Ibid.,* p. 102.

[10]"It is in proximity to death that man has the experience of knowing that he *is* other than the imaginary "I" he *believes* himself to be. Delivered by the word, of the imaginary fiction by which he has alienated himself, he becomes who he is, a Subject that he cannot imagine. This Subject cannot conceive of himself in the image of the "I"; he can only give himself to be recognized by an Other." Vasse, *op. cit.,* p. 102.

[11]The following is according to the noteworthy analysis by François Chirpaz, *Le corps,* coll. SUP, Initiation philos., p. 72 ff.

[12]*Ibid.*, p. 73.

[13]*Ibid.*, p. 74.

[14]A play on words: these doors (or windows) of the house which look over a garden full of fruits are also the openings in garments and the apertures in the bodies of the lovers. The whole text, actually, is built around ambiguous images: the garden is also the body of the beloved and of the lover. Cf. Lys, *op. cit.,* p. 274 ff.

[15]He is one of the greatest contemporary French poets, in my opinion; Jean Malrieu (1915–1976) is shockingly underrated, probably because he never followed the fashion of Parisian literary circles! His major works are listed in the Bibliography for Chap. V.

[16]*Préface à l'amour, suivi de Hectares de soleil* (Honfleur, 1971), pp. 189–120.

[17]"It (the body) is the locus of a presence which finds a place in the world and is oriented towards others (toward the All-Other) and becomes the basis of a field of communication and of encounter. The body is the fleshly density of a presence, a sort of boundary that the presence constantly moves beyond, for its pole is always the other." M. Faessler, *Une interprétation de la Résurrection,* unedited document, AOT, 1976.

Epilogue

[1]Among many other possible examples, one can think of what was said about masturbation in the "Declaration of Certain Questions of Sexual Ethics" published by the Congregation on the Doctrine of Faith, Vatican 1976: a text from another era which debates a question that was long ago resolved, fortunately in an entirely different way!

[2]"Le christianisme et le corps. Réplique d'André Mandouze à Alfred Kastler," *Le monde* (Nov. 19, 1977) p.2.

[3]"Perhaps the current hyper-eroticizing of our societies indicates an identical paradox, the same desire to neutralize sex by sex, the same impatience, the same hope that an end has already been assigned to it which is close at hand and will finally abolish the anguish of being sexed." Bruckner-Finkielkraut, *op. cit.,* p. 40.

[4]It's the same in a relationship with God: ". . .there is only presence because of distance. . . .Not a distance that results from absence for him who experiences it or for him who caused it; not a distance which a mystery maintains because it is fitting to keep hidden that which we are not worthy of and which transcendence would not be able to commit to us. But the distance which is the sacrament of difference, because it's through distance alone that difference can be signified and be effectuated. . . Because God is God, He cannot be present except in the space opened up by this distance—an abolition often required by the believer who would say that unless it is abolished, God is absent." Jacques-Marie Pohier, *op. cit.,* p. 47 ff.

[5]Here are some indications that theological and ethical reflections will not be the prerogative of *man* for long! In Germany, the publication of a new theological collection entitled *Kennzeichen, Studien und Problemberichte aus dem Projekt "Frauen als Innovationsgruppen" des Deutschen Nationalkomitees des Lutheris-*

chen Weltbundes, Gelnhausen/Berlin; the first volume, devoted (very significantly) to the relations of men and women in the history of the Church and of theology is entitled *"Freunde in Christus werden. . . ." Die Beziehung von Mann und Frau als Frage an Theologie und Kirche,* by Gerta Scharffenorth and Klaus Thraede (1977). On the current theological thinking and the struggle for the recognition of the otherness of women in the United States, consult Elisabeth Moltmann-Wendel, *Menschenrechte für die Frau, Christliche Initiativen zur Frauenbefreiung* (Munich, 1974); on the debate in Catholicism, cf. the documents of the General Council on the Lay Apostolate: *Situations féminines* (Brussels, 1976); as well as the collected articles in *Concilium* 134 (1980), "Women in a Man's Church." In French, I must mention, besides the already standard work by Francine Dumas, *L'autre semblable* (Neuchâtel-Paris, 1967) that of France Quere, *La femme avenir* (Paris, 1976). An interesting ecumenical confrontation is found in *La Femme* in the collection, "Eglises en dialogue" (Paris 1968), No. 5, with a triple contribution by Tatiana Struve, "La vocation de la femme" (Orthodox), by Agnes Cunningham "La femme et l'oecuménisme chrétien" (Catholic) and by Françoise Florentin-Smyth, "La femme en milieu protestant."

Excursus

[1]On this question, cf. Marcel Eck, *Sodome, Essai sur l'homosexualité* (Paris, 1966); *Dieu les aime tells qu'ils sont. Pastorale pour les homophiles* (Paris, 1972, trans. from the the Dutch, 1968); Eliane Amado Lévy-Valensi, *Le grand désarroi aux racines de l'énigme homosexuelle* (Paris, 1973); Marc Oraison, *La question homosexuelle* (Paris, 1975); Guy Hocquenghem, *Homosexual Desire,* trans. by Daniella Dangoor (London: Allison-Busby, 1978); G. Durand, *Sexualité et foi* (Montreal, 1977).

[2]Oraison, *op. cit.,* p. 10 (words underlined by the author).

[3]Gen. 19:1–29: the destruction of Sodom and Gomorrah in punishment for crimes of its inhabitants, and especially for the homosexuality of the men of Sodom who tried to rape Lot's guests; Lev. 18:22; 20:13; Deut. 23:18: these are all law-texts; Rom. 1:26–27; I Cor. 6:9; I Tim. 1:10: homosexuality is listed in a series of vices and is not especially pointed out, except in Romans 1.

[4]Jonathan is superbly described by E. Amado Lévy-Valensi, *op. cit.* pp. 122–154.

[5]Oraison, *op. cit.,* p. 172 (words underlined by the author).

Bibliography

Bibliography for Chapter I

Bataille, Georges. *Death and Sensuality.* New York: Walker and Company, 1962.
Benveniste, Emile. *Indo-European Language and Society.* Trans. by Elizabeth Palmer. London: Faber and Faber, 1973.
Brownmiller, Susan. *Against Our Will: Men, Women and Rape.* New York: Simon and Schuster, 1975.
Bruckner, Pascal, Finkielkraut, Alain. *Le nouveau désordre amoureux.* Paris, 1969. 2 Vols.
Caillois, Roger. *Man and the Sacred.* Trans. by Meyer Barash. Glencoe, Ill.: Free Press of Glencoe, 1960.
———. *Man, Play and Games.* Trans. by Meyer Barash. New York: Free Press of Glencoe, 1961.
Chirpaz, Francois. *Le corps.* Paris, 1969.[2]
———. "Dimensions de la sexualité," *Etudes,* March 1969, pp. 409–422.
———. "Sexualité, morale et poétique. Approche philosophique," *Lumière et Vie* 97, 1970, pp. 72–88.
Clastres, Pierre. *Society against the State.* Trans. by Robert Hurley. New York: Urizen Books, 1977.
Cooper, David G. *The Grammar of Living.* New York: Pantheon Books, 1974.
de Coppet, D. "Tabou," *Encyclopaedia universalis.* Vol. XV, pp. 702–705.
Dadoun, Roger. "Sexualité humaine. 3 Les régulations sociales de la sexualité," *Encyclopaedia universalis.* Vol. XIV, pp. 926–928.
David, P. *Psychanalyse et famille.* Paris, 1976.
Domenach, Jean Marie. *Le retour du tragique.* Paris: Editions du Seuil, 1967.
Douglas, Mary Tew. *Purity and Danger.* London: Routledge & Kegan Paul, 1966.
Duyckaerts, François. *La formulation du lien sexuel.* Brussels: C. Dessart, 1967.

Eluard, Paul. *Last Love Poems of Paul Eluard*. Trans. by Marilyn Kallet. Baton Rouge: Louisiana State University Press, 1980.

Freud, Sigmund. *Civilization and Its Discontents*. Trans. by James Strachey. London: Hogarth Press, 1961.

_____. *The Complete Introductory Lectures on Psychoanalysis*. Trans. by James Strachey. New York: W.W. Norton, 1966.

_____. *A General Introduction to Psychoanalysis*. Trans. by Joan Rivière. New York: Liveright Publ. Co., 1935.

_____. *Three Essays on the Theory of Sexuality*. Trans. by James Strachey. London: Imago Publ. Co., 1949.

_____. *Totem and Taboo*. Trans. by James Strachey. New York: Norton, 1952.

Geisindorf, W., Pasini, W. Editors of *Sexologie, 1970–1973*. Geneva, 1974.

Girard, René. *Violence and the Sacred*. Trans. by Patrick Gregory. Baltimore: John Hopkins University Press, 1977.

_____. *Des choses cachées depuis la fondation du monde*. Recherches avec Jean-Michel Oughourlian et Guy Lefort. Paris: B. Grasset, 1978.

Guérin, D. *Essai sur la révolution sexuelle après Reich et Kinsey*. Paris, 1969.

Hesnard, Angelo Marie. *Manuel de sexologie*. Paris, 1959.

de Heusch, Luc. *Essai sur le symbolisme de l'inceste royal en Afrique*. Bruxelles: Université Libre, Institut de sociologie Solvay, 1958.

Jeannière, Abel. *The Anthropology of Sex*. Trans. by Julie Kernan. Foreward by Dan Sullivan. New York: Harper & Row, 1967.

Kinsey, Alfred C., Pomeroy, Wardell B., and Martin, Clyde E. *Sexual Behavior in the Human Male*. Philadelphia: W.B. Saunders Co., 1948.

Lacan, Jacques. *The Function of Language in Psychoanalysis*. Trans. with notes by Anthony Wilden. Baltimore: Johns Hopkins University Press, 1968.

Leclerc, Annie. *Parole de femme*. Paris, 1974.

Lévi-Strauss, Claude. *The Elementary Structures of Kinship*. Trans. by James H. Bell, John Richard von Sturmer, and Rodney Needham, Ed. Rev. ed. Boston: Beacon Press, 1969.

_____. *Structural Anthropology*. Trans. by Claire Jacobson and Brooke Grundfest Schoepf. New York: Basic Books, 1963.

Lorenz, Konrad. *On Agression*. Trans. by Marjorie Kerr Wilson. New York: Harcout, Brace & World, 1966.

Malinowski, Bronislaw. *Sex and Repression in Savage Society*. London: Routledge & Kegan Paul, 1953.

McLean, William. *Contribution à l'étude d'inconographie populaire de l'éroticisme*. Paris: Maisonneuve et Larose, 1970.

Mead, Margaret. *Male and Female. A Study of the Sexes in a Changing World*. New York: W. Morrow, 1949.

Morin, Edgar. *Le paradigme perdu: la nature humaine*. Paris: Editions du Seuil, 1973.

Morin, Violette and Majault J. *Un mythe moderne: l'éroticisme*. Tournai, 1964.

Moscovici, Serge. *Society against Nature: The Emergence of of Human Societies*. Trans. by Sacha Rabinovitch. Hassocks: Harvester Press, 1976.

Oraison, Marc. *The Human Mystery of Sexuality.* New York: Sheed & Ward, 1967.

Rabaut, C. "Oedipe (complexe de)," *Encyclopaedia universalis* Vol. XI, pp. 1090–1092.

Reich, Wilhelm. *The Sexual Revolution.* Trans. by Theodore P. Wolfe. New York: Farrar, Straus and Giroux, 1945.

Ricoeur, Paul. *The Symbolism of Evil.* Trans. by Emerson Buchanan. Boston: Beacon Press, 1969.

Safouan, Moustapha. *La sexualité féminine dans la doctrine freudienne.* Paris: Editions du Seuil, 1976.

Schelsky, Helmut. *Sociologie de la sexualite.* Paris, 1966.

"La sexualité," *Esprit,* 1960, No. 11.

Simon, N. *Comprendre la sexualité aujourd'hui.* Lyon, 1975.

Simon, P. *Rapport sur le comportement sexuel des Français.* Paris, 1972.

Sullerot, Evelyne. (Ed.). *Le fait feminin.* With Odette Thibault. Paris, 1978.

Vasse, D. *L'ombilic et la voix.* Paris, 1974.

Bibliography for Chapters II and III

Allmen, Jean-Jacques. *Pauline Teaching on Marriage.* Trans. from the French. New York: Morehouse-Barlow, 1963.

Allo, Ernest Bernard. *Saint Paul. Première Epître aux Corinthiens.* Paris: J. Gabalda, 1934.

Amado Lévy-Valensi, Eliane. *Le grand désarroi aux racines de l'énigme homosexuelle.* Paris, 1973.

Baltensweiler, Heinrich. *Die Ehe im Neuen Testament.* Zürich-Stuttgart, 1967.

Barth, Karl. *Church Dogmatics.* Trans. by Edwards, Bussey, and Knight. Edinburgh: T & T Clark, 1958.

Bonhoeffer, Dietrich. *The Cost of Discipleship.* Trans. by R.H. Fuller. New York: Macmillan, 1959.

Bonnard, Pierre. *L'Evangile selon saint Matthieu.* Neuchâtel: Delachaux & Niestlé, 1963.

Bonsirven, Joseph. *Le Divorce dans le Nouveau Testament.* Paris-Tournai, 1948.

———. *Textes rabbiniques des deux premiers siècles chrétiens, pour servir à l'intelligence du Nouveau Testament.* Roma: Pontificio Instituto biblico, 1955.

Bornkamm, Günther. *Jesus of Nazareth.* Trans. by Irene and Fraser McLuskey with James M. Robinson. New York: Harper, 1960.

———. "Ehescheidung und Wiederverheiratung im N.T.," *Geschichte und Glaube.* Vol. I. München, 1968, pp. 56–59.

———. *Paul.* Trans. by D.M.G. Stalker. New York: Harper & Row, 1971.

Bovon, Francois. "Orientations actuelles des études lucaniennes," *RTP* 26, 1976, 3, pp. 161–190.

———. "Communauté familiale et communauté ecclésiale dans le N.T.," *Cahiers Protestants,* 1976, 6, pp. 61–72.

Braun, Herbert. *Spätjudisch-häretischer und frühchristlicher Radikalismus; Jesus von Nazareth und die essenische Qumransekte.* Tübingen: J.C.B. Mohr, 1957.

Briend, J. *Une lecture du Pentateuch.* Paris, 1976.

Bultmann, Rudolf Karl. "Das Problem der Ethik bei Paulus," *Exegetica.* Ed. E. Dinkler, Tübingen, 1967, pp. 36–54.

———. *The History of the Synoptic Tradition.* Trans. by John Marsh. New York: Harper & Row, 1963.

———. *Primitive Christianity in Its Contemporary Setting.* Trans. by Rev. R.H. Fuller. New York: Meridian Books, 1959.

———. *Theology of the New Testament.* Trans. by Kendrick Grobel. New York: Scribner, 1951–1955.

Cohen, Abraham. *Everyman's Talmud.* Intro. to Amer. ed. by Boaz Cohen. New York: E.P. Dutton, 1949.

Conzelmann, Hans. *"I Corinthians": A Commentary on the First Epistle to the Corinthians.* Trans. by James W. Leetch. Ed. by George W. MacRae. Philadelphia: Fortess Press, 1975.

Crespy, Georges, Evdokimov, Paul, Duquoc, Christian. *Marriage and Christian Tradition.* Trans. by Sister Agnes Cunningham. Techney, Ill.: Divine Word Publications, 1968.

Dibelius, Martin. *An die Kolosser, Epheser, An Philemon.* Tübingen: J.C.B. Mohr, 1927.

Douglas, Mary Tew. Cf. Bibliography for Chapt. I.

Dupont, Jacques. *Mariage et divorce dans l'Evangile.* Bruges, 1959.

Fitzmeyer, Joseph A. "The Matthean Divorce Texts and Some New Palestinian Evidence," *Theological Studies* 37, 1976, p. 197–226.

Fuchs, Erich. "Chance et ambiguité de la famille selon l'Evangile," *Bull. CPE* 29, 1977, No. 5–6, pp. 38–47.

Gélin, Albert. *The Concept of Man in the Bible.* Trans. by David Murphy. London: G. Chapman, 1968.

Gnilka, Joachim. *Der Epheserbrief.* Herders T.K., 1971.

Goguel, Maurice. *The Primitive Church.* Trans. by H.C. Snape. London: Allen & Unwin, 1964.

Goppelt, Leonhard. *Apostolic and Post-Apostolic Times.* Trans by Robert A. Guelich. New York: Harper & Row, 1970.

Hering, Jean. *The First Epistle of Saint Paul to the Corinthians.* Trans. by A.W. Heathcote and P.A. Allcock. London: Epworth Press, 1962.

Hoffmann, Paul. "Jesus' Saying about Divorce and Its Interpretation in the New Testament Tradition." Trans. by J.T. Swann. *Concilium.* New York: Herder and Herder, 1970. Vol. LV, pp. 51–66.

Humbert, Paul. *Etudes sur le récit du paradis et de la chute dans la Genèse.* Neuchâtel, 1940.

Jacob, Edmond. *Osée.* (Commentaire de l'Ancien Testament). XIa. Neuchâtel: Delachaux et Niestlé, 1965.

———. *Theology of the Old Testament.* Trans. by Arthur W. Heathcote and Philip A. Allcock. London: Hodder & Stoughton, 1958.

Jeremias, Joachim. *Jerusalem in the Time of Jesus.* Trans. by F.H. and C. H. Cave. Philadelphia: Fortress Press, 1969.

Leenhardt, Franz J. "La place de la femme dans l'Eglise d'après le N.T.," *ETR* 23, 1948, pp. 1–50.

———. "La situation de l'homme dans la Genèse," *Das Menschenbild im Lichte des Evangeliums.* Festschrift E. Brunner. Zürich, 1950.

———. "Les femmes aussi. . . A propos du billet de repudiation," *RTP* 19, 1969, 1, pp. 31–40.

Lohfink, Norbert. *The Christian Meaning of the Old Testament.* Trans. by R.A. Wilson. Milwaukee: Bruce Publishing Co., 1968.

Lys, Daniel. *Le plus beau chant de la création.* Paris: Les Editons du Cerf, 1968.

Manson, Thomas Walter. *Ethics and the Gospel.* London: SCM Press, 1960.

Margot, Jean-Claude. "L'indissolubilité du mariage selon le N.T.," *RTP* 17, 1967, pp. 391–403.

Martin-Achard, R. *Essai biblique sur les fêtes d'Israël.* Genève, 1974.

Masson, Charles. *L'Epître de saint Paul aux Ephésians. CNT* IX. Neuchâtel, 1953.

Mehl-Koehnlein, Herrade. *L'homme selon l'apôtre Paul.* Neuchâtel, 1951.

Menoud, Philippe Henri. *Jesus Christ and the Faith: A Collection of Studies.* Trans. by Eunice M. Paul. Pittsburgh: Pickwick Press, 1978.

O'Conner, J. Murphy. *L'existence chrétienne selon saint Paul.* Paris, 1974.

———. "Corinthian Slogans in *I Cor.* 6: 12–20," *CBQ* 40, 1978, pp. 391–396.

Neher, André. *The Prophetic Existence.* Trans. by William Wolf. South Brunswick, N.J.: A.S. Barnes, 1969.

Niederwimmer, Kurt. *Askese und Mysterium. Über Ehe, Ehescheidung und Eheverzicht in den Anfängen des christlichen Glaubens.* Göttingen: Vanderhoeck & Ruprecht, 1975.

Noth, Martin. *Leviticus: A Commentary.* London: SCM Press, 1965.

van Oyen, Hendrick. *Ethique de l'Ancien Testament.* Genève, 1974 (German edition 1967).

Patai, Raphael. *Sex and Family in the Bible and the Middle East.* Garden City, N.Y.: Doubleday, 1959.

Pidoux, G. *L'homme dans l'Ancien Testament.* Neuchâtel, 1953.

Preisker, Herbert. *Geist und Leben. Das Telos-Ethos des Urchristentums.* Darmstadt: Wissenschaftliche Buchgesellschaft, 1968.

von Rad, Gerhard. *Genesis: A Commentary.* Trans. by John H. Marks. Philadelphia: Westminster Press, 1961.

———. *Old Testament Theology.* Trans. by D.M.G. Stalker. New York: Harper, 1962.

———. *Wisdom in Israel.* Nashville: Abingdon, 1972.

Ricouer, Paul. Cf. Bibliography for Chapt. I.

Robinson, John A.T. *The Body: A Study in Pauline Theology.* Chicago: H. Regnery Co., 1952.

Schillebeeckx, Eduard. *Marriage: Secular Reality and Saving Mystery.* Trans. by N.D. Smith. London: Sheed and Ward, 1965. Vols. I and II.

Schmithals, Walter. *Die Gnosis in Korinth*. Göttingen: Vandenhoeck & Ruprecht, 1956.
Schnackenburg, Rudolf. *The Moral Teaching of the New Testament*. Trans. by J. Holland-Smith and W.J. O'Hara from the 2nd rev. German ed. Freiburg: Herder, 1965.
Schütz, F. *Der leidende Christus. Die angefochtene Gemeinde und das Christuskerygma der lukanischen Schriften*. Stuttgart, 1969.
Strack, Hermann Leberecht, Billerbeck, Paul. *Kommentar zum Neuen Testamentum aus Talmud und Midrasch*. München: C.H. Beck'she, 1969.
Tresmontant, Claude. *La docrine morale des prophètes d'Israël*. Paris, 1958.
de Vaux, Roland. *Ancient Israel: Its Life and Institutions*. Trans. by John McHugh. New York: McGraw-Hill, 1961.
Vawter, Bruce. "Divorce and the N.T.," *CBQ* 39, 1977, pp. 528–542.
Vincent Doucet-Bon, Liseron. *Le mariage dans les civilisations anciennes*. Paris: A. Michel, 1975.
Weiss, Johannes: *Der erste Korintherbrief*. Göttingen: Vandenhoeck & Ruprecht, 1910.[9]
Wendland, Heinz-Dietrich. *Ethik des Neuen Testaments*. Götingen: Vandenhoeck & Ruprecht, 1970.
Wolff, Hans Walter. *Anthropology of the Old Testament*. Trans. by Margaret Kohl. Philadelphia: Fortress Press, 1974.

Bibliography for Chapt. IV

A—Ancient Authors and Works (except for Scripture texts)

Quotations have been taken from such series as *Fathers of the Church (FC), Ante-Nicene Fathers (A-NF), Nicene and Post-Nicene Fathers (N-PNF), Ancient Christian Writers (ACW)*. Occasionally there are individual publications of some works. When no English was available, references have come from the famous J.P. Migne edition *Patrologiae Cursus Completus. Series Graeca (PG)*, Paris, 1857–1866, 161 Volumes, and *Series Latina (PL)*, Paris, 1844–1855, 221 volumes. This edition has the advantage of being complete, which is not the case with the more critical editions, some of which are still being published: *Die griechischen christlichen Schrifsteller der ersten drei Jahrhunderten (GCS)*, Berlin, 1897 ff.; *Corpus Scriptorum Ecclesiasticorum Latinorum (CSEL)*, Vienna, 1866 ff.; and *Corpus Christianorum. Series Latina (CCL)*, Turnhout and Paris 1953, ff.

Titles are given in their original language (Greek or Latin) with the English in parentheses whenever a translation is available.

Abelard, Peter. (1079–1142). *Epistolae. (The Letters of Abelard and Heloise.)* Trans. by C.K. Scott Moncrieff. New York: Alfred A. Knopf, 1926.
Acta Apostolorum Apocrypha. (Apocryphal Acts of the Apostles). In *Apocryphal New Testament*. Trans. by Montague Rhodes James. Oxford: Clarendon Press, 1924.

Ambrose of Milan. (335–397 ca.). *De paradiso (Paradise)*. Trans. by John J. Savage. *FC.* Vol. XLII.

———. *Exhortatio virginitatis (Concerning Virginity)*. Trans. by Rev. H. de Romestin. *N-PNF.* Vol. X.

Augustine (354–430). *Soliloquia (Soliloquies)* (387). Trans. by Thomas F. Gilligan. *FC.* Vol. V.

———. *Contra Faustum Manichaean (Against Faustus, the Manichean)* (400). Trans. by Rev. R. Stothert. *N-PNF.* Vol. IV.

———. *De sancta virginitate (Holy Virginity)* (400–401) Trans. by John McQuade. *FC.* Vol. XXVII.

———. *De Trinitate (On the Trinity)* (400–416). Trans. by Stephen McKenna. *FC.* Vol. XLV.

———. *De bono conjugali (The Good of Marriage)* (401). Trans. by Charles T. Wilcox. *FC.* Vol. XXVII.

———. *De Genesi ad Litteram* (401–415). *PL* (Migne).

———. *De civitate Dei (The City of God)* (413–426). Trans. by Gerald Walsh and Grace Monahan. *FC.* Vols. VII, XIV, and XXIV.

———. *De bono viduitatis (The Good of Widowhood)* (414). Trans. by C.L. Cornish. *N-PNF.* Vol III.

———. *De conjugiis adulterinis* (419). *PL* (Migne).

———. *De nuptiis et concupiscentia (On Marriage and Concupiscence)* (419–420). Trans. by Rev. C.L. Cornish. *N-PNF.* Vol. V.

———. *Contra Julianum (Against Julian)* (421). Trans. by Matthew Schumacher. *FC.* Vol. XXXV.

———. *Opus Imperfectum contra Julianum* (429–430). *PL* (Migne).

Letter of Barnabas (125–150ca.). Trans. by Francis X. Glimm. *FC.* Vol. I.

Bonaventure (1217–1274). *Commentaria in IV libros sententiarum P. Lombardi.* In *Opera Omnia.* Parisiis L. Vivès, 1864–1871. Vol. V.

Butzer, Martin (1491–1551). *De Regno Christi* (1550). In *Martini Buceri Opera.* Ed. François Wendel. Paris-Gütersloh, 1955, Vol. XV.

Calvin, John (1509–1564). *Brève Instruction chrétienne* (1536–1537). Ed. *Revue Réformée* 8, no. 30, P. Courthail. Paris, 1957.

———. *The True Method of Reforming the Church.* (1549). Trans. by Henry Beveridge. In *Tracts. CTS* Vol. III. (*CTS* is the series by the Calvin Translation Society, Edinburgh, 1851 ff.)

———. *Commentaries to Timothy, Titus and Philemon.* Trans. by Rev. William Pringle, *CTS.* Vol XLIII.

———. *Commentary on the Epistle of Paul the Apostle to the Corinthians* (1556). Trans. by Rev. John Pringle. *CTS.* Vol. I.

———. *Sermons on the Epistle to the Corinthians.* In *Opera Calvini* (1558). Vol. XLIX.

———. *Institutes of the Christian Religion* (1560). Trans. by Henry Beveridge. Grand Rapids, Mich.: William B. Eerdmans Publishing Co, 1966. Vols. I and II.

———. *Ecclesiastical Ordinances of 1561.* In *Opera Calvini.* Vol X.

_____. *A Harmony of the Gospels* (1562). Trans. by T.H.L. Parker. Edinburgh: Saint Andrew Press, 1972. Vol II.

_____. *Commentaries on the First Book of Moses Called Genesis* (1564). Trans. by Rev. John King. *CTS*. Vols. I and II.

_____. *Commentaries on the Last Four Books of Moses* (1564). Trans. by Rev. Charles William Bingham. *CTS*. Vol. II.

_____. *Commentaries on the Twelve Minor Prophets* (1565).

Caesarius of Arles (Bishop in 503). *Sermones (Sermons)*. *FC*. Vols. XXXI, XLVII, LXVI.

Clement of Alexandria (150–ca. 215). *Paidagogos (Christ the Educator)*. Trans. by Simon P. Wood. *FC*. Vol. XXIII.

_____. *Stromateis*, III. Trans. by Henry Chadwick. In *Alexandrian Christianity*. Vol. II. Philadelphia: Westminster Press, 1954.

Clement of Rome. *Epistle to the Corinthians*. Trans. by Francis X. Glimm. *FC*. Vol. I.

Cyprien. *De habitu virginum (The Dress of Virgins)*. Trans. with comm. by Sister Angel E. Keenan. Washington, D.C.: Catholic University of America, 1932.

Decretalium Collectiones. Ed. Lipsiensis secunda post Ae. L. Richteri curas, instruxit Ae. Friedberg (pars secunda of *Corpus Iuris Canonici*). Graz, 1959.

Didascalia apostolorum (Didache) (ca. 80). Trans. by Francis X. Glimm. *FC* Vol I.

Diogenes Laertius (3rd cent.?). *Lives of Eminent Philosophers*. Trans. by R.D. Hicks. Cambridge: Harvard University Press, 1950.

Letter to Diognetus (200 ca.). Trans. by Gerald Walsh. *FC*. Vol I.

Durand de Huesca. *Une somme anti-cathare: Le Liber contra Manicheos*. Unedited text with notes by Christine Thouzellier. Louvain: Spicilegium sacrum lovaniense administration, 1964.

Epictetus (50–135 ca.). *The Discourses*. Trans. by W.A. Oldfather. Cambridge: Harvard University Press, 1946. Vols. I and II.

Epiphanus (315–403). *Panarium*. *PG*. Vol XLI.

Erasmus, Desiderius (1467–1536). In *Annotationes Novi Testamenti*. In *Opera Omnia*. P. Vander, Lugduni Batavorum (Leyde) 1705. Vol. VI.

Eusebius of Caesarea. (265–340ca.) *Supplementa Questionum ad Marinum*. *PG*. Vol. XXII.

Gospel of Thomas. According to the Coptic text Chenoboskion X, in *New Testament Apocrypha* I. Ed. Wilhelm Schneemelcher. Trans. by Robert Mc L. Wilson. Philadelphia, 1963.

Gregory the Great (Pope from 590–604). *Liber regulae pastoralis (Pastoral Care)*. Trans. by Henry Davis. *ACW*. Vol. XI.

_____. *Epistolae (Letters)*. Trans. by James Barmby. *N-PNF*. Vol. XIII.

_____. *In septem psalmos poenitentiales expositio*. *PL*. Vol. LXXIX.

Gregory of Nyssa (332–ca. 394). *De virginitate (Treatise on Virginity)*. Trans. by Virginia Woods Callahan. *FC*. Vol. LVIII.

Hermas. *Hermae Pastor (The Shepherd)* (ca. 140) Trans. by Joseph Marique. *FC*. Vol I.

Hugh of Saint Victor. (1096–1141). *De sacramentis christianae fidei. PL.* Vol. CLXXIV.

———. *De B. Mariae virginitate. PL.* Vol. CLXXVI.

Ignatius of Antioch (35–107ca.). *To Polycarp.* Trans. by Gerald Walsh. *Fc.* Vol. I.

Irenaeus (120–200ca.). *Adversus haereses I. PG.* Vol. VII.

John Chrysostom (354–407 ca.). *Paraenesis ad Theodorum Lapsum (Two Letters to Theodore after His Fall).* Trans. by Rev. W.R.W. Stephens. *N-PNF.* Vol. IX.

Jerome (345–419 ca.). *Epistolae (Letters).* Trans. by W.H. Fremantle. *N-PNF.* Vol. VI.

———. *Adversus Jovinianum.* L. II *PL.* Vol. XXIII.

———. *De perpetua virginitate Beatae Mariae (On the Perpetual Virginity of Blessed Mary the Virgin).* Trans. by John N. Hritzu. *FC.* Vol LIII.

———. *Commentaria in Epistolam ad Galatas. PL* Vol. XXVI.

Justin (100–165ca.). *Apologia I and II.* Trans. by Thomas Falls. *FC.* Vol. VI.

———. *Dialogus cum Tryphone (Dialogue with Trypho).* Trans. by Thomas Falls. *FC.* Vol. VI.

Kant, Emmanuel. (1724–1804). *Religion within the Limits of Reason Alone.* Trans. by T.M. Greene and H.H. Hudson. New York: Harper & Row, 1960.

Lactantius (4th cent.). *Divinae Institutiones (The Divine Institutes).* Trans. by Sister Mary Francis McDonald. *FC.* Vol. XLIX.

Liber de duobus principiis. Unedited text with notes by Christine Thouzellier. Louvain: Spicilegium sacrum lovaniense administration, 1964.

Luther, Martin (1483–1546). *Treatise on Good Works* (1520). Trans. by W.A. Lambeth. *LW.* Vol. XLIV. (Whenever possible, quotations are from *Luther's Works (LW),* edition from Muhlenberg Press in Philadelphia, 1962 ff.)

———. *To the Christian Nobility of the German Nation Concerning the Reform of the Christian Estate* (1520). Trans. by W.A. Lambeth. *LW.* Vol. XLIV.

———. *The Babylonian Captivity of the Church* (1520). Trans. by A.T.W. Steinhäuser. *LW.* Vol. XXVI.

———. *Judgment of Martin Luther on Monastic Vows* (1521). Trans. by James Atkinson. *LW.* Vol. XLIV.

———. *The Estate of Marriage* (1522). Trans. by William I. Brandt. *LW.* Vol. XLV.

———. *Catechism* (the 6th commandment) (1529). In *Oeuvres.* Geneva. Vol. VII.

———. *Von Ehesachen* (1530). Ed. *M. Luthers Werke.* 30 Bd. Weimar, 1910.

———. *Psalm 117* (1530). In *Oeuvres.* Geneva. Vol. VI.

———. *Sermon for the Marriage of Caspar Cruciger.* In *Oeuvres.* Geneva. Vol. IX.

Methodius (died 311). *The Symposium.* Trans. by Herbert Musurillo. Westminster, Md.: Newman Press, 1958.

Peter Lombard (1100–1160 ca.). *Senentiarum libri quator. PL* Vol. CXCII.

Philo of Alexandria (15 B.C.–50 A.D.ca.) *De vita Mosis.* Trans. by F.H. Colson and Rev. G.H. Whitaker. New York: G.P. Putnam & Sons, 1929.

_____. *Quaestiones et solutiones in Exodum (Questions and Answers on Exodus)*. Trans. by Ralph Marcus. London: William Heinemann Ltd., 1943.

Pliny the Younger (62–120ca.). *Epistolae (Letters and Panegyricus)*. Trans. by Betty Radice. Cambridge: Harvard University Press, 1969.

Psuedo-Clement. *Epistolae duae ad virgines (Two Letters to Virgins)*. Trans. by B.P. Pratton. *ANF*. Vol. VIII.

Rituel Cathare. SC 236, Christine Thouzellier. Paris, 1977.

Stobaeus, Johannes. *Ioannis Stobaei Florilegium*. Lipsiae: B.G. Turner, 1855–1857.

Tertullien (160–222 ca.). *Apologeticum (Apology)*. Trans. by Sister Emily Daly. *FC*. Vol. X.

_____. *De cultu feminarum (The Apparel of Women)*. Trans. by Edwin Quain. *FC*. Vol. XL.

_____. *Ad uxorem (To His Wife)*. Trans. by William P. LeSaint. *ACW*. Vol. XIII.

_____. *De anima adversus philosophos (On the Soul)*. Trans. by Edwin Quain. *FC*. Vol X.

_____. *Adversus Marcionem (Against Marcion)*. Trans. by Ernest Evans. Oxford: Clarendon Press, 1972.

The Testaments of the Twelve Patriarchs. Trans. by Robert Sinker. *ANF*. Vol. VIII.

Theodoret of Cyrus (died ca. 468). *Quaestiones in Genesium*. *PG*. Vol. LXXX.

Thomas Aquinas (1225–1274). *Summa theologica*. Edition by Fathers of the English Dominican Province. New York: Benziger Brothers, Inc., 1948.

_____. *De perfectione vitae spiritualis (The Perfection of the Spiritual Life)*. Trans. by Rev. Proctor. St. Louis: B. Herder, 1903.

B—Modern Authors

Ariès, Philippe. *Centuries of Childhood: A Social History of Family Life*. Trans. by Robert Baldick. New York: Knopf, 1962.

Aubert, Jean-Marie. *La femme. Antiféminisme et christianisme*. Paris, 1975.

_____. *Vivre en chrétiens au XXe siècle*. 2 Vols. Mulhouse, 1976 ff.

Audet, Jean Paul. *La Didachè: Instructions des apôtres*. Paris: J. Gabalda, 1958.

Baer, Richard Arthur. *Philo's Use of the Categories of Male and Female*. Leiden: E.J. Brill, 1970.

Bartmann, B. *Précis de théologie dogmatique*. Mulhouse-Paris, 1951.[7]

Batiffol, P. *Etudes d'histoire et de théologie positive*. Paris, 1968.

Bels, Pierre. *Le mariage des protestants français jusqu'en 1685*. Paris: Libraire générale de droit et de jurisprudence, 1968.

Beyreuther, G. *Sexualtheorien in Pietismus*. München, 1963.

Bezzola, Reto Roberto. *Les origines et la formation de la littérature courtoise en Occident*. Paris, 1966.

Biéler, André. *L'homme et la femme dans la morale calviniste*. Préface de Madeleine Barot. Genève: Labor et Fides, 1963.

Borresen, Kari E. *Subordination and Equivalence: The Nature and Role of Women in Augustine and Thomas Aquinas.* Washington D.C.: University Press of America, 1981.

Borst, Arno. *Die Katharer.* Stuttgart: Hiersemann, 1953.

Bourke, Vernon Joseph. *History of Ethics.* Garden City, N.Y: Doubleday & Company, Inc., 1968.

Broudehoux, J.P. *Mariage et famille chez Clément d'Alexandrie.* Paris: Beauchesne et ses Fils, 1970.

Chelini, Jean. *Histoire religieuse de l'Occident médiéval.* Paris: A. Colin, 1968.

Crouzel, Henri. *L'Eglise primitive face au divorce.* Paris: Beauchesne, 1971.

Dauvillier, Jean. *Le mariage dans le droit canonique de l'Eglise, depuis le Décret de Gratien (1140) jusqu'à la mort de Clément V (1314).* Paris: Recueil Sirey, 1933.

Decret, François. *Mani et la tradition manichéenne.* Paris, 1974.

Delumeau, Jean. *Le christianisme, va-t-il mourir?* Paris: Hachette, 1977.

Demos, John. *A Little Commonwealth: Family Life in Plymouth Colony.* New York: Oxford University Press, 1978.

Denzinger, Heinrich, *Enchiridion symbolorum.* Rome, 1957.[31]

Detienne, Marcel. *The Gardens of Adonis.* Trans. by Janet Lloyd. Intro. by J.P. Vernant. Atlantic Highlands, N.J.: Humanities Press, 1977.

Dumas, André. *Le contrôle des naissances. Opinions protestantes.* Paris, 1965.

Evdokimov, Paul. *La femme et le salut du monde.* Paris, 1958.

———. *Sacrement de l'amour: Le mystère conjugale à la lumière de la tradition orthodoxe.* Paris: Editions de l'Epi, 1962.

Fiorenza, Elisabeth S. "Le rôle des femmes dans le mouvement chrétien primitif," *Concilium* 111, 1976, pp. 13–25.

Flandrin, Jean Louis. *Families in Former Times: Kinship, Household and Sexuality.* Trans. by Richard Southern. New York: Cambridge University Press, 1979.

Foerster, Werner, Haenchen, Ernst, Krause, Martin. *Die Gnosis.* Zürich: Artemis Verlag, 1969.

Foucault, Michel. *The History of Sexuality.* Trans. by Robert Hurley. New York: Pantheon Books, 1978.

Gerest, R.C. "Quand les chrétiens ne se mariaient pas à l'Eglise: histoire des cinq premiers siècles," *Lumière et Vie.* No. 82, 1967, pp. 24–27.

Germain, Gabriel. *Epictète et la spiritualité stoïcienne.* Paris: Editions du Seuil, 1964.

Gilson, Etienne. Le christianisme et la tradition philosophique," *Revue des sciences philosophiques et religieuses* 2, 1941–1942, pp. 249–266.

———. *The Mystical Theology of Saint Bernard.* Trans. by A.H.C. Downs. New York: Sheed and Ward, 1940.

Gisel, P. *Vérité et histoire. La théologie dans la modernité.* Paris-Genève, 1977.

Glotz, Gustave. *Etudes sociales et juridiques sur l'antiquité grecque.* Paris: Hachette et Cie, 1906.

Grant, Robert M. *Gnosticism and Early Christianity.* Rev. ed. New York: Harper & Row, 1966.

Grimal, Pierre. *The Civilization of Rome.* Trans. by W.S. Maguinness. London: Allen & Unwin, 1963.

Grimm, Robert. *L'avortement. Pour une decision responsable.* Lausanne, 1972.

Halkin, L. E. "Erasme et le célibat sacerdotal," *RHPR* 57, 1977, pp. 497–511.

Häring, Bernard. *The Law of Christ: Moral Theology for Priests and Laity.* Trans. by Edwin G. Kaiser. Westminster, Md.: Newman Press, 1961–1966.

Kerns, Joseph E. *The Theology of Marriage.* New York: Sheed and Ward, 1964.

Lähteenmäki, O. *Sexus und Ehe bei Luther.* Turku, 1955.

Lebrun, François. *La vie conjugale sous l'Ancien Régime.* Paris: A. Colin, 1975.

Leipoldt, Johannes. *Die Frau in der antiken Welt und im Urchristentum.* Leipzig: Koehler & Amelang, 1955.

Leisegang, Hans. *Die Gnosis.* Stuttgart: A. Kröner, 1955.

LeRoy Ladurie, Emmanuel. *Montaillou, Village occitan de 1294 à 1324.* Paris, 1976.

Marrou, Henri Irénée. *The History of Education in Antiquity.* Trans. by George Lamb. New York: Sheed and Ward, 1956.

_____. *Décadence romaine ou antiquité tardive?: IIIe-VIe siècle.* Paris: Editions du Seuil, 1977.

Mehat, André. *Etudes sur les "Stromates" de Clément d'Alexandrie.* Paris: Editions du Seuil, 1966.

Mehl, Roger. *Ethique catholique et éthique protestante.* Neuchâtel, 1970.

Meray, Anthony. *La vie au temps des libres prêcheurs, ou Les devanciers de Luther et de Rabelais: croyances, usages et moeurs intimes des XIVe, XVe et XVIe siècles.* 2e ed. Paris: A. Claudin, 1878.

Métral, Marie-Odile. *Le mariage. Les hésitations de l'Occident.* Paris, 1977.

Moore, George Foot. *Judaism in the First Centuries of the Christian Era.* Cambridge: Harvard University Press, 1927–30.

Morgan, Edmund Sears. *The Puritan Family: Religion and Domestic Relations in Seventeenth-Century New England.* Rev. ed. New York: Harper & Row, 1966.

Nautin, Pierre. "Divorce et remariage dans la tradition latine," *Recherches de science religieuse* 62, 1974, pp. 7–54.

Nelli René. *L'érotique des troubadours.* Toulouse: E. Privat. 1963.

_____. *Le phénomène Cathare: perspectives philosophiques, morale et iconographiques.* Paris: Presses universitaires de France, 1964.

Nock, Alfred Darby. *Early Gentile Christianity and Its Hellenistic Background.* New York: Harper Torchbooks, 1962.

Noonan, John T. *Contraception.* Cambridge, Mass.: Harvard University Press, 1965.

Nygren, Anders. *Agape and Eros: A Study of the Christian Idea of Love.* Trans. by A.G. Herbert. New York: Macmillan Co., 1937–1939.

Paul, Jacques. *Histoire intellectuelle de l'occident médieval.* Paris: A. Colin, 1973.

Pinckaers, S. *Le renouveau de la morale.* Tournai-Paris, 1964.

Pinto de Oliveira, C.J. *La crise du choix moral dans la civilisation technique.* Fribourg, Paris, 1977.

Ploechl, Willibald Maria. *Geschichte des Kirchenrechts*. Wein: Herold, 1960.
Preisker, H. *Christentum und Ehe in der drei ersten Jahrhunderten. Eine Studie zur Kulturgeschichte der alten Welt*, Berlin 1927.
Puech, H. Ch. *Le manichéisme, son fondateur, sa doctrine*, Paris 1949.
Quere-Jaulmes, F. *La Femme. Les grands textes des Pères de l'Eglise*, Paris 1968.
Ritzer, K. *Le mariage dans les Eglises chrétiennes du Ier au XIe siècle*, Paris 1970.
Rougement, Denis de. *Love in the Western World*, New York, 1940.
Rousselot, P. *Pour l'histoire du problème de l'amour au Moyen Age*, Munster 1907.
Scharffenorth, G. and K. Thraede. *"Freunde in Christus werden. . . ." Die Bedeutung von Mann und Frau als Frage an Theologie und Kirche*, Gelnhausen/Berlin-Stein/Mfr. 1977.
Schillebeeckx, E. See Bibliography for Chapters II and III.
Schneider, H.W. *The Puritan Mind*, 1966 (s.l.)
Schnucker, R.V. "La position puritaine à l'égard de l'adultère," *Annales E.S.C.* 27, 1972, p. 1379–1388.
Schürer, E. *Geschichte des judischen Volkes im Zeitalter Jesu-Christi*, 3 vol., Leipzig 1901–1909 (4).
Simon, Marcel. *La civilisation de l'antiquité et le christianisme*. Paris: Arthaud, 1972.
Simon, René. *Fonder la morale; Dialectique de la foi et de la raison practique*. Paris: Editions du Seuil, 1974.
Spanneut, Michel. *Le stoïcisme des Pères de l'Eglise*. Paris, 1969.^{2}
Stauffenegger, R. *Le mariage à Genève vers 1600*. Genève, 1966.
Stupperich, Robert Wilhelm. *Erasmus von Rotterdam und seine Welt*. Berlin-New York, 1977.
Sullerot, Evelyne. *Histoire et mythologie de l'amour: huit siècles d'écrits féminins*. Paris: Librairie Hachette, 1974.
――――. *Le fait féminin*. Cf. Bibliography for Chapt. I. Especially these two chapters: "Notes brèves sur le fait féminin au XIIe siècle" (G. Duby, pp. 421–424) and "A propos du destin de la femme du XVIe au XXe siècle" (E. LeRoy Ladurie, E. Sullerot, Michele Perrot et J.P. Aron, pp. 425–445).
Tanner, F. *Die Ehe im Pietismus*. Zürich, 1952.
Taviani, Huguette. "Le mariage dans l'hérésie de l'An Mil," *Annales ESC* 32, 1977, pp. 1074–1089.
ten Doornkaat, J. *Le problème de l'avortement*. Berne, 1952.
Vatin, Claude. *Recherches sur le mariage et la condition de la femme mariée à l'époque hellénistique*. Paris, 1970.
Veyne, P. "La famille et l'amour sous le Haut-Empire romain," *Annales ESC* 33, 1978, pp. 35–63.
Wendel, François. *Calvin: The Origins and Development of His Religious Thought*. Trans. by Philip Mairet. New York: Harper & Row, 1963.
――――. *Le mariage à Strasbourg à l'époque de la Réforme 1520–1692*. Strasbourg, 1928.

"Interruption de Grossesse: Réflexions pour une solution légale et humaine plus juste," *Bull. CPE* 27, 1975, No. 8.

La sexualité. Pour une réflexion chrétienne. Paris, 1975.

Bibliography for Chapter V

Bailey, S. *The Man Woman Relation in Christian Thought.* London, 1954.

Bellet, M. *Réalité sexuelle et morale chrétienne.* Paris, 1971.

Besret, B. *De commencement en commencement. Itinéraire d'une déviance.* Paris, 1976.

Bruckner-Finkielkraut. Cf. Bibliography for Chap. I.

Chirpaz, François. Cf. Bibliography for Chap. I.

Cole, William Graham. *Sex in Christianity and Psychoanalysis.* New York: Oxford University Press, 1966.

Donval, A. *Un avenir pour l'amour. Une nouvelle éthique de la sexualité dans le changement social d'aujourd'hui.* Paris, 1976.

Dumas, Francine. *L'autre semblable.* Neuchâtel, 1967.

Durand, G. *Sexualité et foi. Synthèse de théologie morale.* Montréal, 1977.

Geets, Claude. *Psychanalyse et morale sexuelle.* Paris: Editions universitaires, 1970.

Guindon, André. *The Sexual Language. An Essay in Moral Theology.* Toronto: University of Ottowa Press, 1976.

Kellerhals, Jean. "Couple et famille: ambiguïtés et tensions contemporaines," *Bull. CPE* 29, 1977, No. 5–6, pp. 17–37.

Le Du, Jean. *La sexualité. Elements pour une créativité éthique.* Paris, 1965.

de Locht, Pierre. *The Risks of Fidelity.* Danville, N.J.: Dimension Books, 1974.

Mair, Lucy Philip. *Marriage.* Baltimore: Penguin Books, 1971.

Malrieu, Jean. *Préface à l'Amour.* Paris: Cahiers du Sud, 1953.

_____. *Vesper.* Honfleur, 1908.

_____. *Le nom secret,* followed by *La Vallée des rois.* Honfleur, 1968.

_____. *Nous ne voulons pas être heureux,* s.l. 1969.

_____. *Les jours brulés,* s.l., 1971.

_____. *Le château cathare.* Paris: Le Bouget, 1970.

_____. *Possible imaginaire.* Honfleur, 1975.

Mehl, R. *Société et amour.* Genève, 1961.

Oraison, Marc. *The Human Mystery of Sex.* New York: Sheed & Ward, 1967.

_____. *Vie chrétienne et problèmes de la sexualité.* Paris, 1972.[2]

Piper, Otto. *The Biblical View of Sex and Marriage.* New York: Scribner, 1960.

Pohier, Jacques-Maire. *Le chrétien, le plaisir et la sexualité.* Paris, 1974.

_____. *Quand je dis Dieu.* Paris, 1977.

Ricoeur, Paul. Cf. Bibliography for Chap. I.

Schillebeeckx, Eduard. Cf. Bibliography for Chap. II and II.

Vasse, D. *Le temps du désir.* Paris, 1969.

_____. "Le plaisir et la joie," *Lumière et Vie.* No. 114, 1973, pp. 82–103.

Vincent Doucet-Bon, Liseron. Cf. Bibliography for Chap. II and III.

Sex and Morality. A Report to the British Council of Churches. October, 1966. Philadelphia: Fortress Press, 1966.

Engagement et fidélité. Paris, 1970.

Nouveau livre de la foi. La foi commune des Chrétiens. Ed. J. Feiner and L. Vischer. Paris-Genève, 1976.

The following dictionaries and encyclopedias have been consulted:

Dictionnaire de Théologie Catholique. Ed. A. Vacant, E. Mangenot, E. Amann. Paris, 1903–1950.

Die Religion in Geschichte und Gegenwart. 3rd ed. Ed. K. Galling. Tübingen, 1957–1965.

Encyclopaedia Judica. New York: Macmillan, 1972.

Encyclopedia of Religion and Ethics. Ed. James Hastings. New York: Scribner, 1951 (1955).

Encyclopaedia Universalis. Ed. C. Gregory. Paris, 1968–1975.

Lexikon für Theologie und Kirche. Trans. in *Encyclopedia of Theology.* Ed. by Karl Rahner. New York: Seabury Press, 1975.

Reallexikon für Antike und Christentum. Ed. T. Klauser. Stuttgart, 1950 ff.

Theologisches Wörterbuch zum Neuen Testament. Ed. by Gerhard Kittel and G. Friedrich. Trans. by Geoffrey W. Bromily. (*Theological Dictionary of the New Testament.*) Grand Rapids, Mich.: William B. Eerdmans, 1964.

The following abbreviations have been used:

Bull. CPE: Bulletin du Centre Protestant d'Etudes, Geneva.

CBQ: Catholic Biblical Quarterly

ETR: Etudes théologiques et religieuses

RHPR: Revue d'histoire et de philosophie religieuse

RTP: Revue de théologie et de philosophie

Denz.: H. Denzinger, *Enchiridion symbolorum,* Rome 1957.[31]

TOB: Traduction oecumenique de Bible, 2 Vols. Paris 1972, 1975.

Index Nominum

Biblical Index

288

Thematic Index